The Alliance That Lost Its Way

The Alliance That Lost Its Way

A Critical Report on the Alliance for Progress
by Jerome Levinson and Juan de Onís

A Twentieth Century Fund Study

Chicago
Quadrangle Books
1970

309.223
L 665a
1970

When the trustees of the Twentieth Century Fund first considered sponsoring a critical study of the Alliance for Progress, the United States public seemed almost oblivious of events in Latin America. This lack of interest was understandable. The public was then, as now, preoccupied with the war in Vietnam, the urban crisis, and other domestic issues; those concerned about foreign affairs were too absorbed by the aftermath of the near revolution in France, the intervention of the Soviet Union in Czechoslovakia, and the bloodletting in Nigeria to follow developments in the republics of the Alliance.

But the Fund's trustees, many of whom have frequently demonstrated prescience in selecting subjects for study and some of whom had actually participated in the creation of the Alliance, felt it would be a mistake to ignore Latin America simply because it was relatively quiet. Sensing that this quiet was only relative and only superficial, they called for a review of the Alliance's performance and of the problems involved in speeding economic and social development in Latin America while strengthening and expanding participation in democratic institutions.

The size of Latin America, the variety within it, and the broad scope of the Alliance made such an assignment extremely complex. It proved manageable, however, thanks to the successful collaboration forged between Jerome I. Levinson and Juan de Onís. Mr. Levinson had worked for the Agency for International Development, first as assistant director of the United States AID mission in Brazil and later as deputy director of the Office of Capital Development of AID's Latin American bureau (which had overall responsibility for AID lending in Latin America). Mr. de Onís, a skilled journalist, had had long service in Latin America, first with the United Press and then with the *New York Times*. Both men had been involved with the Alliance from its beginnings, one as a dedicated participant and the other as a professional observer. Their different vantage points and varied experience proved invaluable resources, the essential raw materials for a comprehensive and detailed account of the Alliance's impact.

While Messrs. de Onís and Levinson were engaged in this effort, the fragile and uneasy calm in Latin America was shattered by upheavals in a number of countries, culminating in the tumultuous reception accorded Governor Nelson Rockefeller of New York during his mission on behalf of the Nixon administration. This unrest did not derail the project, for the Fund's research directors, like its trustees, had anticipated turbulence in Latin America. With this awareness they managed to produce what may be the fullest review of the Alliance's accomplishments and failures over the decade of its existence.

Unquestionably their findings and their recommendations are controversial and sobering. Almost any serious comment on the Alliance is bound to be, whether it comes from North America or Latin America. But the special merit of the De Onís–Levinson effort is that it reflects a profound commitment to democratic development of the Americas. This commitment has motivated an uncompromisingly objective, critical appraisal of the Alliance and its influence on the Latin American economies, political systems, and social structures. It has led the authors to clarify a great many issues previously distorted or obscured by both detractors and supporters of the Alliance.

As in all Fund projects, the authors enjoyed complete independence. Their views are their own, not the Fund's.

Their account conclusively demonstrates that the Alliance has not lived up to its initial promise. But the record cannot be considered a complete failure. It reveals the successes as well as the setbacks, and tangible as well as intangible changes wrought by the Alliance. The authors feel that the credit for accomplishments as well as the blame for mistakes must be shared equally between the donors and the recipients of aid. And in identifying the weaknesses and errors of the Alliance, the authors express their deep conviction that this experiment in development must not be abandoned, but must be begun afresh.

M. J. ROSSANT, Director
The Twentieth Century Fund
March 1970

The ambitious and complex venture known as the Alliance for Progress has involved the United States for the better part of a decade in an effort to advance the economic, social, and political development of Latin America. It served two Democratic administrations as the main channel of inter-American relations. But the problems that gave rise to the Alliance in 1961 have not been resolved, and now they face a Republican administration in Washington.

Latin America is on the threshold of a new decade in which pressures for economic growth and social change will sorely test the political strength of the inter-American relationship. At this time a history of the Alliance would be premature, for its tasks are far from finished. But a critical assessment is due. A stocktaking of the Alliance's successes and failures may contribute to the formulation of a more effective program for the future. This book seeks to provide such a critique and audit.

Our opinions and judgments grow out of personal association with the Alliance. We have watched it from two complementary vantage points: that of a United States foreign aid official, involved in the operations of the Alliance in both Latin America and Washington; and that of a correspondent for the *New York Times* in Latin America, for whom reporting on the Alliance has been a continuous assignment.

In these capacities we actually witnessed a number of key incidents and we have included some quotations, paraphrases, and descriptions that cannot be documented because they have never before been recorded. We have also included quotations from our interviews with U.S. and Latin American government officials, businessmen, and other participants in or observers of events concerning the Alliance. Some of these people have asked to remain anonymous. Otherwise, wherever appropriate, we have identified them and the documents, published and unpublished, to which we have referred in our research for this book.

We have judged the Alliance by its own standards and stated

objectives, measuring these against its performance in the setting of the relevant events in both Latin America and the United States which influenced its development. We do not pretend to give a full account of inter-American relations in the past decade. Of necessity we have been selective, paying particular attention to the national and regional experiences that we felt were most characteristic of development problems in the area. The individual characteristics of the Latin American countries make it dangerous to generalize, but we felt that we could not record the particular experience of each and every country without losing our critical focus.

The Alliance experience in Brazil is a recurrent theme in the book, partly because in our respective capacities we both had extended tours in that country. But more important, Brazil is by far the largest country in Latin America; its ninety million people present within one national framework the full range of problems that brought the Alliance into being. We consider Brazil's performance a fundamental test of the Alliance.

We have also drawn heavily on the experiences of Chile, Colombia, Venezuela, and Peru because they provide what we feel are the best illustrations of particular aspects of the Alliance, and have given only passing attention to certain other important countries because they appeared to stand apart from the mainstream.

Argentina and Mexico have had only a marginal relationship to the Alliance in domestic terms, but we do examine the importance of their potential role in the achievement of a major Alliance objective, the creation of a Latin American common market. Central America and the Caribbean countries offer fascinating examples of the problems of small-country development, but their special features fall outside a general study of the Alliance.

This study deals at some length with the significance of the United States in Latin American development. We feel that the Alliance experience shows that the United States does not possess a foolproof blueprint for modern development in Latin America. Even if it did, the United States could not take over the responsibility for sovereign political decisions that Latin American leaders alone can make in circumstances that they understand better than any outsider. Moreover, U.S. policy in Latin America lacks domestic support and shifts under the pressure of interest groups and special pleaders. Thus the past performance of the United States in the Alliance tends to bear out an observation made by President Kennedy in December 1962: "There is a limitation upon the ability of the United States to solve these problems. . . . There is a limitation, in other words, upon the power of the United States to bring about solutions. . . . It is much easier to make the speeches than to make the judgments."

We believe, nonetheless, that the democratic ideal of the Alliance is the true heading for this hemisphere's peace and development, and that the United States, limitations notwithstanding, has a vital part to play in Latin America's future.

We would like to express our thanks to the staff of the Twentieth Century Fund for their assistance in the preparation of this study; we are specifically indebted to M. J. Rossant for his patience and his critical comments on the manuscript in its various stages of development, to Judith Seidel for her sensitive and perceptive editing, and to Pearl Schwartz for her early encouragement.

We would also like to acknowledge the help we received from our research assistants, Alfred Webre and Marlise Simons, as well as the unstinting dedication of our typists, Vera Elena Meehan, Jane Marion, and Catherine Shea.

Thanks are especially due to all those individuals in both the United States and Latin America who made available to us their recollections of key events and in some cases actual documents. We hope that this study justifies the confidence they placed in us.

Our gratitude goes, above all, to our respective wives, Cathy and Marcia, for the understanding and encouragement they have given us throughout our work.

JEROME LEVINSON
JUAN DE ONÍS

CONTENTS

The Alliance That Lost Its Way

The Alliance background

The Alliance:
a preliminary audit

1.

The birth of the Alliance for Progress in 1961 marked a dramatic and fundamental reorientation of Washington's policy toward Latin America. Since World War II, Latin American officials had been appealing for a regional aid program of substantial proportions, an appeal that gathered strength and conviction with the success of the Marshall Plan in Europe. Washington, under Truman, had responded to these appeals by explaining, with a diplomat's tact and a lawyer's logic, that the purpose of the $27 billion in aid that the United States had supplied for the reconstruction of western Europe was primarily to meet the challenge of Soviet communism, but that the development needs of Latin America, where no such security threat was present, could be satisfied largely by private foreign capital, provided the region maintained a good investment climate.

Until shortly before the creation of the Alliance, U.S. public economic cooperation with Latin America was limited to financing exports of U.S. equipment, to long-term sales of agricultural commodities, and to a modest technical assistance program for demonstration and training in health, education, and agriculture. When development funds were mentioned, the Latin Americans were advised to get into line, along with other developing countries, for credits from the International Bank for Reconstruction and Development (IBRD); and they were told that balance-of-payments assistance was available from the International Monetary Fund (IMF).

But in the last years of the Eisenhower administration, Washington's attitude—avuncular, haughty, and parsimonious, mainly because the exigencies of the Cold War diverted its preoccupation and priorities elsewhere—began to change. The cause was clear. A wave of rebellions had swept out of power a number of military dictators whom the U.S. State Department had previously hailed as champions of anticommunist stability in Latin America. Not the least of these rebellions was Fidel Castro's stunning overthrow of the Cuban dictator Fulgencio Batista in 1959. At precisely that juncture the change in Washington became perceptible. The Eisenhower administration put up $350 million as the initial capital of the new Inter-American Development Bank; Congress authorized a $500 million fund for social investments in Latin America, such as low-cost housing, urban water-supply systems, credits to small farmers, and education; and the United States belatedly joined an international agreement to stabilize coffee prices. It was a good start, generous and positive when compared with the help that had been provided before, but modest and unassuming when compared with what was to come.

The fundamental change began when John F. Kennedy, at the very beginning of his administration, spoke in bold and heady terms of billion-dollar aid for a decade of planned economic development and social reform in the hemisphere. His message proposing the Alliance for Progress was an invigorating mixture of compassion and hope, ambition and urgency, which quickened the hopes of millions throughout Latin America. Reformist political ideas, concepts of economic planning, and a host of other notions that had been confined to the fringes of inter-American discussions suddenly found wide audiences. The result was a striking improvement in the U.S. dialogue with the Latin Americans, particularly those whom the Kennedy administration identified as the agents of democratic change and social reform, and an almost euphoric belief in what they could achieve.

Many of these political leaders, economic planners, and intellectual innovators—described loosely as the "democratic left"—as well as younger, more radical exponents of revolutionary change, had risen to prominence in the Latin American rebellions of the late 1950s. The senior figures of the democratic left, President Rómulo Betancourt of Venezuela and President Alberto Lleras Camargo of Colombia, were essentially New Dealers in political outlook, and they fell in naturally with the New Frontier president in the White House. With these leaders, and the expectation that other modern and moderate political reformers would come forward throughout Latin America, the confident policy-makers in the new administration of President Kennedy formulated in the Alliance for Progress a bold and comprehensive ideology of democratic development. It postulated not only rapid economic growth (the dominant goal of the Marshall Plan) and social reform (which has played a part in southeast Asian development programs), but at the same time the strengthening of representative political democracy.

Cuba's growing allegiance to the Communist bloc helped to accelerate and shape the creation of the Alliance as a democratic alternative to Cuba's revolutionary socialist formula for development in Latin America. As its architects in Washington and throughout Latin America conceived it, support from the United States would enable the democratic left to bring about economic development and fundamental social change within a framework of representative political institutions.

If idealism was a strong element in the Alliance, so were overconfidence and even brashness. It was assumed, for instance, that Latin America's ruling classes would refrain from obstructing the process of democratic development, presumably on the grounds that, as President Kennedy said, "those who make peaceful revolution impossible will make violent revolution inevitable." And the United States would protect the process from Castro-inspired or -supported disruption by providing counterinsurgency training and equipment for the Latin American military and maintaining or establishing CIA stations in each country.

7

The quantitative promises

Yet the Charter of Punta del Este, which formally established the Alliance, sought to express the ideology of democratic development in terms of the Latin American reality. The charter enumerated certain objectives, some of them specific, which the Alliance was to achieve by 1970, and which can now be used as yardsticks against which to measure its performance.

The primary objective, on which all others were thought to hinge, was an economic growth rate of "not less than 2.5 percent per capita per year" in each Latin American country. Since the region's population growth rate remained at 3 percent a year[1] (the charter contained no reference to the population question), production of goods and services would have had to increase at a rate of more than 5 percent a year to reach this target. But between 1961 and 1967 the actual average increase per year was only 1.5 percent and only in 1968 did the region as a whole finally reach the target.[2]

The second objective was a more equitable distribution of national income, providing a fairer share of the projected increases to the poorer working class and peasants—the great majorities at the depressed base of the Latin American social structure. According to estimates for nine Latin American countries (including Argentina, Brazil, and Mexico), between 1960 and 1963 the wealthy upper 10 percent of the population received about 42 percent of national income while the poor bottom half received only 14 to 21 percent. A survey taken in 1968 shows little if any change in this structure of gross income inequality.[3] Only Chile seems to have accomplished a significant redistribution of income in favor of the poor.

In the area of trade diversification:

A review of the composition of Latin America's exports during the decade of the 1960's confirms progress in diversification, indicated not only by an increased percentage of exports of manufactures and semi-

1. Statistics in this chapter, when not attributed to other sources, are taken from U.S. House of Representatives, Subcommittee on Inter-American Affairs of the Committee on Foreign Affairs, *New Directions for the 1970's: Toward a Strategy of Inter-American Development, Hearings*, 91st Cong., 1st sess. (Washington, D.C.: U.S. Government Printing Office, 1969); cited hereafter as *New Directions*.

2. *Ibid.*, p. 668.

3. United Nations Economic Commission for Latin America, *Economic Survey of Latin America, 1968*, pt. 1, "Some Aspects of the Latin American Economy Toward the End of the Nineteen-Sixties," E/CN 12/825 (March 1969), pp. 20–31. See also *New Directions*, p. 676.

The Alliance: a preliminary audit

manufactures, but also by a swing away from dependence on only one or two commodities among exports of primary products.[4]

Still another objective was fuller utilization of the region's natural and human resources in the form of increased industrialization and reduced unemployment. But although industrialization has advanced significantly in most Latin American countries, unemployment has not been reduced. According to estimates by the Economic Commission for Latin America (ECLA), the supply of jobs in relation to the size of the labor force has increased more slowly during this decade than during the 1950s, and unemployment, partly disguised as underemployment, has risen from 18 million persons in 1960 to 25 million now. (The current figure is based on a presumed full-employment labor force of 83 million.) The Latin American economies—even those that are growing quite rapidly—are unable to absorb the growing contingents of young job seekers that enter the labor market each year.

The charter proposed "to raise greatly the level of agricultural productivity and output and to improve related storage, transportation, and marketing services." Advances have been made in the agricultural area, with Latin America's food production increasing by 4 percent annually, a step ahead of population growth, while investment in the modern commercial agricultural sector has been strong. But, according to the *Rockefeller Report*, "While overall food production is going up, food production per person, due to the population explosion, is estimated at 10 percent less than it was at the end of World War II. And each year there are eight million more mouths to feed."[5]

The charter recommended agrarian reform, including, "where required," the transformation of "unjust structures of land tenure and use." But progress toward a more equitable structure of land tenure and rural income distribution has been very slow. Mexico, Venezuela, and Bolivia have moved ahead with pre-Alliance agrarian reform programs; Chile and Colombia have made real efforts; and Peru has begun to apply what appears on paper to be the most radical agrarian reform law since Cuba's. Other countries, including Brazil, haven't even tried.

---

4. *New Directions*, p. 677.
5. *The Rockefeller Report on the Americas* (Chicago: Quadrangle Books, 1969), p. 120.

In the lifetime of the Alliance the number of peasants seeking land has grown more rapidly than the number of family lots provided by division of estates, colonization, and entitling of squatters.

In education the goal was "to eliminate adult illiteracy and by 1970 to assure, as a minimum, access to six years of primary education for each school-age child in Latin America." Unfortunately, the decade has seen no significant increase in adult literacy. To be sure, the percentage of children not enrolled in primary schools did decline from 52 percent to 43 percent between 1960 and 1967. But at the end of 1967 an estimated 27 million school-age children—about three-quarters of a million more than in 1960—were still receiving no formal education.

The health goals were to add five years to life expectancy, to halve the infant mortality rate, and, for this purpose, to provide potable water and sewage-disposal systems for not less than 70 percent of the urban and 50 percent of the rural population. In fact, life expectancy has been extended somewhat, the infant mortality rate has been somewhat reduced, and some water systems have been built, but the specific goals are still remote.

The charter also proposed increasing the "construction of low-cost houses for low-income families." However, housing construction during the Alliance decade has not come close to meeting the needs of the growing number of families seeking living space, and urban squatters in Latin America have erected many more square feet of housing than the Alliance has built.

The major countries of Latin America have achieved a somewhat better record in meeting the target of maintaining "stable price levels, avoiding inflation or deflation." Brazil suffered a decline in per capita GNP and a rate of inflation that reached 80 to 90 percent in 1963 and 1964, but in 1968 its per capita growth rate was 2.9 percent and its internal price rise was limited to 24 percent. Colombia's average inflation rate, 16–17 percent in the early Alliance years, had declined by 1968 to 6.5 percent; and its GNP growth, after a long period of stagnation, had also taken an encouraging stride forward, increasing by more than 6 percent. Chile had undertaken an impressive program of social reform, financed largely by increased tax revenues, and was able to reduce its cost-of-living increase from a peak of 46 percent in 1964 to 18.2 percent in 1967, but drought and political pressures pushed up prices 30 percent in 1969.

The charter also called for economic integration ultimately taking the form of a Latin American common market, but:

After more promising initial progress, economic integration in Latin America has reached a plateau from which further significant advances will require considerably more effort on the part of Latin American governments to take the action necessary to achieve stated objectives, as well as substantially more time than had been anticipated.[6]

The first step toward achievement of all these objectives was to be the formulation of national development programs on the principles of self-help and "the maximum use of domestic resources, taking into account the special conditions of each country," but including the "necessary structural reforms."

Specifically, the main economic burden of the development programs was to fall upon those in Latin America who could pay for them, through tax reforms "demanding more from those who have most." At the end of the decade, in Latin America as a whole, tax collections, primarily as a result of improved administrative techniques and organization rather than structural reforms, had increased in real terms by 35 percent since 1961. This increase is about the same as the region's cumulative growth of domestic product and thus is far from spectacular.

During the Alliance decade, domestic savings were to provide 80 percent of the capital for necessary investment. In fact, according to the Inter-American Committee on the Alliance for Progress (*Comité Interamericana de la Alianza para el Progreso*, or CIAP), domestic savings have financed 90 percent, largely because of a shortage of foreign investment.[7]

In the charter the United States undertook for the first time to support Latin American development with a specific long-term financial commitment:

a supply of capital from all external sources during the coming ten years of at least $20 billion [to] be made available to the Latin American countries with priority to the relatively less developed countries. The greater part of this sum should be in the form of public funds.

6. *New Directions*, p. 725.
7. Carlos Sanz de Santamaría (chairman of CIAP), address to the Fourteenth Annual Assembly of the Inter-American Press Association, Buenos Aires, October 15, 1968.

The charter failed to specify whether this figure was to be gross or net (after Latin American repayment on existing debt). Thus between 1961 and 1969 Latin America received over $18 billion from all external sources.[8] However, more than half of its foreign long-term credits were offset by the cost of servicing past foreign loans, an outflow that continues to mount.

The charter made four references to foreign private investment. Though positive, they were brief and vague. The U.S. business community viewed their brevity as a rebuff by the Kennedy administration and their vagueness as a refusal to provide security against expropriation. Thus during the early years of the Alliance new U.S. private investment in Latin America declined considerably, and the business community sought security for existing investments from Congress, through, for example, the Hickenlooper Amendment. However, in 1964, with the Castro threat receding and Thomas Mann, known as a friend of business, in the State Department, U.S. investment in Latin America began to expand once again.

When the Alliance began, many Latin American countries were deeply in debt and virtually unable to meet their debt payments. A substantial amount of early Alliance lending went to refinance the existing debts. At the same time, the trend in U.S. private investment in the region has been toward Latin American–based manufacturing for local markets, generally increasing the region's imports of raw materials without increasing its exports. Thus Latin America's annual payments of principal and interest on loans, together with profit remittances by foreign investors, have been rising much more rapidly than exports. Any drop in export income or cessation in the inflow of foreign capital now could produce a major crisis, precisely the crisis that the Alliance planners sought to forestall.

The United States also agreed at the outset to help prevent undue fluctuation in Latin American earnings from exports of primary products and to "adopt measures necessary to facilitate the access of Latin American exports to international markets." It has not done so. Indeed, according to the Economic and Social Secretariat of the Organization of American States:

During the period covered by the Alliance for Progress, Latin America

---

8. See Table 7.2.

The Alliance: a preliminary audit

seems to have been contributing to an appreciable degree to strengthening the balance of payments position of the United States without the foreign aid provided by that country being sufficient to compensate fully for the deficit accumulated by Latin America in other transactions with the United States.[9]

The qualitative performance

But though the Alliance has not come close to most of its explicit objectives and specific targets, it has had some significant results. The decade has given Latin America a new development consciousness, which has permeated large segments of the population (including two of the region's most tradition-oriented institutions, the military and the church). Economic planning, particularly in Brazil, Colombia, and Chile, has reached an impressive level of sophistication, and throughout the hemisphere young, technically trained people are playing major roles in the key public-sector institutions. At the same time, the private sector contains a growing middle level of successful entrepreneurs and an increasing number of efficient industrial managers.

This new sophistication has been accompanied, in many cases, by a profound disillusionment with the Alliance, based in part on failure to reach the charter's targets. Viewed in retrospect, the targets themselves reflect not only the projections of the Latin American development experts but also the optimism with which the Kennedy administration (intentionally, although not cynically) had infused inter-American relations. But hindsight also shows that the problems of development are more difficult, and the political consequences of unfulfilled expectations more disastrous, than the authors of the charter ever anticipated.

The Alliance, defined as the record of inter-American relations in the past decade, provides additional justification for disillusionment. If it has succeeded in preventing any new Castros from coming to power in the hemisphere, it has done so by military means, failing conspicuously to advance the cause of the democratic left. The United States has intervened openly in the Dominican Republic and less obviously in Brazil and Guatemala to assist not the democratic left but the military

9. Organization of American States, Inter-American Economic and Social Council, *Problems and Perspectives of Economic and Social Development,* CIES/1380 (Washington, D.C.: Pan American Union, May 1969), p. 167.

and civilian forces of conservatism. In disputes between Latin American governments and U.S. corporations, the United States has applied economic pressures against the Latin American governments with a fine disregard for the disputed issues. Loan officials have consistently required that countries seeking financial assistance undertake monetary stabilization programs; they have not required programs of social reform. The U.S. Congress and the executive branch have restricted loan funds to purchases of U.S. goods (particularly those that are not competitively priced) and such other uses as are consistent with a favorable U.S. balance of payments.

These policies have raised serious doubts about both the U.S. commitment to democratic development in Latin America and the Alliance formula for attaining it. They have also given the left and the right in many Latin American countries a common cause: nationalistic opposition to what both regard as a dominating U.S. presence. This opposition has taken forms ranging from restrictions on the acquisition of local banks by U.S. banks to outright expropriation, and has given momentum to at least two successful military coups d'état.

In Latin America today two countries, Venezuela and Mexico, provide solid assurance of economic growth in a constitutional political framework; but both countries benefit from extraordinary access to foreign exchange resources—oil in Venezuela and tourism in Mexico—and neither has been a major recipient of U.S. government aid.

Elsewhere in the hemisphere constitutional government is undergoing the tensions and stresses endemic among rapidly developing nations. In Chile the experiment in social reform initiated by President Eduardo Frei's Christian Democratic party faces strong opposition from both the right and the Marxist left as Chile moves toward the presidential elections of September 1970. In Colombia, the narrow victory of Misael Pastrana Borrero, candidate of the Conservative-Liberal coalition, over the former dictator Gustavo Rojas Pinilla, running on a semi-fascist populist platform in the presidential elections of April 1970, illustrated anew the explosive political potential of Colombia's relatively slow-paced social reform.

The close of the decade also found strong conservative military dictatorships in power in Argentina and Brazil and a populist military government in Peru, among other countries in the hemisphere that had constitutional civilian governments when the Alliance began and have since lost them. The military governments, whether conservative or populist, maintain that development requires the suspension of democratic participation in public decisions, particularly through political parties. They have explicitly rejected the Alliance proposition that economic growth, social reform, and political democracy are mutually reinforcing aspects of an effective development program.

If the Alliance is defined as policy based on this proposition, the pertinent question becomes not whether it has failed but to what extent it has been attempted.

The spirit in which the U.S. Congress agreed to the creation of the Alliance was less one of compassion for Latin America's needy millions than fear of a spread of Castroism. Even when this fear was at its height, the Congress was less generous in its appropriation of funds than President Kennedy had wished. And as the urgency of the Castro threat diminished, so did the annual Alliance appropriation. At the same time, the priority and cost of the Vietnam War were rising. Preoccupied with Vietnam, the U.S. government has treated Latin America as either a means of shoring up the balance of payments or a potential site for revolutions that might endanger the "national security."

The United States has devoted the largest single portion of its regional aid during the past decade to the development program of authoritarian Brazil. Such allocation may be consistent with the size and importance of Brazil, but it is inconsistent with the criteria for Alliance lending set forth in the charter. Although U.S. policy-makers have debated this issue at great length, they have usually resolved it by giving greater weight to a country's economic performance than to its political or social conditions in determining loan allocations.

Of course the United States has also supplied assistance to Latin American countries in which constitutional processes, accountability of public officials, electoral contests, and party debates have both contributed to the establishment of social reforms and proved compatible with good economic management. But the priority of economic considerations goes far to explain the difference between aims and achievements under the Alliance for Progress.

These considerations have traditionally dominated U.S. pol-

15

icy in Latin America. The Alliance was designed to break free of them. Its fate raises vital questions about the purposes and consequences of foreign development assistance for both donor and recipient.

The Alliance: a preliminary audit

Latin American development:
dependence and change

A wealth of diversity is to be expected in a region more than twice the size of the United States and containing the Andes and the Amazon, the pampa and the Caribbean; but the natural environment alone cannot account for the striking contrasts in development among the several countries of Latin America, and for the deep economic, social, and cultural inequalities within each country.

Until a hundred years ago the Latin American countries were twenty poor, backward former colonies of Spain, Portugal, and France, rural-based societies that were essentially unchanged by independence. Their uniformly low level of trade and consumption supplied the wants of only a small number of propertied autocrats and the simple tools used on the plantations and in the mines. Today Argentina and Venezuela enjoy annual per capita incomes of more than $800. A century ago they were at about the same level as Paraguay, Bolivia, and Honduras, which today scrape by on per capita incomes of about $200 a year, while impoverished Haiti's per capita income is $90 a year.[1] These income disparities represent gaps as wide as those between the most developed Latin American countries and the United States. On the basis of per capita income (United Nations figures for 1964), the most advanced countries, including Chile ($690), Mexico ($580), and southern Brazil (about $500), as well as Argentina and Venezuela, seem to have reached a much higher stage of development than Pakistan ($120) and Kenya ($110).[2] However, the distribution of income and social benefits is such that within even the more developed Latin American countries, including Brazil, Colombia, Chile, and Mexico, huge social sectors live under conditions comparable to those of the truly underdeveloped nations.

These disparities, conspicuous even to casual visitors, place Latin America at a sort of intermediate level, encompassing the full range of both the developed West and the underdeveloped "third world." Brazil, the fifth largest nation in the world, with its industrial south, its impoverished, overcrowded northeastern region, and its undeveloped, tropical Amazon, resembles a conglomerate of Austria, Pakistan, and the Congo. In Brazil and Peru especially among the larger Latin American countries, disparities among internal regions have required the formulation of policies to prevent division and maintain national unity. (Even before the Alliance, under the pressure of political discontent, Brazil had started a development program for the Northeast.)

Differences in national income, technology, modernity of outlook, and social conditions are basic problems of development strategy for both individual countries and the region (constituting major obstacles to regional integration programs such as the proposed Latin American common market). The Argentine farmer who plows the black loam of the pampa by tractor to plant wheat for export and the Bolivian Indian peasant who hoes potatoes for subsistence on the rocky Andean slopes are operating technologically in two different worlds. They may even pray for rain to different gods, but ethnic background is not the basic difference between them. The Ecua-

---

1. United Nations Economic Commission for Latin America, *Social Change and Social Development Policy in Latin America*, E/CN 12/826 (February 1969), Table I–2, p. 23.

2. United Nations, *U.N. National Accounts for 1967*.

Latin American development: dependence and change

dorean banana raftsman and the Mexico City truck driver who delivers refrigerated vegetables to a supermarket may both have been raised in an Indian communal village, but their adult lives are totally different. The Venezuelan oil worker and the Haitian cane cutter are separated by an income gap as great as that between a field hand in a Pakistani rice paddy and a French automobile worker.

The vast differences in income and living standards within and among these nations spring from differences in the market values of the Latin American resources that have been brought into production. And the development of these resources, in most cases, has been not an autonomous process, but the work of foreign entrepreneurs.

Development: the first stage

The past century of Latin American history reveals a pattern. Development in a given area has typically begun with major foreign investments, bringing natural resources into production for sale to the industrialized markets of the West. In the nineteenth century the investors were primarily British financiers and entrepreneurs; since World War I, U.S. investors have gradually supplanted the British.

Chile's modern phase began with the mining of nitrates by the British, followed by U.S. investments in copper. Argentina became a major source of beef for Britain and grains for Europe through railroads and ports built by the British to open up the pampa. Cuba became the world's sugar bowl through U.S. investments. Foreign demand for coffee made Brazil and Colombia the world's largest coffee exporters, with production in local hands but marketing controlled by foreign traders. Venezuela came out of poverty and political anarchy through a bonanza in oil, developed by U.S. and British investments. Bolivia was drawn into the world economy by tin, with the ore transported on a British-built railroad to Pacific ports, where it was loaded aboard British ships to be carried to a smelter near London. The United Fruit Company made banana republics of Ecuador and the Central American countries. Panama's major natural resource—a roadway between the Atlantic and Pacific oceans—was developed by the U.S. Panama Canal Company. In more diversified fashion, but still through foreign investments, Mexico and Peru made their way into foreign markets with nonferrous metals, cotton, oil, and fishery products. This process brought Latin America, in a largely passive and dependent role, into the framework of Western industrial capitalism. It had a massive impact on countries that had been relatively isolated from modernizing change after the Spanish and Portuguese colonial enterprises lost their early creative impetus.

Although this form of development is open to the charge of exploitation, it changed economic conditions dramatically. The trade boom raised the export earnings of some countries from tens of millions to hundreds of millions of dollars in just a few years. European immigration moved into some areas even more rapidly than it had into the United States. An extraordinarily large share of the exchange earned by the new exports remained abroad in the hands of the foreign developers, but the capacity of the Latin American countries to import and borrow abroad rose sharply. Their greatly increased consumption, based on foreign products, opened up new avenues of internal commerce. Although this consumption was still confined to a privileged minority, economic expansion significantly enlarged the higher income sectors. Promoted by the new investments, the ports, railroads, sugar mills, mines, and banana plantations served as bases for the first Latin American attempts to form labor unions, gradually giving rise to a wage elite of organized workers. But as Latin America moved into the first stages of economic development a rift opened between the modern sectors and a backward but populous rural society.

Industrialization

During this period Latin America's foreign trade was able to accommodate rising levels of consumption and underwrite domestic development investments. Trade surpluses paid for a whole range of manufactures. Foreign ships calling at Latin American ports brought barbed wire, cement, trucks, gasoline, canned butter, chinaware, textiles, plate glass, and light bulbs. Latin America's function in the international division of labor was to supply raw materials and foodstuffs and to import industrial goods. Throughout the first forty years of this century, export growth stayed ahead of the import demands of a population increasing in size and diversity of consumption aspirations, despite periodic crises that caused severe hardships. In 1900 Latin American exports per capita stood at $18 a year. In 1939, after the Great Depression, the export level per capita rose to $58. But since World War II, although the absolute level of exports has risen (from $8 billion in 1956 to $11.4 billion in 1966), the per capita level has declined. In 1966 it was down to $39. Latin America's exports have not kept up with its population growth. (The contrary is true of most of the rest of the world, particularly the industrially advanced countries.) Latin America's share of world population has risen from 5 percent to 8 percent in the past two decades. Its share of world trade has dropped in proportion, primarily because, although Latin America has industrialized, it has not developed an export-oriented industrial capacity.

In the 1930s, worldwide depression brought about a collapse of raw material prices, forcing Latin America to cut back its imports drastically. The ensuing hardships provided an incentive for the larger countries to develop their domestic industrial capacity for purposes of import substitution. During World War II, Latin America's enforced isolation from normal sources of industrial supplies led to a degree of domestic substitution, which received strong protection through tariffs and industrial credit after the war. The industrialists emerged from the wartime years as a strong interest group that lobbied aggressively in government circles and used political spokesmen and the press to promote the doctrines of economic nationalism in opposition to the free-trade position of the old commercial interests. The military (which had acquired a penchant for state-owned industries), organized labor, aspiring technocrats and economists emerging from the universities, and the political left in general took the side of the industrialists.

During the 1950s the industrialization process advanced rapidly and the larger countries enjoyed relatively high growth rates. In pursuit of import substitution, government policies required foreign suppliers of many industrial goods to invest in domestic production facilities if they wanted to hold onto their Latin American markets. Thus automobile assembly plants, for example, were rapidly expanded into full-fledged production lines. U.S. corporations, the largest suppliers of industrial goods to Latin America, led the way; by 1965 U.S.-

owned plants were generating local sales worth $5.5 billion, $2 billion more than U.S. exports to the region.[3]

By 1960, however, this form of industrialization had demonstrated some serious drawbacks. In the first place, it did not really resolve the trade deficit problem. Some countries did reduce their imports of manufactured consumer goods to as little as 5 percent of total imports, but the reduction was offset by a growing need for imported industrial raw materials and capital goods. As industry in the larger countries advanced to the stage of producing capital goods, it developed a need for greatly increased volumes of capital, higher levels of technology, and modern corporate management, all of which are scarce in Latin America.

Industrial development has thus been a derivative process dependent on external factors, rather than an indigenous process based on what was available locally (such as abundance of low-cost labor). The limited size of national markets, extraordinarily high protective tariffs, the high cost of capital, and entrepreneurial weakness have kept the prices of domestic substitutes for imports high. Latin American industries have nestled in their captive national markets and shown little interest in or aptitude for export. The U.S. manufacturing firms that hold a dominant position in the region make only 7.5 percent of their sales outside of Latin America. These investments thus do not themselves generate the foreign exchange earnings necessary to finance their remittances of profits, royalties, and services. Foreign remittances due to foreign ownership of key parts of Latin America's industry absorb more than 10 percent of its annual export earnings.

Paradoxically, while making extraordinary efforts to subsidize industrial import substitution, the Latin American countries did little to promote agricultural import substitution. As a result, food imports in countries such as Chile and Colombia have risen in proportion to total imports.

Growth points

If poverty, city slums, migrant workers, welfare, and the "bottom fifth" are symptomatic of severe social ills in the

---

3. *Trends and Short-Term Perspectives of National and Foreign Private Investment in Latin America* (Washington, D.C.: Pan American Union, 1967).

Latin American development: dependence and change

United States, they constitute a crisis of society in Latin America. The United Nations Economic Commission for Latin America (ECLA) calculates that more than half the population of Latin America—130 million people—live on an average annual per capita income of $120. This low level is far higher than that in many parts of the developing world, but Latin American expectations, in this age of trucks, transistors, and television, are not what they were when the rural poor stayed down on the farm and lived out their days in immobile resignation. In contrast, according to ECLA's rough estimates, 60 to 70 percent of national income in nine representative Latin American countries goes to the upper 30 percent of the population, and 25 to 30 percent to the privileged upper 5 percent.[4] The upper 30 percent thus enjoy per capita incomes ranging from $500 to $2,500, and have family incomes and standards of living very much like those of the western European countries, while the bottom half of the population lives at or near subsistence level. In between, an insecure 20 to 30 percent seek desperately to enter the upper group or avoid sliding down to the lower half.

The conventional wisdom has it that the inequalities of income in Latin America are perpetuated by hereditary oligarchies of extraordinary wealth—the "ten families" or "hundred families," depending on the size of the country. This cliché corresponds neither to the political realities, since aristocratic families haven't run Latin American countries for a long time, nor to the complex economic and social conditions of Latin American development. Closer observation suggests that these inequalities are the result of an uneven growth process dominated by external factors, and the reluctance of an extended social sector—the middle groups in particular—to spend a major portion of national income on solving the problems of the huge deprived sector. Many members of the middle class deplore the urban shantytowns and the lack of schools for rural children, but they have their own problems and aspirations, such as buying a family automobile.[5]

---

4. United Nations Economic Commission for Latin America, *Some Aspects of the Latin American Economy Towards the End of the 1960's*, E/CN 12/825 (March 1969), p. 23 and Table I–9; cited hereafter as *Latin American Economy*.
5. The figures suggest that this middle-class ambition has not been entirely frustrated. In the seven more industrialized countries, between 1950 and 1960,

---

In 1963, Raúl Prebisch, the outspoken former executive secretary of ECLA, took a critical look at Latin America's development process. Describing the "Westernized" Latin American consumer mentality as inconsistent with the domestic savings and investment necessary for self-sustained development, he observed:

For a century now our economies have been linked to the international economy, and 50 percent of the population is still stagnating in pre-capitalist conditions which are incompatible with its growing economic and social aspirations. The situation of privilege in the distribution of wealth and therefore of income [is] not reflected in a rapid rate of net capital formation, but in extravagant patterns of consumption in the upper strata of society, contrasting with the unsatisfactory living conditions of the broad masses of the population.[6]

These consumption patterns are closely connected with the unusual concentration of wealth in certain "growth points" where the impact of modernizing change in the economy has been strongest. These growth points are usually major metropolitan areas and industrial centers. Buenos Aires and Lima, for instance, account for more than 40 percent of the total gross domestic product of Argentina and Peru respectively. The state of São Paulo generates 25 percent of gross domestic product and 50 percent of industrial production in Brazil. Mexico City and Santiago, Chile, serve much the same function. Some countries contain several growth points. They are characterized by a concentration of capital, modern technology, and a relatively advanced level of economic organization. All are centers of foreign investment and contain the social category that is most open to external influence.

Kalman Silvert has aptly characterized Latin America's "long and varied experience with a portion of European custom and thought not as a superimposition but as a deeply internalized aspect of society."[7] Latin America's permeability to influences from the West (of which it is, of course, a part) is particularly evident in the consumption patterns of the urban middle

---

the number of passenger automobiles grew from 8 per thousand persons to 22 per thousand. Latin America hasn't caught up with Los Angeles, but it is far ahead of the Soviet Union.

6. Raúl Prebisch, *Toward a Dynamic Development Policy for Latin America, ECLA, and the Analysis of Latin American Development*, E/CN, 2/Ac. 61/10 (United Nations Economic Commission for Latin America, 1963), p. 263.

7. Kalman H. Silvert, *The Conflict Society: Reaction and Revolution in Latin America* (New Orleans: Hauser Press, 1961), p. 11.

Latin American development: dependence and change

groups. In their version of the "American way of life," observed by an American newspaperman in Brazil:

People get up in the morning and shave with an American razor blade, brush their teeth with American toothpaste, eat a bowl of American corn flakes, drive to work in an American car to an office cooled by an American air-conditioner and return home at night to their children, who are watching "Batman" on an American television set, drinking an American soft drink.

The wife has seen an American film that afternoon, the son's been to a Boy Scout meeting and the daughter wants a hot dog for dinner. Turn on an American radio and it's Frank Sinatra or the Tijuana Brass.

All the products, of course, are made in Brazil. But they point up the dramatic role of American influence in Brazil, ranging from such recent novelties as cake mix, cowboy hats, and modern bowling alleys to a summer-long school campaign to fly children to Disneyland.[8]

This life style is confined to the upper third of the income structure, but U.S. mass marketing techniques communicate it indiscriminately to the lower 70 percent as well. These techniques have created a consumption-minded middle class, reluctant to bear the austerity of forced savings necessary for domestic investment, and a huge lower class that is constantly reminded of its have-not condition by images of the good life propagated from the growth points.

Mass marketing may also have catalyzed the dynamic imbalance between growth points and heavily populated areas of traditional poverty, producing massive rural migration to the cities. All industrial cities and new urbanized mining and fishing centers are infested with shantytowns so striking that they have required a whole new vocabulary of local names. In Chile, they are called *callampas,* or "mushroom towns." In Mexico they are called "parachute towns." The Uruguayan *cantegril* is ironically named after a luxurious country club. In Rio de Janeiro, the term *favela* came into use in the late nineteenth century to describe what was then a new and curious urban phenomenon, an encampment of poor but independent people, living within the city radius but not fully assimilated by the organized city. There are now 600,000 people living in several hundred *favelas* in Rio.

All of these terms connote rejection. For decades the social core of the organized city has unsuccessfully striven to confine or exclude the squatters, making their settlements synonymous

8. Charles Keely, "Brazil Has Strong U.S. Flavor," *San Diego Union,* April 14, 1968.

with crime, disease, promiscuity, filth, and subhuman conditions. But the shantytowns actually represent an effort by enterprising sectors of the poor to chip off for themselves some of the wealth located in the growth points.

GNP and the marginal millions

In societies with income disparities as wide as those in Latin America, the gross national product may be misleading as a measure of national development. The Alliance prescribed for all Latin American countries an annual GNP growth rate of at least 2.5 percent per capita. In 1968 the Latin American regional product grew 5.4 percent, with a population growth rate of 2.9 percent, and thus achieved the target. But the per capita GNP figure does not refer to actual distribution of the income increase. Did it all remain concentrated in the modern sectors while the bottom half remained as miserable as ever? What portion of the increased income went to saving and capital accumulation for development? Were investments made primarily in the growth points or in backward areas where the need for investment and the accompanying risk were greatest? The GNP statistic provides no answers to these questions. Other signs indicate that the GNP increases in many Latin American countries simply reflect the performance of the growth points and have little to do with the undercapitalized, and therefore far less productive, poorer half.[9] Gino Germani, an Argentine sociologist, has observed that in Latin America "the cleavages tend to become stronger with time, unless there is some form of deliberate intervention to put compensatory tendencies in motion."[10]

This problem has led a growing school of political and socioeconomic analysts in Latin America to the concept of marginality. According to their analysis, society in many Latin American countries consists of an organized core, conducting class and interest-group relations through common institutions, and

9. It is calculated that in Latin America the 10 percent of workers in the modern sectors of industry and agriculture are ten times more productive than the 50 percent of workers in the technologically primitive sectors of traditional agriculture and artisan workshops, which still account for a large proportion of manufactures. See *Latin American Economy*, pp. 66–68.
10. Gino Germani, "América Latina y el tercer mundo," *Aportes*, no. 10 (Paris, October 1968).

Latin American development: dependence and change

another massive sector of "marginals," who are on the fringe of or entirely excluded from these relations and institutions.

The marginals are not recipients of the so-called common wealth: employment, social security, credit, schooling, vocational training, religious instruction, etc. These benefits, which as the name suggests should be common to all, are in fact accessible only to a privileged third of the population, which enjoys them in different degrees, according to the position of each class or subgroup.

For the remaining two-thirds, the "commonwealth" is a constitutional fiction, but not a democratic reality. If we want to save our democracy, we must make that which society holds in common accessible to the marginals. But it will never be possible for the marginals to share in the common wealth—and this is the heart of the matter—unless it is created, oriented, and apportioned with them and by them. In other words, if the marginal sectors are to become beneficiaries of the common wealth, they must be allowed to participate as active forces, and this necessarily implies a redistribution of political power.[11]

Marginals and political radicalism

Despite the frequency of military coups and other manifestations of political disorder, thoughtful observers of the Latin American scene note that these old societies are really quite stable. As one such observer has put it, the "equilibrium mechanisms" of the Latin American societies include "occasional coups d'état, violence, palace revolts, elite replacements, but rarely revolutions."[12] These political disturbances are, in other words, mere safety valves, the means by which the societies have adjusted to relieve pressures or to accommodate new groups within the core.

But today's pressures come from the marginals, a group excluded, by definition, from political participation. The attempts of the left to bring this group into the political arena pose grave threats to the existing power structures. Their traditional safety valves are clearly inadequate to accommodate the marginals, whose growing numbers and demands thus raise the potential for revolution to change the structure of society radically.

On this issue rests the present debate in Latin America between the proponents of "one man, one vote" constitutional government and those who defend authoritarian government in

11. José Galat, *El Tercer Mundo* (Bogotá, November 1968).
12. Anthony Leeds, *A Latin American Research Review*, 3, no. 2 (Spring 1968): 83.

the name of national security and economic management. According to this elitist position, Latin American countries are now ungovernable through open political institutions, because the poor and their political spokesmen would only use them for the redistribution of wealth and, given the scarcity of capital, would wipe out the savings and investments necessary for growth.

The conservative position in Latin America today does not go to the extreme of advocating unregulated privilege. The technocrats in charge of national planning and economic programs in countries like Brazil and Argentina, where the military are in power, believe in taxation as a means of financing accelerated economic growth. As Prebisch has said:

> It is not a matter of taking income away from the upper minority and simply distributing it among the broad masses of the population, for with per capita personal income in Latin America as a whole barely amounting to $370 a year [1963] the benefits of such a redistribution would not stretch very far. But if, on the other hand, restrictions on the consumption of the privileged groups were reflected in a steady increase in net capital formation, the standard of living of the bulk of the population would rise progressively faster.[13]

Measures to induce and allocate savings are clearly part of modern development policy-making, but such planning alone is no guarantee of social reform.

In a conservative political environment hostile to experiment and structural change, planning will be concentrated in the fiscal-monetary area, and stability will be prized above social investment. The planners will favor limiting the state role in social policy and providing incentives for the private sector to make investments under stable market conditions.

In a political environment congenial to reform and change, planners are likely to give equal priority to modernizing the social structure and modernizing the economic system. They will encourage use of the instruments of state to break up obstacles to both economic growth and social mobility.[14]

---

13. Prebisch, *Dynamic Development Policy*, p. 265.
14. The Christian Democrats in Chile and Venezuela have a "humanist" ideology of development that stresses political participation by all members of the national community so that all will share in its responsibilities and benefits. *Acción Democrática* in Venezuela and the Liberal party in Colombia, both of which were influenced by the New Deal and contributed to the political philosophy of the Alliance, adhere to policies that include social reforms as part of national development.

Latin American development: dependence and change

Obviously, the choice of either approach is fundamentally political. The technocrats, however, claim that economic growth alone will gradually alleviate social inequalities even in countries where dissent is repressed by force.

The Latin American intelligentsia, particularly its younger elements, increasingly favors a Marxist analysis of Latin American development problems. The Marxists perceive marginality as a product of the capitalist order and the effect of United States "economic imperialism" on a developing country. They advocate armed revolution—power out of the barrel of a gun—as the only means of achieving genuine social integration.

Radical politics in Latin America is a combination of marginal action, usually with limited, local objectives, such as a land invasion, and the militant rebellion of disaffected core members against the immobility or injustice of the social and political order. The ranks of the disaffected consist primarily of student leaders, but also include progressive intellectuals and concerned professionals, priests, and social workers. Even military officers sometimes reach the conclusion that a society that will not help its poor can't save its rich and so must be changed.

This dissident elite, as it was characterized by the late Jorge Ahumada, an intellectual leader of the Chilean Christian Democrats, becomes disengaged from the core structure and leads a revolutionary movement against the established order from which it has become estranged, subjectively or ideologically. Cuba exemplifies the effectiveness of this formula for revolutionary change.

A more technical and presumably bloodless route to the radical objectives has been postulated by Celso Furtado, a Brazilian political economist:

In Latin America, development cannot be the simple result of the spontaneous operation of market forces. Only the conscious and deliberate action of the central policy-making organs can carry forward this development. What is known today as the "Latin American revolution" consists in a growing consciousness of the problem and in efforts, which are still dispersed and intermittent, to create political institutions capable of bringing about the social changes without which development is not viable. Since the present ruling classes do not understand the nature of the problem and obstinately maintain the status quo, those who work effectively in Latin America for development are playing, consciously or not, a "revolutionary" role.[15]

The special relationship

The fact that Latin America turned to the United States for help in solving its development problems should surprise no American. The United States had sought out and promoted special relationships with the other American republics through both public and private efforts for many years.

In July 1906, Secretary of State Elihu Root attended the Third International Conference of American States in Rio de Janeiro. Shortly after his return he addressed an audience of businessmen, the Trans-Mississippi Commercial Congress, in Kansas City, Missouri, and set the course of subsequent inter-American relations:

The United States have for the first time accumulated a surplus of capital beyond the requirements of internal development. That surplus is increasing with extraordinary rapidity. We have paid our debts to Europe and have become a creditor instead of a debtor nation; we have faced about; we have left the ranks of the borrowing nations and have entered the ranks of the investing nations. Our surplus energy is beginning to look beyond our own borders, throughout the world, to find surplus capital, foreign markets for our manufactures, foreign mines to be developed, foreign bridges and railroads and public works to be built, foreign rivers to be turned into electric power and light.

Immediately before us, at exactly the right time, just as we are ready for it, great opportunities for peaceful commerce and industrial expansion to the south are presented.[16]

Root described the natural resources and trade potential of Latin America in glowing terms and succinctly defined the complementarity of the Americas: "Where we accumulate, they spend."

Since that speech, U.S. investments in Latin America have grown steadily, and with them an elaborate system of regional political and security relations, culminating in 1948 in the Organization of American States (OAS), which absorbed the Pan American Union. The United States has become the most important external political and economic influence in Latin

---

15. Celso Furtado, *Subdesenvolvimento e Estagnação na América Latina* (Rio de Janeiro: Editora Civilização Brasileira, 1966), p. 40 (our translation).
16. Elihu Root, speech quoted in *The Evolution of Our Latin American Policy*, ed. James W. Gantebein (New York: Columbia University Press, 1950), pp. 63–69.

Latin American development: dependence and change

America, and has used this influence in the pursuit of certain permanent objectives, including:

(a) Political stability based on the rule of law in relatively open societies, to ensure equal treatment of foreigners and nationals, protection of the rights of property, and respect for international agreements; what Root called "the safety of property and the certainty of justice."

(b) Economic growth, leading to expanded commercial relations and attractive investment opportunities for U.S. private capital, primarily in natural resources of strategic value, such as petroleum and nonferrous metals, but with increasing emphasis recently on manufacturing.

(c) Prevention of war among Latin American countries by the establishment of procedures for the peaceful settlement of inter-American disputes, particularly to obviate the involvement of extracontinental powers in such disputes.

On the basis of a rather narrow set of interests the United States assumed the right to intervene by force in the turbulent internal affairs of its debtor neighbors of the Caribbean and Central America and acquired the habit of defining good government unilaterally in a number of Latin American countries. The U.S. Marines would come ashore "to protect the lives and property" of U.S. citizens, and hard on their heels the agents of the U.S. creditor banks would follow, taking over the customhouse until the bills were paid. Critics quickly came to characterize U.S. policy in terms of Wall Street, the United Fruit Company, Electric Bond and Share, and other symbols of "economic imperialism."

The New Deal, more sensitive to this charge than the preceding Republican administrations, suspended the humiliating military intrusions. Franklin D. Roosevelt won the goodwill of millions of Latin Americans without spending a cent by announcing that the Good Neighbor Policy rested on the principle of nonintervention. It made little difference to Washington that the "good neighbors" included fledgling dictators such as Rafael Trujillo in the Dominican Republic and Fulgencio Batista in Cuba, or that Argentina, Brazil, and Peru, among others, were under authoritarian governments. Although the New Dealers had no enthusiasm for dictators, the Good Neighbor Policy was not a democratic crusade.

As World War II approached, Roosevelt sought a united hemispheric effort in support of the Allied cause. The Dominican Republic and Cuba were among the first countries to break relations with Germany and Japan. Roosevelt is reported to have said that of course Trujillo was a son-of-a-bitch, but he was *our* son-of-a-bitch. Colonel Juan Domingo Perón, leader of a pro-German military faction in Argentina, was not ours, and the United States bitterly opposed him. (As it turned out, this opposition helped him to be elected president in 1946. The U.S. ambassador at that time was Spruille Braden, and one of Perón's most effective campaign slogans asked who was going to run Argentina: "Braden or Perón?" For a long time this election was used in conservative U.S. circles as an example of the results of meddling in Latin America.)

The cold war added a corollary to the three cardinal objectives of the United States' inter-American policy. It stated that revolution, specifically the overthrow of a government adhering to U.S. rules for inter-American amity by political forces committed to radical social change, was inherently dangerous to U.S. interests and challenged American leadership of the inter-American system. A revolutionary regime that took a nationalist position and had a negligible effect on American private property could resume normalized relations with the United States, as Bolivia did in 1952. But revolutionaries who adopted Marxist ideology, affected large U.S. property interests, and sought political and military support from the Soviet Union to offset American influence would constitute a direct threat to U.S. national security and basic interests in the hemisphere. A result of this reasoning is the CIA-sponsored operation that overthrew the leftist government of Jacobo Arbenz in Guatemala in 1954.

The Kennedy administration sought to place inter-American relations on a new footing and identify the United States with the forces of democratic change and social integration. The old ruling circles in the Latin American countries, the 5 percent who owned property, and the military, on whose collaboration the United States had depended for years, could no longer be counted upon to maintain political stability and provide the conditions for inter-American amity. Only govern-

Latin American development: dependence and change

ments congenial to change could accommodate the political dissent of middle-class social revolutionaries and respond to the pressing demands of the have-nots. The old guard would have to be induced, by persuasion and the carrot-and-stick management of U.S. aid, to make room for new progressive forces.

By giving its support to the democratic left, liberals predicted, the new administration would be able to prevent revolutionary movements mortally hostile to the United States from seizing power. Such a policy would protect United States interests and security without the painful "necessity" of repressive political and military intervention.

As the expression of this theory, the Alliance for Progress did not constitute abandonment by the United States of its traditional policy objectives in Latin America. It was simply the response to what was considered a new situation—emerging revolutionary forces, different in kind and intensity from earlier movements for political and social change. The new dimension that this response added to U.S. policy in Latin America was its explicit recognition of a relationship between the United States' attainment of its objectives and the fate of landless peasants, hungry people in urban hovels, illiterate and diseased children, and young men and women without skills or employment opportunities.

However, the United States still reserved the right of political and military intervention in Latin America *after* the beginning of the Alliance for Progress in 1961.

The inter-American crisis

Unless necessary social reforms,
including land and tax reforms,
are freely made—unless we broaden
the opportunity of all our people—
unless the great mass of Americans
share in increasing prosperity—
then our alliance, our revolution
and our dream will have failed.
John F. Kennedy, 1961

Less than two months after his inauguration, President Kennedy invited the Latin American diplomatic corps and a bipartisan representation of the U.S. Congress to a White House reception. On March 13, 1961, Jacqueline Kennedy, radiant in a silk print dress, led the diplomats and their wives on a tour of the executive mansion, and then President Kennedy delivered the speech that launched the Alliance for Progress.[1]

Instead of mouthing the tired rhetoric of hemispheric unity and the common American quest for the dignity and freedom of man, Kennedy addressed himself to the revolutionary problems and possibilities confronting the Americas. As he saw it, the need of the people of Latin America for homes, work, land, health, and schools was so "staggering in its dimensions" that only a bold program—"a vast effort unparalleled in magnitude and nobility of purpose"—could hope to meet it. The instrument he proposed for this mission, the Alliance for Progress, would be not just a U.S. aid program but a joint effort in which all the American nations would "mobilize their re-

---

1. See Appendix A for text.

sources, enlist the energies of their people, and modify their social patterns so that all and not just a privileged few share in the fruits of progress."

Kennedy outlined a specific ten-point program:

1. A decade of "maximum effort."
2. A meeting of the Inter-American Economic and Social Council (the future Punta del Este meeting) to "begin the massive planning effort which will be the head of the Alliance for Progress."
3. An initial U.S. contribution of $500 million (which Kennedy was about to request from Congress) for the Social Progress Trust Fund, formed by Eisenhower in 1960 for social investment in Latin America.
4. Support for Latin American economic integration through a Latin American free-trade area and the Central American Common Market.
5. U.S. cooperation in "serious, case-by-case examinations of commodity market problems" to stabilize prices in the Latin American countries.
6. Expansion of the Food for Peace emergency program to supply U.S. surplus food to Latin America for school lunches and hunger areas.
7. Sharing of advances in science and research through cooperation among universities and research institutions, and inclusion of Latin American instructors in U.S. science teacher-training programs.
8. Expanded technical training programs and assistance to Latin American universities to supply the trained personnel "needed to man the economies of rapidly developing countries."
9. A renewal of the U.S. pledge to defend all American nations "whose independence is endangered" through the collective security system of the OAS, enabling these nations "to devote to constructive use a major share of those resources now spent on instruments of war."
10. An educational and cultural exchange program to increase appreciation in the United States of Latin American accomplishments in thought and the creative arts.

The success of this program would mean that in 1970 "the need for massive outside help will have passed" and every

American nation would be "the master of its own revolution of hope and progress."

The day after his Alliance speech, Kennedy submitted to Congress a message containing both his request of $500 million for the Social Progress Trust Fund and some further thoughts. He observed that true social progress depended not only on funds, but also "on the willingness of each recipient nation to improve its own institutions, make necessary modifications in its own social patterns, and mobilize its own domestic resources for a program of development." He encouraged United States business concerns to assist in this development by transferring their technical and management skills to Latin American enterprises through licensing, joint ventures, and other private channels. And he added a note of urgency: "Latin America is seething with discontent and unrest. We must act to relieve large-scale distress immediately if free institutions are to be given a chance to work out long-term solutions."

A wave of expectation spread from Washington through the hemisphere. In a tone of enthusiasm and conviction, the appealing young American president had expressed the same positions that the Latin Americans themselves had become weary of restating to uninterested U.S. officials.

The origins of the Alliance

The record of inter-American relations from World War II to 1961 is one long Latin American plea for development assistance, met by U.S. resistance except at moments of crisis. In 1940 the United States sought "active" neutrality from Latin America against the Axis powers. At the second meeting of American foreign ministers, in Havana, Secretary of State Cordell Hull outlined a basis for inter-American economic cooperation when the war was over. He explicitly stated that the United States would support the establishment of an inter-American bank to "foster cooperation in the spheres of long-term development and of money and foreign exchange." In 1942, to accelerate a break with the Axis powers by Brazil and Chile, the Export-Import Bank agreed to finance Latin America's first integrated steel mills at Volta Redonda, Brazil, and the Huachipato works near Concepción, Chile. These plants went into operation after the war, but Latin America had hoped for broader economic assistance in the postwar era. At the inter-American conference on war and peace at Mexico City in 1945, the Latin Americans agreed to back the creation of the United Nations but insisted on retaining a strong organizational tie with the United States. At the conclusion of the conference the United States and the Latin American nations issued a joint statement in favor of economic cooperation among the American nations. They declared that poverty, malnutrition, or ill health among any of their peoples affected all of them jointly, and that education and material well-being were indispensable to the development of democracy. They proposed the equitable coordination of all interests to create an economy of abundance, utilizing natural resources and human labor to raise the standard of living of all the peoples of the continent.

Before these general objectives could be applied in specific programs of regional economic cooperation, the cold war began. Latin America aligned itself with the United States, through the 1947 Rio de Janeiro Treaty of Reciprocal Assistance, which commits its signatories to collective action in defense of any member state suffering "extracontinental" aggression. But Latin America's hopes for economic assistance were subordinated to a higher security priority, the reconstruction of western Europe.

At the Ninth Inter-American Conference at Bogotá in 1948 —the first held after the war—Secretary of State George C. Marshall explained that the United States could not simultaneously undertake the economic reconstruction of Europe and provide massive assistance to the underdeveloped world; Latin America would have to wait until Europe was on its feet. The Latin American leadership, although disappointed, conceded priority to Europe. Moreover, key countries in Latin America still had substantial foreign exchange reserves that they had built up during World War II, and so they did not regard a massive economic assistance program as an urgent necessity. The formation in 1949 of a joint U.S.-Brazilian commission to study the prospects for development and to recommend priority areas of investment in Brazil seemed to lend substance to Marshall's words.

The Eisenhower years

In 1953, following the election of President Eisenhower, the work of the joint commission was discontinued. The economic conference promised by Marshall at Bogotá was shelved, and the fulfillment of commitments that the Latins thought they had received from Hull and Marshall kept receding into the future. At the Tenth Inter-American Conference in Caracas, in March 1954, Secretary of State John Foster Dulles' main purpose was to obtain a joint statement from the Latin American governments that a communist-dominated regime in the hemisphere represented a threat to inter-American security in accordance with the terms of the Rio de Janeiro Treaty of 1947. The threat that Dulles had in mind was the government of Colonel Jacobo Arbenz, who had been elected president of Guatemala in 1951. His regime included communists in key positions and attracted revolutionary followers from all over Latin America, including a young Argentine, Ernesto "Che" Guevara. Continuing the vigorous agrarian reform begun by his predecessor, Juan José Arévalo, a left-wing nationalist, Arbenz had expropriated some lands belonging to the United Fruit Company. Dulles stayed at the conference just long enough to get agreement on the Declaration of Caracas. This declaration provided more or less legal sanction for a plot, supported by the CIA, to overthrow the Arbenz regime. A few months later, a group of Guatemalan exiles under the leadership of a devotedly anticommunist colonel, Carlos Castillo Armas, toppled Arbenz.

Quitandinha

In exchange for the Latin American votes at Caracas, Dulles had to go through with the economic conference that Marshall had promised at Bogotá. In November 1954 the Inter-American Economic and Social Council of the Organization of American States met at the Hotel Quitandinha, in the mountains above Rio near Petrópolis in Brazil. The hotel that gave the conference its name was architecturally a cross between a Swiss chalet and a medieval castle. Quitandinha had been built during World War II as a resort hotel and casino, but with the prohibition of gambling in Brazil in 1945 it had become a white elephant. The main sessions of the meeting were held where the old roulette tables had stood.

The United States was represented at the meeting by Secretary of the Treasury George Humphrey, the strong man of the Eisenhower administration. He was the champion of private-enterprise orthodoxy just as Dulles was the leader of the anti-communist crusade. On the Latin American side, the list of delegates included Eduardo Frei Montalva, then a Chilean senator (later president of Chile from 1965 to 1970); Carlos Lleras Restrepo, then economic policy-maker of Colombia's Liberal party (later president of Colombia from 1966 to 1970); Felipe Herrera, then general manager of Chile's Central Bank (now president of the Inter-American Development Bank); and Roberto de Oliveira Campos, a Brazilian diplomat-economist (ambassador in Washington during the Kennedy administration and later minister of planning, the economic czar of the Castelo Branco government from 1964 to 1967). These sophisticated, self-confident young leaders, clearly destined for national prominence, were eager to set forth Latin America's case for economic assistance and the way in which it should be implemented. Their views largely paralleled the theses developed by the United Nations Economic Commission for Latin America (ECLA) under the direction of Raúl Prebisch, an Argentine economist driven from his country by Perón. Prebisch's strong personality made him the principal spokesman for Latin American developmental theories.

In preparation for Quitandinha, Prebisch had called a conference of Latin American experts, ostensibly to prepare the ECLA annual report but in reality to establish the Latin American position. The chairman of the Committee of Experts, as it came to be known, was Eduardo Frei and the *rapporteur* was Carlos Lleras Restrepo. The committee's report agreed with the diagnosis of Prebisch and his staff at ECLA. It stated that the export boom enjoyed by Latin America as a consequence of the Korean war was coming to an end. At the same time, the "spread of knowledge through communications advances had made the common man aware of the standard of living of other peoples," given the "masses a clear understanding of their own needs, and stimulated more pressing demands than the present rate of growth was capable of satisfying." The resulting "political instability and ever increasing social tensions . . . were frequently transformed into a barren disintegrating struggle to share a communal income which hardly increases at all."[2]

The report indicated that the major constraints on economic development were insufficient domestic savings and inadequate growth of export earnings, the latter due to excessive dependence on the prices of a few major primary commodities, such as wheat, coffee, tin, and copper. Because the prices for these commodities were declining while those of industrial imports were rising, the report concluded, the trend of the "terms of trade" was against Latin America. So long as the Latin economies were dependent on these primary commodities, they would have little chance for sustained advance.

The key to development lay in an aggressive industrialization policy that would substitute domestic manufactures for imports and eventually lead to a more diversified export pattern. However, what Latin America needed immediately was an assured flow of foreign exchange to bridge this transition, through stabilization of the prices paid by the industrialized world for its basic commodities and through long-term low-interest loans to compensate for the insufficiency of savings.

Recommending both international cooperation and domestic self-help for Latin American economic development, the Report of the Experts was a precursor of the Alliance for Progress. It proposed:

1. An annual foreign investment level of $1 billion for ten years, provided by the International Bank for Reconstruction and Development and the Export-Import Bank ($600–650 million), the Inter-American Fund ($50–100 million), and direct private investment ($300–350 million).
2. An inter-American fund for industrial, agricultural, and mining development, primarily financing Latin American entrepreneurs (ultimately the Inter-American Development ment Bank).
3. National planning to establish priorities and allocate investments, private as well as public.

---

2. "Report of the Preparatory Group Appointed by the Secretariat of the United Nations Economic Commission for Latin America," transmitted to the executive secretary by letter dated August 25, 1954, reprinted in U.N. document E/CN 12/359; hereafter referred to as Report of the Experts.

4. Commodity price stabilization agreements for Latin America's major export products.

The Report of the Experts, circulated in advance of the meeting, represented the first time that the Latin Americans had quantified their ideas about external assistance. There was an air of nervous anticipation about the room as George Humphrey approached the dais to present the U.S. position. It was brutally negative. Humphrey urged the Latins to concentrate on attracting private foreign investment to the region and to improve the investment climate through control of inflation and maintenance of realistic exchange rates. To the proposed inter-American development bank the answer was no. Nor would the United States have any part of commodity stabilization agreements or national planning.

The position that Humphrey represented, he said, was a "firm determination to maintain a strong healthy economy in the United States" and an "international system of free trade." Although his government was

aware of your intense and very understandable interest in this problem as it relates to the prices for your products sold in the world market . . . our experience convinces us that if we as governments follow policies which will give our producers everywhere maximum assurance that consumption of their products will enjoy a steady and natural growth and that their access to the international markets will be facilitated, then we will have gone far toward solving this basic problem of prices that concerns us all.

The United States would accept no tampering with the free play of market forces and capital movements.

Humphrey stayed at Quitandinha only two days, just long enough to make his statement and meet briefly with each of the Latin American ministers. Then he left the U.S. delegation in the hands of Andrew Overby, an assistant secretary of the treasury, to clean up the work of the conference.

Another American present was Eugene Black, president of the World Bank, who delivered a speech:

There is a tendency, I regret to say, to think of the bank as a convenient syphon for drawing funds from the public treasury of capital-exporting nations. The fact, let me emphasize, is far different. Our investments in the American republics have been made mostly out of private funds raised by the bank through the sale of securities invested in the United States of America and in many other countries.

On attempts to establish minimum levels of international transfers, Mr. Black said:

In the presentation of calculations of this kind, little attention is usually paid to the heavy burden that would be imposed on the foreign financiers of countries that follow them. The export receipts of the Latin American nations are none too adequate to meet current import needs. We expect that these exports will grow much more rapidly than the demand for increased imports needed for higher standards of living.[3]

The Latin American delegates came away with only a vague exhortation to do the best they could with what they had, which was none too good, and some vague assurance that if they did their homework, prepared better projects, and kept their finances under control, things might get better in the future.

During one of the final sessions of the Commission on External Financing, Lleras Restrepo of Colombia told the story of a Colombian who set up a stand in the marketplace over which he placed a sign that said "Fresh Fish Sold Here." A friend came along and said, "That sign is too long. Why do you say 'Fresh Fish'? Everyone knows that you would not be selling rotten fish." So the man struck out the word "Fresh." Another friend appeared and said, "Why do you say 'Here'? Obviously that's where you are selling the fish." So the sign was reduced to "Fish Sold." Another friend came along and said, "You wouldn't be putting the fish out here if you weren't going to sell them. Why don't you take out 'Sold'?" The man did, leaving just one word: "Fish." Finally, a fourth friend came along and said, "You don't need to say 'Fish.' Anybody can tell what you are selling from the smell." So the man took away the one remaining word. "And that's the way it is with United States aid," said Lleras Restrepo; "after all the discussions we have had here, all that is left is the smell."

Buenos Aires, 1957

Three years passed between Quitandinha and the next major Inter-American Economic Conference, at Buenos Aires in 1957, without any significant change in U.S. policy. Robert D. Anderson, who had succeeded Humphrey as secretary of the treasury, had a more courteous and agreeable personality than

---

3. *Actas de las sesiones del Consejo Interamericano Económico y Social, IV Sesión Extraordinaria* (Washington, D.C.: Pan American Union, 1954).

Humphrey's, but his message was essentially the same. Anderson also stressed the unity of the hemisphere against communism. And he suggested a method by which the Latin American countries could most rapidly and most efficiently develop their resources:

History has demonstrated the vital role of the competitive enterprise system in the economic life of our hemisphere. Just as true leadership is best in the climate of political freedom, so in the economic field the system of competitive enterprise promises the most in the satisfaction of man's material needs. This system produces most of what people want most.[4]

He spoke with satisfaction of the increase in Latin American exports to the United States from $3.4 billion in 1954 to $3.6 billion in 1956, and the $1.4 billion increase of U.S. investments in Latin America between Quitandinha and Buenos Aires.

At that time the U.S. government's Development Loan Fund, to provide long-term, low-interest international loans, was in the works but not yet a reality. Alluding to the possibility of a substantial increase in public capital lending, Anderson cautiously declared, "The extent of our effort will be determined by careful planning, by the ability of the countries to draw capital, and by the assurance of realistic benefits to the economy and the people of the republics involved." It was the language of Eugene Black.

To the inter-American bank proposal Anderson replied, "As far as we can see ahead we believe that the adequacy of capital to meet the needs of sound development is not a question of additional institutions but the full utilization of those in being" (the Export-Import Bank, the World Bank, the International Finance Corporation, and the future Development Loan Fund).

Anderson, like Humphrey, spent only a couple of days at the conference, but his successor as head of the U.S. delegation was C. Douglas Dillon, who had just become undersecretary of state for economic affairs after several years as U.S. ambassador in Paris. This was Dillon's first exposure to Latin American problems, and they intrigued him. As an internationally oriented Wall Street investment banker, fresh from experienc-

4. *Actas de la segunda sesión plenaria de la Conferencia Económica de la Organización de los Estados Americanos* (Buenos Aires, 1957).

ing the "miracle" of western European economic recovery, he looked at Latin America with a positive eye. His experience was eventually to be of considerable significance.

The Nixon trip

The Eisenhower administration was shaken from its position on inter-American affairs not by appeals or polemics but by the violence that Vice-President Nixon encountered during his goodwill tour of Latin America in April and May 1958. Nixon's assignment was to demonstrate U.S. interest in the hemisphere as well as U.S. support for democratic regimes (Colombia and Venezuela) that had recently supplanted dictatorships previously supported by the United States.

In Lima, Peru, an attempted debate with the students at San Marcos University turned into a riot between police and militant students protesting Nixon's visit. Nixon faced the rioters for a brief, tense moment and was spat upon by a demonstrator as he turned back to his hotel. Except for this disturbing incident, the trip was comparatively placid until the last stop —Caracas, the capital of Venezuela. On the road from the airport to the city, a howling mob tried to overturn the official car in which Nixon was riding. Nixon had a moment of real danger as local security police vainly struggled to control the rock-throwing mob. While U.S. Secret Service men were beating off the attackers, the driver of the car saw an opening in the crowd, gunned the motor, and sped Nixon away to the safety of the U.S. embassy residence.

Eisenhower alerted airborne troops to be in readiness for a rescue operation to get Nixon out of Caracas. This effort proved unnecessary; Nixon cut short his visit and Eisenhower gave him a hero's welcome at National Airport. But the violence of this incident, in which the life of a vice-president of the United States had been endangered, told the world that something was seriously wrong in the hemisphere.

One of the Latin American leaders most impressed by the Nixon experience was President Juscelino Kubitschek of Brazil, who regarded it as proof that without a change in U.S. policies the inter-American system was moving toward collapse. He suggested as much to Roy Rubottom, the assistant secretary of state for Latin American affairs, who visited him a week after the Caracas incident. Rubottom saw the incident as evidence of a communist conspiracy in the hemisphere, and he sought Kubitschek's cooperation in a program that would co-ordinate the police forces of the hemisphere to deal with this problem. Kubitschek refused. Then Secretary of State Dulles came to see him. During an all-day discussion Kubitschek attempted to persuade Dulles that the problem was not one for the police, that its source was misery and desperation among masses of people. He suggested a massive attack upon these problems through a dramatic program of economic development which he called Operation Pan-America. Dulles remained immovable until Kubitschek refused to appear with him at a joint press conference. "You explain to the press the result of these talks," Kubitschek said.[5]

Dulles relented and agreed that the United States would hold a regional conference to consider Kubitschek's proposals. A turning point had been reached.

The meeting of American foreign ministers in Washington, in September 1958, was preceded by an announcement that the United States was prepared at last to consider the establishment of an inter-American development banking institution. The proposed bank became an important item on the agenda of the conference, along with plans to implement Operation Pan-America. The conference chose a "Committee of 21" to deal with the problem. The United States was represented on the committee by Rubottom and Thomas C. Mann, then assistant secretary of state for economic affairs.

The United States followed its acceptance of a role in the IDB with other concessions. While it continued to insist on the primacy of private enterprise and on the need for anti-inflationary austerity in Latin American public spending, it also showed a new readiness to provide Latin America with supplementary long-term public capital resources through the Development Loan Fund. At the same time, Mann began to promote U.S. participation in an international coffee agreement, on which negotiations had foundered previously because the Eisenhower administration opposed international price-stabilizing commodity agreements. The favorable reception of these moves by Latin American governments encouraged Eisenhower to make a personal tour of the area. In November 1958

<hr>

5. Interview with Juscelino Kubitschek, Rio de Janeiro, August 1968.

<hr>

he visited Brazil, Chile, Argentina, and Uruguay. Only a minor student incident in Montevideo marred an otherwise highly enthusiastic public reception. But the ensuing sense of triumph was short-lived.

Castro's proposal

Fidel Castro's revolutionary forces entered Havana on January 5, 1959. The fall of the Batista dictatorship in Cuba heightened concern about revolutionary potential throughout Latin America. Commodity problems, particularly those of coffee, and inflationary difficulties, particularly those in Brazil at the end of the Kubitschek regime, began to be looked upon less as technical matters than as aspects of a political crisis. The Committee of 21 convened a second plenary session at Buenos Aires in May 1959. Its discussions were sharpened by the presence of Castro as head of the Cuban delegation.

This international conference was the first face-to-face encounter between the United States and the "new" Cuba. (At this time, relations between the two countries were still marked by courtesy and politeness.) Castro's presence provoked great curiosity. He brought to the conference security police, Klieg lights, pretty girls, and cheering crowds. From the moment he entered the wood-paneled meeting room on the ninth floor of the Industry and Commerce Ministry and took his place at the delegates' table behind a placard reading "Cuba," Castro's every move drew the attention of the room. He nervously jiggled his legs, pulled at his mustache, chewed at the end of his pencil, puffed on cigarettes, made asides to the photographers, and chatted amicably with the Ecuadorian and Colombian delegates, who flanked him.

The room was hushed as the bearded leader rose, in his green fatigue uniform, to address the meeting. He began his speech in a soft voice and jerky sentences, improvising, as is his habit, from a few written notes. He stated that the chronic potential instability of the Latin American governments of the period was the result, not the cause, of economic underdevelopment. (Across the room, Augusto Federico Schmidt, the Brazilian delegate, commented, "Very good. This man really understands the spirit of Operation Pan-America.") Castro said he agreed with the United States that the Soviet threat should not be the basis of Latin American requests for aid.

"We do not want to be a battlefield of political conflicts," he said.

Repudiating the traditional belief that Latin underdevelopment resulted from deficiencies in the Latin character and the enervating tropical climate, Castro declared, "The evil is not in ourselves, but in our economic conditions; the causes are not in the Latin American man, in his capacity for governing himself, in the intelligence of the Latin American man, but in the economies that we have had from the beginning." Castro therefore proposed that the United States supply $30 billion over a ten-year period to support a Latin American development effort, adding:

What we are proposing will not adversely affect the United States. It will benefit future generations, since with a developed Latin America, the United States will have more commerce, just as it has more commerce with a developed Canada than with a backward Canada. Besides, if we solve the economic problems now, we will lay the base for a humanist democracy in the future.[6]

On behalf of the United States and with visible annoyance, Rubottom rejected Castro's proposal. He noted the steps already taken by free-world nations, increasing the resources for economic development by about $15 billion: (1) agreement to establish an inter-American development bank; (2) increases in the resources of the Export-Import Bank; (3) proposed large increases in the resources of the World Bank, the International Monetary Fund, and the Development Loan Fund. "We do not know of any applications for economically sound development loans that have been rejected for lack of funds," Rubottom declared, adding that Castro's proposal "takes no account of the internal measures which capital importing countries must take in order to make international cooperation effective."[7] The Cuban resolution was tabled and Castro never appeared again at an inter-American ministerial conference.

In September 1959, at a meeting of foreign ministers in Santiago, Chile, the United States tried unsuccessfully to persuade the Latin Americans to condemn Cuba's increasing association

6. "Castro Calls on U.S. for More Aid," *New York Times*, May 3, 1959, pp. 1, 35.
7. Press release of U.S. delegation to meeting of Committee of 21, Buenos Aires, May 1959.

with the Soviet Union. The Latin Americans responded by raising the economic issue. In early 1960 the foreign ministers met again in San José, Costa Rica, to deal with Cuba. The Cuban delegation, led by Foreign Minister Raúl Roa, walked out before the other delegates adopted a resolution condemning Cuba for intervention in the domestic affairs of its neighbors.

The conference also considered the attempted assassination of Rómulo Betancourt, the president of Venezuela, by an agent of the Dominican dictator, Rafael Leonidas Trujillo. The agent, using a remote-control detonating device, had placed an automobile loaded with dynamite on the route that Betancourt was riding through Caracas. The car exploded but Betancourt escaped alive, although he was badly burned. The agent was captured and confessed the origin of the plot. The United States reluctantly yielded to Venezuela's demand for a collective blockade of the Dominican Republic—partly in the hope of using it as precedent for similar action against Cuba.

The Social Progress Trust Fund

The United States broke off commercial relations with the Castro regime in June 1960. But Washington's growing anxiety about the possibility of revolution in other Latin American countries heightened its responsiveness to their problems and spurred it to positive action. By the time the Committee of 21 met in Bogotá, Colombia, in September 1960, Eisenhower had announced U.S. willingness to establish a $500 million Social Progress Trust Fund for investment in low-cost housing, public primary education, rural waterworks, health services, and other social projects in Latin America that had never before been eligible for U.S. public loans.

The meeting took place at the Military Casino, a sort of elegant country club for Colombian military officers, on the outskirts of Bogotá. The U.S. delegation was headed by Dillon, who had become a strong advocate in the State Department of a major social aid program for Latin America. Cuba was represented by its minister of economy, Regino Boti, a Harvard-educated economist. Boti again introduced the proposal of a development fund of $3 billion a year to be employed in Latin America over a ten-year period. By this time U.S.-Cuban relations had become openly hostile. Dillon replied sharply to Boti's proposal:

In the first place, there is no indication as to how the $3 billion a year of development capital is to be obtained. I know of no way that a fixed amount of capital can be assured over a long period ahead. No government can foresee what amount of capital might be available annually over the coming ten years. Presently we, in this Committee of 21, are in no position to establish such a fund or even to recommend its creation when we know in our hearts that that cannot come into being. [The subject of Latin American development] is not to be treated as a mere instrument of propaganda.[8]

Boti had boasted that between 1962 and 1965 Cuba's total production would grow annually by "not less than 10 percent and probably not more than 15.5 percent," and that Cuba's per capita consumption would rise by 1965 to 60 percent more than it had been in 1950. Since nobody at the conference could take these assertions seriously, Dillon was able to focus the attention of the delegates on the new social aid fund and the increased availability of development resources that the United States was ready to provide through the World Bank. But Latin America still hoped for something like a Marshall Plan. And the idea of a regional development program, originally suggested by Prebisch's statement at Quitandinha, remained alive.

The Latin American priority

Apart from conditions in Latin America and inter-American relations, many strands of United States politics came together in President Kennedy's Alliance for Progress speech: the New Deal Good Neighbor Policy; the Marshall Plan's reconstruction of western Europe; the success of development planning for economic growth in Puerto Rico; the emergence of Latin America as an issue in the 1960 political campaign; and the international activism of the New Frontier.

Kennedy himself had a strong personal interest in Latin America. Richard Goodwin, who drafted the Alliance for Progress speech, had been one of Kennedy's key speech writers during the 1960 campaign. Goodwin's success as a

---

8. Press release of U.S. delegation to meeting of Committee of 21, Bogotá, September 1960.

speech writer was based not only on his phrasemaking but on his ability to reflect the president's own thoughts. He eventually became Kennedy's "man on Latin America" in the White House. Unlike the great majority of figures in U.S. public life, Kennedy considered policy guidance on Latin America a task too important for second-level bureaucrats. On his first day in the White House he sent a special mission to Bolivia to find out why the Eisenhower administration had suspended aid to that country late in 1960.

David Bell, who served Kennedy as director of the Bureau of the Budget and then as administrator of the Agency for International Development (AID), came into the government with a background focused on southeast Asia through years of work in Pakistan and India. He recalls that "President Kennedy gave a special importance to Latin America. He considered that its problems were right on our doorstep."[9] During Kennedy's lifetime this personal interest was one of the intangible strengths of the Alliance in U.S. government circles.

As a student, Kennedy had traveled to Argentina, with stopovers in other Latin American countries, for a summer visit to the *estancia* (large cattle ranch) of Miguel Carcano, who was then Argentina's ambassador to Britain. The trip had been arranged by Kennedy's father, who had become acquainted with Carcano when he was U.S. ambassador to Britain.

An avid student of American history, Kennedy believed that the Democratic party had contributed to the growth of a special relationship between the countries of Latin America and the United States. He noted that Roosevelt's Good Neighbor Policy had ended the worst abuses of U.S. intervention in the hemisphere and that patient diplomacy had resolved such thorny problems as Mexican nationalization of U.S. oil companies without resort to economic reprisals. Sumner Welles's skillful organization of a wartime front in the hemisphere against the Axis powers demonstrated the positive possibilities of inter-American political and economic cooperation. Kennedy was determined to build on the achievements of his Democratic predecessors.[10]

---

9. Interview with David Bell during American Assembly of Columbia University, Arden, N.Y., November 1968.
10. Telephone interview with Richard Goodwin, New York City, March 1969.

The inter-American crisis

The 1960 campaign

As the Kennedy and Nixon campaigns moved into the decisive early fall months of 1960, the rift between Castro's Cuba and the Eisenhower administration was continually in the news in the United States, heightening public awareness of Latin American problems. For the first time since the Spanish-American War, Latin America was an election issue in the United States.

In May, Cuba had formally inaugurated diplomatic relations with the Soviet Union. In June, with the U.S. Congress in an uproar over Cuban seizures of U.S. property, the Eisenhower administration cut off Cuba's sugar quota and later broke off diplomatic relations. Castro retaliated by stepping up expropriation of American-owned properties, and in July signed a barter agreement with the People's Republic of China calling for an exchange of Cuban sugar for Chinese rice. In September, Cuba became the first Latin American nation to recognize the Peking regime. Almost daily Castro denounced the United States as the instigator of sporadic acts of sabotage and air drops to rebel groups in the Cuban countryside. Neighboring countries in turn accused Cuba of training, transporting, and arming guerrilla groups sent to overthrow their governments.

Despite scruples about criticizing the Republican administration for its handling of the Cuban problem (resolved, according to Arthur Schlesinger, Jr., by Kennedy's observation that the Republicans had not shrunk from holding the Democrats responsible for the "loss" of China in the 1952 election campaign[11]), Kennedy felt that Nixon was vulnerable on Cuba and (in view of Caracas) on Latin America in general. He decided to raise these issues in a speech prepared for delivery in Tampa, Florida, on October 18. Kennedy's delay in reaching Tampa prevented him from delivering the full speech, but he ordered the text to be released as a policy statement.

In it he condemned the Eisenhower administration for its "failure to identify ourselves with the rising tide of freedom" in Latin America and for its "failure to help the people of Latin America to achieve their economic aspirations." But a return

11. Arthur Schlesinger, Jr., *A Thousand Days* (Boston: Houghton Mifflin, 1965), p. 224.

to the Good Neighbor Policy of the New Deal era was not enough:

> We need a new attitude and new approach to the nations of Latin America. Our new policy can best be summed up in the Spanish words *Alianza para el Progreso*—an Alliance for Progress with nations with a common interest in freedom and economic advance in a great common effort to develop the resources of the entire hemisphere, strengthen the forces of democracy, and widen the vocational and educational opportunities of every person in all the Americas.

Although his knowledge of Spanish was rudimentary, Goodwin had coined the phrase in Spanish—*Alianza para el Progreso*—on a bus ride in San Antonio, Texas, and developed the concept in consultation with Karl Meyer, an editorial writer for the Washington *Post*, and Ernesto Betancourt, a Cuban on the staff of the Organization of American States.

The purpose of the Alliance, Kennedy said, would be not merely to combat communism, but to help "our sister republics for their own sake." Kennedy urged both "long-term development loans" and "programs for land reform."

It is unlikely that the half-delivered Tampa speech swayed the narrow margin of voters that gave Kennedy his victory over Nixon, but the text shows that Kennedy had envisioned the rough outlines of the Alliance well before the election.

The Latin American task force

With the election won, Kennedy and his close advisers set about organizing a series of task forces to prepare policy recommendations on major issues. Among the first of these teams was the one on Latin America. Through Theodore Sorensen, the president's special assistant in the White House, Kennedy asked Adolf Berle, Jr., to head up the Latin American study group in late November.

Berle, a prominent New York lawyer and professor of international law at Columbia University, had had a distinguished career in both politics and diplomacy. At sixty-five he was of an older generation than the young president elect and had no personal ties with him. Berle was vintage New Deal, one of the Wilsonian liberals whom Roosevelt had drawn from private careers to public service during the Depression. A brilliant student, Berle had graduated from Harvard College while he was still in his teens and finished law school before most young men are out of college. He was only twenty-four years old when he attended the Versailles Peace Conference as a member of the United States delegation. During the 1920s Berle combined law work with economic scholarship that included groundbreaking studies of the American business corporation as an economic and social institution. His law practice included dealings with Caribbean countries and he thus became interested in Latin American affairs. During the early New Deal years Berle worked in the State Department with Sumner Welles to reconstruct trade ties with Latin America that had been shattered by the Depression. He went on to become assistant secretary of state for inter-American affairs. When World War II ended, he was the United States' ambassador to Brazil, where he encouraged the returning Brazilian officers who had fought with the Allies in North Africa and Italy to overthrow the dictatorship of Getúlio Vargas in 1945.

With Roosevelt dead, he returned to his law practice and teaching at Columbia University, but his East Side townhouse in New York was visited by Dominican exiles plotting against Trujillo, and democratic political leaders such as Rómulo Betancourt of Venezuela and José Figueres of Costa Rica.

Berle also maintained close contact over the years with Governor Luis Muñoz Marín of Puerto Rico, whose *Partido Popular* was the Puerto Rican equivalent of the Democratic party. The island's economic development and political stability and its growing freedom from U.S. control since its achievement of commonwealth status in 1952, Berle felt, made it a model for democratic development throughout the hemisphere.

Berle represented for Kennedy not only a link to the New Deal but a liberal figure in touch with many Latin American leaders whom the Kennedy administration wanted to support. Berle also knew the workings of the U.S. government from within and would base his policy recommendations on this knowledge.

Berle selected the members of his task force from the academic community, of which he was a part, and the government of Puerto Rico. American scholarship after World War II had been largely preoccupied with the political and economic problems of Europe and the Far East, and had paid little attention to Latin America. One of the few experts who combined academic reputation with some practical experience in Latin

American development problems and good Democratic credentials was Lincoln Gordon, an economics professor at the Harvard Business School. Gordon was one of the senior U.S. officials who had taken the Marshall Plan from blueprint to reality. Returning from government service in Paris and London, Gordon had become interested in the role of American private corporations in developing countries, and particularly in the growth of foreign investments in Brazil's automobile industry in the late 1950s. His fieldwork in Brazil was the extent of his Latin American experience.

Robert Alexander, an economist at Rutgers University, was known as an expert on the Bolivian revolution, with which he greatly sympathized, and as an adviser to U.S. groups of Norman Thomas Socialist inclination, interested in supporting anticommunist labor movements in Latin America. Arthur Whitaker was a professor of history at the University of Pennsylvania, specializing in U.S. diplomatic relations with Latin America.

The Puerto Ricans on the task force were members of Muñoz Marín's inner circle. Teodoro Moscoso had headed the Puerto Rican Development Agency, which had carried out the Operation Bootstrap program that industrialized Puerto Rico and improved economic and social conditions throughout the island. Arturo Morales Carrión, who advised Muñoz Marín on international affairs, reflected Muñoz Marín's own bias based on personal relations with the so-called democratic left group of Betancourt, Figueres, and Víctor Raúl Haya de la Torre, the veteran Peruvian leader of the American Popular Revolutionary Alliance (APRA).

The Berle task force pulled together the main strands of American liberalism as they applied to Latin America. Berle represented a continuation of the Good Neighbor Policy and a link with many progressive Latin American political figures. Gordon brought the operational experience of the Marshall Plan and a professional competence in development economics. Moscoso and Morales Carrión added the Puerto Rican development experiences and a Latin feel for political issues and personalities. Alexander and Whitaker provided some experience and perspective on Latin American history. Goodwin, who sat with the group, provided a link to the White House and represented the New Frontier.

The task force met three times: once in late November 1960 at the Harvard Club, the second time in early December at the New York offices of the Twentieth Century Fund (Berle was chairman of the Fund's board of trustees), and the third in Puerto Rico over the New Year's weekend which coincided with Muñoz Marín's inauguration as governor of Puerto Rico for a third term. Berle dominated the group. Speaking in bursts of words "like puffs of smoke," Gordon recalls, Berle insisted upon the need for a "command post" for Latin American policy in either the White House or the State Department.[12] Berle personally favored the establishment of an undersecretary of state for Latin American affairs. So insistent was he that Goodwin at one point thought he would have to report back to Kennedy that "they had a madman on their hands."[13] As it turned out, Berle was more nearly right than anyone had imagined. His proposal, however, was not adopted. President Kennedy, naming G. Mennen Williams as assistant secretary of state for African affairs, had described this position as second to none within State. How then, Gordon asked, could Kennedy create a special status for Latin America?

But organizational structure was not the only problem. Berle wanted an essentially political Alliance for Progress, through which the United States would support the progressive democratic political forces in the hemisphere. He regarded the *Acción Democrática* party (AD) in Venezuela as the type of reformist party the United States should support.

Led by President Rómulo Betancourt, AD was committed to a program of social reform and economic development within the framework of representative democratic institutions. The party had strong support from organized labor, and its agrarian reform program was coupled with political organization of the peasants. Thus it had a popular base for its essentially middle-class leadership, although it was gradually losing its youth movement to more radical forces. In early fall of 1960, AD was beset by extremists of both the right and the left. Berle's idea, supported by Moscoso and Morales Carrión, was to identify the forces in each Latin American country that were

12. Interview with Lincoln Gordon, Johns Hopkins University, Baltimore, Md., August 2, 1968.
13. Telephone interview with Richard Goodwin, New York City, March 1969.

comparable to the AD in Venezuela, and help organize them into political parties that the United States could support. The Berle proposal amounted to a policy of selective intervention on behalf of political parties committed to reform and democracy. Berle spelled it out in its most ambitious form as a sort of "democratic international," analogous to the Communist International.

Gordon and Goodwin were skeptical. Emphasizing economic development, they pressed for a more limited approach. But as a price for its help, the United States would exact a commitment to far-reaching social reform. The members of the group unanimously opposed the employment of U.S. power and resources to prop up inequitable social and economic structures and oppressive political regimes. Goodwin and Schlesinger, sent by Kennedy on a political scouting trip to Argentina and Brazil, were particularly insistent on this point, urging that U.S. resources be used as leverage to bring about fundamental social change. Their position reflected both their pragmatic judgment that any other policy was doomed to failure and their moral indignation, as American liberals, at the perpetuation of intolerable injustice with United States support.

Looming in the background of the task force considerations, however, was the challenge of Cuba. The United States seemed to be in feverish competition with Castro's Cuba for the allegiance of the peoples of the hemisphere. As President Kennedy put it, "If the only alternatives for the people of Latin America are the status quo and communism, then they will inevitably choose communism." The Berle task force sought to come up with a third alternative, believing that for the United States in Latin America, it was one minute to midnight—and the clock was ticking.

The Latin American consultation

Kennedy received the Berle task force report in February, but he was not entirely satisfied that he had a full reading on Latin American attitudes. Late in February, Kennedy personally telephoned José Antonio Mayobre, then Venezuela's ambassador to the United States, and told him that he was planning a major speech on U.S.–Latin American relations. Kennedy asked Mayobre for his ideas and suggestions. Recognizing this opportunity, Mayobre invited nine eminent Latin American economists connected with international organizations to join in formulating his reply. The group included Felipe Pazos, who had been president of the Central Bank of Cuba in the first year of the Castro regime, but had since defected from Cuba; Felipe Herrera, president of the Inter-American Development Bank; Jorge Sol Castellanos, executive secretary of the Inter-American Economic and Social Council; and Raúl Prebisch. At Goodwin's suggestion, Rómulo Betancourt and José Figueres were also consulted. The Mayobre group decided to present Kennedy with a frank statement of the Latin American position. Prebisch drafted the memo and it was reviewed by José A. Mora (secretary general of the OAS), Herrera, and Sol. The document, delivered to Goodwin by Mayobre five days before Kennedy's March 13 speech, made four basic points:

First, although placing the responsibility for development and "transformation" of the archaic Latin American economic and social structure squarely on Latin America, it called for an external program (without specifying an amount) of long-term supplementary capital assistance and commodity price stabilization.

Second, this program

must capture the imagination of the masses: They must be convinced with clear and palpable evidence that the program is not motivated by a desire to create lucrative fields of investment for foreign private capital. . . . There should be cooperation with the countries really willing to make structural social and economic transformations; cooperation should be with the present ruling groups if they propose to do it or with new groups that arrive in power by democratic means. . . . Above all, it is necessary to change the agrarian land tenure system, to correct the regressivity of the tax system, to avoid the restrictive practices and other distortions that impede the functioning of the economic system and favor great inequalities in the distribution of income.

The third point was that the Latin American private entre-preneur's sense of technical and economic inferiority compared with the private foreign investor was politically disturbing. Only the provision of financial and technical assistance to the Latin American entrepreneur could lead to an accommodation between domestic and foreign enterprise on politically acceptable terms.

Fourth, from the political point of view it "would not always be easy to overcome the resistance of the privileged groups without agitation and disturbances." If the United States was going to enter into a program to transform the social and economic structures of Latin American countries, "it must be prepared to understand this fact."

A long road

The Kennedy speech of March 13 drew on ideas from both the Berle task force report and the Mayobre memorandum. The draft was reviewed at the State Department by Dean Rusk and Thomas C. Mann (who had not yet left his Eisenhower administration job of assistant secretary of state for inter-American affairs to take his new post as U.S. ambassador to Mexico). Rusk made one substantive suggestion, which led to the inclusion of a proposal for an educational and cultural exchange program. Mann returned the draft to Goodwin without comment or criticism.

Some members of the Mayobre group expressed concern, after the speech was delivered, that Kennedy was arousing expectations that could not be fulfilled. Others feared that proposals coming from the White House would be interpreted in Latin America as measures about to be imposed by the United States. In general, however, these politically experienced men realized that the dynamics of the New Frontier required a dramatic initiative and not just approval of a Latin American plan. Whatever reservations they had were more than overcome by elation that the United States had finally accepted the Latin American ideology of development. It had been a long road.

The Punta del Este conference

Aid to poor and underdeveloped
countries on a substantial scale has
been accepted by our government and,
I believe, by the American people
as our responsibility. It is an
activity, however, without established
or traditional procedures and without
accepted theory or principle to
inform us how to carry it out. So far,
at least, there is no consensus on
why foreign aid should be given,
to what countries, through what
agencies, with what objectives. . . .
Past experience can afford light as to
errors to be avoided, but little or
no positive evidence.
Jacob Viner, 1961

Little more than a month after his White House speech on the Alliance, President Kennedy authorized the invasion of Cuba by a brigade of 1,100 Cuban exiles organized, financed, trained, armed, and transported by the U.S. Central Intelligence Agency. It was Guatemala in 1954 all over again, but on a scale that made it impossible to conceal the operation's sponsorship. The National Security Council had approved the plan. The joint chiefs of staff had reviewed the invasion tactics. The CIA was convinced that Cubans would rise en masse against Castro when they heard that a U.S.-backed invasion force had landed.

The result was the disaster at the Bay of Pigs, where Castro's forces trapped the invaders in a tidal swamp and captured most of the brigade members after their supply of ammunition was exhausted. With the invasion under hot debate in the U.N. Security Council, Kennedy refused to allow U.S. Navy aircraft to provide air cover for the doomed brigade.

This intervention, violating the basic inter-American agreements, stunned the entire hemisphere as much because of its outcome as because of its auspices. United States prestige was badly shaken. The Kennedy administration's organization of the Bay of Pigs invasion was almost, though not entirely, unilateral. The governments of Guatemala and Nicaragua assented to the planned expedition of Cuban exiles; the CIA used secret camps in their territory for training. Venezuela's President Betancourt was probably informed and may have approved of the plan because pro-Cuban extremists were expanding their urban terrorism and guerrilla operations in his country. But the governments of Argentina, Chile, Brazil, and Mexico, which were advising a conciliatory line toward Cuba, were not officially consulted on the plan.

Adolf Berle had visited President Jânio Quadros of Brazil in February to argue for a common inter-American position against Cuba. Kennedy felt that an overt Latin American stand against Castro would help gain financial support for the Alliance from the U.S. Congress. Berle didn't mention—and probably didn't know about—the invasion plan, but Quadros turned him down and refused to appear with him at a press conference. Employing an old diplomatic formula, Brazilian sources said that the two "had agreed to disagree."

Meanwhile, President Arturo Frondizi of Argentina secretly reported to Kennedy that Argentina's ambassador to Cuba, Julio Amoedo, had had conversations with Castro which the Argentines felt could provide a basis for reconciliation of U.S.-Cuban differences. The Bay of Pigs ended those contacts.

All available evidence indicates that the members of the Kennedy team concerned with the Alliance had no knowledge that the CIA was planning the invasion. As Goodwin recalls them, "These were entirely separate operations running on parallel tracks."[1] After the Bay of Pigs the two tracks were in a sense forced together. The Alliance for Progress became part of a two-pronged effort of the United States both to strengthen Latin American countries by supporting their economic and social development and to align these countries behind a policy of containing and weakening the Castro regime through isolation and economic denial. The administration used this security-with-development approach in persuading conservative congressmen to vote for increased Alliance funds. In an

1. Telephone interview with Richard Goodwin, New York City, March 1969.

appeal to Congress for approval of Kennedy's first foreign aid request, David Rockefeller, the U.S. banker representing the most powerful business interests concerned with inter-American policy, declared, "We have made a firm commitment to Latin America for economic aid and for assistance in containing communist imperialism. I think the situation warrants substantial expenditures on both fronts on the scale proposed by President Kennedy."[2]

To justify this expenditure the Kennedy team had to show Congress that the Latin American countries benefiting from it were lined up against Cuba.

The Stevenson mission

To the Latin Americans Adlai Stevenson was, apart from Kennedy himself, the most prestigious figure of the new administration. During the Bay of Pigs debate in the Security Council, it had become painfully evident that Stevenson, the U.S. chief delegate to the U.N., was unaware of the degree of U.S. involvement in the invasion. He could not be held personally responsible for the action. Kennedy therefore called upon Stevenson to test the administration's new approach to the Alliance. In June, Stevenson set off on a seventeen-day trip to ten South American countries. His assignment was partly to mend the damage of the Bay of Pigs and partly to get a better political reading on chiefs of state such as Quadros and Frondizi, whom Kennedy did not know personally. Stevenson was accompanied by Ellis Briggs, a senior career diplomat with long experience as ambassador to Brazil and other Latin American countries, and Lincoln Gordon, who had become the administration's key adviser on the organization of the Punta del Este conference and who had just been appointed ambassador to Brazil.

The trip was uneventful, but in his talks with the presidents Stevenson learned their views of the future Alliance and the Cuban situation. In Bogotá, Colombia, the last stop, Stevenson met for two days with President Alberto Lleras Camargo, whose lucid view of Latin American problems was combined with a knowledge of U.S. domestic politics which some of the

2. David Rockefeller, speech delivered before the Economic Club of Chicago, April 23, 1962.

other presidents lacked. Like Venezuela's Betancourt, the Colombian president believed that Castro's Cuba must be isolated from the inter-American system in a sort of political quarantine. But he made it clear that Brazil, Argentina, Chile, and Mexico would collectively break with Cuba only if the United States was prepared to make a really major economic commitment at the forthcoming Punta del Este meeting. He explained that the larger Latin American countries, and particularly those most distant from the Caribbean, saw very little connection between the development crisis and whatever subversive intentions the Cuban regime had in Latin America. As one Mexican diplomat put it, "If we publicly declare that Cuba is a threat to our security, forty million Mexicans will die laughing."

Indeed the presence in a small, faraway Caribbean island of a bearded revolutionary who induced the United States to pay attention to Latin America seemed to many like a piece of almost unbelievable good luck. Latin America's astute politicians and businessmen were prepared to accept the popular young U.S. president's social reform program as long as it also provided increased financial assistance. Lleras Camargo said that if the United States made a clear financial commitment at Punta del Este, Colombia would develop Latin American support for a political conference on Cuba. Stevenson accepted this suggestion; on the day he left for Washington, Julio César Turbay Ayala, Colombia's foreign minister, left on a mission to Brazil, Argentina, Uruguay, and Chile to begin consultations that set up a meeting of foreign ministers for January 1962, five months after Punta del Este. At that meeting the participants agreed to exclude the Castro regime from all the organizations of the inter-American system. But this time the Latin Americans got their economic conference before surrendering their political bargaining weapon to the United States.

The preliminaries

In May and June 1961, task forces set up by the Inter-American Economic and Social Council (IAECOSOC) met in Washington to prepare for the Punta del Este meeting. These task forces, composed primarily of Latin American technical experts and political figures, drafted position papers on such topics as economic integration, primary commodities, popular participation, and, most important, planning and development.

The chairman of the task force on this topic was Felipe Pazos, president of the Central Bank of Cuba in the first year of the Castro government, but an anti-Castro exile in 1961.

His group basically followed the line laid down by the Economic Commission for Latin America at Quitandinha seven years earlier. ECLA economic technicians had been experimenting with the construction of macro-economic models to determine the relation of savings and investment to growth rates, the estimated rate of growth of exports, and the foreign exchange gap. Though often highly theoretical, these exercises in model building generated a huge amount of quantitative data and established certain elementary resource estimates.

The task forces were in constant touch with U.S. counterpart teams. Pazos' group, which worked with a Harvard-MIT team headed by Lincoln Gordon, found, Pazos recalls, that the U.S. participants were "totally unprepared." Not only did they lack data on which to base projected growth rates or magnitudes of required external and domestic resources, but also, as far as Pazos could tell, "there was no philosophy, no thinking behind the U.S. position." They were going to do it on will power, "like Guevara in Bolivia."[3]

However, they were clearly in favor of social reform. Goodwin and Schlesinger, politically the most important U.S. participants in the preparatory work, knew that the Latin American governments would be more conservative than the task force members, and were determined that U.S. assistance should not serve to strengthen the status quo. Since the United States apparently favored the experts' reports, the Latin American governments, particularly the foreign offices, began to regard acceptance of these recommendations as the price of U.S. assistance.[4] But without a true commitment to reform on the part of the individual governments, no amount of U.S. support could make the Alliance succeed. And U.S. support itself was to weaken as the full turbulence of social change in Latin America was borne in upon the political leadership of the United States. These eventualities were not immediately ap-

---

3. Interview with Felipe Pazos, Washington, D.C., July 22, 1968. But Gordon claims that he was fully familiar with the Quitandinha proceedings and that the U.S. team wanted the initiative to come from the Latins (interview with Lincoln Gordon, Johns Hopkins University, Baltmore, Md., August 2, 1968).
4. Interview with Ernesto Betancourt, Washington, D.C., July 25, 1968. Betancourt was a member of the task force on popular participation.

parent, however, as the conference of Punta del Este got under way.

Punta del Este

Punta del Este is a delightful beach resort on the eastern tip of Uruguay, a summer playground for wealthy Uruguayans and Argentines. The town contains many small hotels and restaurants and is surrounded by private residences among forests of fir and eucalyptus. The conference of the Inter-American Economic and Social Council, which met there from August 5 to August 17, 1961, had Punta del Este all to itself, because August is the middle of the mild winter in southern South America. Hotels, restaurants, and private residences rented by the delegations had to be reopened out of season. None of the facilities had central heating, and the chill wind blowing off the white-capped South Atlantic kept the delegates in sweaters and overcoats. Like the 1954 conference, held where the roulette tables had stood in the Hotel Quitandinha, the Punta del Este conference conducted its sessions in the halls of the resort town's municipal casino, wired for simultaneous translation in English, Spanish, Portuguese, and French.

Dillon and Guevara

The major dramatic interest of the conference revolved around Che Guevara, who headed the Cuban delegation, and C. Douglas Dillon, the Republican whom Kennedy had appointed secretary of the treasury and who headed the U.S. delegation at Punta del Este. The contrast between the two delegates was striking. Guevara, the guerrilla leader, wore green fatigues, his shirt open at the collar, a black beret, and combat boots. He usually appeared with a long cigar in his mouth, accompanied by four personal bodyguards, all of whom had fought beside him in Cuba's Sierra Maestra. Only after delicate negotiations were the Uruguayan police able to persuade the guards to disarm when entering the conference hall. One day a husky, poorly dressed, unshaven local spotted Guevara from afar and pedaled toward him on his bicycle at top speed. One of the bodyguards reached for his shoulder holster. Guevara reached over and held the guard's arm. The man on the bicycle stopped in front of Guevara, reached out his hand, and said, "*Salud, Capitán.*" To the common people of Latin America,

Guevara, who had triumphed in Cuba beside Castro, was, after all, one of them.

Dillon, tall, blue-eyed, and in blue pin-striped suit, looked the part of a millionaire Wall Street investment banker and skilled diplomat. Reserved, cool, completely unflappable, Dillon had become, since his first inter-American conference at Buenos Aires in 1957, the most knowledgeable high-level U.S. government official on the economic problems of the hemisphere.

The conference opened with a message of greeting from President Kennedy, announcing that the United States would allocate more than $1 billion in development assistance to Latin America during the first year of the Alliance for Progress. The message stated that the United States could and should provide adequate resources for a Latin American breakthrough to self-sustaining economic growth, but only after the nations themselves "formulate the plans, mobilize the internal resources, make difficult and necessary social reforms, and accept the sacrifices necessary if their national energy is to be fully directed to economic development."[5] Heavily stressing social reform as essential for economic growth and political peace, Kennedy's message called for land and tax reform and greater emphasis on education, health, and housing.

It was not until Dillon's opening statement to the conference, however, that the U.S. delegation made banner headlines all over Latin America. Dillon stated that if the countries of Latin America took the necessary internal measures, they could reasonably expect to receive $20 billion in external resources over the Alliance decade. He said the greatest part of this development financing would be in the form of public capital, necessarily from the United States.

This announcement was the long-term commitment of public development funds that Latin America had been seeking from the United States for years—or so it seemed. Actually, Dillon had arrived in Punta del Este without instructions as to the precise amount of aid he could volunteer. There was no broad political consensus in the United States on how the Alliance was to be financed. The two figures in the speech, the $1 billion in U.S. public funds for the first year and the $20 billion for the

5. *Reunión extraordinaria del Consejo Interamericano Económico y Social al nivel ministerial,* OEA/Ser.H/XI, 1 (Washington, D.C.: Pan American Union, 1961), pp. 77–78; cited hereafter as *Reunión extraordinaria.*

ten-year period, represented educated guesses rather than terms that had been worked out in advance with the United States Congress.[6]

Only the day before Dillon spoke, while the speech was being drafted, the delegation had debated the advisability of announcing specific figures. Dillon and Goodwin were in favor of doing so. Edwin Martin, assistant secretary of state for Latin America, said that the delegation had no authority to make such a commitment. Dillon replied that his plenipotentiary powers and Kennedy's general instructions were authority enough.

Guevara sensed this weakness, and in his opening statement he challenged Dillon to make his commitment of $20 billion "concrete," reminding the delegates, "Many times the promises made here have not been ratified up there [in Washington] afterward." Guevara asserted that a "new age" was emerging in Latin America under the sign not of President Kennedy's Alliance for Progress, but of the Cuban revolution. He mockingly told the delegates that any loans they might receive under the Alliance would "bear the stamp of Cuba."[7] And he concluded his improvised two-hour-and-fifteen-minute speech by challenging the delegates to reassemble in 1980 and compare Cuba's performance with that of the rest of Latin America, even with assistance from the United States.

In the working committees Guevara was courteous and even made a few constructive contributions. Several times during the twelve-day meeting he publicly asked Dillon, "Can Cuba expect any benefit from the Alliance for Progress?" He proposed that Cuba and the United States negotiate on ways to halt the hijacking of commercial airplanes, which in those days was being done primarily by Cubans who wanted to escape the Castro regime by flying to the United States. But as the meeting drew to a close and the Charter of Punta del Este was approved

6. In June, Felipe Pazos had raised this issue with his task force's White House contact, Richard Ruggles. Ruggles informed him that no congressional committee declaration in favor of a specific amount of U.S. aid would be forthcoming before the meeting. Pazos therefore urged postponement of the meeting until such a declaration could be made. When Ruggles replied that postponement was impossible, Pazos explained that without a significant financial commitment from the United States, the conference would be a disaster. "Latin America," he said, "is no longer like the savage tribes of Africa to be bought off with trinkets" (interview with Felipe Pazos, Washington, D.C., July 22, 1968).
7. *Reunión extraordinaria*, pp. 212–24.

by all of the delegations except Cuba, Guevara took off the gloves. In the final session of the conference, in a speech reminiscent of Molotov's attack upon the Marshall Plan in 1947 before the Paris committee for European reconstruction, he launched a bitter assault upon the Alliance for Progress as an "instrument of economic imperialism." Dillon, who up to that point had carefully avoided any debate with Guevara, asked to be allowed to reply. In a hushed and crowded room, he sealed the enmity between the Alliance and Castro's Cuba:

The delegate of Cuba has chosen to take one phrase out of this document and tried to twist its meaning so as to gravely misrepresent the position of the United States. He has tried to give the impression that the United States somehow recognizes the permanence of the present regime in Cuba. This we do not do and never will do, because to do so would betray the thousands of patriotic Cubans who are still waiting and struggling for the freedom of their country. . . . We here have shown a spirit of unity and serious effort which bodes well for the success of our efforts. . . . We must now undertake the hard and steady work of making a reality of our dreams. The road to progress lies clear and straight before us. We must march down that road hand in hand.[8]

A burst of applause followed Dillon's short statement. Guevara did not reply. Guevara's attack and Dillon's measured reply in the early-morning hours of the last session were the emotional climax of the conference.

The Charter

The unfolding of the dispute between Havana and Washington did not deflect the conference from its main business, drafting the charter, but this technical task had its own political problems. It threw open all the basic issues of Latin American development, the special U.S. role in the region, and the divergent national viewpoints of the large and small Latin American countries.

The birth of the Alliance for Progress as an inter-American agreement was proclaimed in a "Declaration to the Peoples of America" (see Appendix B), which affirmed the spiritual and political unity of the Americas and itemized the goals of democratic development and the basic commitments of the participating nations that were contained in the charter. The delegates labored long hours to produce this simple synthesis of the charter, itself a complicated document with four titles, seven

---

8. *Ibid.*, p. 260.

chapters, and an appendix. The charter described the Alliance's basic concepts of economic and social development; identified immediate and short-term action measures; defined national planning; stipulated the amounts and form of external assistance; set up an organizational structure, including an expert review mechanism for national plans; and devoted special titles to economic integration and Latin American trade.

The basis of the charter was a prior determination by the conference participants that they must reach a consensus at whatever common denominator they could find. So the charter was necessarily ambiguous on some points and left considerable latitude for interpretation and implementation by each country. Since the charter was not a treaty, the commitments it represented were not legally binding, but depended for their execution on the will and intent of the participants. The charter's statement on trade, Title IV, made vague exhortations but no specific commitments, because the U.S. delegation had no authority to make any special concession to Latin American demands for general or regional trade advantages.

Ambiguity also characterized the charter's Title I, item 6, which stated that the American republics would work together

to encourage, in accordance with the characteristics of each country, programs of comprehensive agrarian reform leading to the effective transformation, where required, of unjust structures and systems of land tenure and use, with a view to replacing latifundia and dwarf holdings by an equitable system of land tenure so that, with the help of timely and adequate credit, technical assistance and facilities for the marketing and distribution of products, the land will become for the man who works it the basis of his economic stability, the foundation of his increasing welfare, and the guarantee of his freedom and dignity.

The obvious qualifying phrases in this statement were insisted upon by those delegates who felt, as Mexico did, that their nations were already making the efforts that were "required," or, as Argentina did, that "in accordance with the characteristics of each country" the problem of land tenure was not the government's concern. Because the text also lent itself to the interpretation that token reforms and colonization schemes in virgin forests would be sufficient, the Peruvian chief delegate, Pedro Beltrán, accepted it willingly; he owned a cotton hacienda employing hundreds of traditionally poverty-stricken peasants. The language of the charter was worked out in private negotiations among all the delegation chiefs, including Che Guevara of Cuba. That it meant whatever each delegate wanted it to mean can be demonstrated by the fact that in the drafting committee's final vote on the agrarian reform statement, to the amusement of the other delegates, Dillon and Guevara raised their hands together; the statement was passed unanimously.

The real commitment of each country to agrarian reform had to be measured after the delegates left Punta del Este for home. To some, the charter provided moral support for programs already under way. To others, it brought political conflicts. To others still, over more than nine years, it has made almost no difference.

Big countries and small countries

In addition to problems of wording, serious conflicts on operational measures also foreshadowed many of the future difficulties of the Alliance. Dillon had stated that the United States was prepared to work "closely and continuously" with Latin American nations to "accelerate economic progress and extend social justice to all America," but only after "the process of planning" had begun in each American country.

The United States draft of the proposed Act of Punta del Este provided that each Latin American country work up a long-term development plan with targets in education, health, housing, land reform, etc., while hitting immediately at acute trouble spots with local funds and the initial $1 billion in U.S. aid. To give these plans strong technical and multilateral backing, the United States proposed that a seven-member Committee of Experts review the plans of each country and report on their acceptability to the Inter-American Economic and Social Council. Argentina and Peru, in particular, recoiled at this proposal. Viewing such a supernational committee as an infringement on their sovereignty, they argued that it should be eliminated from the agreement. Argentina's reservations on this point masked a more fundamental disagreement, to which Frondizi had alluded in a letter to Kennedy shortly after his March 13 speech: Argentina saw the Alliance essentially in terms of trade and industrial development, which were its own major domestic problems. Frondizi told Kennedy that his emphasis on social reform was misplaced and that the primary questions for Latin America were expanded export trade, commodity price stabilization, and industrial investments. Neither Frondizi nor Quadros in Brazil, each elected by a large popular majority, saw any real relevance to the development problems of his big, industrially advanced country in Kennedy's theory of the democratic left. These big-country leaders, who considered themselves progressive nationalists, felt that their political mandates implied not a demand for social reform but a desire for accelerated economic development, mainly in heavy industry. Quadros viewed Brazil's impoverished northeastern region as a special problem apart from the development of the industrial southern region.

After lengthy debate, the delegates adopted a compromise formula for the Committee of Experts, making it a panel of nine planning experts to be nominated equally by the Inter-American Development Bank, ECLA, and IAECOSOC. A country applying for evaluation of its national program would be assigned three of these experts and would select three more. This six-man team would carry out a study that would be submitted to the Inter-American Development Bank as a basis for soliciting international financing. The final draft of the charter stated that the recommendations of the experts would be accorded "great weight" in the allocation of external resources, but it was clear that the committee would face political hostility from the major countries.

The small and individually weak Latin American countries can, and often do, join forces to make their weight felt in inter-American conferences where they represent more than half the votes. At Punta del Este the small countries took issue with the requirement that countries present a national development plan to become eligible for Alliance financing. They said they lacked the technical staffs to prepare the relatively complex plans that would meet the specifications of the charter. Led by Uruguay, Paraguay, and Ecuador, the small countries demanded emergency financing for urgent problems; President Eduardo Víctor Haedo of Uruguay threatened to denounce the Alliance "if we don't see some money fast." The revolt of the small countries was a problem for Dillon, since the United States wanted the conference to be a demonstration of unity. His solution was an announcement that the United States would consider applications for emergency aid submitted within sixty days after the end of the conference. However, the scuffle pointed up the real inability of some smaller Alliance members to draw up development plans of technical quality, a problem that still persists.

The neglected businessmen

Signs of future difficulties also emerged in the area of private enterprise, particularly foreign investment. It was not until about three days before the conference that a White House aide called Richard Aldrich, a director of the Rockefeller-owned International Basic Economy Corporation, and asked him to invite a group of businessmen to Punta del Este as observers (rather than as members of the delegation).

A dozen United States bankers and businessmen representing the International Basic Economy Corporation, Olin Mathieson, the Ford Motor Company, and Standard Oil of New Jersey, among others, attended the conference. They met with delegates from Argentina, Chile, Colombia, and Brazil, and with Felipe Herrera, president of the IDB, and they offered to establish a permanent private enterprise committee to work with the IDB and help formulate national development programs with respect to the role of private foreign investment. This proposal was never followed up.

For other reasons as well the group found the conference unsatisfactory. They felt that the amount of private investment that the draft charter called for was unrealistic. The figure represented simply the average of annual new investment over the five previous years, with no allowance for the deterrent effect of the Castro threat. The participants in the formulation of private investment goals were ignoring reinvestment, depreciation, and depletion considerations, and making no explicit provisions for investment risk guarantees or formulas to assure remittance of profits or royalties free of exchange restrictions.

The final charter stated that self-help, fiscal and administrative reform, monetary stabilization, and more equitable income distribution are "designed to create a framework within which such additional assistance can be provided and effectively used." But U.S. corporate investors did not immediately perceive the relevance of this statement to their own needs. The charter, drafted by international bureaucrats, government economists, and Latin politicians, contained only one paragraph that seemed specifically addressed to the business community. It recommended that national development programs take into account the "promotion through appropriate measures, including elimination of double taxation, of conditions that will encourage the flow of foreign investments."

The businessmen had observed that such tax agreements found little favor at Treasury. Moreover, what they wanted most at the time was security for foreign investments, and the charter offered no specific guarantees against expropriation.

This reticence about foreign private investment was not an oversight. The Latin American representatives of the democratic left had warned President Kennedy in March 1961 that the Alliance would be politically jeopardized if it seemed to be the entering wedge for a great new expansion of U.S. investment. Prebisch and other spokesmen had increasingly stressed the need for foreign public loans to build up domestic private enterprise in Latin America. The Kennedy administration, sensitive to these concerns, was reluctant to include in the multilateral document of the Alliance any language evoking the Eisenhower administration's much-touted "good climate for U.S. private investment."

Dillon and Gordon both believed that foreign investment was important to the economic development of Latin America under the Alliance. They assumed, however, that U.S. corporate management would come to terms, where necessary, with Latin American political pressures. Thus they failed to anticipate both the intensity of Latin American sentiment and the reaction of U.S. businessmen to being, as they saw it, snubbed by the Kennedy administration.

Many of the businessmen who attended the conference had long experience in Latin America. Richard Goodwin did not, and they regarded his lack of receptivity to their ideas as typical of the Kennedy administration's arrogance and immaturity. They were convinced that Lincoln Gordon had bought the ECLA line uncritically and that the entire U.S. delegation was currying favor with the Latin American left at their expense. As one of them was later to say, "Not until Tom Mann came back in 1964 [as Johnson's assistant secretary of state for inter-

American affairs] did the business community feel that it was 'in' again with the United States government."[9]

Despite some misgivings, the Punta del Este Conference ended on a note of high optimism. As the delegates took leave of one another, the atmosphere was one of a job well done. There were smiles, back-slapping, and embraces. In conversation the conference was referred to as a "turning point in American history," the "answer to the communist challenge in the hemisphere." The prevailing spirit was summed up by Clemente Mariani, Brazil's minister of finance, in a closing statement on behalf of all the delegations:

In a gesture of political vision the United States has placed at our disposal the resources which, in conjunction with those of other sources and those we can mobilize ourselves, will be the mainspring of our economic and social development. . . . This economic revolution is to be carried forward with equally needed social reforms. . . . Development is not enough. We need development with social justice. A conscience is being forged, at times in a confused manner, in which the poor, the hungry, the illiterate, the sick, and the despairing clamor to have better days, if not for themselves, at least for their children.[10]

---

9. Interview with Alphonse de Rosso, Standard Oil Company of New Jersey, New York City, July 31, 1968.

10. Press release of the Brazilian delegation to the special meeting of the Inter-American Economic and Social Council at the ministerial level, Punta del Este, August 18, 1961.

The Alliance in action

Political theory undone

*Where a population is divided into
the two classes of the very rich and the
very poor, there can be no real state, for
there can be no real friendship between
the classes, and friendship is the essential
principle of all association.*
Aristotle

The spirit of optimism and new purpose with which the delegates left Punta del Este was shattered within ten days of the
signing of the charter by the resignation of Jânio Quadros as
president of Brazil. His astonishing abandonment of duty,
which started Brazil on a roller coaster to political calamity,
was followed nine months later by a military coup d'état in
Argentina which overthrew President Arturo Frondizi. And
before the end of the Alliance's first year, the Peruvian military toppled President Manuel Prado.

The breakdown of constitutional normality in three major
countries not only broke the initial momentum of the Alliance,
but began as well the undermining of the democratic left theoretical structure on which the Kennedy administration had
based its hopes for democratic reform. During the first eight
years of the Alliance, sixteen military coups took place in the
Latin American countries. These coups, and the way in which
the United States reacted and in some cases contributed to
them, have largely determined the fate of the Alliance.

U.S. policy in Latin America during the Alliance decade has

passed through three distinct phases. From 1961 through 1963 it sought to apply the Kennedy administration's ideology of democratic development. From 1964 through September 1968 it was dominated by economic concerns and maintained political neutrality except toward communist or potentially communist regimes. Since October 1968 it has been based on what might best be described as perplexity.

This evolution began with Quadros in Brazil.

Phase I: The breakdown of ideology
Brazil: Round one
On August 18, the day after the close of the conference at Punta del Este, Che Guevara stopped in Brasília at the invitation of President Jânio Quadros. In an apparent demonstration of independence from U.S. influence, Quadros bestowed Brazil's highest decoration, the Order of the Cruzeiro do Sul, on Guevara. Six days later, on August 25, Quadros submitted his resignation to Congress. The motivation behind this act was the condition of the Brazilian polity, an impasse resulting from the lack of consensus on goals, priorities, and means. Quadros himself admitted, in a 1966 article in the Brazilian magazine *Realidades*, that he had intended his resignation to generate popular demand for his return. He believed that such a mandate would force the opposition within Congress to give him executive emergency powers. What Quadros did not say in his article was that he expected Brazil's military leadership to back him. His plan amounted to political blackmail; he thought that rather than permit Vice-President João Goulart to assume the presidency, the armed forces would compel Congress to reject his resignation. Quadros had some sound reasons for expecting this gamble to work, but he was only half right.

Goulart, the Brazilian Labor party leader, who had been visiting Communist China, returned and took over the presidency only after a split within the military that brought Brazil to the brink of civil war. The compromise by which he took office led to two and a half years of harrowing political tension and economic deterioration, after which he was ousted. The military then consummated Quadros' plan, but they took over only to set up a military regime that tore up Brazil's constitution and dismantled the nation's political parties.

Argentina: Round one

Nine months after Quadros resigned in Brazil, the Argentine armed forces overthrew President Arturo Frondizi, who had taken office in 1958 after a landslide electoral victory. Frondizi had been the candidate of the moderate left wing of the *Unión Cívica Radical* (UCR) party. Like Quadros in Brazil (elected as an independent), Frondizi had extended his electoral base beyond his own party, primarily by wooing the outlawed Peronists (followers of the former populist dictator, Juan Perón) with campaign pledges of social legislation, nationalism, and state control of heavy industry. The week before the election, reports circulated that Frondizi had made a deal with Perón to legalize the Peronist *Justicialista* party. But once elected, he acted upon his own view of the immediate economic and political realities and did the opposite of what he had pledged.

He opened up the oil industry to foreign investment and initiated an IMF-type economic stabilization program; the peso was devalued, multiple exchange rates were scrapped, tight credit restrictions were imposed, consumer subsidies were eliminated, wage increases not linked to production increases were discouraged, and a determined effort was made to balance the budget. Labor felt betrayed, particularly when Frondizi called in the military to break major strikes. Financial austerity hit consumers, and businessmen chafed at credit restrictions.

In his efforts to steer his way among the various interest groups of Argentine society, Frondizi offended all of them. In order to garner Roman Catholic support he placed private religious educational institutions on an equal footing with state schools, and thus incurred the wrath of anticlerical liberals and socialists. In order to conciliate the Peronists, he returned control of labor unions to elected Peronist leaders, and thus angered the right-wing military. In order to curry favor on the left, he espoused a policy, like Quadros' in Brazil, of noninter-vention in the hemisphere and neutrality toward Cuba, and thus infuriated Argentine conservatives. Like a circus performer on a shaky highwire, Frondizi moved from one breathtaking crisis to another, until, in March 1962, he lost his political footing and fell.

In the general elections of March 1962, Frondizi allowed the

Peronists to compete openly under the colors of their own political party, the *Frente Justicialista*. The *Frente* won 35 percent of the vote, more than Frondizi's own party (28 percent), and gained forty-five of the eighty-six contested seats in the Chamber of Deputies and nine of the fourteen governorships. The military forced Frondizi to prevent Andrés Framini, a Peronist labor leader who had been elected as governor of Buenos Aires province, from taking office. A wave of Peronist-led strikes ensued and Frondizi had to call on the military to control them.

The military was increasingly divided between those pushing for an outright coup and those who, concerned that the whole world was watching, wanted just to keep Frondizi under control. Frondizi tried to check the rising conspiracy of anti-Peronist politicians, particularly in the right wing of the UCR, and military chiefs, particularly in the Navy, by collaborating with the wing of the military opposed to a coup, but in the showdown the constitutionalist military lost out. The U.S. military attachés in Buenos Aires strongly advised the Argentine military against a coup, but to no avail. On March 29, 1962, Frondizi was arrested at the presidential residence by military officers and imprisoned on Martín García Island. The Supreme Court invested as president José María Guido, president of the Senate and constitutional successor to the presidency. The military justified its action, in what was to become a standard line throughout the hemisphere, as "necessary to maintain democratic procedures."

Peru: Round one

The dominant fact of Peruvian politics is the implacable enmity between the military and the *Alianza Popular Revolucionaria Americana* (APRA). The leader of this party, Víctor Raúl Haya de la Torre, founded it in 1924 while he was in exile. Although he originally planned it as an international party, it never attracted much of a following outside Peru. Within Peru it became an important political force.

An intellectual potpourri, initially radical in outlook, APRA called for the nationalization of land and industry, a united front of workers and intellectuals, the unity of "Indo-America" against U.S. imperialism, and the internationalization of the

Panama Canal. As an indigenous socialist party it was attacked not only by the propertied community of bankers, conservative landholders, and foreign investors, but also by the communists, with whom it competed for popular support.

The blood feud between APRA and the military dates back to 1931. In an APRA raid on an army barracks in the town of Trujillo a number of army officers were shot to death. The army retaliated by rounding up virtually the entire male population of the town and executing all those identified as *apristas*.

APRA was part of the political coalition in power under President Manuel Prado (1956–62). By that time it had lost most of its radicalism, but the army's attitude toward it had not softened. Haya was a presidential candidate in the elections of June 1962 and emerged with a plurality of the votes but without the one-third required for election by the Peruvian constitution. The choice fell to the Congress. The other two candidates were Fernando Belaúnde Terry, a forty-nine-year-old architect who had made a spectacular political debut in the 1956 presidential race, and Manuel Odría, a former general who had been strong-man president of Peru from 1948 to 1956. The army made it clear that it would not accept Haya as president. Haya tried to make a deal first with Belaúnde and then with Odría. When Haya and Odría seemed to be reaching agreement on a formula whereby Odría would have the presidency and APRA a majority of the cabinet, the army took action. On July 18, 1962, a Sherman tank, supplied to Peru under the U.S. military assistance program, crashed through the iron gates of the presidential palace in Lima. A U.S.-trained ranger officer routed seventy-three-year-old President Manuel Prado out of bed with the news that he had been deposed and a military junta installed.

The United States interrupted diplomatic relations, canceled $81 million in aid, as well as military assistance, and recalled its ambassador to Peru, James Loeb. Loeb, a well-known liberal and a founding member of Americans for Democratic Action, had established close ties with APRA. He returned to Washington on the same plane as Teodoro Moscoso, then U.S. coordinator of the Alliance for Progress, who was on his way home from Chile. Loeb and Moscoso agreed that the United States ought to stand firm and not recognize the military junta that had seized power.[1] Until then, the standard U.S. statements on unconstitutional changes in government in Latin America had been limited to an expression of regret or concern over fulfillment of international obligations. President Kennedy departed from this precedent in a forthright statement:

The declaration of the peoples of America adopted at Punta del Este set forth the aim to improve and strengthen democratic institutions through the application of the principle of self-determination within a framework of developing democratic institutions. In the case of Peru this great cause has suffered a severe setback.[2]

Nine Latin American countries joined the United States in breaking diplomatic relations with the junta.

However, the U.S. business community in Peru feared that continued nonrecognition would only cause the Peruvian junta to unleash nationalist reprisals against them. Peter Grace, president of W. R. Grace and Company, and executives of U.S. mining companies called the White House to protest this policy.

Meanwhile, in Peru, the military takeover had met with public apathy. APRA's attempt to stage a general strike was a flop. The United States began quietly looking for a way to heal the breach. After hearing that the junta promised "clean" elections for the following June (1963), on August 17, 1962, barely one month after breaking relations, the United States restored them and resumed economic, but not military, aid. Loeb did not return to his post.

In the elections of June 1963, Belaúnde won and Haya ran second best, as the military had planned. For a moment, Peru seemed to have solved its domestic political problems and become ready to participate actively in the Alliance for Progress.

The missile crisis

As the Alliance moved into its second year, a dramatic event produced a significant change in the U.S. outlook on Latin American problems. In October 1962 the United States discovered that the Soviet Union was placing offensive missiles

---

1. Interview with Teodoro Moscoso, San Juan, Puerto Rico, August 20, 1968.
2. White House statement, July 19, 1962.

---

in Cuba. In the ensuing confrontation, the Soviet Union backed down and removed the missiles. Despite President Kennedy's desire to underplay this triumph, it was seen in Latin America as a restoration of U.S. hegemony. It was also a turning point in Cuba's influence in the hemisphere.

Whether Castro had accepted the missiles reluctantly as the price of Soviet economic assistance or welcomed them eagerly as protection against the United States, he no longer seemed so independent. His potential disciples in Latin America had seen him humiliated; the great powers had made a decision about his country in which he had no say.

The United States stopped feeling that it was one minute to midnight in Latin America. The political failures in Brazil, Argentina, and Peru seemed less disastrous. The democratic left dwindled in importance because an alternative to Castro was no longer an urgent necessity. The first manifestation of this decline came early in 1963.

Guatemala

Guatemala is a country of approximately 4.8 million people, over half of whom are Indian. Most of the Indians do not speak Spanish and live outside the money economy, beyond the scope of modern society. The illiteracy rate of the adult population is 62 percent (90 percent of the Indian population cannot read or write); over 70 percent of the land is owned by less than 2 percent of the population. The infant mortality rate in the rural areas is among the highest in the world. Until recently it was not unusual for army units to be used to transport entire Indian communities to the coastal plantations to work under conditions of virtual peonage. By general consensus Guatemala's landowning and commercial interests are among the most retrograde in Latin America.

In 1945, Juan José Arévalo was elected president. Arévalo initiated a modest series of social reforms, including an agrarian reform law under which all unused lands exceeding ninety hectares (222 acres) were to be expropriated and distributed to landless farm workers. But the law was not really enforced until Jacobo Arbenz Guzmán, a retired army colonel, became president in 1951. Among the lands that the Arbenz government expropriated were some properties of the United Fruit Company. The 1954 meeting of foreign ministers in Caracas produced the Caracas Declaration, and shortly thereafter a CIA-sponsored exile invasion brought Arbenz down.

The new government, the military dictatorship of Carlos Castillo Armas, reversed the reforms of Arévalo and Arbenz. "The country was placed again in the hands of its most reactionary elements: the same combination of landowners, wealthy businessmen, and military men who tried to turn the clock back a full generation and who have resisted openly and consistently the concepts of the Alliance for Progress."[3]

In 1957 Castillo Armas was assassinated by a palace sentry and replaced by General Miguel Ydígoras Fuentes. (As president, Ydígoras permitted the CIA to use Guatemalan territory as a training base for the Cuban exiles preparing for the Bay of Pigs invasion.) Elections were scheduled for November 1963 and the leading candidate appeared to be ex-president Arévalo, who meanwhile had written *The Shark and the Sardines,* a book widely read in Latin America, which denounces U.S. "imperialism."

Within the United States government a debate began as to whether Arévalo should be "allowed" to become president of Guatemala. No agency of the United States government accused Arévalo of being a communist, but, as one high-level official put it, "I don't give a damn whether he is or is not a communist. He talks like a communist, he acts like a communist, and if he's elected he'll be soft on the communists." The opposing argument was that the case against Arévalo was no different from the case at one time against Rómulo Betancourt of Venezuela, who was now "our best friend in Latin America."[4] Kennedy, however, had been burned politically by the Bay of Pigs debacle. If Arévalo turned out to be not another Betancourt but another Castro, the Democrats would be accused of having lost another country to communism, a charge that Kennedy himself had employed in the 1960 campaign. Thus domestic U.S. politics, which had originally provided a stimulus for the Alliance, now became a restraint.

On the night of March 30, 1963, Ydígoras was deposed and

<hr />

3. Arnold R. Isaacs, "Anti-Red Policy Fails to Aid Guatemala," *Baltimore Sun*, May 5, 1968.
4. This account of the debate on Arévalo was supplied, in an interview, by a participant in the debate. He has requested that his name not be disclosed, but his report has been corroborated by others who, although not actual participants, had knowledge of the debate and its results.

Political theory undone

Colonel Enrique Peralta Azurdia, the fifty-five-year-old minister of defense, was installed as president. The elections scheduled for November 1963 were not held. The exercise had fulfilled its purpose: Arévalo was not allowed to become president of Guatemala.

Whether the CIA actually sponsored the coup against Ydígoras or, as is more likely, merely refrained from trying to head it off is not clear. What is clear is that the Kennedy administration would not risk its prestige and influence on a reformist leader whose political base seemed too radical, even if the only alternative was a right-wing military regime.[5]

The Dominican Republic: Round one

An even clearer example of the shift in U.S. policy is the Dominican Republic. On May 30, 1961, Rafael Trujillo, the sixty-nine-year-old dictator who had ruled that unhappy country for thirty-one years, was gunned down on a lonely country road by assassins from within his own regime. His relatives then attempted a coup d'état, which failed in part because of the dispatch of American warships, containing 1,200 Marines, off the coast of Santo Domingo.

In December 1962 the country held its first free elections in thirty-eight years. Juan Bosch, a fifty-four-year-old poet who had spent the greater part of his life in exile, writing and plotting against Trujillo, was elected president. Bosch was counted by Muñoz Marín and Betancourt as one of the brotherhood of the democratic left, and the Kennedy administration was determined to make the Dominican Republic a showcase of free men working through democratic institutions.

The showcase lasted seven months. Unlike Betancourt, Bosch turned out to be a weak administrator, not a tactician but a speechmaker. In Washington (and Caracas) disillusionment with Bosch's ineffectual leadership coincided with CIA reports that Dominican communist groups were infiltrating his administration. The same reports came from AFL-CIO labor organizers working with labor groups that Trujillo had suppressed. In September 1963, Bosch attempted to oust certain

---

5. Lincoln Gordon reports that the United States did use its influence with the Guatemalan military several years later to help ensure the investiture of a moderately reformist president, Julio César Mandez Montenegro. (Interview with Lincoln Gordon, Johns Hopkins University, Baltimore, Md., August 2, 1968.)

key military commanders with whom U.S. attachés and military advisers maintained close personal relations. Rumors of a coup were rife in embassy circles. The attachés advised the United States not to oppose the military, who were the country's only sure strength against "communists." When the coup finally took place no U.S. warships were standing offshore.

The Dominican military ousted Bosch and installed a junta. But under U.S. pressure for a civil regime, Donald Reid Cabral, whose brother had been killed by Trujillo, emerged as president. The United States provided $100 million in economic assistance to the Reid government, substantially more than the former showcase, the disorganized Bosch government, had received, but this support proved insufficient to avert the Dominican disaster three years later.

Painful reappraisal

In July 1963, Carlos Julio Arosemena, a drunkard who had moved up from vice-president to succeed José María Velasco Ibarra as president of Ecuador after a military crisis, was in turn toppled by the military. In October President Ramón Villeda Morales of Honduras was replaced by a military regime. Confronted by the implacable succession of military coups, the Kennedy administration began a formal reappraisal of U.S. policy on governments that came to power through the overthrow of constitutionally elected authorities.

The first product of this reappraisal was a statement by Edwin A. Martin, assistant secretary of state for Latin American affairs, that was approved by President Kennedy[6] and published in the *New York Herald Tribune* on October 6, 1963. In this statement Martin sorrowfully observed that the basic political principle of the Alliance—"that free men working through the institution of representative democracy can best satisfy man's aspirations"—was beyond attainment in the near future in individual Latin American countries. Martin noted that military coups "thwart the will of the people, destroy political stability and the growth of the tradition of respect for democratic constitutions, and nurture communist opposition to their tyranny." But the crux of his statement was that the United States must recognize the traditional importance of the

6. According to Teodoro Moscoso in the interview cited above.

military in Latin American politics and the futility of "keeping a man in office by use of economic pressure or even military force, when his own people are not willing to fight to defend him." Martin recommended that the United States give its support to the educated middle class as the strongest force for peace and democracy in the Latin American countries, and encourage the military "to assume the more constructive peacetime role of maintaining internal security and working on civic action programs."

Where military coups did occur, Martin said:

We must use our leverage to keep these new regimes as liberal and considerate of the welfare of the people as possible. We must support and strengthen the civilian components against military influences and press for new elections as soon as possible so that these countries once again may experience the benefits of democratic legitimacy. . . .

I fear that there are some who will accuse me of having written an apology for coups. I have not. They are to be fought with all the means we have available. Rather, I would protest that I am urging the rejection of the thesis of the French philosophers that democracy can be legislated—established by constitutional fiat. . . . We cannot simply create the plant and give it to them.

A turning point

The administration's reappraisal of the policy underlying the Alliance was interrupted by the assassination of President Kennedy on Friday, November 22, 1963. This event had special poignance to Latin Americans. Kennedy had made several trips to Latin America during his presidency. He had dedicated Alliance projects in Colombia, Costa Rica, Venezuela, and Mexico. Like many young, educated Latin Americans, he was a liberal Catholic who wanted to reform the old order. In backland villages of Colombia, Peace Corps volunteers had found photographs of Jesus and Kennedy as the only adornments in humble homes. The stunning impact of the assassination was written on the faces surrounding the news kiosks in Rio, Santiago, and Bogotá.

Phase II: The eclectic approach

The Johnson administration placed the Alliance in a new perspective dominated by pragmatic judgments and technical standards. Dismissing Martin and Moscoso, Johnson united both State Department and AID functions in the person of Thomas C. Mann, assistant secretary of state for economic affairs in the last years of the Eisenhower administration and ambassador to Mexico under Kennedy.

Mann was an ardent advocate of U.S. business interests in Latin America. In March 1964 he convoked a three-day meeting of U.S. ambassadors to the Latin American countries and, speaking off the record, announced the new line.[7]

What became known as the Mann doctrine consisted of four basic objectives: (1) to foster economic growth and be neutral on internal social reform; (2) to protect U.S. private investments in the hemisphere; (3) to show no preference, through aid or otherwise, for representative democratic institutions; and (4) to oppose communism.

Mann's new policy was a far cry from Martin's reluctant confrontation of the military's role in Latin America. Mann expressed no political or moral reservations about cooperating with military governments. In his view, so long as a government was not communist-controlled, or in danger of becoming so, it should be acceptable to the United States. The Mann doctrine redefined the political objectives of the Alliance for Progress within the United States government. This new approach would soon find application in Brazil and the Dominican Republic.

Brazil: Round two

President Goulart's failure to implement an economic stabilization agreement concluded between Brazil's finance minister and David Bell in 1963 had led the United States to suspend virtually all economic assistance to the Brazilian federal government. Adopting an "islands of sanity" strategy, the U.S. mission made loans instead to the major state governments that appeared to offer a political counterpoise to Goulart's increasingly reckless populism. In general these loans were technically sound, but through them the U.S. assistance program under the Alliance served U.S. political and security interests in Brazil. By early 1964 the U.S. government was deeply concerned about reports of growing communist influence in Gou-

7. There is no official transcript of the meeting, but Mann's remarks were reported by Tad Szulc in the *New York Times* of March 19, 1964. Mann was later to claim that the Szulc report was distorted, but other participants in the meeting (who ask that their names be withheld) have corroborated Szulc's report.

lart's government and the labor unions that were his base of support.

During the week before the military moved to oust Goulart, two huge civic marches for "God, nation, and family" took place in São Paulo and Belo Horizonte, the capitals of the states where the insurrection began. U.S. businessmen resident in Brazil, who were in close contact with the CIA representatives there, helped to organize and finance these demonstrations.

On March 25, the day of the São Paulo civic march, a complaint within the Brazilian Marine Corps over the alleged inadequacy of food escalated into a mutiny led by a young corporal. (The press luridly paralleled this event with the Potemkin mutiny in Russia in 1917.) Goulart refused demands of Navy officers that the mutineers be severely punished, and on the night of March 29, at a meeting of the Association of Brazilian Army Sergeants, he delivered a speech that seemed to be pitting the sergeants against their officers. On the morning of March 31 the liberal newspaper *Correio da Manha* ran an editorial entitled *"Fora!"* ("Out!"), which signaled that the end was near. In the state of Minas Gerais, General Olympio Mourão Filho and Governor José Magalhães Pinto went on the radio to announce that the revolution to save Brazil from communism had begun.

It turned out to be virtually bloodless. At the president's residence in Rio, Santiago Dantas, Goulart's former finance minister, told Goulart that the United States had promised the Brazilian conspirators to support a "free government" established in opposition to the Goulart regime.[8] This opposition government-in-arms was to have been set up in São Paulo if Goulart had managed to hang on in Rio.

São Paulo businessmen have confirmed that early in 1964 Ambassador Lincoln Gordon was told of the plan to establish this government and was asked whether the United States would assist the São Paulo rebels. Gordon replied that he would put the issue to Washington.[9]

---

8. Interview in Rio de Janeiro, Brazil, August 1968, with a former aide and close friend of Dantas who has asked not to be identified.
9. Whether this assistance was in fact promised or merely represented by the conspirators as promised is not clear. In any case, Goulart's government fell with surprisingly little resistance. It did not need an external push.

Deciding that resistance was hopeless, on April 1 Goulart and his immediate entourage drove to the municipal airport in Rio and flew to Brasília. From there Goulart escaped to his immense ranch in Rio Grande do Sul with his wife and two children. Two days later they drove into exile in Uruguay, across the thinly guarded border.

Twelve hours after the provisional government took office in Brasília, President Johnson sent his "warmest wishes" and a tender of "our intensified cooperation." Next day, Secretary of State Rusk sent the new regime a congratulatory telegram describing the coup d'état as a "move to insure the continuity of constitutional government."[10] An editorial in the *New York Times* of April 7, 1964, commented, "It would be hard to figure out from the public and official pronouncements who got more satisfaction in the overthrow of President Goulart, the Brazilians or the United States State Department."

On April 9, seven days after receiving Rusk's telegram, the military high command issued an "institutional act" (in effect a constitutional amendment by decree) drafted by Francisco Campos, an eminent legalist who had written the 1937 constitution, *O Estado Novo,* propagated by Getúlio Vargas in his second attempt to introduce a document that would legitimize his dictatorship. The act empowered the three chiefs of the armed forces to arrest whomever they pleased without judicial or administrative recourse and to suspend political rights arbitrarily for as long as ten years.

Thousands of people were arrested without charges. Four hundred officials lost their political rights. The blacklist included three ex-presidents (Goulart, Kubitschek, and Quadros), six state governors, fifty-five congressmen, labor leaders, and intellectuals, among them Celso Furtado, the head of Brazil's Northeast Regional Development Agency (SUDENE).

Ambassador Lincoln Gordon, who had recommended Washington's immediate recognition and endorsement of the new government, was shocked by the institutional act and the wave of arrests and punitive acts that followed. Gordon had initially endorsed the coup as a move to protect constitutional processes. Now he felt that the new regime's abuse of such processes made it impossible for him to stay on as ambassador. The political

10. *New York Times*, April 3, 1964, p. 1; April 4, 1964, p. 1.

counselor of the embassy persuaded him not to resign by arguing that U.S. power and influence could help the moderate wing of the Brazilian military to oppose the hard-line military, who wanted an undisguised military dictatorship.[11] This argument was to be used successfully on several subsequent occasions.

Chile

Chile was to hold a presidential election in September 1964. Salvador Allende of the *Frente de Acción Popular,* or FRAP (a Socialist-Communist alliance), seemed a promising candidate. He had lost the 1958 election to the conservative Jorge Alessandri by a mere 33,500 votes. The Alessandri government had failed to step up economic growth, and copper prices remained low. The government's monetary stabilization program had failed to stem inflation. The price level had risen nearly fourfold but salaries had increased at lower rates, with a consequent decline in real wages. In its six-year term the Alessandri government had grown increasingly unpopular.

Now Allende was again the candidate of the FRAP. Alessandri's conservative coalition nominated Julio Durán, a middle-of-the-road member of the Radical party. The Christian Democratic party nominated Eduardo Frei Montalva.

Late in 1963, in order to prevent a recession in the economy, which the United States thought would work to favor Allende, the United States loaned $40 million to the Alessandri government for general commodity imports. However, the United States was not the only source of external interest in the Chilean election. The FRAP was obviously receiving financial support from the Soviet Union and other Eastern-bloc countries. The Christian Democrats were receiving help, financial and organizational, from their counterparts in Italy, France, and West Germany. Chile in 1964 had become a cold war battleground.

The Christian Democratic party in Chile had been formed in the 1930s as a rather narrow Catholic-action party. But as their movement grew in national stature, the Christian Democrats became more secular and their ideology more progressive

---

11. Interview with Lincoln Gordon, Johns Hopkins University, Baltimore, Md., August 2, 1968.

and reformist. Deriving its theoretical orientation from such Catholic European intellectuals as Jacques Maritain, the party advocated a "humanist revolution" in Chilean society within the framework of representative democratic institutions. Its leadership had come up through university student politics and its strength was in the professional and intellectual sectors of the middle class. But the party set out to compete with the Communists and Socialists on their home ground, in the slums surrounding Santiago, among the rural landless laborers, and in the labor movement. By 1964 its years of organizational work had begun to pay off. Frei, not Durán, emerged as the major alternative candidate to Allende.

The Christian Democratic party platform called for a revamping of Chilean education, which had been patterned after the elitist French system. The party advocated an agrarian reform program in which land would be expropriated and redistributed to the landless after an initial period of technical assistance and orientation in farm management. The Christian Democratic land reform proposal differed from that of the FRAP in that it was to provide compensation for the expropriated lands.

Another major issue in the 1964 campaign was the status of wholly U.S.-owned copper companies in Chile. Braden, Anaconda, and Kennecott together provided more than 75 percent of Chile's total export earnings. Allende called for outright nationalization of these companies and had nothing specific to say about compensation. Frei and the Christian Democrats advocated a policy of gradual "Chileanization" of the mines, a process whereby the government would buy an ownership interest in the companies as part of a larger program of new investment and expansion of production.

The United States ambassador in Chile, Charles Cole, a former president of Amherst and an early Kennedy appointee, was convinced that the United States could not live with the Christian Democratic position on the copper companies. He initially favored Durán, the candidate of the Conservative-Radical coalition. However, in the spring of 1964, in an important congressional election, the Conservative-Radical candidate was resoundingly defeated by the FRAP candidate. The interpretation of this election result was that Durán had no chance to win the presidential election in September and that by staying in the race he would only divide the non-FRAP vote, possibly permitting Allende to win. Durán accordingly withdrew and threw his support to Frei.

Ambassador Cole's policy of support for Durán had been questioned in the White House by, among others, Ralph Dungan, a Kennedy appointee. The AID mission director in Chile, John Robinson, had maintained open lines to the Christian Democratic leadership despite Cole's policy. With Durán's withdrawal, the United States shifted its support to Frei, who won a decisive victory with 56 percent of the votes (although the Christian Democrats themselves received only slightly more than 36 percent). Allende got 38 percent on the combined FRAP ticket and the remaining 6 percent were divided among minor candidates.

Frei's dramatic win was in a sense misleading. Many conservatives voted for Frei merely as the lesser of two evils and had no intention of endorsing the reform programs of the Christian Democrats. Nonetheless, the United States seemed at last to have found a second democratic left alternative (Venezuela being the first) in the hemisphere. Ambassador Cole resigned to return to Amherst. The appointment of Dungan to replace him showed that the United States was backing the Frei government.

Bolivia

Two months after Frei was elected, the commander in chief of the Bolivian armed forces gave President Víctor Paz Estenssoro the choice of the airport or the cemetery. Paz understandably chose the airport.

This coup was especially significant because, outside of Cuba and Mexico, Bolivia had been the only country in Latin America to undergo a genuine social revolution, and it was one that the United States had supported with substantial resources (nearly $200 million between 1952 and 1964). In the initial years of the Alliance for Progress, the United States had shown special solicitude for Bolivia, both because of its geographic location (in the heart of South America, with no access to the sea), and in order to demonstrate identification with the social reform objectives of the Bolivian revolution. One of Kennedy's first acts had been to send Ben Stephansky, a labor attaché in the U.S. embassy in Mexico, well known in Latin American labor circles, on a special mission to assure Paz Estenssoro of U.S. support.

But by 1962 the ruling Nationalist Revolutionary Movement (MNR) party had lost control of the nationalized tin mines to Trotskyite and other radical labor leaders. The continued losses incurred by the nationalized mines, along with the demands and the apparent revolutionary potential of the miners (who were already Bolivia's labor elite), led the United States to encourage the rebuilding of the Bolivian army (destroyed in the aftermath of the revolution) as a counterweight to the miners. The economy had achieved impressive growth rates in 1963 and 1964. However, the increasingly evident corruption of the regime, Paz's inability or unwillingness to use the army (as it had been used in the prerevolutionary period) to crush the miners (his traditional constituency), the reemergence of an articulate middle class demanding an end to political repression, and the ambitions of an aggressive military establishment together led to Paz's overthrow in November 1964.

The Dominican Republic: Round two

For nearly six months an unnatural calm seemed to prevail in the hemisphere. But on April 24, 1965, a rebellion broke out in the Dominican Republic. Younger army officers allied to Juan Bosch's party initiated a revolt against the Reid Cabral government. On April 25, Thomas Mann, then undersecretary of state for economic affairs, cabled the embassy in Santo Domingo, expressing Washington's fear that "Castroite extremists" might emerge in control of the rebel movement, noting that the embassy had not yet reported that American lives were in danger, and instructing the embassy to inform Washington promptly of any such danger. Almost immediately the embassy sent back a report of danger to American lives.

As Theodore Draper and other writers have documented, the purpose of sending United States Marines to the Dominican Republic was not to protect the lives of U.S. citizens but to prevent the rebels (led by "Castroite extremists") from prevailing.[12] The reasoning behind this intervention directly affected the Alliance for Progress.

The preeminent objective of U.S. policy in the Alliance for Progress was to prevent other Latin American countries from following the example of Cuba. U.S. support of moderate progressive forces (i.e., the democratic left and social reform) was preeminently a means to that end, a means that experience had not proved effective. The moderate progressive forces in Latin America (except in Chile, Colombia, and Venezuela) were apparently not sufficiently competent to find safe channels for the revolutionary ferment in their countries.

The United States must therefore find and support other forces within these countries to prevent a new Castro from emerging—even if these forces consisted of reactionaries like General Wessin y Wessin, the Dominican general who "requested" U.S. intervention.

The difference between the coup against Goulart in Brazil and the coup against Reid Cabral in the Dominican Republic lay in the relative strengths of the sides favored by the United States. In Brazil, Goulart's opponents were strong enough to prevail without overt U.S. intervention. In the Dominican Republic, "our Dominicans" were losing and time was of the essence. U.S. policy in both cases was based on a venerable principle: the "security interest" of the United States must take priority in Latin America. Kennedy himself had stated it in a comment to Arthur Schlesinger shortly after the assassination of Trujillo: "There are three possibilities in descending order of preference: a decent democratic regime, a continuation of the Trujillo regime, or a Castro regime. We ought to aim at the first but we really cannot renounce the second until we are sure that we can avoid the third."[13]

Pragmatism

In January of 1966, Lincoln Gordon replaced Jack Vaughn as assistant secretary of state for inter-American affairs. As

---

12. See, for example, Theodore Draper, "The Dominican Crisis: A Case Study in American Policy," *Commentary*, December 1965.
13. Arthur Schlesinger, Jr., *A Thousand Days* (Boston: Houghton Mifflin, 1965), p. 769.

---

one of the formulators of the Alliance, Gordon was a figure of considerable stature in Latin American affairs. He had been appointed ambassador to Brazil by President Kennedy and maintained independent access to the White House. Although Gordon's relationship with President Johnson was never as close as his relationship with Kennedy, there was never any doubt that Gordon was in charge of United States Latin American policy.

An economist in his own right, Gordon made economic development the keystone of U.S. foreign policy in Latin America. He had a natural affinity for such economic planners as Roberto Campos, minister of planning in the government of General Humberto Castelo Branco, who had been elected president by Brazil's congress in April 1964, in accordance with the institutional act decreed by the military.

The Castelo Branco government, supporting sound financial management policies carried out by apolitical technicians, inspired Gordon with a new vision of the military role in Latin American politics. He cast the military not merely in the traditional and essentially negative role of bulwark against communism, but in a positive development role as well. The military was to ensure the political stability within which a new coalition of apolitical economic and financial technicians (of whom Roberto Campos and later Adelberto Krieger Vasena, minister of economy in the Onganía government of Argentina, were the models) and the more modern progressive members of the industrial and agricultural establishment would promote economic development and institutional modernization. Brazil, then, provided the proving ground for a new theory to complement that of the democratic left. This new coalition, the theory ran, would be more receptive to foreign investment, foreign policy collaboration with the United States, and orthodox economic management theories.

In June 1966 Argentina tried the Brazilian solution. In 1963 the military had arranged a presidential election in which the Peronists were not permitted to run a candidate. Ten other parties did, however, and the candidate of the People's Radical Civic Union, Arturo Illía, won with only 25 percent of the popular vote. His administration proved to be as weak as his popular support, and after three years the military deposed him and installed an outright dictatorship, headed by General Juan

Carlos Onganía. Both Gordon and the U.S. ambassador in Argentina, Edwin Martin, tried to convince the Argentine military that the United States was opposed to the coup. But the Argentine military saw no need to justify actions the clear purpose of which was to clean out the alleged corruption of weak and ineffective civilian governments and set the economy right. Moreover, the officers had observed Brazil's "unnecessary" crisis in October 1965, when the opposition succeeded in electing the new governors of Minas Gerais and Guanabara, and diagnosed its cause: after ousting Goulart, the Brazilians had maintained a façade of representative political institutions and the rhetoric of democracy. Determined not to repeat this "mistake," the Onganía government dissolved the Congress and the political parties and set no timetable for the reestablishment of representative political institutions. However, by freezing wages and following the prescriptions of the International Monetary Fund, the Onganía government endeared itself to the international financial community. The rate of price increases dropped dramatically and the foreign exchange position improved. U.S. officials stilled their qualms over the absence of representative political institutions by admiring Argentina's economic picture.

Thus by the end of 1966 U.S. policy in Latin America was solidly centered in its pragmatic phase, as favorable to the authoritarian governments of Brazil and Argentina as to the democratic governments of Chile and Colombia. The common denominator among these four governments was their acceptance of the economic policy recommendations made by the International Monetary Fund or their AID equivalent.

But as the Alliance lost its social and political content, it also lost popular appeal. In Latin America, in a play on the word *para*, which means both "for" and "stop" in Spanish and Portuguese, the Alliance was increasingly referred to as the Alliance That Stops Progress.

Punta del Este: Round two

In 1967 President Johnson proposed a summit meeting of Western Hemisphere chiefs of state to discuss ways in which the nations could cooperate to achieve Latin American economic integration. Characteristically, Gordon was more impatient with the slow pace of integration than many of his Latin

American counterparts. Indeed, Gordon was impatient with the pace of the meetings to arrange the summit. On a visit to one country he refused to attend a black-tie dinner. "They have to realize the days of clipper ships are over," he said. The more cynical Latin Americans attributed the U.S. government's pressure for speed to a desire to enlarge the market for U.S. multinational companies.

The conference finally convened in April 1967 at Punta del Este. The topic of the meeting was itself an indication of the state of the Alliance. The first meeting at Punta del Este had produced a call for political and social reform; the second dealt with essentially technical concerns.

But the 1967 meeting was at least an attempt to find common ground for hemispheric cooperation. The Latin Americans decided to concentrate aid resources in education and agricultural development. Johnson offered to finance a Pan-American highway system if studies on the program went forward quickly. (These studies are still awaiting completion.)

On April 28, 1968, in an interview for the *Washington Evening Star*, Covey C. Oliver, who had replaced Lincoln Gordon as assistant secretary of state in June 1967, expressed considerable optimism about Latin America. He pointed out that the last military coup had been the one in Argentina two years earlier. He praised Brazil, Chile, and Argentina for their achievements in economic stabilization. He was cautiously sanguine about Brazil's prospects for return to representative political institutions. Noting that the inflation that had ravaged the major countries in the early years of the Alliance was now under control, Oliver explained that these countries could now give greater emphasis to social reform, particularly in agriculture and education.

Less than six months later, Peru, Panama, and Brazil erupted in a new burst of military assertiveness. And in May 1969 Argentina's much-publicized stability went up in smoke.

Phase III: Perplexity
Peru: Round two

On October 3, 1968, the Peruvian military deposed President Belaúnde and installed a junta. The main purpose of this coup, like that of 1962, was to prevent an APRA victory in the presidential elections scheduled for 1970. The approaching retirement of General Juan Velasco Alvarado as chief of staff of the army, and a dispute between Belaúnde and Velasco over which general should be war minister, added to the tension. But the Peruvian military was also impressed by the examples of Argentina and Brazil, in which authoritarian military regimes had apparently achieved political and economic reconstruction.

The military had apparently changed during the Belaúnde period. The language of development and social change, the rhetoric of the Alliance, had penetrated the army staff school and war college. Starting with the problem of "nation-building," the war college had become a major social science research center. Its students—colonels and lesser officers, often from the ranks of the lower middle class—began to see themselves as the spearhead of fundamental change in the economic and social structures of the country. With the coup, the colonels moved from the war college, where they had merely studied and talked theory, to the presidential palace, where they had the opportunity for action.

By a series of obscure decrees, these young officers brought the ramshackle system of government agencies and state enterprises under corrective ministerial control for the first time. They placed the Office of Planning right in the president's office and provided it with financial resources. They systematically purged the Central Bank of competent technicians who they thought would oppose social restructuring because of its financial consequences. They established a think tank of young officers in the presidential palace. These officers consulted with lawyers, sociologists, and economists, and then held brainstorming sessions themselves. Out of this process, on June 24, 1969, emerged the most extensive agrarian reform law in the hemisphere since Cuba's.

Government comptrollers swiftly moved in to seize the books of the major sugar companies and of W. R. Grace and Company, the first objects of expropriation. The wealthy landed families of Peru and their allies in banking and industry shuddered. Following a venerable tradition, they tried to coopt the colonels, inviting them to garden parties in the magnificent residences of the elegant suburbs of Lima. But the officers either didn't accept or, as one puzzled host expressed it, "didn't even seem to have a good time."

Whether this reformism might in time give way to a more traditional politics remained to be seen. But the Peruvian coup and subsequent events destroyed the United States stereotype of the Latin American military as a stabilizing, conservative force in Latin American society. Panama destroyed another illusion.

Panama

Since World War II the United States had maintained large military assistance groups in the Latin American countries. Through these groups, it was argued, the United States influenced the Latin American military toward a higher degree of professionalism and a greater respect for constitutional processes. The U.S. military assistance program had generally been considered one of the most effective technical assistance efforts in the hemisphere. To those who remembered the parades of goose-stepping troops with their *Wehrmacht*-style helmets in Chile, Bolivia, Argentina, and Brazil in the prewar period, the pervasive U.S. influence in the postwar period seemed nothing short of miraculous.

The U.S. armed forces spared no expense in connection with this program. They trained promising young officers at United States bases. They regularly engaged in joint planning with the general staffs of the Latin military. The Department of State and AID were often forced to send to the field key personnel who were poorly prepared in language training and cultural background. U.S. military attachés, however, were given plenty of time for study and stepped off the plane fluent in the language and knowledgeable about the country. Basic to the program was an effort to create a sense of belonging to a hemisphere-wide fraternity: all for one and one for all.

Nowhere was the American military presence more marked than in Panama, home base of the U.S. Southern Command. And the most perfect product of the entire assistance program was the National Guard, Panama's army, equipped virtually down to its last shoelace by the United States.

In October 1968, however, the Panamanian National Guard deposed the newly elected president, Arnulfo Arias, and established a military junta to run the country. Arias was a familiar figure on the Panamanian political scene. A member of one of the old families that have profitably passed the government back and forth among themselves for many years, Arias was also a demagogue of considerable talent, who had been elected president twice before—and had been deposed by the military on both occasions. He had great support among Panama City's slum dwellers, who pressed in against the Panama Canal Zone, where the U.S. equivalent of the French colony in prerevolutionary Algiers resided. Although the incumbent government had tried to throw the election to David Samudio, former finance minister, Arias' margin of victory was so substantial that modification to ensure his defeat was impossible. But when Arias as president attempted to change the top command of the Guard, apparently in the hope that officers of his own choosing would permit him to serve out a presidential term for a change, constitutional processes once again went out the window. Arias was overthrown for the third time and shipped off to exile in the United States.

Barely a month after the Peruvian coup, in a country that was considered little more than a U.S. satellite and in which U.S. military presence and influence were supposedly preeminent, the Panamanian coup demolished the credibility of U.S. military assistance in Latin America as an aid to constitutional government. The U.S. ambassador in Panama, Charles Adair, attempted to disclaim U.S. influence over the National Guard and was ridiculed by U.S. correspondents.

Perhaps inspired by the Peruvian military, the Panamanian National Guard adopted the rhetoric of social reform to justify its ouster of Arias. The junta brought into office a young, technically competent ministry. But unlike Peru's junta, Panama's subsequently exiled its more radical members to Miami. The Panamanian coup was thus less important as a source of change in Panama than as a blow to a major justification for continued U.S. military assistance in the hemisphere.

Brazil: Round three

Following the 1964 coup that toppled Goulart, the United States supplied major economic assistance to Brazil (an estimated $1.6 billion between 1964 and 1968 in bilateral resources alone). First Gordon and then Oliver had insisted that Brazil was steadily making its way back to constitutional processes and that U.S. assistance had played a crucial role in easing the way. They explained the removal of governors, the closing of Congress, and other regressive political acts as regrettable but temporary aberrations in otherwise steady progress toward a return to democratic political processes and constitutional restraints.

On December 13, 1968, however, even the United States government became unable to accept this argument. On that date Marshal Artur da Costa e Silva, who succeeded Castelo Branco as president in 1967, signed a new institutional act, assuming full dictatorial powers. He abolished the writ of habeas corpus for political offenses and shut down Congress indefinitely. The occasion that prompted these measures was relatively trivial: Congress had refused to deprive a federal deputy of his congressional immunity so that he could be prosecuted under the national security law for insulting the military in an Independence Day speech. This pretext, however, hid a more fundamental issue. Since 1964 the Brazilian military had assumed for the first time responsibility for managing the country's affairs. Unused to the cut and thrust of politics, and bedeviled by the nation's economic and social problems, the military increasingly suffered the opprobrium of Brazilian public opinion, previously reserved for civilian politicians. (And in retrospect the civilian politicians, particularly Juscelino Kubitschek, looked better to a significant part of urban middle-class Brazil.) Girls on the beach at Ipanema refused to date military cadets, and called them gorillas. Sergeants requested permission to wear civilian clothing on trains to the working-class suburbs of Rio because uniforms aroused the hostility of the other passengers. The military was increasingly resentful of the public's "lack of understanding," and the refusal of the Congress to deny immunity to the federal deputy was the last straw. The result was the Fifth Institutional Act.

Making use of his new powers, Marshal da Costa e Silva deprived almost two hundred persons, including ninety-one federal deputies, of their political rights. On December 14 a new decree was issued empowering the president to expel within forty-eight hours any foreigner who "attempts action against national security or public order." Three foreign worker-priests were immediately expelled from the country. On February 25, 1969, another decree was issued providing for the suspension or expulsion from academic activities of any student who "organizes or participates in strikes, marches, unauthorized meetings," or who was caught with "subversive" material. By the summer of 1969, approximately six hundred students had been expelled.

On April 27 and 29, 1969, without prior warning, a new decree expelled professors from the Universities of Rio de Janeiro and São Paulo and barred them from teaching in any public institution in Brazil. The professors, some of them internationally renowned, represented a variety of academic disciplines and political positions. Some were communists; others seem merely to have supported university reform. Since the decision to expel the professors was essentially a star chamber proceeding, no one could be sure of the precise reasoning behind it.

Costa e Silva expressed some concern to his cabinet about the reaction of the U.S. government to the Fifth Institutional Act. His finance and planning ministers assured him, however, that so long as Brazil continued to talk about economic stabilization measures, "the Americans would go along with anything." Antonio Delfim Neto, the finance minister, made a public statement to this effect. The Fifth Institutional Act was justified to the Brazilian public (and indirectly to the U.S. public, as one aide to the finance minister later explained[14]) as necessary to the economic stabilization program.

U.S. officials in the field called upon Delfim Neto to protest his public statement. Lincoln Gordon himself headed a list of professors in the United States who sent a telegram to Costa e Silva protesting the expulsions of professors. Influential congressmen warned the administration that any attempt to authorize increased financial assistance for Brazil would meet with resistance.

Meanwhile, as the Brazilian economy improved, the political situation continued to deteriorate. During the summer of 1969 urban terrorism, in the form of bank robberies and shootouts, became an almost daily occurrence in Rio and São Paulo.

On August 29, 1969, President da Costa e Silva suffered a paralyzing cerebral hemorrhage. Rather than permit the civilian vice-president, a conservative elderly politician, to as-

---

14. This aide, who is still an official in the Brazilian government, must remain unidentified.

sume the presidency in accord with the Brazilian constitution, a military junta took over the government.

Less than a week later, the United States ambassador in Brazil, C. Burke Elbrick, was kidnapped by terrorists who demanded (and obtained) the release of fifteen political prisoners in exchange for the release of Ambassador Elbrick. They also insisted that the political manifesto that they had left in the ambassador's car be widely publicized and broadcast.

This manifesto called the kidnapping of the ambassador not an isolated incident but

> only one more act of the revolutionary war which advances every day and which this year began its urban guerrilla stage. . . . With the kidnapping of the ambassador we want to demonstrate that it is possible to defeat the dictatorship . . . if we arm and organize ourselves. We show up where the enemy least expects us and we disappear immediately, tearing out the dictatorship, bringing terror and fear to the exploiters, the hope and certainty of victory to the midst of the exploited.[15]

The document was signed in the names of two groups, one led by Carlos Marighella, a former Communist party federal deputy, and the other the Revolutionary Movement of October 8 (the date of Che Guevara's death), a student activist group.

The kidnapping and release of Ambassador Elbrick (and the release of the government's political prisoners) seemed to open a new phase of political violence in Brazil. In October, Carlos Marighella was gunned down in São Paulo. Marighella, aging and unwell, had been preparing to leave the country for medical treatment in Moscow. His death was a psychological blow to the Brazilian underground, but it did not lead to any easing of the government's political repression.

Torture of political prisoners became increasingly commonplace and known to the public. On November 20 Michael Field reported in the *London Daily Telegraph:* "Brazilian students, including girls, arrested for subversive political activity, had been stripped naked, beaten unconscious, given electric shocks, hung upside down for hours, trussed like chickens, and submitted to many other forms of physical and mental torture." On December 3, in a story datelined Rio de Janeiro, the *New York Times* reported: "A young Brazilian former medical student who had gone underground apparently to join a guerrilla

---

15. "Text of Manifesto from Kidnappers of U.S. Ambassador to Brazil," *New York Times,* September 6, 1969, p. 2.

group late last year was arrested as a terrorist recently. Four days later, his body was returned to his family."

On October 7, 1969, the Brazilian military junta selected General Emílio Garrastazú Médici, commander of the Third Army and former head of the Brazilian Intelligence Service, to succeed Artur da Costa e Silva. The junta convoked the Congress to ratify this decision and then immediately adjourned it. At first Médici candidly acknowledged that Brazil was not living in democratic normality, and seemed to promise a return to democratic political processes by the end of his term, 1974. But early in the new year the government imposed prior censorship of newspapers and television, including variety shows, and at the end of February Médici retreated from his moderate hopes for a return to democratic processes and instead implied an indefinite continuation of the dictatorship. In 1974 the ten-year period for the original *cassacões* (loss of political rights) following the 1964 coup runs out. Brazil can almost certainly expect continuing political upheaval in the coming decade.

The 1970 USAID congressional presentation showed $187 million programmed for Brazil. In the spring of 1970, reports from U.S. intelligence sources about widespread torturing of political prisoners led the Nixon administration to cut back—but not end—U.S. economic assistance to Brazil. (Brazil's foreign exchange reserves of nearly U.S. $1 billion softened the impact of the cutback.)

Argentina: Round two

In March 1969 a World Bank team returning from its annual appraisal of the Argentine economy brought back glowing reports of Argentine economic performance, attributed primarily to an effective program of economic stabilization that had apparently won the acquiescence, if not the support, of Argentine wage earners.

On May 15, 1969, during student demonstrations against the rising prices of meals at the canteen of the National University in Corrientes, a student was shot and killed by the police. The students, who had long resented the Onganía government's supervision of the universities, responded with a series of unexpectedly massive and violent demonstrations. They were soon joined by workers and labor organizers embittered by the wage freeze and by the suppression of strikes, through which the government had achieved its "political stability and good economic performance." By the end of May, bloody street battles had occurred in Córdoba, Rosario, and other cities. As violence and bloodshed spread, urban guerrilla terrorists became more bold. Central Bank reserves fell as capital fled the country. In an attempt to save his position, President Onganía fired his cabinet, including Krieger Vasena, the architect of the economic policies so acclaimed by the World Bank, and the government resorted to even more brutal repression of its opponents. In June 1970 Onganía himself was replaced by a new general chosen by the chiefs of the Argentine armed forces.

By eliminating or emasculating their political parties and discrediting the political process as a channel for dissent, the governments of Argentina and Brazil drove political opposition into extrainstitutional channels. In both countries, elements of the Catholic church increasingly took on the task of social protest. Worker-priests became the organizers of labor opposition in Argentina, setting up strike funds and leading protest marches. In Brazil the churches often became headquarters for student activism. Acts of terror shocked those who believed that violence was not a part of the Brazilian character. In Recife, Father Henrique Pereira Neto, a professor of sociology and assistant to Dom Helder Camara, the progressive archbishop of Recife and Olinda, was found hanging from a tree with his throat slit. He had been tortured. In São Paulo a U.S. army captain was shot down in the driveway of his home while his wife watched and his nine-year-old son was removed from the line of fire.

The prospect

Entering office in January 1969, the Nixon administration found a small heap of discredited approaches to the dilemmas of Latin American development. The idealistic theory of U.S. assistance through representative political institutions had been undermined by a succession of military coups. This approach had then given way to new pragmatism that increasingly favored the benevolent authoritarianism of military governments. But these military governments had turned out to be neither completely benevolent toward their own people nor completely dedicated to U.S. policy objectives. The Catholic church, a bastion of conservatism at the beginning of the decade, had become a sanctuary for student activists and militant young priests.

The countries of Latin America were struggling to find institutional means by which new groups could take their places within the traditional structure of political power and economic privilege. As this struggle grew in intensity, an otherwise deeply divided society found a degree of cohesion in assertive nationalism. This spirit has served to unite conservative businessmen, concerned about foreign competition, with leftists opposed to imperialistic exploitation behind political campaigns for economic liberation from U.S. business.

The limitations of foreign aid

When Governor Rockefeller undertook his fact-finding mission to Latin America for President Nixon early in 1969, he was amazed to discover that there was no single organizational entity called the Alliance for Progress, no building or group of offices specifically devoted to the work of the Alliance. The Charter of Punta del Este merely stated that the governments of the individual Latin American countries should formulate long-term development programs; a group of experts called the Committee of Nine would be available to evaluate and make recommendations regarding the programs; and the "inter-American credit institutions, other international credit agencies, and other friendly governments" would determine the allocation of assistance funds.

Each national development program was to be prepared "if possible within the next eighteen months," and was to set forth "mutually consistent targets to be aimed at over the program period in expanding productive capacity in industry, agriculture, mining, transport, power and communications, and in improving conditions of urban and rural life, including better housing, education and health." It was also to state the target priorities and specific methods and projects to achieve the targets, and to include detailed cost estimates for major projects and the entire development program year by year over the program period, the internal resources available for the program, the estimated amount of external resources required, the effect of the program on the balance of payments, measures to direct the operations of the public sector and to encourage private action in support of the development programs, fiscal and monetary policies to permit implementation of the program within a framework of price stability, and the administrative structure to be used in carrying out the program.

The Committee of Nine, which was to coordinate external assistance with the internal self-help and planning efforts, consisted of Paul Rosenstein-Rodan and Harvey Perloff of the United States; Raúl Sáez of Chile; Jorge Sol Castellanos of El Salvador; Felipe Pazos, former president of the National Bank of Cuba; Hernando Agudelo Villa of Colombia; Jorge Grieve of Peru; Ernesto Maleccorto of Argentina; and Manuel Noriega Morales of Guatemala.

The charter did not describe the form the Alliance would take within the governments of the member nations. The Kennedy administration considered setting up a separate organization, like the Peace Corps, within the U.S. government. Adolf Berle also favored making the Alliance a self-contained, high-ranking operation. But in 1961 the Agency for International Development (AID) was newly established, succeeding the International Cooperation Administration and representing a new, untried approach to foreign aid. On the grounds that Latin America was sufficiently popular with Congress to carry other parts of the foreign aid program past hostile budget-cutters, President Kennedy placed the Alliance within the AID–State Department structure.[1]

---

1. Even as late as 1963, after completing his study of the Alliance for the Inter-American Economic and Social Council, former president Juscelino Kubitschek of Brazil recommended to Kennedy that the Alliance be given a new status and organizational structure patterned after the War Production Board, authorized to cut across agency lines and report directly to the White House (interview wtih Juscelino Kubitschek, Rio de Janeiro, August 27, 1968).

The conjunction of AID and State, with their parallel regional and national desks, represented an innovative attempt to politicize development assistance and to make policy responsive to development needs. Teodoro Moscoso, the first AID regional director for Latin America, became the U.S. coordinator of the Alliance for Progress, responsible for carrying out U.S. financial and technical assistance commitments in the region. Edwin A. Martin, assistant secretary of state for inter-American affairs, was responsible for the foreign aspects of the Alliance. Richard Goodwin, as Kennedy's assistant on inter-American affairs, was responsible for coordinating the activities of USAID in Latin America, the State Department's Bureau of American Republics Affairs, and the White House.

The expansion of the U.S. aid program in Latin America also required a large new staff in Washington, better staffed missions in eighteen Latin American countries, a new subregional office in Central America, and a special office for the Brazilian northeast. AID missions became a vital part of U.S. embassy staffs in nearly every country. The United States also had to upgrade its representation at the Inter-American Economic and Social Council and maintain a director at the Inter-American Development Bank. (Both of these institutions hold important annual meetings dealing with Alliance policy.)

Because the Kennedy administration assigned high priority to the Alliance, the Latin American bureau began to attract highly motivated young Foreign Service officers and outside talent who had shunned Latin American affairs in the Eisenhower years. Kennedy himself was in almost daily contact with Moscoso and Martin, and even lowly State Department desk officers for Peru or the Dominican Republic sometimes picked up the telephone on weekends and found Kennedy on the line asking for information or giving instructions. Kennedy's interest also affected Congress; Title VI of the Foreign Assistance Act of 1962 singled out the Alliance for a separate appropriation. This special standing, however, was short-lived.

The limitations of planning

Essential to the Alliance concept of national development was a belief in the necessity and value of planning. But the framers of the charter did not take into consideration the conditions under which such planning would take place. These technical and political conditions soon emerged as obstacles to implementation of the charter's recommendations. For example, in the early years of the Alliance the Latin American countries lacked the wherewithal to plan. Despite ECLA's yeoman work in educating and influencing a new generation of political and economic leadership, national governments had no planning ministries staffed by technically trained personnel who could formulate operational plans. They had no projects ready for financing by even the most modest standards. Some of the first AID loans under the Alliance financed feasibility studies—research to determine the optimum structure and to estimate the cost of a development project—rather than actual projects. Even these preliminary technical studies were hampered by the lack of statistical data on such basic questions as income distribution, employment, agricultural production, and education. From a technical standpoint, the allowance of eighteen months for preparation of development programs was much too short. But from a political standpoint it was too long.

The Kennedy administration was under pressure at home to show speedy results. A sign over Moscoso's desk said, "Please be brief. We are already twenty years late." President Kennedy continually pressed Moscoso, asking why they couldn't do more and do it faster.[2] This pressure led to shortcuts.

According to the charter, the recommendations of the Committee of Nine were to be "of great importance in determining the distribution of public funds under the Alliance for Progress." This wording, in practice, allowed impatient U.S. officials to bypass the committee. On a trip to Chile early in 1962 Moscoso and Goodwin wound up promising the Chileans a large loan without consulting the committee. They did much the same thing in Argentina. The larger Latin American countries preferred to deal bilaterally with the United States rather than with a multilateral institution. At Punta del Este these larger countries had refused to submit their plans to a screening committee and insisted on wording the charter so that only at the invitation of a government could the experts formally evaluate its development program. Personal frictions and rival-

2. Interview with Teodoro Moscoso, San Juan, Puerto Rico, August 20, 1968.

ries within the committee also played a part in reducing its effectiveness. However, the elimination of the committee's voice in Alliance decision-making did not mean that lending procedures flowed smoothly.

The United States government: the war within

When C. Douglas Dillon committed the United States to a major program of long-term capital resource transfers, Latin America assumed that there was a cohesive United States government that could be committed. Insofar as the Alliance for Progress was concerned, however, the U.S. government was divided among warring bureaucratic and political fiefdoms, each pursuing its own special interest. The Congress was at war with the executive; the Treasury was at war with AID; and AID was at war with itself. The Bureau of the Budget served as a sort of arbiter among the contenders. The Export-Import Bank, regarding the others with disdain, generally remained on the side lines, while the Agriculture and Commerce Departments, parochial in outlook, entered the fray from time to time on behalf of beet-sugar producers, textile interests, and other nervous constituencies. The Alliance for Progress was merely a pawn in the interdepartmental competition for power and favor within the United States government.

The executive branch

The executive branch of the United States government consists of a disparate group of entities created to protect and carry out special functions. The function of the Treasury Department in the international field is to protect the United States balance of payments. The Department of Agriculture serves to promote the interests of the United States agricultural sector. The Commerce Department responds to the concerns of the U.S. business community and, in the international sector, of U.S. exporters. The Export-Import Bank finances U.S. exports abroad. The Alliance for Progress touched on all of these functional interests.

The Treasury saw the Alliance as a dangerous conduit for foreign exchange leakage from the United States. The Commerce Department wanted to make AID a vehicle for U.S. exports. The Department of Agriculture feared that the Alliance would finance the production of commodities in Latin America which might compete with U.S. producers in foreign markets. Anticipating these problems, Congress provided, in the Foreign Assistance Act, for the establishment of a Development Loan Committee (DLC) to advise the administrator of AID on possible conflicts with other aspects of U.S. policy.

The members of the DLC were the administrator of AID, the president of the Export-Import Bank, the secretary of the treasury, the secretary of agriculture, and the secretary of commerce. Sitting as observers were the director of the Bureau of the Budget and the president of the Federal Reserve Board. At first the DLC held actual meetings, chaired by the AID administrator, David Bell. But the process of considering every individual AID loan proved too cumbersome. Eventually the DLC turned over the task of harmonizing AID loans with other government policies to the Development Loan Staff Committee (DLSC).

In the first years of the Alliance, the Latin American Bureau of AID was able to implement its program with a minimum of interference from the representatives of other agencies. The special status of the Alliance became something of a joke within AID. At one meeting of the DLSC, a loan proposal was submitted with the comment that the AID field mission assigned a very high priority to the project. Phillip Golden, representing AID in Washington, said the committee could relax, for it was clear that this was a low-priority item. The loan officer making the presentation protested. But Golden explained, "We all know there are only three categories of loans in the Alliance for Progress: very high priority, hysterical, and if-we-don't-make-this-loan-the-Communists-will-take-over-the-country. On that scale, this loan has a very low priority."

Under the imaginative leadership of Philip Glaessner, the deputy assistant administrator for capital development, AID pioneered new lending techniques and took chances that the more conventional international lending agencies shunned. (For example, AID supplied $200 million for the establishment of privately owned development financing institutions in Latin America, providing long-term, low-interest loans to Latin American entrepreneurs. The other international lending agencies, which had regarded this kind of lending as too risky, began to make funds available for similar purposes when AID's experiment proved successful.) But as the Castro threat receded, other concerns within the United States government gained precedence and stifled this innovative spirit.

AID and the Congress

The Alliance was designed to serve a long-term planning effort in which the governments of the Latin American countries would know well in advance what external resources would be available to supplement their own. The United States Congress makes its appropriations on an annual basis. To harmonize the demands of planning with congressional procedure, President Kennedy requested a three-year authorization of $3 billion for the initial Alliance for Progress fund. Congress, however, not only cut the request by $600 million, but stipulated that the administration would have to request appropriations annually. As a result of this measure, recipient countries could not formulate long-range programs on the basis of a specific amount of external resources from the United States on which they could depend. And the U.S. administrators of the Alliance were under pressure to use up appropriated funds by the end of each fiscal year.

Effective development planning takes time. Preparation of an adequate feasibility study showing the relative costs and benefits justifying investment in, say, a construction project may take as long as two years. But if the Alliance failed to use up the funds appropriated in the previous fiscal year, administrators feared that an already reluctant Congress would reduce the following year's appropriation correspondingly.

So each year, by the end of June, the AID loan staff would produce a pile of loan proposals for authorization. This task was more desperate and difficult than it seemed. The perennially understaffed missions in the various countries were dealing for the most part with underdeveloped borrowers and Latin American law. For example, AID routinely required of borrowers a statement that they had the legal authority to enter into a loan and carry out its terms and conditions. But it often took months to get this statement from a ministry of finance that did not have a full-time legal staff. The AID standard loan agreement had other clauses totally unfamiliar to lawyers in a different legal system. Solving all of these problems took time. And because new programs did not get started until late in the fiscal year, authorizations were late again the next year.

The June bulge aroused the suspicions of the congressional committees dealing with foreign assistance. Individual congressmen—most notably Otto E. Passman, chairman of the subcommittee on foreign operations and related agencies of the House Appropriations Committee, charged that, in its haste to authorize funds, AID was financing poorly planned projects and programs. And in some cases these charges were well founded. Congressional cutbacks in funds and refusal to agree to a long-term commitment made the AID administrators feel that Congress was not really committed to the Alliance. AID's late authorizations, on the other hand, made Congress ever more reluctant to authorize more funds. Mistrust escalated on both sides.

After the 1964 election, David Bell, the administrator of AID during the Kennedy administration, resigned and was replaced by his deputy, William Gaud, who had previously been assistant administrator of AID operations in the Near East and southern Asia. Gaud was convinced that Congress had overfunded Latin America by comparison with the rest of the underdeveloped world, and the economists who staffed the central AID Washington office felt that Latin America's economic performance was inferior to that of other regions. Lincoln Gordon and his deputy, David Bronheim, tried to preserve the special status of the Latin American program, but as 1965 moved into 1966, Gaud and the central AID bureaucracy assigned ever higher priority to Vietnam. When Gaud was asked by the Bureau of the Budget where cuts in the AID program should come from, he said, "Take it out of the Alliance." In 1968 Gaud informed a meeting of AID mission directors in Latin America that their programming decisions were easier than those of the other parts of the agency, since Latin America had always had more funds than it could effectively use. Word got around, and it was not surprising that Congress soon afterward slashed the Alliance appropriation request for the next year.

AID against itself

Title VI of the Foreign Assistance Act of 1962 stipulates that Alliance funds are to be appropriated separately from development loan funds for general AID use in other areas of the world. This provision gives the Alliance a degree of special status. But the uses of the Alliance appropriation, like those of the rest of the AID appropriation, are subject to the governing provisions of the Foreign Assistance Act.

The Foreign Assistance Act is a maze of conflicting objectives. It sets out the U.S. intention to "assist the people of less developed countries in their effort to acquire the knowledge and resources essential for development, and to build the economic, political and social institutions which will meet their aspirations for a better life, with freedom and in peace." But the act also reflects at least two other considerations: U.S. balance-of-payments constraints and the particular orientation of special-interest groups in the United States.

Under the Marshall Plan, the funds provided by the United States to the countries of western Europe had been "untied"; they could be used to purchase goods and services anywhere in the world. As it happened, however, most of these funds were spent in the United States, because in the years immediately after World War II only the United States among the highly industrialized nations had an unimpaired productive capacity. The U.S. balance of payments was overwhelmingly favorable and seemed likely to remain so. Economists worried over whether Europe could ever compete with the United States and earn enough dollars to pay for imports, services, and other dollar charges.

By the early 1960s, however, the U.S. balance of payments showed a chronic deficit. Economists now worried about the soundness of the dollar. The franc and the deutschmark appeared to be strong currencies. In key industries western Europe and Japan were more competitive than the United States. U.S. goods were increasingly priced out of the market.

Congress responded to this competitive pressure by stipulating, in the Foreign Assistance Act of 1962, that purchases financed by appropriated funds must be made in the United States, unless the president made a special finding that such procurement would not be consistent with U.S. interests. And the governing legislation contained other provisions favoring the interests of special groups. The act placed transportation of commodities financed by the program under Section 901.b of the Merchant Marine Act of 1936, which provides that at least 50 percent of commodity tonnage financed by appropriated funds must be carried on U.S. vessels. It stated that small U.S.

business "insofar as practicable" was entitled to "participate equitably" in the supply of commodities under the program. The act also demanded that the services of U.S. private enterprise, "particularly experts and consultants in technical fields such as engineering, be utilized wherever practicable." Expensive reports by U.S. private consultant firms became almost mandatory on project loan applications.

AID established the Office of Material Resources to administer the procurement provisions of the act, and gradually came to consist of two bureaucracies: one, the operators in the field (loan officers, economists, technicians, etc.); the other, the staff officers, most of them in the Office of Material Resources, in Washington. Each bureaucracy had its constituents. The field operators, who dealt primarily with Latin Americans, came to represent the development interests. The staff officers, who dealt primarily with congressmen, lobbyists, and other government agencies, came to represent them.

The pressures of all these groups had ramifications of harrowing complexity for the actual work of the Alliance.

Fertilizer for Brazil

In 1964 AID authorized a $15 million loan to the government of Brazil to finance imports of fertilizer from the United States. The dollars made available under the loan were to be sold to Brazilian importers, who would use them to pay U.S. exporters of fertilizer. The Brazilian importers would pay the Bank of Brazil for the dollars with local currency. This local currency would then be placed in a special fund to finance the purchase of the fertilizer by Brazilian farmers. This system was designed primarily to assist small farmers who did not have access to normal channels of credit.

The Brazilian government was particularly anxious that the loan be implemented promptly. In 1964 Brazil was in the throes of a spiraling inflation and its foreign exchange reserves were virtually exhausted. It was hoped that the fertilizer would arrive by September 1964, when the planting season would begin. In accordance with the terms of the Foreign Assistance Act, the loan agreement stated that at least 50 percent of the tonnage financed by AID would be shipped on U.S. vessels.

But the cost of shipment on U.S. vessels was more than double that of shipment on foreign vessels. Fertilizer is usually shipped on tramp steamers in large lots. (The minimum is 10,000 tons.) Shipment on a U.S. tramp under U.S. Maritime Administration guidelines cost approximately $19.50 a ton. Shipment on a non-U.S. tramp could be obtained for approximately $9 per ton. Understandably, Brazilian private importers balked at paying the excess cost of shipping on U.S. tramps.

After protracted negotiations, the Brazilian government agreed to offer preferential financing with AID loan funds to the fertilizer importers. The government also agreed to absorb the price differential of shipment on U.S. and non-U.S. tramps, up to a maximum of $10 per ton.

But during the fall of 1964 a food crisis in India and the demand of the Vietnam aid program put a heavy burden on U.S. tramp shipping. U.S. vessels were carrying wheat to India and commodities to Vietnam. Since fertilizer is a "dirty" (undesirable) cargo, few U.S. tramps were available for transporting fertilizer to Brazil.

The AID mission in Brazil requested AID in Washington to make a finding that U.S. tramps were not available, and to have the shipping division of the Office of Material Resources (MR) issue a "certificate of nonavailability" (CNA). They set up a procedure whereby the Brazilian importers would attempt to charter U.S. tramps. If within three working days they had not been able to do so, MR would issue a CNA. But MR then declared that the CNA did not mean what it said. Nonavailability of U.S. ships, MR claimed, did not relieve the Brazilians of the obligation to ship an equivalent amount of tonnage on U.S. vessels at a later date.

This ruling confronted the Brazilian government with a dilemma. Fertilizer had to be shipped within four months to arrive in time for the planting season. U.S. ships might well take more than four months to become available. But according to MR, even if all the fertilizer were shipped on non-U.S. tramps, the government of Brazil must refund to AID an amount equivalent to the cost of shipping 50 percent of the tonnage at U.S. rates.

The Brazilian government refused to license further shipments under the AID loan. When the AID mission reported to MR the consequences of its ruling, MR responded that it had merely followed the statute. The mission lawyer, Peter

Hornbostel, demanded that MR cite the statute it had followed, and AID found that the MR ruling was merely an administrative interpretation that could be, and was, changed by administrative action without violating the statute. The issuance of a CNA now meant what it said: No U.S. ship was available and the Brazilians did not have to ship equivalent amounts of cargo on U.S. tramps at a future time. The loan was reactivated and the fertilizer was shipped.

In the meantime, six months—one planting season—had been lost. But once under way, the program was so successful that the Brazilian government requested, and the mission agreed to recommend, a second fertilizer import loan. Both the mission and the Brazilian government assumed that the shipping issue had been resolved and that the procedures that had finally been agreed upon under the first loan would continue to apply. They were mistaken. AID discovered that individual importers were having their small fertilizer parcels consolidated and shipped on non-U.S. tramps. MR decided not to issue the CNA until the individual parcels first had been offered to U.S. tramps and then to U.S. liners. This complication led to a whole new set of negotiations.

In April 1967 a new Brazilian government entered office. The process of initiating an entirely new group of Brazilian officials in the mysteries of AID procedure began. The Brazilian foreign exchange position improved. By now the importers did not want to come anywhere near the AID loan. But the finance minister did not want to lose the $20 million. Desultory negotiations continued for another year. In the fall of 1968 the Brazilian government finally agreed upon new procedures. But by this time the Maritime Administration had increased the applicable U.S. tramp rate for Brazil from $19.50 to $25.46 per ton, thus requiring the Brazilian government to increase its subsidy of fertilizer imports. It was estimated that $4–5 million of the $20 million loan would go to subsidize shipment on U.S. vessels. The Brazilians concluded that the loan was too expensive, despite AID's forty-year repayment terms. In April 1970, still unable to come up with a formula for the use of the loan that was acceptable to the Brazilians, AID canceled the unused portion, $19 million, of the $20 million fertilizer loan.

In this instance, among others, the Foreign Assistance Act provisions intended to protect noncompetitive U.S. industries worked against both the development objectives of the Alliance for Progress and the ultimate interests of the industries themselves. Congress, however, blamed the results entirely on the administration of the Alliance for Progress. In 1968 the House Committee on Government Operations, in evaluating the goals of the Alliance for Progress, criticized the AID program for its failure to assist the small farmer and its lack of emphasis upon agrarian reform.[3]

The Treasury and "additionality"

In 1965 Henry Fowler became secretary of the treasury and the balance of power within the United States government shifted sharply in favor of the Department of the Treasury. The Treasury staff sought to counteract the financial drain of the Vietnam war and the deterioration of the U.S. balance of payments.

Treasury was in a strategic position to influence AID lending under the Alliance for Progress by virtue of its membership in the DLC. Moreover, in 1965 President Johnson initiated a "new commitments procedure," under which every loan of $10 million or more had to obtain his personal approval. Each loan proposal also had to be accompanied by a memorandum signed by the director of the Bureau of the Budget and cleared by the secretary of the treasury. In addition to its delaying effect (which was substantial), this procedure made Treasury the gatekeeper of the White House.

In 1967 a cabinet-level committee was appointed to find ways to limit the adverse effects of United States overseas programs on the balance of payments. A subcommittee was appointed to measure the balance-of-payments effects of foreign assistance and to establish procedures to minimize its adverse consequences "wherever practicable" and consistent with the purpose of the foreign assistance program. Thus as each loan came up before the Development Loan Staff Committee, Treasury insisted on more restrictive financial conditions. The final au-

3. U.S. House of Representatives, Committee on Government Operations, *USAID Operations in Latin America Under the Alliance for Progress: 36th Report by the Committee on Government Operations,* 90th Cong., 2nd sess. (Washington, D.C.: U.S. Government Printing Office, August 5, 1968), pp. 24–27.

thority on the purposes of the foreign assistance program was, of course, the president, but since State and AID could not bring every disagreement on every loan to his attention, for the most part they tended to seek accommodation with Treasury.

Foreign aid provides resources that a recipient country would otherwise not have to purchase goods and services essential to its development. AID has divided its funding for this purpose into several categories. Loans in category A supply funds to pay for imports in connection with a particular project. For example, a country that wants to build a hydroelectric plant may not have factories that can produce the necessary equipment. AID may then authorize a project loan, supplying dollars to finance the purchasing of equipment for the project in the United States and its shipment to the recipient country.

Loans in category B finance projects in such fields as education, agriculture, and housing. These funds usually go to pay local expenses for labor and for simple construction materials and equipment that can be produced in the recipient countries. AID provides financing by making an arrangement with the recipient country's central bank (or equivalent institution) whereby the AID dollars are deposited in a U.S. account. The country then uses the AID dollars so deposited to finance U.S. imports. The central bank supplies AID with an equivalent amount of local currency, in which AID pays its share of the cost of the project.

In the category C or program loan, AID supplies dollars to a central bank or ministry of finance for general commodity imports. The central bank resells the dollars to individual importers, who use them to pay for goods and services imported from the United States. The country then uses the local currency generated by the sale of the dollars as a "noninflationary" means of financing budget expenditures or special programs with the agreement and supervision of the local AID mission.

The Treasury Department sought to confine AID project lending to category A (procurement of goods from the United States for a specific project being financed) on the theory that these loans would produce "additional" imports from the United States. Treasury believed that projects in category A were unlikely to be carried out without AID financing, and would result in purchases of equipment that would not otherwise have been imported from the United States. These purchases would be "additional" to the usual import flow from the United States.

Treasury also reluctantly accepted category C, program loans, which also promoted U.S. exports and provided some leverage on the economic policies and performance of the recipient.

In fact, Treasury's objections to AID lending were generally confined to category B, projects requiring the conversion of dollars into local currency, on the grounds that such loans—primarily in agriculture, education, and housing—did not result in additional U.S. exports, but involved, for the most part, "local cost" financing.

Part of the reason for Treasury's insistence on "additionality" in loans to Latin America was that the Export-Import Bank, the principal financer of U.S. exports, had curtailed its lending in the region since 1960. EX-IM has substantial support in the Congress, and its president at that time, Harold Linder, had a particularly strong personality. Rather than tangle with Linder, Treasury tried to use AID as a substitute for EX-IM in promoting U.S. exports.

In spite of development priorities, AID found itself making more and more loans for the sake of additionality.

In August 1966 President Johnson delivered a speech about the Alliance for Progress, stating that the three development fields of highest priority were to be agriculture, education, and health. The secretary of the treasury objected to this new emphasis on social investment, and Charles Schultz, the director of the Bureau of the Budget, noted in a memo to the president that projects in these fields required local-cost financing. The president replied that he was willing to make local-cost financing available for such projects.

But Treasury was still concerned about the fact that AID dollars supplied for a category B loan would increase the country's capacity to import, without providing assurance that these additional imports would come from the United States. Treasury now insisted that AID work out procedures with each country to ensure that dollars made available under categories B and C were used to finance only those imports that the coun-

The limitations of foreign aid

try would not otherwise be likely to obtain from the United States—that is, additional imports. Thus the goods most eligible for financing were those in which the United States had a relatively low share of the local market—or, in other words, was least competitive. At every meeting of the DLSC, representatives of the Department of Commerce sat poring over their trade statistics to determine the categories in which the United States was least competitive. Behind them was the Treasury Department, represented at the working level by Ralph Hirshtritt, an exceptionally able career civil servant. AID had to negotiate each loan individually with Hirshtritt, and these negotiations were infinitely more difficult than those with the recipient countries.

In 1968 President Lleras Restrepo had to intervene personally in the negotiations for a program loan to Colombia. It took him four months to get a realistic list approved. "Colombia has received two program loans under the Alliance," he said before the compromise was reached; "I don't know if we can survive a third."

In 1967 AID authorized a $10 million loan to Chile to accelerate a dramatic program of education reform. Largely because the U.S. government was unable to decide on the commodity list and procedures of financing, AID was unable to obtain local currency for six months and had to borrow from the Chilean government to cover its share of the program.

In Panama, AID authorized a $3.4 million loan for cooperative housing. The loan was delayed for three months until Treasury received assurances of additionality, despite the fact that Panama uses the dollar as its national currency, has no import controls, and found it virtually impossible to meet Treasury's conditions.

In 1967 the AID mission in Rio decided to focus on modernization of Brazil's secondary education system. The Brazilian government committed itself to provide matching contributions in local currency for a major project in secondary education and to implement important structural reforms in curriculum and methods of teaching. However, Brazil, which has the most developed industrial plant in Latin America, prohibits the importation of foreign-financed equipment if an equivalent Brazilian product exists. Since Brazil had the capacity to produce virtually all the secondary school equipment necessary, an AID loan to meet this development need would not result in direct dollar imports from the United States. Treasury therefore pressed AID to concentrate on higher education, in the hope that funds for a university program might divert purchases of university laboratory equipment from Germany to the United States. In this case, AID executives were so convinced of the importance of secondary education that they resisted pressure from the Treasury staff and threatened to take the matter to the president. At this point, realizing that President Johnson took a special interest in education loans, the Treasury staff backed down.

In January 1968 the House Committee on Government Operations conducted an investigation of the AID program in Brazil and other Latin American countries. At the hearings in Rio, Congressman Benjamin Rosenthal, a New York Democrat, sharply criticized AID's lending priorities, pointing out that in 1966 Brazil had received much more money from AID for highway equipment than for housing and education.

The response of the AID mission director, Stuart Van Dyke, to this criticism illustrates the ravages of the war within the U.S. government. The AID bureaucracy believed, not entirely without cause, that Congress was generally hostile toward the foreign aid program and that Treasury's priorities would prevail over any opposition. Even when Rosenthal tried to suggest the true explanation for AID's lending in Brazil, Van Dyke still felt that any admission would give Congress a weapon against AID and worsen relations with Treasury. Instead he insisted that it was impossible to determine the Brazilian priorities. Rosenthal disagreed, and he was right.

Brazil does need improved maintenance of its road network. However, in 1966 the AID mission considered education Brazil's second most serious problem, surpassed in urgency only by inflation. AID also considered its chance of obtaining Treasury approval for education loans virtually nonexistent. (President Johnson had not yet announced the new priorities of the Alliance.) AID chose to authorize loans for highway maintenance equipment because they would involve direct imports from the United States and therefore win the approval of Treasury, and because AID had to use up the Alliance appro-

The limitations of foreign aid

priation somehow in order to keep Congress from cutting the next year's appropriation.

Tractors for Chile

In July 1967, AID authorized a $24 million agricultural loan to the government of Chile. Of this amount, $2 million was to purchase tractors for the agrarian reform program carried out by the *Corporación de Reforma Agraria* (cora) of the Chilean government. (Another $4 million was earmarked to finance tractors for the private sector.) The AID mission to Chile presented the loan as an opportunity for the United States to identify itself usefully and visibly with a Latin American agrarian reform effort.

The loan also presented an opportunity to sell tractors. The AID mission noted that tractors produced in the United States were not competitive with tractors produced in western Europe. The share of U.S. tractors in the Chilean market had declined from 79 percent of total tractor imports in 1951 to 9 percent in 1966. The Chilean government had adopted a policy of limiting tractor imports to two or three makes in order to obtain quantity price discounts and to ensure an economical supply of spare parts and adequate maintenance. It had also established a maximum delivery price level for all tractor imports. This ceiling led to the withdrawal of all U.S. exporters except the John Deere Company of Peoria, Illinois. John Deere had been exporting approximately 160 tractors a year for the seven previous years, receiving annual export earnings of approximately $550,000. The company was deliberately sacrificing profit on its tractors to maintain its market for the more profitable agricultural implements that were sold with the tractors.

The John Deere tractor was made in the United States and used no imported components. Delivered to the Chilean farmer, the Deere tractor cost approximately $5,700. Its major competitor was a tractor produced in England by a wholly owned subsidiary of the Ford Motor Company and selling for $5,300. Ford (like other U.S. companies) follows the practice of assembling identical tractors both in the United States and overseas, using in about equal quantities components produced both in the United States and overseas. The tractor that Ford produces in the United States has approximately 50 percent English components and is identical to the English Ford tractor, produced with 50 percent U.S. components.

But Alliance loan funds are "tied." AID regulations (M.O. 1414.1) require not only that goods financed by AID be of U.S. source and origin, but also that no less than 90 percent of their components be manufactured in the United States. John Deere was the only supplier that met both Chilean requirements for tractor imports and AID requirements for componentry and production.

The AID mission had been assured that if the 90 percent rule were waived, Ford would produce its tractors for the Chile market in the United States with English components, instead of producing in England with imported U.S. components, as it was then doing. Ford also offered a 25 percent discount on public-sector bulk purchases, bringing its price for the tractors to be delivered to the Agrarian Reform Agency below $3,900. Since English Ford already had the lion's share of the market (selling approximately 1,100 tractors a year, or seven times as many as Deere), and since Chile's policy was to rationalize its tractor fleet by reducing the number of brands, the Chilean government was reluctant to make a one-shot AID-financed purchase of the more expensive Deere tractors.

The AID mission therefore proposed that the 90 percent componentry rule be waived in this one case, and reset at 50 percent. Ford could then bid, introduce an element of competition, possibly bring down the Deere price, and enable the United States to provide direct support to the Chilean agrarian reform effort.

The procurement division of AID's Office of Material Resources and the Central Programming Office (primarily concerned with congressional presentation) opposed the waiver. The Programming Office argued that the political benefits of assisting the agrarian reform effort were offset by the risk of adverse congressional reaction to the waiver. It also noted that by permitting the percentage of imported components to increase from 10 to 50 percent, the waiver would cause the United States a balance-of-payments loss of approximately $3 million. It recommended abandoning the tractor loan and assistance to the Agrarian Reform Agency, rather than risk antagonizing the Congress.

John Deere had informed AID that it would oppose the waiver and, if necessary, take its case to the Congress. Since the loan touched upon both balance-of-payments and export considerations, the Departments of the Treasury and Commerce became involved in the decision-making process. In view of Ford's promise to shift its production for the Chilean market to the United States, Commerce was initially in favor of the waiver. But after a meeting with John Deere executives, Commerce changed its recommendation. Treasury went along with Commerce, and the mission's request for the waiver was finally denied.

The process of negotiation within AID, between AID and John Deere, between Commerce and Treasury, and finally with the Chileans took seven months. The tractors were bid on the basis of the 90 percent componentry rule. John Deere was the low bidder on the CORA tractors. International Harvester also submitted a bid, which was $1,200 higher than Deere's on a somewhat heavier tractor. The Chilean government's bid evaluation committee determined that John Deere had not complied with the power takeoff specifications and recommended the purchase of the International Harvester tractors. The AID mission concurred in the committee's findings. The Procurement Division of AID in Washington, however, feared congressional repercussions from Chile's failure to accept the low bid and was unconvinced that Deere's deviation from the specifications was material. The division therefore directed the mission to ask the Chileans to reconsider their decision.

By this time the issue had reached the ambassadorial and presidential level. President Frei explained to the United States ambassador that he was neither legally nor politically empowered to repudiate the recommendation of the bid committee.

In December 1968 AID was still debating the relative dangers of political repercussions in Chile, the wrath of the congressional allies of International Harvester, and the wrath of the congressional allies of John Deere. And as of that date, a year and a half after the authorization of the loan, not one tractor had arrived in Chile. The order had not even been placed. Not until 1969 was the loan finally activated and the shipment of International Harvester tractors delivered in Chile. It is not surprising that Chilean officials, and Latin Americans in general, began to wonder whose development the Alliance for Progress was supposed to promote.

The role of CIAP

In 1963 Raúl Sáez, chairman of the Committee of Nine, asked two former presidents, Kubitschek of Brazil and Lleras Camargo of Colombia, to evaluate the Alliance for Progress and recommend improvements. The 1963 meeting of the Inter-American Economic and Social Council (IAECOSOC) at São Paulo focused on the presidents' reports. (Each had prepared one.)[4] They recommended (1) that a new inter-American committee be established to give political direction to the Alliance for Progress and to emphasize its Latin character; (2) that the countries of Latin America agree among themselves on the allocation of funds; and (3) that some operative agencies of the Alliance, such as the Inter-American Development Bank, be physically located in Latin America.

Using the conclusions of the presidents' reports (which they had helped to formulate), the Committee of Nine, led by Sáez and supported by Chile, Colombia, and Venezuela, sought to invest the proposed Inter-American committee with the authority that the Committee of Nine had failed to obtain at Punta del Este: the right to determine criteria, allocate funds, and establish the conditions for lending.

Within the U.S. government the Bureau of the Budget, the Treasury Department, and the central AID bureaucracy opposed any concession limiting the freedom of decision of the United States. They did not fear that the new committee's lending conditions would be too lenient, but merely that they might conflict with U.S. interests. For example, the committee might produce an adverse report on a particular lending program that the United States wished, for political reasons, to carry out. However, within the Latin American Bureau of State and AID a small group led by William Rogers and David Bronheim sought to make some concession to the presidents' reports. They agreed that the United States could not commit itself to

---

4. Juscelino Kubitschek, *Report on the Alliance for Progress* (Washington, D.C.: Pan American Union, September 25, 1963); Alberto Lleras Camargo, *Report on the Alliance for Progress* (Washington, D.C.: Pan American Union, September 25, 1963).

accept in advance the decisions of the entity to be established. Such a commitment, amounting to a treaty obligation, would require Senate approval, which, given the fragility of congressional support of the program, would probably not be forthcoming and might even be dangerous to request. U.S. officials finally agreed to recommend the formation of a special committee of the Inter-American Economic and Social Council, authorized to make annual estimates of funds needed for the Alliance and available from domestic and external sources, but not to establish criteria for the allocation of funds or conditions for individual loans.

The U.S. position was communicated to Sáez before the São Paulo meeting. Chile, Colombia, and Venezuela did not have enough voting power to support their position against opposition from the three major Latin American delegations and the United States, and the final agreement largely reflected the U.S. position. It established a special permanent committee of the Inter-American Economic and Social Council, the *Comité Interamericana de la Alianza para el Progreso* (CIAP), in which seven permanent members (six elected by Latin American countries and one by the United States) and a large technical secretariat would carry out a continuing review of national and regional development plans, the availability of domestic resources in each country, and the availability and distribution among the several countries of external funds under the Alliance for Progress. CIAP was also to cooperate with the Inter-American Development Bank and help to coordinate negotiations between the individual countries and potential sources of external aid. In a provision that applied primarily to the United States, the member states agreed to give "special consideration" to the recommendations of CIAP in the allocation of public external funds under the Alliance for Progress, when providing financial and technical assistance through their own agencies and "when instructing their representatives in the various international organizations that provide such assistance."[5]

The United States did make what its delegates considered a major concession in accepting Raúl Prebisch as chairman of

5. Inter-American Economic and Social Council Resolution 1–01/63, approved November 1963 at second annual meeting in São Paulo.

CIAP.[6] But Prebisch declined the honor (possibly because CIAP had been given no real power), as did Lleras Camargo. Carlos Sanz de Santamaría, a former Colombian minister of finance and an able diplomat, but without the prestige of a Prebisch or a Lleras Camargo, became chairman.

The Committee of Nine continued to function, and CIAP was to take its recommendations into account. In 1966, however, increasing friction between the two groups led to the committee's resignation, an event welcomed by the United States.

In 1966 the U.S. Congress attempted to strengthen CIAP through the Fulbright Amendment to the Foreign Assistance Act. This amendment requires that social and economic development projects and programs financed under the act must be "consistent" with the "findings and recommendations" of CIAP in its "annual review" of national development activities.[7]

The CIAP annual reviews now provide a useful forum within which the representatives of the financing entities explore with the country representatives—usually the ministers of finance and planning—the issues confronting the country and its plans for resolving them. The finance minister expresses the commitments he will be expected to give in return for loan funds in a formal letter of intent to CIAP, but he does the actual negotiation of gut issues with the AID mission in his country and the headquarters staff in Washington.

CIAP has no power to enforce its recommendations and is, in any case, reluctant to take controversial positions. As a broker, it does not wish to offend either of its clients, the borrower or the lender. Its members, elected by individual countries, also prefer not to endanger their own or their colleagues' positions by voicing unpopular opinions. The large Latin American countries accept CIAP because it does not interfere with their relations with the United States, and the international financial agencies accept it because it does not materially affect their relations with the individual countries. As for the United States,

---

6. According to David Bronheim (in an interview on July 31, 1968) and William Rogers (in an interview on August 15, 1968), Prebisch's responsibility for the ECLA theses, particularly with respect to the terms of trade, the positive role of the public sector, and the limitations of private enterprise, had not endeared him to the State Department.

7. Foreign Assistance Act of 1961 (as amended), sec. 251(h).

as long as it tries to make its aid program serve its short-term political and commercial interests, it cannot risk subjecting decisions with respect to the amount of funds or the conditions attached to them to a multilateral decision-making body.

The financial balance sheet

The advent of Fidel Castro in Cuba dramatized Latin America's critical situation, but behind the political crisis was an economic crisis of towering dimensions. In the 1950s the major Latin American countries had adopted industrial promotion policies to substitute domestically produced industrial hardware and raw materials for imports. In order to import capital goods and raw materials for their new domestic manufacturing plants, they incurred large debts in short-term, high-interest loans and suppliers' credits. By the end of 1964 the Latin American countries owed close to two-fifths of the $33 billion aggregate public indebtedness of developing countries.[1]

Latin America's industrial promotion policies had also attracted foreign capital in huge quantities. Between 1950 and 1959 the book value of U.S. direct private investment in Latin America increased from $4.6 billion to $9 billion, almost two-thirds of all U.S. direct private investment in developing areas.

---

1. International Development Assn., *Annual Report, 1968* (Washington, D.C.: International Bank for Reconstruction and Development, 1968), p. 52.

In 1956 and 1957, Venezuela's new oil concessions produced a billion-dollar boom in foreign investment, but Mexico, Peru, and Cuba also registered substantial gains, and Brazil's influx of capital was second only to Venezuela's.[2]

In trade, until the middle of the 1950s, Latin America's position was favorable. In 1955 Latin America enjoyed a U.S. trade surplus of $200 million. But after the Korean war the commodity price boom ended. From 1956 to 1960, Latin American export earnings remained at about $8 billion a year. The average price of all Latin American exports, excluding petroleum, fell 18 percent in the four years before the Alliance. Only large increases in commodity export volume held earnings steady.

In 1960, trade, debt, and investment conditions converged. As a result of overproduction, falling coffee prices threatened to tip the already precarious political balances in Brazil, Colombia, and Central America. With Castro sympathizers already mounting guerrilla operations in depressed rural areas, the Eisenhower administration stopped mouthing the rhetoric of free competition and signed the International Coffee Agreement to halt the price slide. The United States also poured large balance-of-payments loans—known as "bailouts"—into the shaky treasuries of Brazil, Colombia, Chile, and Argentina. These government loans and similar U.S. private bank loans guaranteed by Latin American currency reserves held in New York were little more than expensive stopgaps. Often the borrowing country never even saw the principal, which passed directly from the New York banks to the creditors. Each year, however, the interest payments rose.

The creators of the Alliance wanted to take inter-American economic relations out of the hands of the bankers and attract popular support for the hemispheric development program. Social reform, national economic planning, and long-term government loans got the headlines at Punta del Este. But behind the publicity was what amounted to a financial salvage operation. In the early years of the Alliance, a significant part of the U.S. foreign aid funds channeled to Latin America served merely to refinance debt payments to bankers, including the

2. Data from U.S. Department of Commerce, *U.S. Business Investments in Foreign Countries* (Washington, D.C.: U.S. Government Printing Office, 1960), pp. 7, 11.

Export-Import Bank.[3] This use of U.S. public funds may have prevented some major Latin American countries from suspending foreign payments, but it did not add to the visible accomplishments of the Alliance. When addressing their people, Latin American politicians seldom point to debt payments, however necessary they may be, as examples of national accomplishment or social progress. Many people in Latin America therefore began to wonder whatever had happened to the millions of dollars for development they had heard so much about, but could not see in the form of jobs, houses, schools, or credit.

Trade

In the 1960s, Latin America's balance of trade with the United States continued to deteriorate steadily:

(a) Between 1960 and 1968, U.S. exports of goods to Latin America increased from $3.8 billion to $5.3 billion.

(b) In the same period, U.S. receipts from transportation services and travel by Latin Americans more than doubled, increasing from $580 million to $1.2 billion.

(c) In 1968, the United States posted a record $1.7 billion surplus in its balance of trade on goods and services with Latin America. In the same year, it registered a $1 billion deficit with western Europe including the United Kingdom, and a $1.4 billion deficit with Japan. In other words, U.S. earnings from Latin America made up nearly two-thirds of the U.S. deficit in trade with western Europe and Japan.

(d) On the basis of receipts for U.S. goods and services, Latin America has ranked second only to Canada as a market for the United States during the decade.

(e) Between 1960 and 1968, U.S. imports of Latin American merchandise rose only from $4 billion to $5.2 billion, while total U.S. imports more than doubled, reaching $33 billion in 1968. In that period Latin America's share of United States merchandise imports fell from 27.2 percent to 15.8 percent.[4]

During the Alliance years, Latin America has paid for this imbalance with increased exports to western Europe. Instead of receiving a net transfer of resources from the United States

---

3. In 1958 the Export-Import Bank embarked on a policy of reducing its Latin American lending and committing new funds, in key countries of Latin America, only in amounts equivalent to its expected take-out. Between fiscal 1961 and 1969, EX-IM transactions with Latin America yielded net repayments to the United States of $437 million, including interest (Agency for International Development congressional presentation, fiscal year 1970).
4. Felipe Herrera, "Inside the Economy," *American Banker*, September 4, 1969.

through trade to supplement Alliance aid, Latin America has devoted surpluses accumulated from western Europe to cover its commercial deficits with the United States.[5]

Debt service

The Alliance for Progress was handicapped from the beginning by the level of public indebtedness in Latin America. In 1960 the figure was over $10 billion. In 1966 it was $12.9 billion, and debt service in Latin America amounted to about 90 percent of grant and loan disbursements (public and private), a proportion higher than that in any other region of the underdeveloped world. (It was 32 percent in Africa, 20.4 percent in South Asia, and 22 percent in East Asia.) Between 1963 and 1967, annual service payments on outstanding external public debt rose from $1.3 billion to $2 billion, although the rate of increase in the level of public indebtedness slowed in 1965 and 1966. According to the World Bank, in 1966 the three largest Latin American economies—Argentina, Mexico, and Brazil—"had to earmark one-fifth to one-third of their export earnings for debt service."[6]

Private investment

Since World War II the United States has provided 75 percent of foreign private investment in Latin America. But in 1961 U.S. businessmen were undertaking few new ventures in the region. Cuba's seizure of nearly $1 billion in U.S.-owned sugar mills, hotels, banks, nickel mines, factories, and other assets had been a psychological as well as a financial blow. Brazil, Chile, Colombia, and Argentina, suffering from inflation accompanied by high debt payments and low export earnings, generated additional apprehension. During the first few years of the Alliance, although reinvestment of profits by subsidiaries remained relatively steady, new investments were sharply curtailed. But after 1964, with Cuba well isolated from the hemisphere by a collective diplomatic and economic blockade and Brazil under a military regime friendly to the United States, a new mood of optimism arose in the U.S. busi-

5. United Nations Economic Commission for Latin America, *Economic Survey of Latin America, 1968*, E/CN 12/825 (March 1969), p. 134.
6. International Development Assn., *Annual Report, 1968*, Table 6, p. 35; Table 7, p. 52.

ness community, producing an upsurge of investment in Latin America.

Since 1950 the major emphasis of U.S. investments has been on manufacturing. It has given rise to a wide range of U.S.-owned enterprises, from automobile factories to cosmetics plants, devoted mainly to production for the local market. These investments create jobs and generate production and tax revenues that local capital, at the present stage of domestic savings and technology, might be unable to provide. The U.S. corporate system in Latin America includes more than a million local employees of U.S.-owned companies and a huge structure of subcontractors, distributors, and service agents.

Companies that produce only for the local market do not generate foreign income. They usually require, nonetheless, a large volume of imports of raw materials for their production. The presence of U.S.-owned companies has thus had a profound effect not only on patterns of consumption but also on the allocation of foreign exchange income in Latin America. The annual rate of take-out in profits and capital repatriation by U.S. companies is 12 to 15 percent of investments, more than 12 percent of Latin America's annual export earnings. (See Table 7.1.)

As of 1969, the level of direct U.S. private investment in Latin America was $12 billion. The March 1969 issue of the U.S. Department of Commerce *Survey of Current Business* reports a gradual shift in investment emphasis from Canada and western Europe to Latin America and other countries. With substantial gains in all industries, capital investment in Latin America showed the largest increase of all major areas for 1968, easily surpassing the 16 percent gain registered in 1967.[7]

The role of the Alliance in stimulating these new investments is difficult to assess. They are not the result of public financing; virtually all private-sector loans made by USAID and the IDB have been to Latin American entrepreneurs, either through di-

---

7. ECLA suggests that in order to circumvent balance-of-payments restrictions on new overseas investments, international corporations obtained financing for ventures in Latin America from European capital markets. According to ECLA estimates, in 1968 capital expenditures by U.S.-owned companies in Latin America were $1.7 billion, 42 percent more than the 1967 figure. U.S. subsidiaries had their own growing profits from which to finance increased investments; in 1967, sales of U.S. manufacturing subsidiaries in their Latin American markets exceeded $6 billion, compared with U.S. export sales to Latin America of $4.1 billion.

Table 7.1.

Summary of U.S. private investment in Latin America, 1961–1968

(in millions of dollars)

	reinvested earnings	direct investment from U.S.[a]	income received in U.S.[a] (profits and earnings)	net inflow to U.S.[a]
1961	$ 255	$ 173	$ — 730	$ — 557
1962	268	— 32	— 761	— 793
1963	173	69	— 801	— 732
1964	216	143	— 895	— 752
1965	306	176	— 869	— 693
1966	302	191	— 965	— 774
1967	172	191	— 1,022	— 831
1968[b]	210	481	— 1,087	— 606
Total	$1,902	$1,392	$ — 7,130	$ — 5,738

SOURCE: U.S. Department of Commerce, *Survey of Current Business*, October 1968 and predecessor issues.
[a] A negative number reflects a net flow to the United States.
[b] Estimated.

rect loans for larger projects or through loans to national development banks and other credit institutions specializing in medium and small borrowers. Moreover, the EX-IM Bank has made no changes in its regular lines of credit to finance purchase of U.S. equipment for overseas projects. In 1962 USAID began offering investment guarantee insurance to promote investments in all developing countries. A major share of this insurance, which protects new investments against loss through war, revolution, expropriation, and nonconvertibility, has gone to firms making investments in Latin America. However, major corporations do not base their investment decisions on the availability of risk insurance. From all indications, the most important ways in which the Alliance has encouraged foreign investment are through its general support of monetary stabilization within programs to reduce inflation and its dollar loans to Brazil, Chile, and Colombia, which, by easing their chronic balance-of-payments problems, promote essential imports and free remittance of profits.

Public capital assistance

According to figures compiled by USAID, in the first eight years of the Alliance (fiscal years 1961–1969) the U.S. government, the United Nations, international financial institutions, the European Common Market, and the Development Assistance Committee members authorized $18 billion in assistance to Latin America.

Table 7.2

Economic assistance programs in Latin America, fiscal years 1961–1969: net obligations and loan authorizations (gross less deobligations and cancellations)

(in millions of dollars)

United States	
AID total	$ 4,418.5
U.S. contributions to Social Progress Trust Fund	
(Inter-American Development Bank)	535.0
Food for Freedom (Public Law 480)	1,417.8
Export-Import Bank (long-term loans)	2,118.6
Other U.S. economic programs	1,796.2[a]
Total U.S. economic assistance	$10,286.1[b]
International organizations	
Inter-American Development Bank (Fund for Special	
Operations and ordinary capital resources)	$ 2,456.9
International Bank for Reconstruction and Development	2,600.9
International Finance Corporation	117.1
International Development Association	132.1
U.N. agencies	420.3
European Economic Community	73.0
Total international organization aid	$ 5,800.3
Other	
Development Assistance Committee bilateral aid	
(exclusive of U.S.)	$ 3,215.4[c]
U.S. private aid	387.6[d]
Total other aid	$ 4,603.0
Grand total economic assistance	$18,119.4[e]

SOURCE: Constructed from congressional presentation figures of the Agency for International Development, fiscal year 1970.
[a] Includes U.S. subscriptions to the IDB Ordinary Capital Fund and Fund for Special Operations totaling $1.57 billion.
[b] Includes 1969 preliminary figure of $325.9 million.
[c] Calendar year gross disbursements of loans and grants.
[d] Includes Ford, Kellogg, and Rockefeller Foundations grants, U.S. voluntary agencies, and U.S. Partners Program.
[e] Excludes U.S. contributions to the IDB in note b above to avoid double counting.

On a *net* disbursement basis (gross disbursements less repayments and interest), however, the Latin American countries participating in the Alliance for Progress received only $4.8 billion from the United States from all sources: USAID, EX-IM Bank, and Public Law 480, Titles I and IV.

Table 7.3

U.S. direct official net disbursements, fiscal years 1961–1969:
gross disbursements less repayments and interest

(in millions of dollars)

AID	$3,257.8
Public Law 480	1,355.2
Export-Import Bank	− 437.0
Inter-American Development Bank Social Progress Trust Fund	458.3
Other economic aid (Peace Corps, Inter-American Highway)	185.0
Total	$4,819.3

SOURCE: Constructed from congressional presentation figures of the Agency for International Development, fiscal year 1970.
NOTE: The AID Direct Official Flow total shows $5.2025 billion. This figure is $383.2 million more than the figure shown above. The difference is accounted for by the fact that AID counts as an official U.S. flow the U.S. paid-in subscriptions to the IDB ordinary capital resources and U.S. contributions to the Fund for Special Operations. It seems to us that these figures should be shown as U.S. authorizations or obligations but should not be counted as part of U.S. flows. This seems to us misleading. IDB disbursements do not (and cannot) allocate disbursements among contributors to both funds. Yet IDB net disbursements are usually shown (and properly so) as part of the official flows to Latin America. Hence, if the U.S. contributions to the FSO and ordinary capital resources are also shown as flows, there is a double count. (Cumulative net disbursements of IDB and IBRD during the period 1961–1967, respectively, were $815 and $676.1 million.) See "Development Perspectives Under the Alliance for Progress" (paper prepared by the General Secretariat of the Organization of American States for the special meeting of the Development Assistance Committee, February 3–4, 1969).

William T. Dentzer, Jr., former deputy U.S. ambassador to the Organization of American States, observes:

If one further deducts the net flow of capital income payments to U.S. private investors in the United States, that is to say, gross remittances less new investments and reinvested earnings, that flow is about nil, in terms of bilateral U.S. capital flows. Capital income payments to U.S. investors in Latin America in the years 1964 to 1967 averaged about $514 million. . . . When you look at net capital flows and their economic effect, and after all due credit is given to the U.S. effort to step up support to Latin America, one sees that not that much money has been put into Latin America after all.[8]

During the first seven years of the Alliance (1961–1967) the cumulative net disbursements of the IDB and IBRD were $815 million, or about $110 million per year, and $676 million, or about $95 million per year, respectively.[9]

8. U.S. House of Representatives, Subcommittee on Inter-American Affairs of the Committee on Foreign Affairs, *New Directions for the 1970's: Toward a Strategy of Inter-American Development, Hearings*, 91st Cong., 1st sess. (Washington, D.C.: U.S. Government Printing Office, 1969), pp. 44–45.
9. Development Perspectives Under the Alliance for Progress" (a paper prepared by the General Secretariat of the Organization of American States for the special meeting of the Development Assistance Committee, February 3–4, 1969).

In 1967 Hollis Chenery, then director of AID's Office of Programming and Planning, stated:

The net effect of the first five years of the Alliance is to leave external assistance to Latin America at relatively low levels. Before 1960, the net flow of official funds to Latin America was less than half the per capita level for other regions. It has now almost reached the average ($4.00 per capita), but this is a much smaller proportion of development expenditures than in other areas. The net inflow of long-term foreign capital finances only slightly over 10 percent of total investment compared to the 20 percent to 30 percent which is common in Asia and Africa among countries that are following reasonably effective development policies. Since more than half of foreign long-term lending is offset by amortization of past loans, the net resource contribution of foreign capital to Latin America has been relatively small. [However, without this foreign assistance] a debt burden which existed at the beginning of the Alliance period in Latin American countries would have led to national bankruptcies accompanied by severe reductions in production and amortization.[10]

Overall, the Alliance balance sheet is disappointing. The flow of public funds from the United States to Latin America may well have prevented national bankruptcies, unilateral moratoria on debt repayment, and economic stagnation. But in financial terms, the Alliance for Progress has done more to avert, or at least to postpone, economic disaster than to stimulate economic development.

10. Hollis Chenery, "Toward a More Effective Alliance for Progress," Agency for International Development discussion paper no. 13 (1967).

The role of U.S. business

*Our foreign aid program constitutes a
distinct benefit to American business.
The three major benefits are: (1)
foreign aid provides a substantial and
immediate market for U.S. goods
and services; (2) foreign aid stimulates
the development of new overseas markets
for U.S. companies; (3) foreign aid
orients national economies toward a
free enterprise system in which U.S.
firms can prosper.*
Eugene Black, 1965

In 1961 the Mayobre memorandum warned President Kennedy that the Alliance was doomed if Latin America viewed it as an entering wedge for U.S. private investment. But since 1964 U.S. private investment in Latin America has been on the rise and U.S. banks, led by the First National City Bank of New York and the Chase Manhattan Bank, have greatly increased their operations in Latin America, often by buying out local banks. In 1967 Brazil, Peru, and Argentina all imposed restrictions on foreign acquisitions of national banks, and Brazil and Peru adopted selective credit measures to favor national industry.

The response of most Latin American countries to foreign investment is ambivalent. Latin America welcomes foreign technology and needs foreign capital to stimulate economic growth, but at the same time it fears foreign economic domination and the long-term implications of overdependence on direct foreign investment for Latin America's balance of payments. Each country has the problem of maintaining access to the capital and technology that foreign investment provides without definitively mortgaging national sovereignty to the international corporations managed from New York, Detroit, and New Orleans.

The Servan-Schreiber syndrome

In 1968 the best-selling foreign book in Latin America was Jean Jacques Servan-Schreiber's *The American Challenge*, analyzing U.S. investment in Europe. If Servan-Schreiber's analysis applies to Europe, it has even greater significance for Latin America. U.S. investments in the European Common Market countries in 1966 ($7.5 billion) accounted for approximately 2.5 percent of total production. U.S. investments in Latin America ($11 billion) accounted for 10 percent of production —including one-third of all Latin American exports—and employed one-fifth of all industrial workers.[1] The Latin American entrepreneurial elite used the Servan-Schreiber book to justify its perennial preoccupation with U.S. economic penetration, and the nationalist left used it to justify its perennial denunciation of U.S. "economic imperialism." For Servan-Schreiber's analysis addressed in contemporary terms issues that date back to the early days of U.S. investment in the hemisphere. These investments developed huge, untapped mining and petroleum resources, installed public utilities such as power and telephone companies, and organized production and foreign marketing of tropical commodities such as sugar, coffee, and bananas. Latin America has waged a long, often bitter political struggle to obtain a larger share of the earnings of these operations through higher taxes and improved wages and working conditions. Most U.S. corporations have responded to this pressure to improve their standing as good corporate citizens in their host countries, but the names United Fruit, Electric Bond and Share, Standard Oil, and City Bank still produce in many Latin Americans a sentiment of nationalist ill feeling that no public relations campaign has been able to extirpate and which no Latin American politician can ignore.

In its favor, foreign investment creates jobs, tax revenues, and new production. Without such investment Latin America would either be poorer or have to find an alternate way to ob-

---

1. U.S. Department of Commerce, *Survey of Current Business*, September 1967.

The role of U.S. business

tain the same benefits, probably through increased domestic savings (assuming that the technology is for sale). But foreign investment also has drawbacks, especially where the investors produce for the internal market but contribute practically nothing in the way of export earnings. The importing of raw materials for internal production that yields no compensatory export earnings, as well as the remittance drain, places a burden on the balance of payments that is a potentially explosive political issue in Latin America.

The balance of payments would improve if Latin American interests purchased the foreign-owned enterprises. But the local capital required for this investment is badly needed for other activities, and the technology and applied research involved in operating these businesses are not a part of the domestic industrial know-how at present. From time to time the Latin Americans propose joint ventures, in which they would share ownership with U.S. investors. The response to such proposals has generally been negative, except when a Latin American government has made shared ownership a condition for authorizing major "strategic" investments.[2]

The Hickenlooper amendment

At the beginning of 1962, foreign ownership of public utilities had become a major political issue in Brazil. The Goulart government, seeking to halt inflation, was reluctant to grant rate increases to the power and telephone companies, both of which were in large part owned by American investors. Without rate increases, maintenance and new investment declined, and as service deteriorated, public dissatisfaction mounted. The companies became an easy target for demagogic politicians.

The International Telephone and Telegraph Company, a major provider of telephone services in Brazil, owned an old local company valued at about $6 million in Pôrto Alegre, the capital of Rio Grande do Sul, the southernmost state of Brazil. The governor of the state, Leonel Brizola, who was President Goulart's brother-in-law and an influential member of the rul-

2. The U.S. business community has, however, shown some concern for the political implications of the remittance burden. In a speech to the Council for Latin America in December 1968, David Rockefeller urged that U.S. companies, whatever their orientations, undertake at least one export promotion project to increase Latin American exchange earnings in an amount at least equal to the volume of their remittances.

ing Brazilian Labor party, expropriated the IT&T subsidiary. The ensuing controversy triggered a national campaign by the left for expropriation of all foreign-owned utilities. To some U.S. investors it appeared that all American companies in Brazil were under attack.

To protect the interests of American companies abroad, Senator Bourke B. Hickenlooper, urged on by Harold Geneen, the president of IT&T, introduced an amendment to the Foreign Assistance Act of 1962.[3] This amendment required the president to suspend all economic assistance to any country that expropriated the property of a U.S. company, repudiated a contract with a U.S. company, or made a U.S. company subject to discriminatory taxation or administration. Suspension of all forms of economic assistance included not just foreign aid, but such legislation as that allotting sugar quotas to favored nations. A country had six months in which to take "effective steps" to provide compensation for expropriated property in "convertible foreign exchange." Thereafter the president was allowed no discretion to waive enforcement of the amendment.

President Kennedy opposed the proposed legislation because it would invade his right to make foreign policy and embroil the U.S. government in quarrels between U.S. companies and foreign governments, regardless of the merits of each case; but Kennedy was not prepared to make a public fight about it.

In a feverish attempt to head off passage, Lincoln Gordon, then ambassador to Brazil, pressed Goulart to settle the IT&T issue promptly. Goulart, however, feared that settlement would alienate the left, which he saw as his defense against the military coup d'état being organized by Carlos Lacerda, the powerful governor of the state of Guanabara. While Goulart vacillated, Harold Geneen, supported by other U.S. companies with interests in the hemisphere, pressed for passage of the amendment. The amendment was a statement of congressional policy, tying the foreign assistance program to protection of United States overseas investments.

Goulart finally settled the IT&T case. The company agreed to reinvest 75 percent of its compensation in diversified invest-

---

3. Foreign Assistance Act of 1961, as amended 1962, sec. 620(e).

ments outside the utility field in Brazil. But the mere availability of the Hickenlooper Amendment became a powerful factor in the dispute between the American and Foreign Power Company (AMFORP) and the Brazilian government.

In April 1963, during an official visit to Washington, Goulart suggested to President Kennedy that it was politically undesirable for United States companies to control Brazilian industries that were in effect public utilities. He proposed that Brazil buy out these interests. Kennedy was enthusiastic about the idea as long as the companies agreed. He commented, Goodwin recalls, that every month, when the electric bill came due, thousands of Brazilians were bound to think, "It's that damned U.S. company."[4] Late in April 1963, AMFORP and the Brazilian government announced an agreement by which the government would purchase the company's holdings, valued at $135 million; the company would reinvest 75 percent of this price in nonutility enterprises in Brazil; and the government would pay the remaining 25 percent in dollars over twenty-two years, with interest. The Kennedy administration greeted this agreement with relief. Governor Brizola attacked it as a betrayal by Goulart of the nationalist left (now supported by the communists). Carlos Lacerda attacked it from the right, claiming that the equipment to be purchased was obsolete and overvalued. Goulart again procrastinated. His two key ministers, for war and economy, who had approved the purchase terms, were forced to resign. The agreement was never consummated.

In 1964, immediately following Goulart's overthrow, the United States offered the new Brazilian government a $50 million program loan, future capital assistance, and debt renegotiation, contingent on, among other things, fulfillment of the AMFORP contract. President Castelo Branco, unlike Goulart, favored increased foreign enterprise. The new authorities felt that Brazil's resources could be better utilized in productive enterprises than in paying for expropriated properties, and therefore requested AMFORP to reconsider the contract. The government promised to set electric service rates that would assure the company an adequate return on its investment. (And it ultimately kept this promise.) The AMFORP management,

4. Interview with Richard Goodwin, New York City, June 1969.

however, insisted that the Castelo Branco government honor the contract signed by the Goulart government, invoking U.S. government assistance as a bargaining weapon.

The new regime submitted the agreement to the Brazilian Congress for ratification. By this time the institutional act under which over fifty-five congressmen had been stripped of political rights had effectively excluded the left wing from legislative decisions. But until the Brazilian executive branch stationed military units at the doors of the Congress, it was unable to persuade reluctant congressmen to approve the contract. As a result of this episode, the Castelo Branco government, which had begun with considerable possibilities of consolidating popular backing, was immediately characterized as an American puppet. It lost substantial support among the nationalistic Brazilian urban middle class and alienated democratic and reformist groups.

The AMFORP affair also convinced many Brazilians that although the U.S. government was not above twisting the arm of the Castelo Branco government, it would do so for the benefit of U.S. companies rather than for the social objectives of the Alliance for Progress.[5]

In an interview in August 1968, Rafael de Almeida Magalhães, vice-governor of Guanabara under Lacerda, one of Brazil's leading young politicians and hardly a radical leftist, declared, "U.S. aid in Brazil simply reinforced the existing inequities of Brazilian society. . . . Since you intervened here so extensively, why didn't you at least do so for the right reasons?"

The IPC case

When the Peruvian military deposed President Fernando Belaúnde Terry, its public justification was that Belaúnde had betrayed the national interest in settling the long-festering dis-

---

5. One of the chief Brazilian negotiators (who has asked to remain anonymous) in the AMFORP case claims that members of the U.S. embassy actively lobbied for AMFORP in the corridors of the Congress. He also reports that while pressing for approval of the AMFORP settlement, the Brazilian government was also abandoning a key provision of the agrarian reform bill then pending in the Congress, which would have vested taxing authority in the federal government rather than in the municipalities, most of which were controlled by the large landholders. He maintains that the uproar over the AMFORP settlement diverted attention from the agrarian reform bill and indelibly marked the priorities of the Castelo Branco government.

pute with the International Petroleum Company, a wholly owned subsidiary of Standard Oil of New Jersey. The new military regime immediately nationalized the IPC oilfield and subsequently took over all the company's properties in Peru, charging that IPC owed more than $600 million in back taxes. This action generated broad public support for the regime in Peru. It also presented the incoming Nixon administration with a conflict of major proportions and repercussions throughout the hemisphere. And it brought under examination not only the future of $500 million in U.S. investments in Peru, but a series of events and policy decisions that made up one of the tragedies of the Alliance for Progress.

Peruvian law has traditionally held that subsoil mineral resources, including petroleum deposits, are the inalienable property of the state. Thus private enterprise could not own such resources outright and could exploit them only through concession with payment of royalties. However, during the nineteenth century a British developer gained title to a property covering 419,000 acres of land in northwest Peru, including a tar pit that had been exploited in outright ownership. This became La Brea y Pariñas oilfield. The claim to ownership was upheld through a series of transfers of the property, but in 1922 it was submitted to international arbitration after strong representation by the British government on behalf of a British oil company that by then had become the owner. The arbitral award confirmed the company's title to the subsoil resources and also declared that the favorable income tax treatment that the company had been receiving was to remain in force for fifty years; that is, until 1972. Two years later, through IPC (its subsidiary), Standard Oil of New Jersey acquired full ownership rights and the benefits of the fifty-year tax provision from the British company.

Once in possession of the field, IPC grew to dominate all aspects of Peru's petroleum industry, including production, exports, refining for the local market, and distribution to the public. In 1966 IPC accounted for 76 percent of the 23 million barrels of oil produced in Peru. By then, having developed new fields, the company depended on La Brea y Pariñas for only 30 percent of its production. The key to IPC's operation was a refinery at Talara which produced 90 percent of the petroleum products consumed in Peru.[6] According to the company, IPC's total assets in Peru represented an investment of $200 million.

In 1963 no country in Latin America had greater need for the social reforms of the Alliance than Peru. The development of great mineral and agricultural resources had given Peru a high and diversified export income and a start on industrialization. But gross inequality of income distribution meant that a small urban core of wealthy, high-living consumers was surrounded by relentless poverty. The Andean highlands held five million Indian peasants who could either remain in their abysmal rural poverty or migrate to the glittering cities and become squatters. In the growing urban working class, public education for vast numbers of new pupils was an almost desperate demand.

Belaúnde, elected president in 1963, had both a respectable majority of the vote and the goodwill of the military. An architect by profession, Belaúnde was a politician by instinct and genteel family tradition. His political program, little more than an application of the Charter of Punta del Este to the particular conditions of Peru, appealed to both young urban professionals and provincial voters. His *Acción Popular* party seemed to promise new blood, a departure from the dominance of Peru's political affairs by conservative banking and landholding interests, and an escape from the sterile impasse between the military and the labor-based APRA party. A new class of national industrialists financed Belaúnde's campaign and he enlisted the cooperation of a large number of young managers and technicians, recent graduates of Peruvian and foreign universities. Fifty years old, educated at the University of Texas, and friendly toward the Kennedy administration, Belaúnde represented no threat of radicalism.

During the 1963 presidential campaign, left-wing nationalistic circles, including a segment within Belaúnde's party, had raised the issue of IPC's ownership of the La Brea y Pariñas oilfield. Belaúnde took a moderate nationalistic position and announced in his inaugural address that within ninety days he would submit a bill to the Congress laying the basis for reas-

---

6. Only in 1967 did the Peruvian government complete a state-owned refinery processing 20,000 barrels a day, about a third of IPC's capacity.

sertion of Peru's sovereignty over the disputed oil properties once and for all.

The Congress was dominated by an opposition coalition of APRA and conservative National Union party members, which outnumbered the *Acción Popular* bloc 110 to 75. The *apristas* saw Belaúnde as an upstart who had come to power solely because of the antagonism between them and the military, and as a populist competitor for the rural and labor votes that made up APRA's electoral base. If Belaúnde succeeded in his programs to expand education, promote rural community development, and carry out an agrarian reform in a country where 1.3 percent of the landholders owned 84.6 percent of the farmland, APRA would lose whatever popular appeal it had as the party of reform in Peru. Within the Congress APRA could rely on support from the National Union party against any meaningful reforms. Belaúnde regarded the proposed legislation on IPC as a national issue, above partisan debate, but it became part of the struggle between him and the Congress.

When, after ninety days, Belaúnde failed to come up with his bill, the Congress took the initiative. It revoked Peru's ratification of the international arbitration award, claiming that the subsoil rights of La Brea y Pariñas were the inalienable patrimony of the nation and could not have been ceded legally to a private company. The United States and British governments officially protested this decision. In February 1964 the Congress passed another law directing Belaúnde to resolve the IPC problem through negotiation and requiring him to submit any settlement terms to the Congress for ratification.

The Peruvians demanded back taxes, contending that the company had been operating the oilfields illegally. They also demanded that, once the fields were turned over to Peru, IPC adopt a policy of preferential purchase of La Brea y Pariñas crude oil.

Standard Oil of New Jersey saw some wider implications in the Peruvian demands. According to one of its executives,[7] the corporation feared:

1. Loss of its freedom to select the sources of crude oil used in its refineries (that if it agreed to the Peruvian demand

---

7. The Standard Oil executive has asked to remain anonymous.

for preferential purchase, it would find itself pressured in Italy, for example, to process Russian crude oil purchased by the Italians).

2. Potential competition for Peruvian crude oil (that once the Peruvians got control of La Brea y Pariñas, they would invite other interested companies, such as Occidental Petroleum, to establish refineries, and thus leave IPC dependent on Peruvian import licenses for crude oil for its Talara refinery).

3. The unilateral repudiation of an international arbitral award (that if it took a soft line with Peru, other major oil-producing nations such as Venezuela, whose huge Creole Petroleum Company is also a subsidiary of Standard Oil of New Jersey, might be tempted to apply a "Peruvian solution" to their own needs).

Belaúnde and IPC opened negotiations, working toward a possible solution whereby the company would cede the subsoil rights in return for an operating contract and termination of the claim for back taxes. The terms of the operating contract then became the crucial issue. Belaúnde feared that a settlement too favorable to the company would be repudiated by a Congress intent on embarrassing him. IPC feared that a settlement too favorable to the government would set dangerous precedents for its parent company's operations elsewhere in the world. Teodoro Moscoso quotes a high executive of Standard Oil of New Jersey as explaining, "Our flexibility is limited by our worldwide commitments."[8]

Moscoso, as coordinator of the Alliance for Progress, paid a visit to Belaúnde at about this time, shortly after his inauguration. Belaúnde described his plans to Moscoso and seemed not to understand that a sizable United States assistance package was dependent upon settlement of the IPC case. Moscoso therefore explained to him the implications of the Hickenlooper Amendment and, before returning to Washington, authorized the AID mission in Peru to process projects for authorization. But in Washington he also suggested to Assistant Secretary of State Edwin Martin that the United States should freeze the loan authorizations pending the outcome of the IPC

8. Interview with Teodoro Moscoso, San Juan, Puerto Rico, August 2, 1968.

negotiations. Moscoso regarded this measure as strictly temporary, serving only to provide Belaúnde with an incentive to reach accommodation with IPC. The engineering studies that had to precede actual work on the major projects for which Belaúnde had requested financing—roads, rural community centers, irrigation projects, and housing—would not be completed until the spring of 1964. The State Department assumed that before that time the IPC issue would be resolved. And since Moscoso considered the measure only temporary, the government made no effort to ascertain the merits of the dispute. But by freezing loan funds for Peru the United States threw its influence on the side of the company.

Moscoso's temporary freeze became permanent after the assassination of President Kennedy, when both Martin and Moscoso were replaced by Thomas Mann. Mann was convinced that Peruvian repudiation of an arbitration award, followed by company agreement to an "unduly favorable" operating contract (that is, one that was not completely satisfactory to the company), would encourage other governments to break their contracts and impose extortionate settlements on the oil companies. Mann felt that he understood how to deal with the Latins. It was a matter of psychology. "They don't think like us. Their thought processes are different. You have to be firm with them," he said. One of his techniques in being firm with the Latins was, having made a demand, not to keep repeating it, but to delay in producing something the Latins wanted. Eventually they would get the idea and come around.[9] Mann used this technique with Peru. AID authorized $36 million in development loans in June of 1964 but did not inform the Peruvians that it had done so. Mann expected the Peruvians to get the idea, relate the slowdown in aid to the IPC dispute, and then come around.[10]

Belaúnde and the Peruvians did not immediately get the idea.

9. Interview with William Rogers, Washington, D.C., August 15, 1968.

10. William Rogers reports that when he and David Bronheim attempted to initiate a study of the merits of the dispute, their efforts were brushed aside.

Throughout the IPC dispute, the U.S. embassy in Lima constantly equated U.S. interests with the interests of IPC. In 1965, when Robert Kennedy visited Lima on his trip through Latin America, he had a bitter argument with Ernesto Siracusa, the U.S. deputy charge of mission in the Lima embassy, over this issue. (Interview with Thorborne Reid II, former deputy director of the Peace Corps in Peru, October 24, 1969. Reid was in an automobile with Kennedy and Siracusa when the argument occurred.)

They blamed the delays in financing generally on the fabled inefficiency of AID and specifically on the incompetence of the AID loan officer in Peru, Frank Kimball.[11] Eventually, of course, Belaúnde realized that Kimball was not the source of the problem and that without a settlement of the IPC dispute he could not expect substantial U.S. assistance. He did not feel strong enough politically, however, to resolve the issue on terms that would be satisfactory to the company. Moreover, he was confident that Peru's strong financial situation would allow him to get along without United States assistance. Having committed himself to a dramatic development program in his campaign, he determined to push ahead on Peru's own resources and foreign credit.

Belaúnde expanded public-sector spending enormously. Average annual expenditures in education grew at the rate of 33 percent between 1963 and 1966. Public education as a percentage of total government expenditures rose from 19 percent in 1963 to 30 percent in 1966 and 1967.[12] Even starting from a low base, these percentage increases were impressive. And Belaúnde's emphasis on rural education was a completely new departure for Peru. As the visionary architect of a "new Peru," Belaúnde also initiated impressive projects to develop the interior, particularly a highway along the edge of the Amazon basin.

Public expenditure as a percentage of gross domestic income soared from 21 percent in 1962 to over 29 percent in 1966. Belaúnde drew on Peru's ample but expensive credit with foreign banks to pay for long-term development projects. Obligations piled up and Peru's gold reserves began to dwindle.

Belaúnde's development projects had in many cases been hastily planned and were obviously wasteful of resources. The conservative forces in the Congress used these failures of planning as arguments against any increase in taxes. APRA, concerned by the government's increasing popularity, was also

11. Kimball, a twenty-nine-year-old business-school graduate, was one of the brightest and most able loan officers, but he reports that Belaúnde called him the slowest in the hemisphere. It was typical of the early years of the Alliance that the president of an important Latin American country should identify a relatively obscure AID officer as a significant obstacle to Peru's development.

12. Inter-American Committee for the Alliance for Progress, *Domestic Efforts and the Needs for External Financing for the Development of Peru* (April 9, 1968).

reluctant to authorize resources that might advance the cause of a rival party. After his fast start, Belaúnde found his programs held up for lack of funds. Inflation drove prices upward 17 percent in 1965. Demands for wage increases by government workers cut further into public investment. By 1966 Belaúnde was in bad financial trouble.

In February 1966, Lincoln Gordon became assistant secretary of state for inter-American affairs. Gordon considered it intolerable that the United States should sacrifice the Alliance program in an important country to the interests of one company, especially without ascertaining whether the company or the government was right. Within five days of taking office, he ended the freeze of more than two years and made Peru eligible to receive AID development loans.

By 1966, however, it was too late. Weakened by inflation and loss of political momentum, the Belaúnde government was unable to implement the unpopular measures demanded by the international lenders as the price of assistance—budgetary cuts, a tax reform program proposed by an OAS team, and a possible devaluation of the sol.

In 1967 prices rose 20 percent. In September 1967 the government was forced to take measures that amounted to a 40 percent devaluation of the sol. Strikes broke out sporadically and there was increasing talk of a military coup.

In July 1967 the Peruvian Congress passed a bill, which Belaúnde signed, nominally nationalizing the subsoil deposits of La Brea y Pariñas oilfield by transferring ownership from IPC to the government. The bill also stated that "the Executive shall establish a regime more consistent with the national interest for exploitation of the reserves in accordance with the petroleum code," and thus did not preclude the possibility of an operating contract between the government and IPC. In August 1967 the government registered the oil reserves of La Brea y Pariñas as national property and referred the question of IPC's back taxes to a special tax commissioner. Until November the government permitted the company to continue paying taxes on the basis specified in the arbitration award. In November, however, on the eve of important municipal elections, the tax commissioner ruled that IPC had been "unjustly" enriched and owed the government $144 million in illegally acquired profits. In mid-November the government initiated suit to collect the back taxes. This suit confronted the State Department for the first time with the prospect of actual injury to the company, grounds for mandatory application of the Hickenlooper Amendment. The suit was being litigated in the Peruvian courts, however, and the State Department legal counsel found that until the courts gave a ruling, the Hickenlooper Amendment would not be applicable.

In 1968 the APRA leadership began to have hopes of winning the congressional and presidential elections in 1969. Realizing that further deterioration of economic conditions could lead to a military coup that would wipe out these hopes, APRA agreed to Belaúnde's seizure of emergency powers to decree tax measures and administrative reforms. These measures significantly improved Peru's fiscal prospects and bolstered the shaken confidence of the business community.

APRA also concluded that if power was at hand, the time had come to resolve the IPC dispute and eliminate this obstacle to good relations with the United States. APRA leaders advised Belaúnde they would not stand in the way of a settlement with the company. New management in IPC was able to convince the parent company that the political situation was favorable for a settlement. In August 1968, IPC ceded the subsoil rights to the government. In return, the government abandoned the tax claim. The U.S. company and the Peruvian State Petroleum Monopoly negotiated an operating contract acceptable to both sides—but for one explosive detail.

Meanwhile, imminent resolution of the IPC dispute and progress in meeting the fiscal crisis did not restore Peru's eligibility for U.S. assistance within the Alliance for Progress. In 1968 the Peruvian military had decided to modernize the Peruvian Air Force and buy French Mirage supersonic jets. Within the United States Congress this purchase brought to a head the issue of military expenditures by underdeveloped countries receiving United States economic aid and produced two congressional amendments to the Foreign Assistance Act.

The first, proposed by Representatives Silvio Conte and Clarence Long and known as the Conte-Long Amendment, provided that funds appropriated for a country were to be reduced in the same amount as its purchases of unnecessary sophisticated weapons. Supersonic jets were clearly sophisticated weapons within the meaning of the statute. The Symington

Amendment, also named after its author, Senator Stuart Symington, provided for the termination of assistance to a country spending an unnecessarily large percentage of its domestic resources on its military.

Undersecretary of State Nicholas Katzenbach sought to convince the Congress that the executive branch would enforce these amendments. United States relations with Peru had deteriorated to a point where he saw little danger in making an example of that country. He did not consider the fact that only by consenting to the purchase of the Mirage jets could Belaúnde maintain peace with the Air Force and avoid a military coup. AID froze two more newly authorized but not yet negotiated development loans.

As a result of the IPC dispute, AID's total loan authorization for Peru (population 12.5 million) during fiscal years 1962 to 1968 was $74.5 million. The comparable figures for Chile (population 9 million) and Colombia (population 16 million) were $500 million and $450 million respectively.[13] As one high Peruvian official put it: "We have no illusions. We have received little and we will receive little. First IPC, then fiscal irresponsibility, now the jets and military spending. Always you will find a reason that you cannot give us aid."[14]

The final reason was yet to come. Belaúnde had withheld some details of the August agreement from the public. In September the director of the State Petroleum Monopoly resigned, announcing that the last page of the agreement, reported to include an important clause specifying what IPC was to pay in dollars for crude oil purchased from La Brea y Pariñas, was missing.

Belaúnde was attacked by important figures of his own party. The cabinet resigned. APRA was certain to win the coming election. The conditions for a military coup were set, and on October 4, 1968, at gunpoint, Belaúnde boarded a chartered plane for Argentina and political exile.

On October 9 the new military government nullified the IPC contract and expropriated the company's properties, including

13. The source of these figures is the Agency for International Development, Office of Capital Development, Latin American Bureau. Total lending to Peru between fiscal years 1962 and 1968 was $105.4 million, of which $30.9 million were deauthorized or deobligated.

14. Interview with Cecilio Morales, formerly Inter-American Development Bank representative in Peru, July 20, 1968.

the Talara refinery, gas lines, and docks, as well as La Brea y Pariñas. The political effect was impressive. The military, in one stroke, established a base of popular support and a nationalist issue to justify its permanence in power. The Johnson administration handed the problem over to the new Nixon administration as its first Latin American crisis. In March 1969, President Nixon dispatched John D. Irwin, a New York lawyer and former assistant secretary of defense, as a personal emissary to Lima, and the Peruvian military agreed to negotiate with Irwin on a settlement of the dispute. On April 7, 1969, Secretary of State William Rogers announced that the United States was deferring invocation of the Hickenlooper Amendment while IPC pursued an administrative appeal procedure regarding the $690 million it allegedly owed the government in back taxes. This confrontation was the most serious threat to U.S. property interests in a Latin American country since Cuba.

If, as the evidence shows, United States policy on the IPC dispute contributed to the downfall of Belaúnde, was this policy really in the interests of IPC and Standard Oil of New Jersey? Belaúnde told one official of an international agency that he could not come to an agreement with IPC until he had a dramatic development program under way, and that if the United States supported him in this effort, he could present settlement with IPC as necessary to maintain the momentum of the development effort.[15] Accepting such an alternative would have meant investing substantially in a development program on the basis of a political promise. Belaúnde, who had no great talent for power politics, might still not have been able to deliver. But cooperation with Belaúnde would have enabled the United States government to associate itself with development and reform in Peru, and it is difficult to see how the result could have been worse from the company's point of view than what did occur.

The "Chileanization" of Chile's copper

In 1964, when the status of the U.S. copper companies was one of the hottest issues of the Chilean presidential campaign, Eduardo Frei Montalva, the Christian Democratic party candi-

---

15. *Ibid.*

---

date, proposed what he called the "Chileanization" of the foreign-owned copper producers. These companies were preparing to expand their output considerably. By purchasing an equity position in the companies (through investment in this expansion), the Chilean government would acquire not only a share of their earnings but also a voice in their management, and thus, in view of the economic importance of copper to Chile, enhanced political sovereignty.

Frei's electoral victory reflected not only Christian Democratic strength but also the desperate opposition of conservative circles to the Communist-Socialist alliance. Recognizing the need to capitalize on the political momentum of his victory, Frei immediately appointed Raúl Sáez, one of the founding fathers of the Alliance, as his special negotiator. Discussions with company representatives and U.S. officials began even before Frei took office in November 1964.

By this time the IPC stalemate in Peru had taught the U.S. government something of the virtues of compromise. The copper companies were seeking financing from U.S. government sources for the huge investments required by their expansion plans. The government therefore agreed to have the Export-Import Bank supply this financing on condition that the Chilean government participate in the companies' expansion under terms that, according to the Christian Democratic leadership, the Chilean Congress would ratify. The companies, recognizing the Christian Democrats as the rising political force in Chile and as a bulwark against the extreme left, accepted this condition.

Even under such favorable conditions, agreement was reached only after excruciating negotiations. The Chilean government had to grant the companies special tax concessions, liberal dividend repatriation rights, import privileges, and loan guarantees for domestic financing. Most important, it allowed the companies to retain their share of exchange earnings from foreign sales in the United States instead of depositing those earnings in Chile and then making remittances. In return, the companies allowed a Chilean state copper company to purchase ownership of 25 percent of Anaconda's newest mine, 25 percent of a Cerro de Pasco property, and 51 percent of Kennecott's subsidiary, Braden Copper. The Export-Import Bank authorized $200 million in new loans to the copper companies, and AID guaranteed the new investments against expropriation. The program was designed to raise production to more than a million tons a year by 1972. The total investment came to $456 million.

In March 1965 the Christian Democrats won a majority position in the Congress. Despite bitter last-ditch opposition from the Communist, Socialist, and Radical parties, by the end of 1966 the Congress had passed and Frei had signed the basic legislation incorporating the terms of the settlement. The Communist-Socialist coalition steadily attacked each measure implementing the agreements, however, and even the Christian Democrats grumbled that Frei, misled by windfall gains resulting from the high level of international copper prices from 1966 to 1968, had made the agreements too favorable to the U.S. companies. In June 1969, with a presidential election scheduled for 1970, Frei negotiated an agreement with Anaconda nationalizing the huge Chuquicamata and El Salvador copper mines over a period of years, but giving the government only a minority interest in the company's new La Exótica mine. The U.S. ambassador in Chile, Edward Korry, a former journalist whose first ambassadorial assignment had been in Ethiopia, played a key role in bringing about this settlement. Learning again from events in Peru, the U.S. government was able to distinguish, to some extent, between its interests and the demands of the company.

Thanks to these agreements, Chile will be able to hold its place in the world copper market of the 1970s. Copper prices are bound to come down after the Vietnam war is over, but with increased production and aggressive marketing of Chilean copper by the big U.S. companies, Chile's exchange earnings will be hurt less than if the copper expansion program had not been carried out.

Radomiro Tomic, former Chilean ambassador to the United States, had, along with the Chilean left, criticized the Anaconda agreement as not going far enough in nationalization of the copper mines. As the Christian Democratic party's candidate to succeed Frei in the 1970 presidential elections, Tomic has muted his criticism of the agreement. However, since he appears to be seeking an alliance or accommodation with the Chilean left, the durability of the copper agreements remains to be seen.

U.S. business and the national interest

During most of the Alliance, U.S. business interests, and in several cases the interests of a particular corporation, have taken precedence over the U.S. national interest in Latin America. The reason for this precedence lies in the interest-group nature of U.S. domestic politics. At least since the New Deal, a diverse lot of interest groups—labor, farmers, and consumers, as well as the business community—have organized to protect their respective interests when government action affects them. In domestic affairs a number of such groups must come to terms on their conflicting interests. But only one interest group has a permanent stake in the U.S. Latin American policy. And it has organized itself, as any other interest group would, to present its point of view to both the executive branch and the Congress.

Initially as the Business Group for Latin America, some twenty to thirty chief executives of corporations involved in Latin America, headed by David Rockefeller, advised U.S. government policy-makers on the views of the business community with respect to the Alliance for Progress. In 1965 the Business Group expanded into the Council for Latin America (CLA), again led by Rockefeller and representing some 224 corporations, approximately 85 percent of all U.S. companies doing business in Latin America. Its membership list includes such giants as Du Pont, Caterpillar, Standard Oil of New Jersey, and the Chase Manhattan Bank. CLA holds regular meetings with State, AID, IBRD, IDB, CIAP, and other government agencies whose work may affect U.S. business interests in Latin America. Its board of trustees meets two to three times a year for consultation with U.S. government officials in Washington.

The Council for Latin America also includes area subcommittees corresponding to the State and AID desks responsible for particular geographic areas—Brazil, Peru and Ecuador, Bolivia and Chile, Central America, etc. The subcommittees meet informally with their State and AID counterparts two or three times a year to exchange views on economic and political trends and investment climate. The relationship is important to both sides. The business community depends heavily on the official assessment of a region's and an individual country's economic and political prospects in planning its immediate and long-term investments. And because it has a permanent stake in the area and benefits directly from AID-financed orders for the sale of goods, business can be an effective ally for the AID program in the Congress or a powerful enemy if offended.

The institutionalized relationship of the business community with the State Department and the influence of individual companies with the Congress, in the absence of countervailing pressures from other organized domestic interest groups, predispose the policy-makers automatically to favor individual companies or the interests of the business community as a whole. In dealing with the IPC dispute the State Department seemed to some observers more zealous on behalf of IPC than the company itself might have dared to demand. Moscoso was not responding to specific pressure from the Standard Oil Company of New Jersey when he decided to freeze development loans to Peru. He simply assumed that the business interest was the most important component of U.S. policy in Latin America, and he based this assumption on his consultations with people outside the U.S. government who were concerned about that policy. The overwhelming majority of these people were leaders of the U.S. business community. (The business community, of course, is not always of one mind. On IPC, other U.S. companies refused to support Standard Oil of New Jersey because of the widespread feeling that IPC had hardly been a model of corporate responsibility.)

It is easy to condemn the State Department for identifying uncritically with United States business. But business is the only interest group that consistently presents its viewpoint on Latin American affairs to U.S. government policy-makers.

A Latin American advisory group

In the decades ahead, the rising tide of nationalism in the hemisphere will demand a different accommodation between the U.S. business community and government than has prevailed to date. In its relations with Latin America, the U.S. government must consider more than the interests of individual U.S. companies, however legitimate these interests are.

What is needed is a permanent Latin American advisory group, with members appointed by the secretary of state from a representative range of U.S. institutions—labor, business, universities. This group could meet on a regular basis with responsible government officials to advise them on major Latin American policy issues. The responsibility for decisions must rest with the elected and appointed U.S. officials. But it is arguable, for example, that if Mann in 1964 and 1965 had had to account to such a group for the freeze policy in Peru, the IPC dispute would have come in for a more searching inquiry than it in fact received. U.S. policy in Brazil between 1964 and 1968 might also have been different if a broader perspective had been brought to bear upon its underlying premises. The point is that, in the absence of pressures to countervail those of business, a group that has neither direct responsibility for policy nor material interests to protect can represent the national interest when it differs from the interests directly involved in a given issue.

The basic form of economic relations between the United States and Latin America is not aid but trade. One of the great ironies of the Alliance is that during the past decade Latin America's export trade has been unable to capitalize on the spectacular growth of its biggest market. The financial effect of U.S. policy in the 1960s—increasing Latin America's debt burden without facilitating export flows to finance the servicing of the debt—calls into question the concept of foreign aid in general and the effectiveness of the Alliance in particular.

One of the major objectives of the delegates at Punta del Este was the expansion of Latin America's export market. The Latin American delegates pressed the U.S. delegates for specific commitments on commercial policy, commodity price stabilization, removal of trade restrictions, and compensatory financing for exchange losses through price declines. But the U.S. delegation had been given no authority by the Kennedy administration to make regional commitments or concessions beyond the basic policies of the United States as a worldwide trading nation. The Kennedy administration itself had obtained no assurance of approval from the U.S. congressional leadership for measures liberalizing access to the U.S. market for exports from Latin America or other developing countries.

As a result, the charter's chapter on trade (Title IV, Basic Export Commodities) was particularly vague. It stated that "importing member countries should reduce and if possible eliminate, as soon as feasible, all restrictions and discriminatory practices affecting the consumption and importation of primary products, including those with the highest possible degree of processing in the country of origin." It urged member countries to "eliminate within a reasonable time export subsidies and other measures which cause instability in the markets for basic commodities." It recommended that the "industrialized countries" make "maximum efforts to create conditions so as to permit the rapid expansion of their markets" and extend "maximum cooperation to less developed countries so that their raw material exports will have undergone the greatest degree of processing that is economic." It also stated, "Member countries should support the efforts under way to improve and strengthen international commodity agreements and should be prepared to cooperate in the solution of specific commodity problems."

These propositions are the basis of a debate on trade policy that has gradually sharpened since Punta del Este, fluctuating in shrillness with the latest statistics on commodity price movements and Latin America's balance of payments.

Recovery and reflection

Between 1961 and 1966, Latin America's annual export income rose from $8.4 billion to $11.5 billion. This trend had little direct relation to any Alliance measures, although the exchange rate devaluations that were part of monetary stabilization programs probably helped. More important was a worldwide increase in the prices of raw materials and commodities of major importance to Latin American trade—copper in Chile, tin in Bolivia, sugar in the Dominican Republic, and wheat in Argentina. The volume of Latin America's basic exports also rose with the levels of economic activity in the industrialized countries. Demand for raw materials and grains in western Europe and Japan took up what slack was left by the low rate of commodity purchases in the United States. Between 1961 and 1965 the level of imports to Latin America rose only 11 percent, from $7.9 billion to $8.8 billion. Argentina, Brazil, Chile, and Colombia were austerely devoting their favorable trade balances to foreign debt payments and the rebuilding of monetary reserves, and with exports rising at a healthy 6 percent a year, external trade did not appear to be constraining Latin American development.

In 1965, however, world trade figures showed that Latin America's export increase of 6 percent a year after 1961 was below the annual rate of expansion—more than 8 percent—of world exports. In 1950 Latin American exports represented 10.6 percent of world trade. By 1960 the Latin American share had dropped to 7 percent and by 1968 to 5.6 percent.

Recent analyses of trade trends suggest that the Latin American countries, particularly those that are more industrialized, are caught in a double bind. The African countries, which can sell raw materials and tropical commodities at lower prices, are rapidly expanding their markets in the industrialized countries. And the industrialized countries not only grant domestic subsidies and place restrictions on such Latin American exports as wheat, sugar, and beef to protect their own agricultural producers, but also block Latin American efforts to open up new trade in simple manufactures to protect their own industries. What tightens the bind is Latin America's need to import raw materials and machinery so that its domestic industries may substitute their products for finished imports.[1]

Since 1965 the rising demand for imports has shifted the trade balances in key Latin American countries. In 1967 the rate of export expansion slowed somewhat because of a drop in prices for coffee, beef, hides, tin, fish meal, lead, zinc, copper, and fibers. And although exports rallied in 1968, reaching a record level of $12 billion, their average annual rate of expansion for 1966, 1967, and 1968 was only 3.2 percent, while imports pressed ahead at more than 5 percent. Anticipating an end to the war in Vietnam, the Latin American countries feel very shaky about the outlook for commodity prices, particu-

---

1. See Organization of American States, Inter-American Economic and Social Council, *Latin America's External Gap, 1968–1973,* CIES/1369 (Washington, D.C.: Pan American Union, December 1968).

larly in nonferrous metals, for which wartime demand has kept prices very high.

Foodstuffs, raw materials, fuels, and metals have been, and will continue to be for many years, the export products that determine Latin America's exchange income, but one of the objectives of the Alliance was to diversify export production. USAID, the IDB, and the IBRD have given high priority to loans for the development of new export products in agriculture and industry. In the period from 1955 to 1966, however, the proportion of simple manufactures, chemicals, and machinery in Latin America's total exports (including those within the region) grew only from 2.9 percent to 5.1 percent. Even in the 1964–1966 period, almost 95 percent of Latin America's trade income came from primary commodities.[2]

The industrialized countries have sought to reduce agricultural imports by promoting domestic production or substituting synthetics for traditional natural products, and the United States, western Europe, Canada, Australia, and New Zealand have mounted strong government-subsidized export promotion programs that Latin America cannot afford to match. As a result, in the four categories of primary products on which Latin America's exchange earnings depend, exports from the developed countries have grown faster, except in nonferrous metals, than exports from Latin America. The real value of Latin American agricultural exports (for the purpose of purchasing essential imports) was no more in 1966–1967 than in 1955–1956. As the manufactured goods that Latin America must import (for example, tractors) become more expensive, both the region's share of world agricultural exports and the unit value of these exports decline.

The Latin American countries are pressing the United States to join in international price stabilizing agreements for individual commodities, negotiations for elimination of restrictions on the access of Latin American commodities to the U.S. market, and creation of a financial system to cushion against severe exchange losses through commodity price declines. They have also noted the contradiction between an Alliance foreign aid

2. United Nations Economic Commission for Latin America, *Latin American Foreign Trade Policy*, E/CN 12/816 (April 1969), Table 2, p. 9.

policy that promotes Latin American export diversification and a Treasury and Commerce policy that raises protectionist barriers against the new Latin American products, particularly manufactures.

Trade and aid

Under the foreign aid program, the United States has sent advisers on textile export marketing to Colombia, but the Department of Commerce has restricted U.S. imports of Colombian cotton textiles. U.S. loans have helped livestock ranchers in Costa Rica and other Central American countries to develop their cattle herds, but the Department of Agriculture has blocked beef shipments to the United States. The U.S. government has restricted imports of tomatoes from Mexico, terry-cloth towels from Brazil, raincoats from Costa Rica, and other items too numerous to list. A Brazilian banker comments, "Each case may be insignificant in itself. What is serious is that the example set discourages all new exports."

The Latin Americans have asked the United States at least to enter into a "standstill" agreement, to set no new restrictions on existing Latin American exports. This proposal reflects anxiety generated by the Washington lobbies for restrictions on Venezuelan petroleum imports to make room on the east coast for Alaskan oil, the pressure from livestock interests to prohibit imports of Argentine cooked beef, and proposed restrictions on the importation of soluble coffee from Brazil. The vulnerability of these multimillion-dollar operations, vital to the countries concerned, to unilateral U.S. action corrodes the economic solidarity that is supposed to be the keystone of the Alliance.[3]

3. The CIAP report to the annual Alliance ministerial meeting held in Washington in July 1968, expressing alarm at the "resurgence of protectionism" in the U.S. Congress, declared: "The United States is a natural market for Latin America. Despite trends in recent years, it still accounts for one-third of the exports from the region. Any subsequent limitation on this trade would have an adverse effect, and, by the same token, favorable change would represent a dynamic prospect for development in many countries. The loss in Latin America's position in the U.S. market is the principal factor causing the general deterioration in its share of world trade. . . . This factor should be borne in mind in the efforts which should be made by the Alliance in the next period in order to offset, through mutual cooperation, the adverse factors which at present appear to restrict Latin American exports" (Organization of American States, *Report of the Inter-American Committee on the Alliance for Progress to the Inter-American Economic and Social Council*, CIES/1315

U.S. policies are not, of course, solely responsible for the Latin American trade impasse. The British and European markets have also adopted protectionist positions that limit Latin American exports, particularly in agriculture. The European Common Market has embarked on a program to increase beet sugar production, mainly in France, scheduling the six-nation area to be a net exporter by 1970. The governments of these nations are promoting this production through subsidies at prices high above what it would cost to import Latin American sugar. The Common Market also extends preferences to associated African states, particularly the former French colonies, for tropical commodities that compete with Latin American products. Some Latin American countries have proposed that the United States should grant such preferences to Alliance members. Others, notably Argentina, which compete with the United States in Temperate Zone agricultural exports, fear that a special hemispheric arrangement would jeopardize their established positions in the British and European markets. The Latin American nations therefore favor a general system of nonreciprocal preferences for all developing countries.

In April 1967, President Johnson announced to his fellow · American chiefs of state at Punta del Este that the United States was "ready to explore with other industrialized countries —and with our people—the possibility of temporary preferential tariff advantages for all developing countries in the markets of all the industrialized countries." However, not until

---

[Washington, D.C.: Pan American Union, June 1968], pp. 45–46; cited hereafter as CIAP Report).

A year later, with the Nixon administration reviewing the Alliance, the Economic and Social Secretariat of the OAS explained even more explicitly the effect of trade restrictions on Latin American development:

"The insufficiency of exports and the limitations that undoubtedly exist for the substitution of imports in the majority of Latin American countries have been probably the most important causes for the region not having reached during the past eight years the minimum rate of growth foreseen in the Charter of Punta del Este   It is external strangulation that frustrates internal efforts which would otherwise result in much greater savings and investment, wider employment opportunities, and a more rapid attainment of the basic objectives of economic and social development contained in the Charter of Punta del Este. . . .

"The commercial policies of the United States and other industrialized countries tend at this time to create very serious obstacles for efforts to increase and diversify exports, and in some cases block the achievement of the desired objectives" (Organization of American States, Inter-American Economic and Social Council, *Problems and Perspectives of Economic and Social Development*, CIES/1380 [Washington, D.C.: Pan American Union, May 1969], pp. 292–93).

the end of 1969 did President Nixon commit the United States to seek adoption of a liberal system of tariff preferences from the other industrialized countries.

This Western economic community approach may well be the best solution for Latin America's trade and aid problems. Given the regional distribution of Latin America's trade, with western European markets growing faster than the U.S. market, Latin America has more to gain from a system of preferences that includes these markets than from purely hemispheric concessions. Moreover, in commercial and financial competition among themselves, the industrialized Western nations have systematically exploited Latin America's foreign aid needs, through "tied" loans and high interest rates for development capital, to shore up their own balance-of-payments positions. Cooperation among the Western donor countries to liberalize trade and cut the costly strings that are now attached to nearly all forms of bilateral aid would enrich the trade-aid mix and help Latin America to achieve the growth rate and development goals of the charter. The Latin American countries are not responsible for, and cannot themselves remove, the external constraints that have thwarted the Alliance. Nor is Latin America responsible for the U.S. balance-of-payments problem, which Robert McNamara, president of the IBRD, has pointed out as

a problem of balance among the rich economies and not of balance between those countries as a group and the rest of the world. Very little of the money lent in aid stays in the developing countries. Almost all of it returns quickly in payment for the goods purchased in the richer countries.[4]

The socialist markets

Since World War II a growing number of Latin American countries have explored the development of trade with the centrally planned socialist markets. All the major Latin American countries now maintain commercial relations with the Soviet Union, and Argentina has entered the grain trade with mainland China. This trade serves to provide new outlets for tradi-

4. Robert McNamara, address to the board of governors of the International Bank for Reconstruction and Development, Washington, D.C., September 1968.

tional products in oversupply in Western markets; it has not stimulated the development of any new products.

The Soviet Union has welcomed these trade ties particularly during this decade because they fit in with the Soviet Union's post-Castro policy of establishing a politically low-key presence in Latin America through commercial and cultural relations. However, despite frequent exchanges of commercial missions and the opening of permanent offices in the major Latin American countries, the volume of trade remains small. Between 1960 and 1966, exports from the Latin American countries to the socialist group rose only from 3.5 percent to about 7 percent of Latin America's total trade. Since 1966 exports have diminished somewhat, probably because of agricultural recovery in the Soviet Union and mainland China. The prospects for expansion of trade between the socialist countries and Latin America are unimpressive.

The reason for this sluggishness seems to be incompatibility between Soviet and Latin American approaches to trade. The industrial capacities of the larger Latin countries—Argentina, Brazil, and Mexico—are ahead of the Soviets in many areas of consumer goods, but the Russians have not shown interest in importing manufactures. The major Latin American countries can also produce many of the capital goods that go into a hydroelectric station or an oil refinery. They want foreign investment in such projects to cover only financial costs and such equipment as must be imported. The Soviets specialize in complete installations, and they are averse to the public bidding on projects which is customary in Latin America. The Soviets also have had difficulty working in convertible currency, particularly to set up long-term credits. They refuse to supply local-currency financing for civil works or production of components by local industries and therefore don't win project contracts. Trade stays in the rut of exchanging Latin American coffee, hides, and other commodities for Soviet petroleum and industrial raw materials. Latin America's trade with the socialist countries is a last resort when other doors are not open.

The Latin American common market

The idea of a Latin American common market is sprinkled through the records of all the inter-American economic conferences since Quitandinha in 1954, when the impact of the then recently established European economic community was still fresh in Latin American minds. Raúl Prebisch, from his command post at ECLA, became a tenacious advocate of Latin American economic integration. A new school of regionalist economic thought argued that heavy industry could prosper under competitive economic conditions only if Latin America's compartmentalized national markets were opened to each other in one great economic space.

The Charter of Punta del Este, building on the then recently established Latin American Free Trade Area and the small Central American Common Market, declared that one purpose of the Alliance for Progress was

> to strengthen existing agreements on economic integration, with a view to the ultimate fulfillment of aspirations for a Latin American common market that will expand and diversify trade among the Latin American countries and thus contribute to the economic growth of the region.

An entire chapter (Title III) of the charter describes ways in which the Alliance for Progress would contribute to the "economic integration of Latin America."

The movement for integration swelled as new regional organizations were formed (among them the Inter-American Development Bank, which its president, Felipe Herrera, refers to frequently as the "bank of integration"). And of all the ideas on trade and development that have come out of Latin America, the proposal to form a common market is the one that has attracted the largest following in the United States.

In 1965, after more than forty years of shaping political opinion on all aspects of U.S. international relations, Walter Lippmann made his first extended visit to Latin America. The distinguished columnist traveled to Argentina, Chile, and Peru to see what the Alliance for Progress was all about and came away convinced that the whole program was "doomed to fail" unless it were reoriented toward a great new purpose. "The central task is to stir up and finance the South American equivalent of the opening of the West in North America," Lippmann wrote in the first of two syndicated columns devoted to ways in which the Alliance might be saved.[5]

He described the Latin American countries as a "string of

5. Walter Lippmann, "A Look at South America," *New York Herald Tribune*, December 14, 1965, p. 24.

islands" surrounded on one side by the oceans and on the other by an "unpenetrated wilderness" that made it easier and cheaper for the Latin Americans to trade with Europe or North America than with each other. Lippmann felt that South America could not flourish until this wilderness were conquered. He therefore considered the region's needs "not primarily ideological or sociological," but rather material, in the form of roads, canals to interconnect the Amazon, Orinoco, and Paraná-Paraguay river systems, airfields, tropical medicine, and air conditioning "to make the jungle lands habitable."

The opening of the South American heartland will open more land for the landless than can possibly be provided by the best-intentioned agrarian reform. It will make possible a common market which is essential if South American industry is to develop on the scale which makes possible low costs of production. . . .

There is no other way, it would seem, to provide the channels through which the mounting internal pressure of population and urbanization can find safe and satisfactory outlets. All of the South American countries are chronically unstable because the problems that confront their governments are insoluble within the narrow confines of their existing economic boundaries. Instability threatens all the governments, be they oligarchies, military governments, leftist governments, or Christian Democratic governments.[6]

Lippmann's judgments on the state of the Alliance and his recommendations for a bold new departure aroused unusual interest in Washington. His views harmonized not only with those of the technocrats in the regional agencies but with sectors of the U.S. government and business community that had been engaged for some months in reviewing the lagging performance of the Alliance and the possibilities of activating the growth process through regional integration. Lippmann's idea of "opening the South American heartland" as the basis for the common market even had some political appeal for Congress. It was a big, strategic scheme that was simple to grasp and seemed to offer a way out of Latin America's disconcerting domestic political disputes, social distress, and angry words about relations with the United States.

Early in 1965 President Johnson had called a White House dinner meeting of all congressional leaders involved in foreign aid legislation as well as the top executive officials in the foreign

---

6. Walter Lippmann, "Toward the Making of a Continent," *New York Herald Tribune*, December 16, 1965, p. 24.

aid field. The guests exchanged views on ways to make foreign aid requests more palatable to Congress, and concluded, however reluctantly, that large annual appropriations for external assistance programs were on the wane. They further noted that in seeking support for foreign aid, they did have recourse to one influential "constituency"—the U.S. corporations with overseas operations. These corporations favored the establishment of a Latin American common market, by which they meant one large regional market within which the production and sales divisions of their Latin American subsidiaries could operate in essentially the same way as their counterparts in the United States. David Rockefeller, leading the U.S. Business Advisory Council of the Alliance, had been urging a vigorous push by the United States to make Latin America one undivided economic space.

In 1966 four leaders of the inter-American financial and economic institutions—Raúl Prebisch, Felipe Herrera, Carlos Sanz de Santamaría, and José Antonio Mayobre (then executive secretary of ECLA)—prepared a statement entitled "Proposals for the Creation of the Latin American Common Market." This document, drawn up at the request of President Frei of Chile and circulated to all the Latin American chiefs of state, called for unity of political purpose and a sense of regional identity to overcome Latin America's anachronistic, narrowly based nationalisms:

These countries cannot carry the weight they should in a world where, in addition to the countries that were already large, vast economic blocs have emerged. The full advantages of industrialization will not be secured if the Latin American countries . . . persist in trying to produce every type of goods and doing, within their own frontiers, everything that the others are doing within theirs. . . .

We must learn to work together; we must form the community of Latin American peoples. Up to now we have been unable to undertake this great task to any meaningful extent because we have not been able completely to escape from the pattern in which our development began in the nineteenth century. Thus separated one from another, without active relationships closely binding them together, each of our countries in those days was attracted, in isolation, toward the world's major economic, political, and cultural centers. We lived in the reflection of those centers, and this had a far-reaching effect not only on Latin America's past but also on its present. . . .

It is not enough for us merely to respond to the requirements of technology, or to work together to create a great economic base and widen our cultural, scientific, and technological horizon. Our action in this sense must also be for the purpose of securing greater political influence internationally.

The four "wise men" specifically proposed the formation of a common market over a ten-year period, at the end of which, behind a common external tariff, all national duties for trade within the region would be reduced to a maximum of 20 percent, except in the smaller, least developed countries, which would be allowed a longer period of protection for their infant industries. They also urged the creation of a strong regional executive agency to lead the integration process and guide industrial planning on a regional scale, particularly in iron and steel, nonferrous metals, heavy chemicals and petrochemicals, including the production of fertilizers, and the manufacture of motor vehicles, ships, and heavy industrial equipment. In addition, they recommended the creation of a payment union, based on periodic liquidation of large trade imbalances in convertible currencies, and coordination of investments in transportation and communication.

Back to Punta del Este

By late 1966 President Johnson's advisers had convinced him of the value and urgency of U.S. support for a Latin American common market. He called for a meeting of American chiefs of state, which took place in April 1967. Johnson's statement at Punta del Este drew on the ideas of both the "wise men" and the U.S. corporations. He announced, "If Latin America decides to create a common market, I shall recommend to the Congress a substantial contribution to a fund that will help ease the transition into an integrated regional economy." He also pledged United States assistance, through contributions to the Inter-American Development Bank, for "great multinational projects that will open up the inner frontiers of Latin America" to provide a "physical basis for Simón Bolívar's vision of continental unity." He said he had also urged the Export-Import Bank to give "sympathetic attention" to loan applications from Latin American countries for earth stations providing access to the Intelsat system for satellite communications (a project in which Senator Jacob Javits of New York and the International Telephone and Telegraph Company had shown particular interest). He further stated that the United States stood ready to finance a regional program of fertilizer plants (in which United States chemical companies were strongly interested). In the field of education, he offered U.S. support for pilot projects in educational radio and television, an Inter-American Foundation for Science and Technology, studies in marine science, and the possibility of regional programs in peaceful uses of atomic energy.

At the conclusion of the three-day meeting, Johnson, the nineteen Latin American presidents, and the prime minister of Trinidad-Tobago (which had just joined the OAS) agreed to form a Latin American common market, with United States support, over a fifteen-year period beginning in 1970. (Johnson had hoped that the process would take only ten years and would start in 1968, but the Latin American presidents felt that more time was needed.) They also agreed to a "vigorous and sustained" effort to create land transportation links among the member countries, mentioning in particular the Pan-American Highway, which is supposed to run from Mexico to Argentina, and the Andean Piedmont Highway, which is supposed to girdle the Amazon basin from Venezuela to Bolivia, tie in with the Trans-Chaco Highway from Bolivia to Paraguay, and run from there to Brazil and Argentina. The presidents agreed on a common effort to mobilize public and private resources, both from outside and within the continent, to "promote industrial development within the process of integration and the national development plans." Resources were to be earmarked particularly for preinvestment studies of industrial projects by multinational Latin American enterprises. When these studies established economic feasibility, international resources as well as local capital would fund the projects.

These presidential pronouncements were hailed as "historic" and may yet be looked back on as such. However, the actual preparations for the common market have been at a virtual standstill since the meeting, largely because of the widespread fear in Latin America that a common market would be dominated, even more than the national markets are now, by the big U.S. corporations. In providing the official Latin American interpretation of the conference, President Gustavo Díaz Ordaz of Mexico raised two issues with profound implications for the U.S. role in the formation of a Latin American common market. The first issue is the presence of foreign investors:

The integration of Latin America is (and we should fight to keep it so) an exclusively Latin American process. We have asserted this with the utmost conviction, and at the same time with great cordiality toward the United States and Canada. It is not a matter of proceeding against anybody, but of uniting efforts to help us to help ourselves. . . . Whatever can be done to reach this goal, to the extent of our effort, we have agreed to do through the Latin American world itself, and not through large enterprises alien to it.[7]

The second is the relationship between international trade and Latin American economic integration:

When fair prices are paid for our raw materials, when they do not suffer unexpected and at times disastrous fluctuations, we can hold in reserve a due proportion to pay for manufactured articles; when the principle prevails of meeting the needs created by injustice and, with expectations of reciprocity, preference is given to countries of relatively lesser development . . . when the rule is observed that no state may exercise economic or political pressure to subdue the sovereign will of another state and obtain advantages; in other words, when there is really just and equitable treatment in international trade, then, and only then, will fair and durable foundations be laid for the integration of Latin America, making it possible to think of balanced economic development among the different regions of the world and of greater tranquillity and social peace.[8]

Regional obstacles

With the exception of the United States, all countries that belong to the Organization of American States are eligible, in principle, to become part of the Latin American common market. These twenty-two countries, from tiny Barbados to huge Brazil, extend over an area of 7.2 million square miles, nearly two and a half times the size of the United States.

The massive Andean range, soaring to snow-capped peaks 23,000 feet high, runs the length of South America, blocking off the countries on the Pacific coast from easy access to their eastern neighbors. The natural resources of the Amazon basin, which occupies the center of the continent, are still largely unexplored; the huge rain forest is frequented only by primitive Indian tribes, hunters of game and treasure, gatherers of rubber and Brazil nuts who push their dugout canoes beyond civilization, and air-force teams and missionaries who have cut some landing strips in the jungle. South America is also cut off from overland contact with Central America, Mexico, and the Caribbean islands.

7. *Meeting of American Chiefs of State, Punta del Este, Uruguay*, OEA/Ser. C/IX, 1 (Washington, D.C.: Pan American Union, April 1967), p. 158.
8. *Ibid.*, p. 159.

The region contains only 200,000 miles of surfaced roads. (The United States contains three million miles of highways.) Passage by ship from Buenos Aires to Veracruz, Mexico, is longer than the sea route from San Francisco to Shanghai. Air transportation has, of course, put all the capitals within a few hours of each other, but natural barriers and distances are still formidable obstacles for heavy shipments. Latin America's railroads were built almost exclusively to bring goods from the interior of each country to coastal ports for shipment to the United States and Europe, not to link up the Latin American countries.

The differences among these countries are vast, not only in size but in level of economic development. Electric power consumption is generally regarded as a measure of economic and industrial development. The installed capacity in Latin America is 118 kilowatts per thousand persons, compared with 77 kilowatts per thousand in Asia and 32 kilowatts per thousand in Africa. But within the region, per capita consumption of electricity in 1967 ranged from 985 kilowatt hours in Venezuela to 770 in Chile, 718 in Argentina, 106 in Honduras, 92 in Paraguay, and 24 in Haiti.

Brazil and its neighbor Paraguay illustrate the extremes of Latin American development. Brazil, with ninety million people, has a large, expanding internal market for many manufactures. She pours four million tons of steel a year and generates thirty-two billion kilowatt-hours of electric power. Brazil is the world's eighth largest automobile maker and is industrialized to the point of producing machine tools and heavy chemicals. She is also one of the world's principal producers of cattle and tropical crops, such as cotton, coffee, and cocoa.

Paraguay, with fewer than two million people, is a land of dirt farmers, huge undeveloped forests, and dry grasslands where cattle run almost wild. Cotton, meat, and lumber exports are the bases of her economy. Industrialization has not gone beyond meat packing and the production of simple cotton textiles, shoes, beer, and building materials. Paraguay's first hydroelectric power station was opened in 1968.

Such pronounced differences in development and economic structure present obstacles to the creation of a common market. The smaller and less industrialized countries, which can export only agricultural products and raw materials, have no assurance that a common market would increase their sales, because the big countries also produce these goods. Moreover, they point out, if they opened their markets on a preferential basis to their big neighbors, they would be flooded with manufactured goods more expensive than those they have been buying from suppliers in the United States and Europe.

Latin American manufactured goods are indeed expensive. More than two decades ago, in their efforts to promote the growth of import-substituting industries, the more industrialized nations instituted protective tariffs, many of which ran over 100 percent on competitive imports. Today, having grown up behind massive tariff walls into virtual monopoly control of the domestic markets, these industries have no experience of cost competition and no interest in export markets. Many of the domestic raw materials from which they manufacture their products are also protected by prices higher than those prevailing on the world market, but a monopoly industry can easily shift this cost over to the consumer.

The sales manager at Chile's Hauchipato steel mill has convinced government authorities that this relatively small plant, producing 1.2 million tons a year, can't break even unless it charges at least 25 percent more than the Pittsburgh price for equivalent semifinished products. The Volkswagen plant in Brazil charges double the West German price for the same car. The prices for nationally produced chemical fertilizers on the domestic market in Argentina are 50 percent above international market prices. Venezuelan cattlemen, cement producers, and textile manufacturers desperately resist legalizing the entry of far cheaper Colombian cattle, cement, and fabrics, although the same Venezuelan ranchers are happy to buy contraband Colombian cattle, which they can fatten and sell in their local urban markets at high prices. Mexico has adamantly refused to reduce protection for its domestic wheat production, although Argentine wheat is much less expensive.

The small, least developed countries have argued in common market conferences that they should be allowed special tariffs to protect their infant industries. The big countries agree to this demand but refuse to commit themselves to buy from new plants, to be built in the small and medium-sized countries, on a planned basis. Argentina in particular is opposed to the creation of a supranational planning board within the common market to allocate industries on a regional basis. Chile argues that without such planned location of industries, the majority of large-scale foreign investments will go to the three big countries, which will thus dominate the common market.

As a further obstacle, in some Latin American countries the military is deeply involved in certain state-owned industries (steel in Argentina and petroleum in Brazil) and invokes arguments of national security against proposals for diversifying in steel products or fuels on a regional basis through complementary plants.

Historically, the political experience of the Latin American republics does not lend itself to unity. Despite a common colonial, cultural, and religious heritage, each nation feels today a strong sense of separate identity, the fruit of three hundred years of colonial administration. Starting at the time of the Conquest, the intrepid captains and missionaries of Spain and Portugal penetrated to the deepest recesses of the continent and explored the great heartland rivers from their origins to the sea. Deep in the Colombian Amazon on the Putumayo River, where the jungle is so impenetrable that helicopters are used to supply oil rigs drilling there now, one finds the ruins of a Franciscan missionary church. In 1968 the builders of the Andean Piedmont Highway had to float bulldozers up the length of the Amazon to Chachapoyas, Peru, which was settled by Spaniards three hundred years ago.

The Spaniards had laid claim to all these interior lands when independence came, and relations between the republics during the nineteenth century consisted mainly of wars and arbitration to determine national boundaries. Latin America's nationalisms fed on these conflicts, which smolder on today in rivalries between Argentina and Brazil, Argentina and Chile, Chile and Peru, Bolivia and Chile, Peru and Ecuador. A few still unresolved territorial disputes (particularly those between Bolivia and Chile and between Peru and Ecuador) further limit the opportunities for political and economic cooperation among these countries.

Apart from rivalries, the obstacles to formation of a common market are greater in Latin America than they were in Europe. Western Europe had a long tradition of intracontinental trade, transportation and communications networks, and a level of administrative competence and political stability that is lacking in Latin America. In monetary and fiscal management the European countries followed convergent policies. In Latin America, countries caught in chronic inflationary processes find it difficult to coordinate plans with countries that have solid, stable currencies. Political instability also undermines the long-term planning required for the formation of a common market. In Latin America, coups d'état have repeatedly interrupted attempts at cooperative programs.

The Latin American fear that a common market would serve only to increase the predominance of foreign corporations prompted the authors of the "Proposals" to write:

Foreign capital undoubtedly has an important part to play in the development of our economies, particularly when it operates in association with local entrepreneurs in industries which are so technically complex or so capital-intensive that access to them is difficult for Latin American entrepreneurs alone at their present stage of development. Foreign firms generally have considerable exporting experience, and this experience, in conjunction with the efforts of our own entrepreneurs, could be of great use in ensuring better exploitation of the opportunities offered by the common market, and particularly in promoting the export of industrial goods to the rest of the world. There are already a number of highly positive examples of these forms of association in various Latin American countries.

If the Latin American entrepreneur is to be enabled to take an efficient and equitable part in this type of association, the rules for foreign investment will have to be founded on the principle that the regional market must be an instrument to strengthen the position of our entrepreneurs and confirm their paramount role in the development of Latin America.

Thus foreign investment must be brought into line with the fundamental objectives: that is, it must bring with it modern techniques of production, and it must serve increasingly as an efficient vehicle for the transfer of such techniques to our technicians and entrepreneurs and their genuine incorporation in the processes of business management.

The establishment of such a foreign investment code would represent a substantial departure from present conditions of investment in Latin America. It would be difficult to accomplish because:

1. The great majority of corporate investors in the United States resist participatory ownership schemes that limit managerial control of their organizations and products.
2. Few Latin Americans are prepared to assume the major personal investment risks and heavy duties of modern corporate management.
3. The difficulties of mobilizing private capital in Latin

America on a major corporate scale are enormous, not only because capital is scarce but because investors have little enthusiasm for ownership when they exercise no influence on management decisions.

4. Technological research and development in Latin America are rudimentary and will take many years to reach a level comparable to that of their foreign counterparts in meeting the requirements of industrial development.

These conditions are unlikely to change quickly. However, the "Proposals" accurately state the need for a system of international financing that will underwrite ventures by Latin American entrepreneurs on a larger scale than the Inter-American Development Bank and the International Finance Corporation now provide. In a fresh approach to Latin American entrepreneurship, government development agencies in Mexico, Venezuela, Colombia, and Chile have taken an equity share of future large foreign investments in basic industries and mineral development. The Latin American countries increasingly demand national control of major corporate investments. The vision of a common market, far from presenting a reassuring prospect of increased control, accentuates the fear of economic domination by huge foreign companies.

An economist of the nationalist left declares, "Latin American economic integration can be justified only if it is understood as a definition of common policy among national states, and not as a combination formed by great foreign enterprises that want to operate in the region."[9]

Multilateral moves

Within the Alliance the Inter-American Development Bank has assumed the role of promoter of the common market. Under Felipe Herrera's imaginative leadership, the IDB has made loans of more than $300 million, in line with the presidential recommendations on integration, to finance highways and electric power projects involving two or more countries, exports of capital goods within the region, studies for joint development of multinational areas, and telecommunications through satellites. These funds have come largely out of the

---

9. Celso Furtado, *Subdesenvolvimiento e Estagnação na América Latina* (Rio de Janeiro: Editora Civilização Brasileira, 1966), p. 40 (our translation).

special operations or "soft loan" section of the bank. The bank has also created an Institute for Latin American Integration, based in Buenos Aires, as a training and information center.

The IDB and the OAS economic staff provide technical assistance to the Latin American Free Trade Association (LAFTA), a group of eleven countries accounting for 85 percent of intraregional trade, which was established in 1960 with headquarters in Montevideo. This precursor of a common market was to free from tariff restrictions most articles traded within the area by 1972. In this goal it has failed. Negotiations on tariff concessions on a product-by-product basis, now covering nine thousand items, have become virtually paralyzed, with only 50 percent of the products freed from tariff restrictions. In 1966 and 1967 LAFTA trade reached $1.4 billion, or about 11 percent of the member countries' total trade. But without new liberalization, regional trade growth tends to level off. The across-the-board tariff cuts that would really open up this market require not technical but political decisions, and these decisions are not apparently forthcoming.

However, the proponents of a Latin American common market are heartened by the example of the small Central American Common Market, comprised of Guatemala, El Salvador, Honduras, Nicaragua, and Costa Rica. Although it has had its share of political turmoil, this common market, founded in 1960 with United States financial support, has managed to increase intrazonal trade from $12 million in 1960 to $20 million in 1968. This market, with twelve million people in an area the size of California, has attracted quantities of foreign investment undreamed of by the five little countries individually. Its members have liberated 90 percent of their nonagricultural production from tariff restrictions. In recognition of this effort, Johnson met in 1968 with the Central American presidents in San Salvador, the capital of El Salvador, and announced a $30 million loan for a Central American integration fund to strengthen the transportation and communications systems of the region. The proposed Latin American common market requires LAFTA to unite with the Central American Common Market.

Within LAFTA a six-nation bloc known as the Andean Group has organized its own subregional plan of integration. The countries involved—Chile, Bolivia, Peru, Ecuador, Colombia, and Venezuela—maintain that by virtue of their limited industrial development and relatively small internal consumption they should be classified within LAFTA as countries with "insufficient domestic markets." Argentina, Brazil, and Mexico, the "Big Three," have agreed not to demand automatic access to tariff concessions that the Andean Group may provide each other. In 1969, when the group was formed, Venezuela refused to join for six months. Without a high degree of cooperation, the Andean Group, which now represents about 20 percent of Latin American trade, will be unable to achieve an industrial capacity capable of competing in a common market with the three bigger countries, which now account for 75 percent of Latin America's industrial output. The fate of the Andean Group may well determine the chances for a full Latin American common market.

Meanwhile, arrangements among industrial sectors in various countries also work in the direction of integration. For instance, Mexican automotive engines are being sold duty free under a $10 million contract to Venezuelan automobile assembly plants. The Andean Group is working out sectoral complementation plans for petrochemicals and metal fabricating industries. LAFTA has reached tariff-cutting agreements on components of business machines and electronic valves. But a true common market is still remote.

As the proposed date of 1970 for the drafting of a common market treaty approached, preparatory staffwork lagged and was assigned a low priority in most countries, including Brazil and Argentina. A CIAP report to the annual meeting of Alliance ministers in 1968 criticized the "general abandonment of efforts to plan development with a long-term outlook, and a growing concentration on short-term policies dictated by circumstances."[10] Prebisch commented, "The immediate problems are becoming more serious and more acute because no basic decisions have been made, while such decisions are not being made because of the constant pressure of the immediate problems."[11]

As the 1970s began, the prospects for Latin America's exports seemed more favorable than at any time in the previous

10. CIAP Report.
11. Interview with Raúl Prebisch, New York City, October 1968.

decade. The region's traditional export commodities were more profitable than they had been since the early 1950s. Within the terms of the International Coffee Agreement, clever management had substantially reduced excess coffee stocks, and in 1969 a severe frost in Brazil reduced them still further, bringing coffee production into balance with demand. In February 1970 the price of Brazilian coffee (Santos 4S) reached its highest level in sixteen years. (The price quoted in New York was 52 cents per pound. Colombian coffee, considered of higher quality, was quoted at 57.5 cents per pound.)[12] Prices over the first few years of the new decade promised to remain relatively high and stable. This prospect is particularly significant for Brazil, Colombia, and several of the Central American countries, which are heavily dependent on coffee for their export earnings.

The outlook for certain other export commodities is also encouraging. In February 1970 copper prices, particularly important for Chile and Peru, were at an all-time high (68 cents per pound in London) and seemed likely to remain high at least for the duration of the Vietnam war. Prices for tin, the mainstay of Bolivia's economy, were also at record levels ($1.74 per pound in New York).

Over the late 1960s, the economies of important Latin American countries had become more diversified. The industrialization effort begun in Argentina, Mexico, and Brazil during the 1950s was starting to pay off in an increasing variety of exports. Colombia discovered a major new oilfield that added substantially to her export earnings, and also found that stable, realistic exchange rates helped to boost new exports.

In June 1969 Gabriel Valdez, the foreign minister of Chile, delivered to President Nixon an ECLA document, *The Latin American Consensus of Viña del Mar*, representing the views of delegates from twenty-one Latin American countries who had met earlier in the year to discuss trade, aid, and development. Like older Latin American documents, the *Consensus* stressed the need for increased aid, but it also reflected the Alliance experience in a realistic shift of emphasis from aid to trade, accompanied by easier terms for debt service and removal of the restrictions on existing aid funds.

---

12. *New York Times*, February 5, 1970, p. 63.

The *Consensus* also echoed earlier statements (including those in the Charter of Punta del Este) of Latin America's need for access to the markets of the industrialized countries. But the trade barriers about which it expressed the most concern were not those against primary products, but those against manufactured and semimanufactured goods. This shift reflects the progress of the Latin American countries in diversifying their economies.

President Nixon responded cautiously to these proposals. At the annual Alliance for Progress meeting of IAECOSOC at Caracas in February 1970, the U.S. delegation agreed to establish a permanent trade consultation mechanism that would hear Latin American grievances over U.S. trade restrictions case by case and explore ways to boost Latin American exports to the United States.

At the same time, the Nixon administration reduced the restrictions on use of U.S. aid by Latin American countries by allowing U.S. loans to be applied to purchases of equipment produced by Latin American manufacturers if at least 50 percent of the equipment components were produced in the region.

By 1970 Latin America's relatively high earnings from basic exports had taken some of the sharpness out of its complaints about its trade situation and were facilitating further export diversification. But the basic problem of increased access of competitive Latin American exports to the world's major markets still remains unresolved.

Self-help, planning, and politics

The idea of self-help is not alien to the Latin American mind. The Spanish proverb *"Quien se ayuda, Dios le ayuda"* (He who helps himself God will help) is part of Latin America's Iberian heritage, not a translation of the English "God helps those who help themselves." In writings on economic development, self-help refers to the necessary domestic efforts that external assistance can support but not replace. The report of the Latin American experts at the Quitandinha conference in 1954 strove to clarify this point: "Attempts to modify this situation [economic inequality between the United States and Latin America] are fundamentally the responsibility of the Latin American countries. It is a dangerous illusion to believe that external assistance can represent the dominant factor in achieving higher standards of living."[1]

---

1. "Report of the Preparatory Group Appointed by the Secretariat of the United Nations Economic Commission for Latin America," transmitted to the executive secretary by letter dated August 25, 1954; reprinted in U.N. document E/CN 12/359.

In proposing the Alliance for Progress, President Kennedy expressed his own view of self-help:

Let me stress that only the most determined efforts of the American nations themselves can bring success to this effort. They and they alone can mobilize their resources, enlist the energies of their people, and modify their social patterns so that all, and not just a privileged few, share in the fruits of growth. If this effort is made, then outside assistance will give vital impetus to progress; without it, no amount of help will advance the welfare of the people.[2]

Under the Alliance, self-help would consist not merely of domestic policies to stimulate economic growth but of an effort in which all the people would participate, achieving through democratic processes a national consensus on the priorities and responsibilities of development.

President Kennedy envisioned the United States as actively supporting this democratic development effort wherever it was manifest in Latin America. The Charter of Punta del Este declared, "The United States will assist those participating countries whose development programs establish self-help measures and economic and social policies and programs consistent with the goals and principles of this charter." Thus U.S. assistance was contingent on an evaluation of each country's performance. Such evaluation was in theory the task of the Committee of Nine, and later of its successor, CIAP. In practice the loan officials did their own evaluating, and they gradually established their own performance criteria. Some of these criteria were the products of specific Latin American situations within which officials struggled to accelerate development. Others reflected the special viewpoints of U.S. officials involved in the program and the global standards of such international agencies as the International Monetary Fund and the International Bank for Reconstruction and Development.

The meaning of country performance

Underlying the very concept of a national development program is faith in the efficacy of national planning. This faith, shared by U.S. and Latin American officials alike, gave the Alliance much of its initial appeal and momentum. As Felipe

---

2. John F. Kennedy, "Address at a White House Reception for Members of Congress and for the Diplomatic Corps of the Latin American Republics, March 13, 1961," in *Public Papers of the Presidents of the United States, 1961* (Washington, D.C.: U.S. Government Printing Office, 1962), p. 172.

Self-help, planning, and politics

Pazos has observed, "Planning represented a break with the mentality of an earlier generation which accepted Latin American poverty as a natural consequence of Latin inferiority."[3] Those who formulated the Alliance had an almost mystical belief in the power of planning to solve Latin America's problems, reform its social structures, and stimulate its economic growth.

The charter placed equal stress on economic and social objectives, calling on the one hand for a growth rate of "not less than 2.5 percent per capita per year," and, on the other, for raises in "the income and standard of living of the needier sectors of the population" and reforms in land tenure and public education. Many Latin American economists had come to believe that these objectives were not only reconcilable but complementary. They argued, for example, that farm production was held back by a near-feudal pattern of land tenure, largely unresponsive to price incentives; thus agrarian reform was in the interests of social justice as well as long-term economic growth. The charter provision dealing with the problem of inflation and price stability took a similar line.

At the beginning of the 1960s, two schools of economic thought were vehemently debating the causes, remedies, and functions (or disfunctions) of inflation in Latin American development. The "monetarist" school saw inflation mainly as a consequence of financial mismanagement—large budget deficits, excessive expansion of the means of payment through "easy" credit policies, and overvaluation of exchange rates, which in effect subsidized imports. They proposed to cure this economic disease with the tools of monetary management, austerity, and incentives to promote exports and discourage unnecessary imports. Maintained with pious fervor by the IMF, the IBRD, and economic conservatives in general, this school dominated U.S. official thinking throughout the Eisenhower administration.

The "structuralist" school, on the other hand, traced the causes of inflation back to Latin American economic structures, which, being monopolistic, were unresponsive to free market forces. The structuralists believed that these structures, and the social inequities they supported, had to be broken

---

3. Interview with Felipe Pazos, Washington, D.C., July 22, 1968.

down and replaced, because the traditional order could not accommodate economic growth without inflation. Many structuralists, believing that unregulated market mechanisms worked to benefit the propertied private interests, favored government intervention in the market. More concerned with growth than with stability, this school saw little merit in balanced budgets without accompanying structural reforms, particularly in land ownership and use. The structuralists had their citadel in ECLA, where a group of Latin American, United States, and European economists had developed a technical analysis based more on empirical regional studies than on established economic growth theories.[4]

The charter brought these two views together, urging its signatories "to maintain stable price levels, avoiding inflation or deflation and the consequent social hardships and maldistribution of resources, always bearing in mind the necessity of maintaining an adequate rate of economic growth."

Inflation is more than an economic problem. According to the economist W. Arthur Lewis, "The price spiral is, in the last analysis, a political phenomenon, arising out of political tensions in society, and aggravated by poor fiscal policies. . . . If prices are increasing by 25 percent or more every year . . . this is because the society is sick rather than because it is developing."[5] Lewis views social equity as essential to development because it makes possible a national consensus on the priorities of development and the distribution of the sacrifices it may require. Without such a consensus a developing country can become subject to inflation because its old and new interest groups, unwilling to postpone their own consumption aspirations for the sake of development, will make conflicting claims on property and income. The government, unable to reconcile these claims, may attempt to appease the claimants by distributing nominal purchasing power to all of them through monetary expansion. Eventually the economic conflict manifests itself as political confrontation.

The Latin American countries have shown a relatively greater

---

4. The best English-language summary of the two points of view is still to be found in Albert Hirschman, ed., *Latin American Issues, Essays, and Comments* (New York: Twentieth Century Fund, 1961), pp. 69–123.
5. W. Arthur Lewis, closing remarks, Conference on Inflation and Growth in Latin America, Rio de Janeiro, January 1963.

Self-help, planning, and politics

propensity than other developing countries for sustained inflation. The exceptions—Mexico and Venezuela, for instance —have maintained relative price stability during periods of intensive growth. However, these countries enjoy a high level of foreign exchange earnings, sufficient to finance all imports necessary for development, and this income may have contributed to their price stability. More characteristic, however, and more intriguing to economic analysts is the endemic upward spiral of prices accompanied by chronic balance-of-payments problems in Brazil, Chile, Colombia, Argentina, and Uruguay.

Between 1962 and 1964, in a number of vital countries, inflation became critical. In 1963 the cost of living in Brazil, Colombia, and Chile rose 81, 46, and 45 percent respectively, well above the average for the 1960–1962 period and the already high average of the 1950s.

Table 10.1

Annual increases in cost of living, 1959–1966, and average annual increases, 1961–1966 and 1950–1958, in selected Latin American countries

(in percentages)

	increases in cost of living								average annual increases	
	1959	1960	1961	1962	1963	1964	1965	1966	1961–1966	1950–1958
Brazil	43%	32%	43%	61%	81%	85%	41%	46%	60%	17%
Chile	33	6	9	27	45	39	26	17	27	38
Colombia	5	7	5	5	46	2	15	14	15	9

SOURCE: International financial statistics, International Monetary Fund, Washington, D.C.

By the end of 1963, U.S. officials were convinced that halting inflation was essential to the success of the Alliance in the three countries that, for all practical purposes, were its main fronts. They were especially concerned about Brazil, where the problem was most acute and had been worsening steadily. But since 1964 the Brazilian government has made a massive effort to combat inflation and its outstanding achievements in this area have been decisive in the formulation of U.S. definitions of self-help and country performance. It is therefore worthwhile to look at the Brazilian experience in some detail.

The Brazilian background

President Juscelino Kubitschek (1956–1960) had been elected by the strange coalition of conservative rural interests and organized urban labor that had supported Getúlio Vargas. An immensely dynamic individual with a taste for modernity, Kubitschek sought to transform economic development into a political mystique. He captured the Brazilian imagination by building a new federal capital, which he called Brasília, in the interior. He gave a major boost to Brazilian industrialization through the extension of easy credits to São Paulo's national entrepreneurs, and a successful drive to attract foreign investments, particularly for the automotive, electrical, and capital goods industries, substituted "made in Brazil" products for imports. On foreign credits he established state-owned steel and petrochemical companies, huge hydroelectric power plants, and shipyards. He also began a massive road construction program.

Kubitschek's development promotion gave Brazil a GNP growth rate of nearly 7 percent a year for the 1957–1961 period. A boom psychology developed, and plant capacity for the entire capital goods sector, as well as for many lines of consumer products, was increased well beyond existing demand, which was heavily urban.

Kubitschek did little, meanwhile, to improve conditions in the rural sector. Rural conservatives had backed his industrial and public investment efforts on the condition that he avoid upsetting their political and social order. Kubitschek maintained high coffee price supports while the international price for Brazil's main export collapsed. The government spent hundreds of millions of dollars to stockpile 50 million worthless 132-pound bags of coffee. Enough money for a massive campaign against Brazil's rural illiteracy, through the establishment of rural schools, went instead to subsidize the large planters.

Kubitschek's "developmentalism" stirred Brazil deeply. Heavy industry, great public works, and Brazil's triumph in the 1958 world soccer championship contributed to a feeling that the country was on the move. With a growth of industries and state enterprises, the managerial and technical sector grew in size and influence. Rural migrants flocked to the urban centers. Labor unions became more active politically. University student enrollment rose rapidly, even though rural children remained without schools, and student organizations led the clamor for social reforms. Even the impoverished Northeast obtained a federally financed regional development agency of its own.

At the same time rising inflation, food shortages in the cities, tolerance of corruption, and extravagant displays of wealth by the "new class" of industrialists and promoters generated public resentment. By the end of Kubitschek's term, the country was ready for a leader with a different style and message. Ten million voters chose Jânio Quadros, former governor of São Paulo, the "man with the broom" who had promised to halt inflation, punish corruption, and extend the social benefits of development to the poor of the city shantytowns and the landless peasants of the Northeast. To fulfill these commitments Quadros had to contend, of course, with the industrialists, the labor leaders, the coffee planters, the Kubitschek forces powerfully represented in Congress, and the military, always suspicious of political leaders with a large popular following.

The economic and financial legacy that Quadros received in 1961 included an industrial plant that had been expanded in excess of existing consumer demand, a vastly enlarged public sector unaccompanied by administrative rationalization, inflation fed by wage policies and federal subsidies that the benefited groups considered "political conquests," and an extremely heavy external debt burden. Two billion dollars was due during Quadros' presidential term, $600 million in the first year. Kubitschek had bought development at a high price and the bills were falling due.

Quadros' task was to accommodate the foreign creditors without alienating the popular vote that had elected him. He launched the most thoroughgoing anti-inflationary campaign since that of the 1954–1955 interim government following Vargas' suicide. He devalued the cruzeiro by 100 percent, simplified the exchange-rate system, and drastically reduced subsidies on wheat and petroleum. These reforms earned IMF approval. Foreign creditors agreed to extend their deadlines for payment of the debt, and Secretary of the Treasury C. Douglas Dillon, during a visit to Brazil, promised Quadros $500 million in Alliance development credits.

Quadros courted the left with proposals for social and nationalist legislation, including agrarian reform, a profit remittance law, and an antitrust statute. He pursued an aggressive, "independent" foreign policy, contemplating the opening of diplomatic relations with the Soviet Union, closer ties with Africa and the "nonaligned" countries, and "correct" relations with Cuba. He also launched a series of investigations of irregularities involving government money, thus fulfilling his campaign promise to sweep out the corruption that had characterized the previous regime, but also incurring the enmity of the opposition majority in the Congress, which had the most to lose by such investigations. The result was a congressional deadlock, especially in the economic and financial sphere, but also on foreign policy and social and political issues. In a desperate and ill-conceived move to break this deadlock, after eight months in office Quadros resigned.

João Goulart, who succeeded Quadros, spent the next year and a half in a losing battle against the problems that had caused Quadros to resign. In 1962 the cost of living in Guanabara increased 52 percent; it had increased 43 percent in 1961. Between 1961 and 1962, the GNP growth rate dropped from 7.3 percent to 5.4 percent, a figure that, though still respectable, indicated a general slowing down of the economy. In 1962, debt repayment and profit remittance reached \$564 million, 45 percent of the value of all Brazil's exports in that year. Terms of trade continued to decline and foreign direct investment and supplier credits fell off sharply.

At the same time, new alignments within the major parties indicated a sharpened focus on social change. Leonel Brizola, Goulart's brother-in-law and a left-wing nationalist, was elected federal deputy in Guanabara, receiving 269,000 votes, the highest number ever given a federal deputy in Brazil.

An undisciplined "new left" emerged as a force in Brazilian politics, adding to a roughly structuralist view of Brazilian development a revolutionary ideology. This new left included Marxist intellectuals, pro-Castro students, left-wing nationalist politicians, and younger Roman Catholic priests and laymen who were in the process of organizing direct participation movements among factory workers, slum dwellers, and peasants. These groups were willing to accept support but not control from the Communist party. Their common platform was radical social change through agrarian reform, massive adult literacy campaigns, and a thorough overhaul of the education system, with emphasis on widening opportunity and modernizing the curriculum. Unconcerned, for the most part, with administrative and technical rationality, the new left regarded rising inflation almost as an ally in bringing about a crisis. They were interested not only in reforms, but also in power. Through Brizola and other spokesmen within the palace inner circle, they put constant pressure on Goulart. Brizola believed that with the support of Goulart and the new left he could reach the presidency by election.

The conservative coalition in Congress, backed by key state governors, resolved to oppose all the reforms for which the radical left was agitating.

During 1963 the Kennedy administration made a resolute effort to help Goulart pull back from the brink. After a plebiscite in which he easily won a popular mandate to resume full presidential powers, Goulart made an official visit to Washington. Kennedy assured him of continuing cooperation on such political issues as the U.S. public utilities that the government wanted to nationalize. Goulart presented Celso Furtado's three-year program designed to reduce inflation to a 10 percent annual increase in prices while maintaining a GNP growth rate of 7 percent a year. Goulart also named Santiago Dantas, the most respected member of the Brazilian Labor party, as minister of finance. Dantas successfully negotiated with David Bell the so-called Bell-Dantas agreement, under which the United States agreed to a combined program-loan and project-financing package of $398.5 million. The IMF provided Brazil with a new standby credit of $85 million. This was Goulart's last chance, and he blew it.

The Bell-Dantas agreement required the Goulart regime to take austerity measures that would be politically unpopular but were considered indispensable for the short-term fight against inflation. Even before the agreement was signed Dantas had eliminated costly wheat and petroleum subsidies. He also decreed a 30 percent exchange-rate devaluation. These measures raised the price of bread and gasoline as well as of imports in general. Dantas had agreed on maximum wage increases of 40 percent—less than the cost-of-living increase—for the military and civil service. He also established ceilings on credit, and thus incurred the wrath of the industrial sector. To placate the military Goulart authorized a 70 percent wage increase and granted a similar raise to the civil service. In June 1963, as a result of Brizola's agitation, Dantas was forced to resign.

In 1963 the cost of living in Guanabara rose 75 percent. The U.S. government, convinced of Goulart's incompetence, cut back its assistance program. Brazil would soon be unable to meet its external debt payments, and the radical left was campaigning for a unilateral moratorium on debt repayment. By early 1964 inflation seemed completely beyond control. Having antagonized the conservative coalition in the Congress, the middle class in the cities, and his natural allies on the left, Goulart was on the point of a desperate decision. Quadros in a similar situation had resigned. Goulart adopted the program of the radical left.

On March 13, 1964, at a political rally attended by 150,000 people, Goulart announced the expropriation of "underutilized properties" of over 120 acres situated within six miles of federal highways or railways and lands of over 70 acres located within six miles of federal dams or irrigation or drainage projects. He nationalized by decree all private oil refineries, giving Petrobras, the state oil company, a full monopoly. He went on to list other areas in which he was planning to issue decrees (rent control) and propose legislation to the Congress (tax reform and voting rights for illiterates). In one fell swoop Goulart was attacking the rural social structure, expanding the state role in industry at the expense of private enterprise, striking at the middle-class owners of small rental properties, and, by incorporating millions of rural illiterates into the electoral rolls, threatening politicians of the urban middle class and the rural political "colonels" who had been in power since 1930.

The middle class, important elements of which had supported agrarian and educational reform, responded to this apparent attack on social status and economic position by aligning itself with the extreme right. Rather than tolerate an inversion of the social pyramid, the middle class supported the military coup of March 31, 1964, which toppled Goulart.

The Brazilian solution

For Alliance purposes, the task now facing the Brazilian military was to build a political and social consensus on which to carry forward an orderly development program. But the group that came to power under the presidency of Humberto Castelo Branco, the former army chief of staff, did not see the problem that way. Nor did the U.S. officials responsible for the economic assistance program, or the staffs of the IMF and the IBRD, also instrumental in establishing performance standards.

Roberto Campos was minister of planning in the new military government. He had resigned as Goulart's ambassador in Washington after the collapse of the Bell-Dantas agreement. Campos had definite views as to the relative priorities of capital accumulation and social reform. As early as 1955 he had written:

Given the . . . painful choice between acceleration of economic development and distributive equity . . . the option of development implies acceptance of the idea that it is more important to maximize the rhythm of economic development than to correct social inequity. If the rhythm of development is rapid, then inequality is tolerable and can be corrected in time. If the rhythm of development is slow through lack of adequate incentives, the exercise of distributive justice transforms itself into a division of poverty.[6]

The Castelo Branco government gave top priority to the economic stabilization effort, an urgent necessity with inflation raging at a projected annual rate of 144 percent in the first quarter of 1964. The IMF recommended a drastic program of monetary, wage, and fiscal restraint designed to bring prices down precipitously. Close associates urged Campos to adopt this program and blame the economic consequences on the chaos left by Goulart. Campos, however, feared that such policies would enable foreign buyers to take over the under-capitalized Brazilian industries, and therefore refused. The government established a more gradual program, reducing the annual rate of price increase from more than 80 percent in 1963–1964 to 25–30 percent in 1965, and after 1966 leveling off price increases at 10 percent a year (regarded as a "tolerable" rate of inflation). The plan was also to achieve a growth rate in national production of 6 percent in 1965 and 7 percent thereafter. The proposed wage policy was essentially a freeze in real wages, with annual adjustments for inflationary loss of purchasing power.

Things did not move as fast or as well as planned, but Cam-

---

6. Roberto de Oliveira Campos, *Ensáios de História Económica e Sociológica* (Rio de Janeiro: APEC, 1964), pp. 92, 115 (our translation).

pos' program did reduce inflation and restore growth. The cost-of-living increase in Guanabara declined from 86 percent in 1964 to 46 percent in 1966. The Costa e Silva government further reduced this rate of increase to an annual level of approximately 25 percent in 1967 and 1968. By 1968 Brazil had achieved (in real terms) an increase of more than 6 percent in gross national product, the highest rate since 1961. And for 1969 the finance minister proudly claimed a real growth rate of 9 percent.

The Campos period also brought a host of overdue administrative reforms. The Castelo Branco government established a central bank and improved budgetary and planning procedures. It tightened tax collection and significantly reduced the fiscal deficit. The National Housing Bank emerged as a major financier of low-income housing and the major social success of the postcoup government. The government removed price controls on key agricultural commodities, and stimulated substantial increases in noncoffee export and foodstuff crops through increased farm credit and an agricultural price-support program. In 1966 the government cut the domestic support price for coffee 45 percent (in real terms) to discourage the coffee planters from playing their traditional game, overproduction at government expense. The Castelo Branco government also initiated a courageous program of import liberalization, forcing many of Brazil's overly protected industries to become more competitive.

On the other hand, the Castelo Branco government maintained tight control of the trade-union movement and dealt with all signs of resistance to government policy by arresting or suspending the political rights of uncooperative union leaders. From 1964 to 1967, despite its stated intention of preserving real wages, the Campos wage policy proved to be regressive. By 1966 industrial wages had dropped back to the 1962 level. The government had reduced the fiscal deficit at least in part by holding back expenditures for education, a policy that contributed to the student riots of 1967 and 1968. The postcoup regimes treated education as a fiscal orphan and student unrest as a matter for the police. In northeast Brazil, the government abruptly terminated an incipient agrarian reform movement, took over the agrarian labor unions, arrested and exiled their leaders, and reestablished the dominance of the landowners.

In the name of its crusade against inflation, the Castelo Branco government thus crushed the unions, withered the incipient social reforms of the Goulart period, and deprived the political institutions of all genuine representation. Instead of presenting a strong program in agrarian reform, education, and urban development, which would have given meaning and purpose to sacrifice and austerity for the Brazilian majority, the military government viewed any effort to mobilize popular consent and participation as demagoguery. For a brief period after the coup d'état, the government had the opportunity to develop a social and political consensus, particularly among the middle class and organized labor. It ignored this opportunity.[7]

The United States government supported the Castelo Branco regime despite some reservations. In 1961 Ambassador Lincoln Gordon had visited Venezuela with Adlai Stevenson and had been enormously impressed by Rómulo Betancourt's success in building popular support for economic development and social reform. Gordon tried to persuade Castelo Branco of the need for an effective political base to sustain the economic effort, but Castelo Branco either did not understand what Gordon meant (as Gordon thought) or wasn't interested.[8] Both Castelo Branco and Campos considered politics an intrusion on rational decision-making and, given their military backing, saw no need for political accommodation. Finding himself unable to communicate this need to them, Gordon went on to examine their economic stabilization program and concluded, as an expert in this field, that it merited U.S. support.

In the fall of 1964 AID authorized a $150 million program loan. The agreement required the Brazilian government to

---

7. Campos claims that the Castelo Branco government did not adopt a more aggressive policy of social reform in the early years because it was caught between IMF demands for a tight credit and fiscal policy (backed by the United States after its initial support for a gradualist policy) and the demands of the "inflationist" state governors of Minas Gerais, Guanabara, and São Paulo: Magalhães Pinto, Carlos Lacerda, and Adhemar de Barros. He explains that before the Second Institutional Act (October 1965) the Castelo Branco government was actually a weak government with limited room for maneuver. (Interview with Roberto Campos, Rio de Janeiro, August 1968.) However, the Castelo Branco government never sought to repair this weakness, if weakness it was, by presenting a program that could attract support from the urban centers. It is on the possibility or feasibility of such a program that the debate over postcoup policy in Brazil has turned.

8. Interview with Lincoln Gordon, Johns Hopkins University, Baltimore, Md., August 2, 1968.

---

meet fiscal, monetary, and exchange targets roughly corresponding to the IMF tests for anti-inflation programs. AID scheduled quarterly reviews of performance in meeting these conditions. This program-loan agreement also included references to agrarian reform and education, but both sides ignored them. The Brazilian officials knew that the way to obtain economic assistance was through monetary stabilization.

When Castelo Branco issued the Second Institutional Act, Jack Vaughan, then assistant secretary of state for Latin American affairs, ordered the suspension of negotiations for a new program loan, pending review of the effects of the act. Gordon, however, urged the United States to support Castelo Branco against the hard-line military, who wanted to establish an overt military dictatorship.

Later, testifying before a subcommittee of the House Appropriations Committee, Gordon justified supporting the regime on the grounds that Castelo Branco had assumed dictatorial powers "for the extremely nondictatorial purpose of insuring the inauguration into power of two opposition governors elect." Gordon explained that Castelo Branco and his supporters "were not able, unfortunately—and they are just as unhappy about this as the Chairman or anybody else—to return at once to full democratic institutions. . . . This is a transitional transformation . . . headed in the right direction." Moreover, the Brazilian economic stabilization program spoke well for the regime; "their self-help record is indeed one of the best in the hemisphere."[9]

On Gordon's recommendation, early in 1966 AID authorized another $150 million program loan. The conditions of this loan concerned fiscal and monetary restraint, exchange-rate management, and related measures, such as the internal coffee domestic support price. The agreement contained nothing on education, nothing on agrarian reform, nothing on more equitable income distribution.

In 1966, when Gordon became assistant secretary of state for inter-American affairs, he selected John C. Tuthill to succeed him as ambassador to Brazil. Tuthill, a career Foreign Service officer and former U.S. ambassador to the Organization for

9. U.S. House of Representatives, Committee on Appropriations, Subcommittee on Foreign Operations and Related Agencies, 89th Cong., 2d sess. (Washington, D.C.: U.S. Government Printing Office, 1966), pt. 2, pp. 659–60.

Economic Cooperation and Development, was due to retire from the Foreign Service in 1968; he had reluctantly accepted Brazil as his last ambassadorial assignment. He arrived in Rio de Janeiro in June.

In August 1966, new governors were elected in several Brazilian states by the state legislatures (which the Castelo Branco government considered more amenable to manipulation than the voting public). Nonetheless, in the state of Rio Grande do Sul the opposition candidate (who had supported the 1964 revolution) appeared to have a majority in the state legislature. Castelo Branco therefore stripped four opposition state legislators of their political rights for ten years and thus obtained a majority for the government candidate. The advent of a new ambassador and the *cassacões*[10] in Rio Grande do Sul provided the occasion for a searching review of U.S. policy toward Brazil.

Early in October 1966, Gordon and his chief aides met in Washington to conduct the Brazilian segment of AID's annual program revision.[11] Tuthill described the political and social consequences of Brazil's regressive wage policy for both the Castelo Branco government and its main pillar of support, the United States. He suggested that a review of wage policy be made part of the annual program-loan negotiations. Others went on to question the advisability of supporting a government whose negative social policies and arbitrary political acts seemed likely to destroy whatever chances it had of constructing a sound, long-term political base. Unless the Brazilian government was prepared to modify these policies, the United States should not support it with program-loan assistance. For, though the U.S. government privately frowned on undemocratic procedures, the Brazilians tended to interpret U.S. financial support of the Castelo Branco government as approval of its actions.

The counterargument was that after three years of stringent austerity the rate of price increases was at last declining. Once

10. The Brazilian term designating a loss of political rights.
11. One of the functions of these program reviews was to bring together the political and economic perspectives, represented in theory by the State Department and AID respectively, within the U.S. government. In practice whatever representation the political principles of the Alliance received at these meetings usually came not from the State Department but from AID officials.

inflation was under control, the Brazilian government could undertake social programs and the political base would fall into place; besides, the only available alternative to the Castelo Branco government was an even more authoritarian military dictatorship that would probably be hostile to the United States.

Although Gordon had been deeply distressed by Castelo Branco's action in Rio Grande do Sul, he decided that the United States would continue to support the Castelo Branco government. AID did not conduct a review of wage policy, although it did authorize an independent study.[12] Subsequently, Castelo Branco closed the Congress when it refused to ratify removing the political rights of six opposition deputies.

The closing of the Congress did not change United States policy. Using the same arguments, AID authorized another $100 million program loan, under an agreement to include import liberalization. Monetary stabilization and import liberalization had become the key objectives of the AID program in Brazil.

Tuthill's reports of the deteriorating political situation and the absence of a political base for the government became steadily more pessimistic throughout 1968, but State and AID rejected his analysis and that of his chief political officer, Frank Carlucci. The economists within State and AID argued that, in view of Brazil's good economic indicators, a political crisis was unlikely. On December 13, 1968, the Costa e Silva government issued the Fifth Institutional Act, which closed the Congress and established an overt military dictatorship.

The sources of performance criteria

The tendency to focus on economic criteria is a habit that certain key U.S. officials involved in the Alliance had acquired while working on development problems in other parts of the world. Lincoln Gordon had learned a great deal from his Marshall Plan experience. Donald Palmer, deputy assistant secretary of state for economic affairs, Latin America, from 1964 to 1968, was an exceptionally able monetary economist who had also served as a Foreign Service officer in Greece during the Marshall Plan. As Hans Morgenthau has said, "It was

---

12. This study showed that real wages in 1966 had fallen to the 1962 level, but it also argued that industrial wages between 1962 and 1964 had risen at an unrealistically high rate.

not the purpose of the Marshall Plan to bring about a structural transformation of European society."[13] The Marshall Plan had financed the rebuilding of the western European economies on preexisting foundations of national organization and managerial-technical competence. The Alliance, through external effort and domestic resources, was to finance the transformation of the Latin American economies to new, modern forms. The task, then, was to make the structural changes necessary for sustained economic development in Latin America. Such changes obviously included reorganizing tax bureaus and modernizing collection offices by supplying them with business machines in order to increase public revenues and balance the budget. Change was also necessary in agrarian conditions. Working on the Marshall Plan had familiarized Gordon and Palmer with various techniques for increasing agricultural productivity. It had not given them any experience in tampering with the social and political supports of an underdeveloped agricultural sector. Gordon and Palmer therefore supported an agricultural policy involving removal of production disincentives, such as price controls on foodstuffs and the extension of credit to the commercial agricultural sector—that is to say, the larger farmers. Gordon was cool toward agrarian reforms that seemed likely to lead to social or political disruption and could not be shown to have a direct relationship to improved economic efficiency. In later years Palmer was to modify his view and give greater weight to social reform, but the AID program continued to emphasize financial considerations.

The central AID economic staff reflected the specialized experience of important development economists from Harvard and Yale in India and Pakistan. The office of Program Planning was headed first by Hollis Chenery, professor of economics at Harvard, and subsequently by Gustav Ranis, head of the Growth Center at Yale. Chenery questioned the monetary stabilization emphasis of the AID program in Latin America:

Economists now generally agree that stabilization cannot be achieved in Latin America without accompanying growth. Stabilization alone will not lead to development, and excessive emphasis on price stability may actually hamper growth. The principal lesson to be learned from the success of aid programs in other parts of the world is that accelerated

13. Hans Morgenthau, *In Defense of the National Interest* (New York: Knopf, 1951), p. 179.

growth makes possible a restructuring of the economy and a rapid approach to viability.[14]

Latin America needed "to move toward more outward-looking and increasingly integrated economies. . . . The central problem is how to move in this direction from the present set of inefficient protected economic units." An increased flow of external resources could "support liberalization of imports of raw materials and capital goods together with realistic exchange rates for a period long enough to raise output and also to provide an incentive for increased production of new agricultural and manufactured exports." This strategy was one of the key features "of the remarkable success of the U.S. aid policy in Taiwan, Greece, Pakistan and Korea." External assistance could also support more

rapid growth for a period long enough to increase substantially the domestic resources available for development purposes, provided the countries had (a) the ability to increase their rate of investment and production once the balance of payments constraint was alleviated, and (b) the ability to capture a substantial share of the increase in GNP for development purposes, through private savings and taxation.[15]

Chenery noted that countries like Greece, Israel, and Taiwan had achieved viability within a decade through a strategy of rapid growth which depended upon their siphoning off 25 percent of the increment of GNP for development purposes.

The State Department and AID thus arrived at a definition of necessary "internal measures" which combined Palmer's concept of monetary stabilization and Chenery's theory of growth through import liberalization and increased savings. The two approaches were obviously compatible. Palmer acknowledged the need for economic growth. Chenery did not deny the value of monetary stabilization. The question was one of emphasis in particular circumstances. Neither the monetary stability nor the growth thesis involved deliberate social reform. Both Palmer and Chenery could consider Greece—which had experienced little social reform but which showed high growth rates—an example of a successful aid program. They had two other cogent reasons for adopting this approach.

First, monetary stabilization and high growth rates do have

_____
14. Hollis Chenery, "Toward a More Effective Alliance for Progress," Agency for International Development discussion paper no. 13 (1967).
15. *Ibid.*

important social consequences. Price stability clearly benefits the lower classes, who suffer most from inflation. High economic growth rates, too, are almost invariably accompanied by increased employment, which gradually draws the marginals into the economy. (But the assumption of the Alliance planners was that unless economic growth were accompanied by political and social reforms, the rate of social integration would be too slow to meet Latin America's needs.)

Second, the idea that economic growth is all that is needed to remedy social inequalities is a traditional assumption of U.S. domestic policy. With two relatively brief exceptions (the New Deal and the War on Poverty) the United States has shied away from redressing domestic inequalities by direct government intervention.[16]

To solve its agrarian problem in the post–Civil War period, the United States established the Homestead Act, which opened up new lands. But it never carried out an agrarian reform of the southern plantations (the closest parallel in the United States to the latifundia of Latin America) to distribute land to the newly freed slaves. The industrial North and the southern agricultural oligarchy came to terms strikingly similar to those of the São Paulo industrial leadership and the interior rural landowners in Brazil today.

In pursuit of monetary stabilization and economic growth, State and AID employed macro-economic models and sophisticated techniques of financial management. But this pursuit represented a reversion to traditional concepts of development and foreign assistance and the abandonment of innovation. The Alliance for Progress, as originally conceived, represented a new theory of development which stressed social reform and

---

16. Joseph Kraft has pointed out that in the 1930s the share of the poorest fifth of the population in total income went up by more than one-quarter, while that of the richest 5 percent fell by nearly a third. But as Kraft has noted:

"The postwar reaction to the New Deal made the Democrats defensive about the inequality issue. Instead of harping on the heated theme of social inequality, they came on with antiseptic talk about 'growth' and 'consensus.' Instead of stressing a larger slice of pie for the poor, they talked about expanding the pie as a whole. And with the Democrats not hitting on the issue of inequality, the Republicans also left it severely alone.

"As a result, distribution of income throughout the postwar period has stayed almost constant. The poorest fifth of the population received 3.7 percent of the total income in 1966 as against 3.5 percent in 1947. The richest fifth received 45.8 percent of the total in 1966 as against 43.8 percent in 1947" (*Washington Post*, February 9, 1969).

---

democratic political processes as much as economic growth. This emphasis on deliberate policy measures to speed up the process of income redistribution and redress social injustices gave the Alliance its revolutionary impact and uniqueness. Without this democratic and reformist orientation it became just another aid program.

In 1966 David Rockefeller stated in an article in *Foreign Affairs* that the "new concept of the Alliance for Progress with its emphasis on economic development" was more conducive to a confident investment attitude than the "overly ambitious concepts of revolutionary change" in the early (1961–1963) years.[17] However, in another *Foreign Affairs* article in 1967, President Frei of Chile stated that the Alliance had "lost its way" precisely because it had abandoned its emphasis upon "revolutionary social change."[18]

Country performance: new definitions

Thus, as the working standards of country performance under the Alliance evolved, social reform measures became secondary.[19] This is not to say that the United States automatically opposed governments that were committed to fundamental social change. In Chile the United States provided some $400 million, the highest per capita allocation in the hemisphere, to support the Frei government's ambitious development and social reform program. In Colombia the United States was likewise generous in support of the Lleras Restrepo reform program. But this support went only to those governments that

---

17. David Rockefeller, "What Private Enterprise Means to Latin America," *Foreign Affairs*, April 1966, p. 408.

18. Eduardo Frei Montalva, "The Alliance That Lost Its Way," *Foreign Affairs*, April 1967, p. 444.

19. Assistant Secretary of State for Inter-American Affairs Covey Oliver (1967–1968) attempted to revive the social reform emphasis of the Alliance but was unable to make any really significant inroads on the established priorities. Besides, by 1967 it was too late. Even a small revolt in the U.S. Congress proved ineffectual. In 1966 a bipartisan group of liberal congressmen had obtained the passage of Title IX of the Foreign Assistance Act, which says:

"In carrying out programs authorized in this chapter, emphasis shall be placed on assuring maximum participation in the task of economic development on the part of the people of the developing countries, through the encouragement of democratic private and local governmental institutions."

Title IX urges the use of U.S. aid funds to support grass-roots development efforts by private and local groups. The idea is laudable, but only a trickle of funds moves through these channels, partly because they are hard to supervise.

were able to meet the same financial and monetary stabilization requirements that applied to Brazil. If a country undertook significant reforms in agriculture and education within the framework of representative political institutions, but fell short of IMF standards or the AID equivalent of such tests, AID loans in support of education and agriculture would be suspended. But the converse was not true. A country that did little in the areas of social reform and progressively limited representative political institutions, but met the IMF tests and, later, import liberalization commitments, continued to receive substantial economic assistance. Nowhere did AID make progress in agrarian or educational reform a condition of its major lending (program loans) or consider it relevant whether a country closed a fiscal gap through regressive or progressive taxes.[20] If a government could not control its wage policy in an opposition-dominated congress, and inflationary forces resurged, officials noted only bad performance, financial mismanagement. As an official of one international financial institution put it, "Look at Chile. They have done all the things called for under the Charter of Punta del Este. And what a mess!" If efficient financial management is the sole criterion of neatness, this observation is not inaccurate. But what a look at Chile also suggests is that fundamentally transforming social, economic, and political relationships within the framework of genuinely representative political institutions may have to be both expensive and messy. Authoritarian governments like those of Brazil and Argentina can achieve stabilization neatly by imposing a regressive wage policy and suppressing political institutions. The accompanying costs, being social and political rather than financial, don't show up on IMF balance sheets.

These governments may not even realize that they are merely sweeping the mess under the rug, because without representative institutions a political system gives off no signals as to how

20. In 1969 a Senate Foreign Relations Committee staff report commented on the performance standards of the Colombia aid program:

"These standards were aimed at economic stabilization—at controlling inflation and balancing the country's international accounts. They took into account considerations of economic development, but mainly from the point of view of maintaining an adequate level and appropriate distribution of imports to support industrial activity. Even less did the standards take account of the need for social reform. The basic problem, of course, was the difficulty of inducing economic growth while simultaneously applying the brakes to an inflationary economy. But in the process, the rhetoric of the Alliance for Progress was lost in the arcane world of international finance."

the people feel about the economic policies imposed on them. Economic technicians formulate policy without an effective political checkpoint. The international financial agencies, which value economic rationality above all else, congratulate the policy-makers on their technical proficiency and the absence of political calculation revealed in their policies. This international praise confirms the policy-makers in their belief in the irrelevance of public opinion.

In March 1969, regional disparities between East and West Pakistan set off riots in the east that ultimately led to the resignation of President Ayub Khan. The political system in Pakistan, lacking representative political institutions, provided no way short of violence for the public to register its discontent. In the *New York Times* of March 9, 1969, Joseph Lelyveld quoted a Pakistani businessman on the role of the U.S. government and the international financial agencies in the Pakistan crisis:

You didn't have to denounce Ayub, but you also didn't have to give him your stamp of approval. . . . That just made things worse. Every time someone here tried to say, "Can't we set things right?" he would be told, "What do you mean, set things right? We're a great success. Everyone says so. Look at what the World Bank says, look at what the International Monetary Fund says, look at what the Agency for International Development says."

It is entirely conceivable that in the 1970s a Brazilian or Argentine businessman may express these sentiments with equal vehemence.

The Charter of Punta del Este originally postulated an evaluation of country performance which would consider economic, social, and political progress all on the same plane. Table 10.2 illustrates this approach, rating the three major aid recipients under the Alliance on a roughly indicative scale of 1 to 5, with 5 being the highest rating.

For the past few years loan officials have evaluated performance only under column A, according to which Brazil is an outstanding performer and Chile a poor one. But if a country's performance is evaluated in all three categories, its relative rating changes. Moreover, in the development process, the relationship between political, social, and economic components at any given time is likely to be distorted. Development is as likely to occur in a series of spasmodic lurches as in a straight-line progression. In 1969 the Frei government in Chile found itself

Table 10.2

Rating of three major aid recipients under the Alliance for Progress on economic, social, and political progress

(on scale of 1 to 5)

	A macro-economic management (fiscal, monetary, and exchange policy)	B social reform (education, housing, and agriculture)	C representative political institutions	total
Brazil	4.5	2.5	1.0	8.0
Chile	2.0	4.0	5.0	11.0
Colombia	4.0	3.5	4.0	11.5

in financial difficulties after an ambitious taxation, wage, and social investment program in agrarian reform and educational expansion that accomplished some degree of income redistribution. A rebellious Congress defeated Frei's attempt to keep the wage increases demanded by the labor unions from exceeding the 25 percent price increase. Important elements of the middle class increasingly resented the high tax burden incident to the social investment program. Inflation became more serious (Column A) and Chile requested economic assistance from the United States. The AID staff viewed such assistance as betrayal of economic performance standards. Following issuance of the Fifth Institutional Act in Brazil, however, AID noted that country's outstanding self-help performance (Column A) and was reluctant to include such extraneous factors as deteriorating political conditions (Column C) in its review. Supporters of a high level of U.S. aid to Brazil considered a cutback "unjust." James Fowler, then deputy coordinator of the Alliance for Progress, testified before a House subcommittee:

I want to make it very clear that while we did say that there have been some disturbing developments in Brazil, certainly I would not describe the situation there as pessimistic or a total problem. Development in Brazil, particularly economic development, is going ahead in a very satisfactory fashion. I just wanted to be sure there wasn't any misunderstanding on that.[21]

Shortly thereafter, AID programmed $187 million in development loans for Brazil, nearly 30 percent of the total AID request, for fiscal year 1970.

21. U.S. House of Representatives, Subcommittee on Inter-American Affairs of the Committee on Foreign Affairs, *New Directions for the 1970's: Toward a Strategy of Inter-American Development, Hearings*, 91st Cong., 1st sess. (Washington, D.C.: U.S. Government Printing Office, 1969), p. 33.

Certainly the three-column approach is not without problems. Categories B and C are not easily quantifiable and call for the exercise of judgment tailored to the individual case. Mexico, for example, until recently has had a political system based upon one party. Yet that party has provided more effective representation of a broader range of major interest groups within the society than multiparty systems in other countries. The adjustment called for is therefore fairly sophisticated and difficult. But its absence may invalidate assessments of country performance under the Alliance for Progress.

The assumption underlying the hard-line position characteristic of AID, the IMF, and the IBRD is that the Latin Americans, left to themselves, lack both the requisite competence and the political courage to make hard economic decisions. The international lending agencies must therefore make the Latin Americans toe the mark. This essentially paternalistic stance has inspired an increasingly critical attitude among Latin American governments toward what the agencies tell them they need for their development.

In 1966 the IMF, backed by AID and the IBRD, demanded that the Colombian government devalue its currency immediately. The purpose of this devaluation was to stimulate minor exports and cure an exchange imbalance, but the sharp internal price increases that it would also cause were politically unacceptable to a new government seeking to consolidate its position. As President Lleras Restrepo of Colombia saw it:

It became clear that the USAID program loan hinged on our being in full agreement with the IMF. . . . We differed with the IMF on how technically to face the structural imbalance of our payments. And we differed on the degree of autonomy that should be preserved by countries, even though they need loans, in handling their economic policies.[22]

Lleras Restrepo therefore announced that rather than devaluate, he was prepared to give up the $65 million U.S. program loan. He pointed out that if prices got out of control as a result of the devaluation, the Colombian people would hold him, not the IMF representative, responsible. Reluctantly, the AID mis-

22. U.S. Senate, Committee on Foreign Relations, *Survey of the Alliance for Progress in Colombia: A Case History of USAID*, a staff study prepared at the request of the Subcommittee on American Republics Affairs (Washington, D.C.: U.S. Government Printing Office, February 1, 1969), p. 45.

sion provided the program loan on Colombia's terms. Time has proved that devaluation would not have been wise. Colombia's exports have gone up through alternative incentives; capital flowed in as it became clear that the peso rate was firm; and internal price levels have remained relatively stable. Investments, both foreign and domestic, went through a period of uncertainty and then began to increase. The threatened suspension of the program loan also pushed the Colombians to seek out domestic sources of development money. A Harvard advisory group hired by Lleras has completed a full-scale tax-reform study. Colombian planners hope to increase internal resources for investment to a level that will permit fulfillment of the goal of an annual growth rate of 6 percent.

When the Costa e Silva government assumed power in early 1967 the Brazilian economy was on the verge of a severe recession resulting from the stringent financial measures of the Castelo Branco administration. The new minister of finance, Antonio Delfim Neto, agreed with the São Paulo industrialists that Brazil's most serious inflationary pressures did not come from excessive demand but from high costs due to underutilized plant and very high interest rates. Against the advice of the international financial agencies, Delfim Neto relaxed credit and wage restrictions to stimulate the economy. AID suspended disbursements under the program loan to Brazil. But in retrospect, Delfim Neto's decision is considered responsible for the improvement in Brazil's growth rate in the second half of 1967 and 1968. Later, when the Brazilian inflation showed signs of reviving, Delfim Neto accepted the arguments of the international agencies for new stabilizing measures (and AID reinstated disbursement), but by this time Brazilian businessmen had recovered their optimism, and growth continued to be strong in 1969.

These examples prove neither that the international financial agencies are invariably wrong nor that Latin American governments and political leaders are always lucid and courageous in their economic policy decisions. They do suggest that the lending agencies' hard line is not the only approach to development that produces good results. Aid decisions must be based on both technical criteria and the judgments that only local leaders can make about the political possibilities and consequences of accepting these criteria. No external agent, multilateral or bilateral, can have the same sense of a country's political situation that its own leadership has.

The level of development sophistication in Latin America today is incomparably higher than it was at the beginning of the sixties. This change may well be the most lasting accomplishment of the Alliance. Ministries of planning are increasingly well run and influential. Many of these ministries are staffed with able young technicians, many of whom have studied in the United States, often thanks to AID grants. The improvements have been outstanding in Brazil, Chile, Colombia, Argentina, Mexico, and Venezuela, and pockets of technically trained officials can be found in Peru, Ecuador, the Dominican Republic, and the Central American countries. Increasingly, political leadership recognizes that it needs this generation of young technicians to run more and more complex government and development agencies.

Between 1966 and 1970, President Lleras Restrepo of Colombia devoted most of every Tuesday to a meeting of the National Council of Political Economy, the government's top coordinating body for economic and social development planning. Ministers and agency heads attended the meeting. Lleras Restrepo, a skilled economist as well as a strong-willed political leader, acted as chairman, carefully preparing each session with the top staff of the planning department, which reported directly to him. Lleras Restrepo had been developing this department as a personal project since 1958. Headed by Edgar Castro Gutiérrez, a Harvard graduate with a Ph.D. in economics, the staff included ten other senior economists with Ph.D. degrees from American and European universities and salaries ($10,000 a year) that kept them from being hired away by private companies. Another forty staff members had M.A. degrees. A Harvard University development advisory group assisted the Colombian staff.

With this expertise, the Colombians had drawn up a five-year development plan that regulated public-sector investment and presented a wide range of technical judgments that influenced policy decisions on all aspects of the Colombian economy, including exchange, foreign trade, industrial promotion, agricultural development, and social investments. The plan operated on a year-to-year basis, and systematically underwent performance checks and revisions that controlled both budgetary commitments and fulfillment of physical targets.

This technocratic management of Colombia's economic policy produced friction between planners and cabinet ministers, criticism from champions of private enterprise, and vigorous confrontations between the Colombian executive and Congress.

The planning department greeted this criticism with confidence and good humor. Castro Gutiérrez delighted his audience at a meeting of the American-Colombian Chamber of Commerce in Bogotá by reading aloud a letter from an anonymous U.S. businessman in Colombia, addressed to a representative of an international agency in Washington, which Castro Gutiérrez said had been forwarded to him through undisclosed "good offices." It said:

There is a sect, or a caste, composed of high-level bureaucrats in Colombia. I have been told that this caste makes a professional career of government, where it devotes itself to controlling the private sector. The caste comes from the upper- and middle-class families of society who have had enough money to educate their sons abroad, but not enough to place them in prosperous enterprises. For this reason, there is always a sort of resentment in this caste toward businessmen. The members of this caste are usually well educated, and frequently have high university degrees. They have the best intentions. But I consider them a sect because, like the priests of the Middle Ages, they all consider that because they have knowledge and the best of intentions, they have all the right to manage the country! It seems that President Lleras is the archbishop of this sect. He has placed the country in the hands of these all-powerful individuals. . . .[23]

Although planning continues to spark debate in private circles, it is now generally recognized as the way business is going to be done in Colombia.

In Chile a young team of technical people within the Ministry of Education did much of the planning that has led to the success of the educational revolution. In Brazil, the Ministry of Planning developed the controversial university and educational reform program that deepened the rift between modernizing and conservative sectors in the Costa e Silva regime. Staffed by young *técnicos*, the Ministry of Planning is likely to emerge with a more authoritative voice in the future, particularly as this younger generation of technically prepared people spreads throughout the public sector in Brazil.

23. Edgar Castro Gutiérrez, speech delivered to a meeting of the American-Colombian Chamber of Commerce, Bogotá, August 1968.

As this human infrastructure of technical competence develops, in cooperation with a more assertive political leadership, the Latin American governments will become less willing to accept uncritically the strictures of the international lending agencies with respect to self-help performance and more willing to present their own ideas on this subject. Obviously the U.S. government has a responsibility to the U.S. Congress and the taxpayer not to waste public resources. It might therefore approach the problem of lending by setting a standard of minimum acceptability, rather than by making its own economic criteria the price of assistance. In the Goulart era in Brazil, the financial chaos accompanying social and political turmoil made it impossible to employ public resources effectively for development purposes. The Goulart government would thus have fallen below the minimum acceptability standard. Above this level, the United States might well improve relations without sacrificing long-run performance under the Alliance if it deferred more to the borrowing country's judgment on the details of economic and sector programs. To the extent that the United States is prepared to provide development funds through the multilateral channel of the IDB, it does show this interest. For most of the smaller Latin American countries, as well as for Argentina, Venezuela, and Mexico, the IDB is already the major source of Alliance resources. Friction with the United States over general economic policy questions arises primarily in the three countries (Brazil, Chile, and Colombia) that are the major recipients of program loans. The balance-of-payments and domestic budget aspects of these loans carry the USAID mission in these countries perilously far toward direct involvement in domestic policy-making. There is much to be said for so-called sector loans, in which the United States provides broad financing on a selective basis for areas of high priority, such as agriculture and education. Generally, such AID financing complements IDB and IBRD loans in the same areas. But unless the lending agency judges the country's overall stability or the government's competence as insufficient to permit effective use of the loan for its stated purpose, development lending in general must be consistent with the priorities of the recipient government. In the end, after all, Latin American development is Latin America's problem.

The social question

The social balance sheet

We are poor, sir. We barely produce enough to eat. Very little is left over to sell, and not every year. Some years it rains well, but other years it rains little and there is drought. Other years it rains a lot, and our fields are flooded. We work the land of our community all together. We plant potatoes, quinoa, and barley. One year potatoes, another year quinoa, the next year barley. We can keep few animals.

We were six brothers. One by one they left here to look for work in other parts because they saw that here it wasn't possible to live. I too had gone to Tacna when I was a child. But when I was twelve years old my father was left all alone because my mother died, and I came back to work with him. I had to come back because I was the oldest. Now my father is dead.

I took a woman, and we made a family. We had three children. Two died.

With what we harvest there is barely enough to eat and pay our debts. We sell a bit in Ilave.

Many leave to look for work because here they can't earn enough to eat. They go far away: to Cananá, to Tacna, as far as Lima. Sometimes the whole family goes.

That's the way it is, sir.

This statement was made by Eusebio Maquera, an Indian peasant, to Cecilio Morales of the Inter-American Development Bank, on the high, wind-blasted Andean plateau at Camicachi, Peru. Maquera spoke for the millions of "marginals" in Latin America who await the day when they or their children can become part of the modern society they know is around them, but beyond their reach.

Latin America today presents the corrosive paradox of an ever growing number of poor in the midst of the potential for plenty. The past decade has served less to solve this basic problem than to develop an awareness of the inequities of economic opportunity and cultural access in Latin America. The Alliance let out the genie of awareness; no one can coax it back into the bottle again. Today the issue of poverty has considerable political potency, particularly among the young.

The attainment of some of the objectives of the Alliance seems even more remote in 1970 than it seemed in 1961. The social problems identified by the Alliance for priority action have turned out to be much bigger, and therefore much more difficult and costly to overcome, than had been imagined. Early in 1969 a frank report by USAID in Washington to the U.S. Congress commented on some of the goals of the Alliance:

Agrarian reform

Almost a million Latin American families were settled or resettled during the period of 1960–67. . . . An estimated 10 to 14 million families in Latin America remain to be settled or resettled. This figure is increasing faster than the current rate of resettlement. At an average cost of $1,000 per family, close to $15 billion in agricultural credit would be needed now for agrarian reform purposes—a sum approaching total annual gross investment for the entire region.[1]

Education

It is expected that there will be about 69 million children of primary-school age in 1970. This is almost twice the number enrolled in school in 1967. If the present trend of 6 percent increase in school enrollment annually were to continue, enrollment would not reach the level of 69 million children until 1979. By that time, of course, the school-age population would be well above that level, or about 92 million, so there would still be 23 million children not enrolled in school. Not until 1986 would the entire school-age population be enrolled, if present rates of population growth and school expansion continue. . . . If the current rate of increases in school enrollment were to be stepped up from 6 per-

1. U.S. House of Representatives, Subcommittee on Inter-American Affairs of the Committee on Foreign Affairs, *New Directions for the 1970's: Toward a Strategy of Inter-American Development, Hearings*, 91st Cong., 1st sess. (Washington, D.C.: U.S. Government Printing Office, 1969), p. 699.

cent to 9 percent per year, the entire expected school-age population of 85 million would be enrolled in school in 1977.[2]

Health

Although detailed and up-to-date information on changes in the expectation of life in Latin America since 1960 is scarce, the Pan American Health Organization has been able to estimate that the average future life span increased from 60.2 years to 62.5 years between 1960 and 1966. (The Alliance target for the decade was a five-year increase.) ... Progress in increasing life expectancy depends largely on the success of another general goal of the Charter, to reduce childhood mortality by 50 percent. ... This implies reducing deaths by children under five by one-fourth by 1966. Infant mortality decreased by only 12 percent, or less than half this goal during the first five years.[3]

Low-cost housing

The goal of adequate housing for all is obviously desirable, but realistically one which cannot be soon realized. The total need for housing in Latin America has been estimated as being between 15 and 20 million units. This deficit is increasing by at least one million units a year. Squatter settlements continue to mushroom. Given higher priority needs for the use of scarce internal and external resources, the countries of Latin America will not be able to meet the housing need in the foreseeable future. ... The greatest need for housing is for low-income families. Unfortunately, persons in this income category can make little or no contribution to the cost of their housing, and generally require some form of public subsidy. This raises the hard economic question of the feasibility and desirability of allocating large amounts of capital to low-rent housing.[4]

Employment

Aggravating Latin America's social problems is the inadequacy of productive employment available to a rapidly growing labor force. According to ECLA estimates, during the Alliance decade the Latin American population of working age (fifteen to sixty-five) has increased by 2.3 million men and women each year, reaching a total of 136 million people in 1969. Of these, 84 million are "economically active," that is, in the labor market, but ECLA estimates that only about 60 million are fully employed. The remainder are unemployed or underemployed, particularly in the rural areas, where ECLA estimates that 11 million are unemployed in an economically active population of 35 million.

The low rate of absorption of rural manpower is held respon-

---

2. *Ibid.*, p. 704.
3. *Ibid.*, p. 710.
4. *Ibid.*, p. 715.

sible for an actual slowdown in job openings during the Alliance period; only about 60 percent of the new job seekers gained employment during the sixties, compared with 62.5 percent during the 1950s. The percentage of the economically active population engaged in agriculture has declined from 53.4 percent in 1950 to 47.2 percent in 1960 and an estimated 42.2 percent in 1969. Over the same period, the rate of employment in industry, mining, construction, and public services has increased only from 23.5 percent of the total to 24.8 percent. The major increase for the period has been in "miscellaneous services," from 13 percent to 17.3 percent. It results from the transfer of many job seekers to various marginal forms of livelihood in the urban areas; in short, the displacement of rural poverty to the cities. According to ECLA, the annual per capita income of about two-thirds of the agricultural population, including children and inactive adults, averages less than $90 a year, which implies an annual income per economically active person of approximately $275. Latin America's average per capita annual income is $510.[5]

Latin America's inequities of income distribution and employment thus derive from the structure of the rural economy, in which a disproportionate amount of good land is concentrated in large farms, some modern and highly productive, but many more traditional, using low-productivity peasant labor at subsistence wages. The lack of employment, even at very low wages, for landless peasants (particularly the sons of peasant families with tiny holdings) is a direct cause of migration to the cities. The desperate problems of rural and urban poverty in Latin America are entirely interdependent. Summarizing an extensive study of the problem, the IDB said:

Though the nature of the problem varies among countries and zones, the chronic imbalance between relatively abundant land resources and rural poverty remains typical of the Latin American region; the highly unequal access to natural resources is, of course, one of the main causes

5. United Nations Economic Commission for Latin America, *Economic Survey of Latin America, 1968*, pt. 1, "Some Aspects of the Latin American Economy Toward the End of the Nineteen-Sixties," E/CN 12/825 (March 1969), pp. 50–60. The figure of $510 for the regional average is based on new ECLA calculations that take into account price-level differential in various countries. The calculation is in constant 1960 dollars, and the dollar level, with adjustment for relative price levels in the United States and Latin America, brings the real value of Latin per capita income higher than before the 1969 calculations.

of the extreme discrepancies in the distribution of rural incomes. Some social welfare-type help has penetrated to the very lowest rural income groups, while economic development programs undertaken under the Alliance for Progress have mostly benefited the middle levels of farmers. However, the vast bulk of rural families are still landless or in the dwarf-holding class, with insufficient access to income-earning possibilities. . . .

Looking at the region as a whole, the continued slow progress must be viewed against the backdrop of increasing rather than diminishing structural problems. The growth of the labor force proceeds at a much faster annual rate than the increase in the number of new jobs in nonagricultural activities, and overcrowding of the big cities by rural migrants is getting worse. It is also becoming evident that the capacity of the urban sector to create productive employment is likely to be limited by virtue of accelerated adoption of advanced technology. Yet some of the best land in the already settled areas of most countries continues to be very much underutilized and could offer employment and income opportunities to many *campesinos*.[6]

The Alliance balance sheet in all these areas and its overall response to the social question reflect two major influences. The first is the weakening of the Alliance commitment to social integration. The commitment to integrate Latin America's marginal masses into the core society was based largely on fear. In order to compete effectively with Castro, the charter called for the elimination of adult illiteracy and for six years of primary education for every school-age child, for agrarian reform to change land tenure conditions, for housing and decent living conditions for the low-income masses.

As the political theory of the Alliance was undone and the threat of Castro lost its urgency, technocratic considerations supplanted these social objectives. The Alliance focus shifted from adult literacy and universal primary education to technical and higher education, from equitable land distribution to improving the productivity of commercial farmers, from housing the poor to housing the middle classes and then to dropping housing objectives altogether. Abandoning the task of social integration, the Alliance sought to improve conditions within the core society and perhaps to expand the core over an extended period of time.

The second influence on the social balance sheet was the failure of the Alliance to deal with the issue of population.

6. Background document submitted by the Inter-American Development Bank to the Development Assistance Committee meeting in Paris, February 3–4, 1969, p. 19.

Population

If Latin America's social problems already raise revolutionary pressures and a backlash of political repression, one can only surmise what confrontations lie ahead as population soars and migration further congests the cities.

In 1900 Latin America had a population of 63 million, growing at an annual rate of 1.8 percent, which added 1.1 million people a year. In 1920 the population was 90 million and it took almost thirty-seven years to double. During the last two decades the rate of population growth for the region has climbed to 3 percent a year. Latin America's population in 1970 is estimated at 275 million, with an annual increment of 7 million people a year. At this rate, the region's population will double in about twenty-three years.

Latin Americans have been slow to grasp the implications of this accelerated population growth for the region's development. The first leader to point out the dangers publicly was President Alberto Lleras Camargo of Colombia. In his opening address to the 1960 meeting of the Committee of 21 in Bogotá he said:

This population explosion is notable chiefly in terms of the impact it has upon the psychology of the governing classes, who until recently greeted the increase in inhabitants of each nation as a sign of progress and strength, but have suddenly realized that without economic development impelled with a purpose and speed heretofore unimagined, the problem by itself becomes unmanageable.

However, Lleras Camargo stopped short of the crucial question: Should Latin American countries adopt population control as part of their development policies? At that time, this question was considered politically taboo, partly because the Latin American elites were predominantly Roman Catholic, but also for entirely secular reasons. The developmentalist school of Latin American economic planners had utilized population pressure as an argument for increased external economic assistance. They tended to regard U.S. proposals for population control as subtle attempts to avoid having to give more aid to Latin America. Communists even suggested that population control was part of a plot by "white imperialists" to hold down the rise of the developing brown peoples.

The Charter of Punta del Este made no mention of population growth as an influence on Latin America's economic and social development, although Kennedy had referred to this problem in his White House speech of March 1961. During the early years of the Alliance, population policy was a matter of concern only to specialized medical groups and private international organizations that sought to promote interest in family planning.

Population control became public policy in Latin America for the first time when the Christian Democratic government of President Frei made family planning services part of Chile's national health program. After 1966 the U.S. government began to emphasize the need for population policies in all developing countries. In September 1967 the OAS held a meeting of government experts in Caracas to discuss population policies in relation to development. The meeting recommended that CIAP henceforth "include demographic factors" in its annual review of Latin American development programs. By 1968 the U.S. government had set aside $25 million under the aid program for Latin America to finance family planning programs, scientific research in reproduction, and population studies. (The United Nations had also established a regional demographic center in Santiago, Chile.) Seventeen Latin American countries now have some organized form of family planning services; Chile, Colombia, and Honduras have publicly supported programs.

Latin American interest in population policy has grown with the realization that the rate of population increase was an obstacle to attainment of the Alliance targets for growth and social development. The United Nations said that an annual increase of 5 percent in gross national product was desirable for all developing countries during the sixties. In Latin America, with an annual population increase of more than 3 percent, the achievement of this target would increase per capita income by a little less than 2 percent a year. At this rate, a country would take forty years to double its per capita gross national income. On the other hand, if Mexico, Colombia, Brazil, Chile, and Venezuela were able to halve their present birth rates and maintain an annual 5 percent increase in GNP, they would double their per capita income in twenty-five years.

The reasons for the accelerated growth of Latin America's population are in some ways obvious and in others still unclear. Generally acknowledged as a major determinant is the reduction of death rates through improved nutrition, effective campaigns to wipe out yellow fever and malaria in many rural areas, and the very wide use now made of antibiotics and other wonder drugs. Migration to the cities, which offer better public health services than the countryside, may also have played a part.

On the other hand, Uruguay and Costa Rica are often bracketed as socially comparable countries, little democracies with a predominance of small farmers owning their own land; yet Uruguay has the lowest population growth rate in the hemisphere, about 1.4 percent, and Costa Rica has the highest, an estimated 3.8 percent. The reason for this difference is so far unknown.

A comparison of Latin America with slow-growth industrialized regions suggests that the level of female employment may affect the propensity to have many children. For instance, in the Soviet Union 41.4 percent of women of working age are economically active, and birth rates are well below 20 per thousand, whereas in Brazil, with a birth rate of 38 per thousand, only 12 percent of women of working age are employed.[7]

The opposition of the Roman Catholic church has been generally considered an effective deterrent to family planning. Some superficial observers even attribute the proliferation of children to the *machismo* (masculine vanity) of Latin American men.

Regional variations in the level of *machismo* are difficult to detect. However, variations in the power of the church do not noticeably correlate with population growth. Argentina, a strongly Roman Catholic country, has a population growth rate of 1.6 percent a year, and a birth rate of 20 per thousand, above the low European averages but below those of Australia. Mexico, which is officially anticlerical and on a par with Argentina in industrialized urban centers, has a population growth rate of 3.4 percent and a birth rate of 43 per thousand, double the rates of Argentina and close to those of India. The main difference between the two countries is in their populations' respective levels of education, with Mexico lagging far behind Argentina in rural areas.[8]

---

7. United Nations, *Demographic Yearbook*, 1967; and *Programa Estratégico de Desenvolvimiento, 1968–1970* (Rio de Janeiro: Ministerio de Planejamento, June 1968), vol. 1, pt. 2, chap. 3, Table 6.
8. Social Progress Trust Fund, *Eighth Annual Report* (Washington, D.C.: Inter-American Development Bank, 1968).

During the Alliance decade, the advent of the birth-control pill has had considerable social impact on Latin America. Despite the opposition of the Roman Catholic church, an estimated 2.5 million Latin American women, predominantly of the middle and upper classes, have made use of the pill. Religious beliefs have also failed to deter poorer women from availing themselves of family planning care in privately organized services, although these services have concentrated their efforts in the cities.

It is noteworthy that leaders of progressive Latin American governments, such as Frei in Chile and Lleras Restrepo in Colombia, a very Catholic country, have given public support to family planning, while leaders of the major authoritarian regimes, Onganía of Argentina and Costa e Silva of Brazil, have thundered against it. Costa e Silva was the first chief of state to send a telegram of congratulations to Pope Paul VI for his encyclical *Humanae vitae*, proscribing the use of the pill. Brazil's military leaders hold to a geopolitical beatitude that says: "Blessed are the poor that multiply, for they shall occupy the Amazon wilderness." Robert McNamara, president of the IBRD, disagrees:

It is a false claim that some countries need more population to fill their land or accelerate their economic growth. There are no vacant lands equipped with roads, schools, houses, and the tools of agricultural or industrial employment. Therefore, the people who are to fill these lands, before they can live at even the current low standard of living, must first eat up a portion of the present scarce supply of capital—it is this burden which defeats a nation's efforts to raise its standard by increasing its population.[9]

In the chapters that follow we shall examine the problems of schools, housing, and agricultural employment. Slower population growth in most Latin American countries would eventually help to solve these problems. But fifty million new job seekers will enter the labor market during the coming decade. They are all alive now. No birth-control program can alter this fact or resolve the Latin American development problems of the 1970s.

9. Robert McNamara, speech at the annual meeting of the International Bank for Reconstruction and Development, September 1968.

The agrarian impasse

*We must emphasize the needs of rural
Latin America. Here half the people
of Latin American live. And it is
here, in the countryside, that the
foundation of a modern economy
will finally be built.*
Lyndon B. Johnson, 1965

In the fifty years before the birth of the Alliance, revolution shattered the traditional landholding structures of three Latin American countries. In Mexico, Bolivia, and Cuba, private estates and plantations were either seized by the peasants or expropriated by the new governments. The redistribution of land had vast implications for modernization and development in all three countries.

The Mexican revolution began in 1910 and continued for ten bloody years. Peasant rebellion against the exploitative hacienda system contributed to the conflagration, and peasant demand for land was a burning issue over the next twenty-five years. Between 1934 and 1940, the "radical" agrarian policies of President Lázaro Cárdenas extended communal village ownership to nearly half the land of Mexico, including many of the best estates that had resisted seizure until then. Cárdenas also nationalized foreign oil companies, placing them under the control of a state monopoly corporation, Petróleos Mexicanos (Pemex), which became the symbol of Mexican nationalism.

The Cárdenas period consolidated and stabilized the revolution. Since 1940 Mexico has maintained one of the strongest rates of economic development in Latin America through a mixed system of state and private enterprise. Foreign investment has poured in from the United States and Europe for large-scale industrialization. Agriculture has grown impressively within a strong system of state credit, irrigation, research, and extension services that has particularly benefited private commercial farmers. Food production has more than kept pace with a population increasing at the rate of 3 percent a year, from 20 million in 1940 to 45 million in 1968.

But in the midst of this stable growth, the landless peasant is still a forgotten man. As a result of Mexico's population explosion, there are as many rural laborers without land today as there were when the revolution began. Mexico has made greater use of Alliance credits than any other country to build new irrigation projects to increase arable land for new settlers, and Mexico's strong rate of development has increased absorption of rural manpower into Mexico's growing industrial and service sectors. But social justice for the poor peasantry is again a subject of active debate in political, intellectual, and labor circles.

The Bolivian revolution erupted in 1952, led by young nationalists of the professional class and labor organizers, and inspired, to some degree, by the Mexican example. It began in the cities and large mining camps and spread to the rural areas as the military regime toppled. The peasants seized and divided up the large estates of the high plateau and the valleys of Cochabamba, Chuquisaca, and Tarija. By offering land titles to legitimate the seizures, the new government was able to organize the peasants in rural unions and armed militia, and the propertied peasants became a strong force for stability, siding with the government against the more radical miners in moments of crisis. But agricultural development has been very slow.

Bolivia is far poorer than Mexico. Its annual per capita income is $150; Mexico's is $500. Seventy percent of Bolivia's four million people are peasants, nearly all of them small landholders living in primitive conditions on poor land. But in the tropical grasslands cattle ranches are spreading, and large private commercial farms have made Bolivia self-sufficient in rice and sugar. In the eastern region, virgin agricultural land awaits colonization. Under the Alliance, Bolivia has been receiving aid to finance colonization settlements and build highways to the new lands, but the settlements undergo severe hardships and produce little for the market. At the outset the Bolivian revolutionaries nationalized the country's three largest tin mines; but, as in Mexico, the government subsequently encouraged new foreign investment.

In 1963 the Gulf Oil Company invested heavily in a rich oil and natural gas concession in Santa Cruz. Six years later, in 1969, a bloodless military coup established General Alfredo Ovanda Candia as president of Bolivia. Advocating social reforms, Ovando announced that his regime would be one of "leftist nationalism" and that he hoped to establish an "ideological federation with Peru."[1] His government expropriated Gulf holdings valued by the company at $141 million.[2] If Bolivia's newly nationalized oil industry can maintain and expand production, and if the Ovando regime can fulfill its promise, this oil wealth may benefit the peasant population; or, like the fruits of Bolivia's other developed resources, it may remain in the hands of the urban sectors, which still control Bolivian politics.

In 1959 the Cuban agrarian property structure was tied to major U.S. private property interests far more extensively than those of revolutionary Mexico and Bolivia had been. Castro's first agrarian reform decree, in 1959, expropriated U.S. properties representing a total investment of $300 million and claimed all private farms larger than 660 acres, including a number of large U.S.-owned cattle ranches. The reaction of these business interests did much to bring about the U.S.-Cuban confrontation. But the really radical aspect of Cuba's agrarian reform was still to come. In 1962 Castro reduced the size limit on private farms to sixty-six acres, consolidating 70 percent of Cuban agriculture in state farms.[3] The Cuban approach to the agrarian problem was ultimately a centrally

---

1. As reported by Malcolm Browne, "Bolivia Espouses New Nationalism," *New York Times*, September 28, 1969, p. 26.
2. "Gulf Urges a Halt in U.S. Aid for Bolivia," *New York Times*, October 31, 1969, p. 63.
3. It is hard to say to what extent this act represented the growing influence of Marxist-Leninist ideology or simply an attempt to solve the problem of middle-sized farmers (relatively numerous and powerful within the Cuban rural structure) who by 1962 had turned against the regime and were supplying and harboring counterrevolutionary guerrillas in several provinces.

planned agricultural system under which a majority of peasants became state employees. Since 1964, after a misguided, premature fling at industrialization, Castro has concentrated his resources on agricultural development. The results of this effort will make or break Cuba's socialist experiment.

Cuba's adoption of this system could not have been foreseen early in 1961, but even then, the Kennedy administration regarded peasant unrest in Latin America as a warning signal of incipient Castro-style revolution.

Kennedy and his liberal advisers looked upon agrarian reform as a historical imperative for Latin America. Impressed by the political moderation that. Mexico and Bolivia had achieved after the breakup of the big estates, they argued that the United States should support land redistribution following the Mexican and Bolivian patterns. They regarded the Cuban revolution, on the other hand, as a negative example to which the Alliance for Progress must provide a bold but peaceful alternative. When newspapers published reports about Francisco Julião's "Peasant Leagues" in Brazil's Northeast, Kennedy met at the White House for more than two hours with Celso Furtado, the reform-oriented economist who was superintendent of Brazil's Northeast Development Agency. Furtado convinced Kennedy that an emergency program for the Brazilian Northeast had to be one of the priorities of the Alliance for Progress, and that agrarian reform was a necessity in the backward sugarcane zone of the region. George McGovern, Kennedy's first Food for Peace coordinator, accompanied Schlesinger on his Latin American trip in 1961, and brought back from the Northeast appalling reports of nutritional deficiencies, sickness, subhuman housing, illiteracy, and exploitation of labor, including children. Kennedy subsequently appointed Merwin Bohan to lead a Northeast task force that produced a $131 million program for the region.

The signs of peasant unrest were not confined to Brazil. Throughout the continent observers reported that the peasants, making up 60 percent of Latin America's working population, were awakening to a new demand for social justice. If Latin America's governing classes were not prepared to accept redistribution of the land and a new place for the peasant in the social and political order, then revolution was imminent.

A group of agricultural economists working in a Latin American regional office of the U.N. Food and Agriculture Organization formulated a theory that acquired wide currency in Latin American economic development circles. They attributed low farm productivity, nutritional deficiencies, and rising food imports in Latin America to the land-tenure system, which crowded 90 percent of the rural producers onto 10 percent of the land in most countries. The big estates, they said, were holding back a dynamic agricultural development in Latin America.

These strong views, along with past agrarian revolutionary experience and apprehensions about the potential for rural violence, gave Washington a rationale for supporting agrarian reform. Washington would encourage deliberate policy decisions and legal measures to change agrarian structures throughout Latin America as constructively as revolutionary unheaval had changed it in Mexico and Bolivia. This approach would, at one stroke, open the way for modernization of agriculture in underfed Latin American countries and eliminate peasant unrest as a weapon for *fidelista* extremists.

An orderly agrarian reform requires that a society commit itself to heavy investment in its peasants. The peasants of most Latin American countries are numerous, deprived, and excluded from participation in politics. Therefore an effective public program to give them land, capital, education, technical services, equal access to the market, and a voice in political affairs amounts to a social revolution. It is also enormously expensive. The Alliance for Progress gave this great and costly social change high priority in its program for inter-American cooperation.

The Charter of Punta del Este included a broad statement of purpose tailored to accommodate the wide range of positions that the delegates held on agrarian reform. The subsequent performance of each country has demonstrated its commitment to this objective. The U.S. commitment, in the form of financial contributions to structural changes in Latin American land-tenure systems, has been neither substantial nor specific. The U.S. delegates at Punta del Este had in mind a tidy rural social reform that would extend to peasants a greater share of national income and social services through credit programs and rural modernization. They regarded land tenure, however, as a domestic problem for the Latin Americans to solve in their own way and in their own time. And the United States further curtailed its financial support of agrarian reform programs as its priorities shifted to monetary stabilization and increased agricultural production through development of the private commercial farming sector—that is, the sector that already owned the productive land.

The United States has often used monetary stabilization and the liberation of exchange rates as conditions for aid to Latin American countries. It has never used land redistribution as a condition for aid. The United States has exercised its leverage to induce Latin American countries to carry out general tax reforms that have greatly increased government revenues and helped balance the budget in some countries, but it has never pressed strongly for the establishment of a general rural property tax with teeth in it to back up an agrarian reform.

Whereas the targets of the Alliance for Progress in housing and education were quantified in the Charter of Punta del Este, agrarian reform goals, in terms of the number of peasants to be given land or the desirable ratio of family farm owners to farm laborers, were never specifically stated. The United States offered no new ideas on agrarian reform, but simply urged the Latin Americans to adopt the modern U.S. agricultural system of farmer-businessman, supported by "agri-business" services, with some special emphasis on cooperatives for the small farmer. This approach is what U.S. agriculture officials know about. Redistribution of privately owned land as an object of public policy is outside of U.S. experience.

The United States made it clear from the outset that it would not finance land expropriations. According to rules established by the United States in 1962 for the IDB's use of the Social Progress Trust Fund, agrarian reform projects involving land-tenure reforms are eligible for financing, but "the countries must bear the entire cost of land purchase; no part of such costs can be charged to SPTF."[4] Land acquisition rarely represents more than 10 percent of the cost of an agrarian reform settlement. The bulk of the expense comes from land improvement, production credit, machinery and fertilizer, roads, irrigation, and essential services for the peasant families, which the IDB

---

4. Social Progress Trust Fund, *First Annual Report*, annex 2 (Washington, D.C.: Inter-American Development Bank, 1961), p. 235.

and USAID have financed in limited amounts. By themselves these agrarian reform measures create conditions for increased production that benefit not the landless but those who already have productive farms.

U.S. officials opposed the purchase of land with aid funds on the grounds that a Latin American government with the determination to carry out agrarian reform could acquire land without using external resources, through expropriation mechanisms with long-term payment in local currency. This argument had merit on technical and self-help grounds, but in some countries it allowed strong conservative resistance to withhold from the government "confiscatory" legal powers over land and the funds to put agrarian reform laws into effect. In 1965 the presidents of Chile and Peru proposed that the United States create a reserve fund to guarantee Latin American agrarian reform bonds. The United States rejected this proposal as "impractical," although its only purpose was to make the bonds more readily marketable and therefore more acceptable to landowners. Events in Chile and Peru have subsequently opened to question the practicality of the U.S. government's policy. A few case histories of agrarian reform efforts during the Alliance period may serve to illustrate the social and political aspects of an issue that the United States has generally viewed in purely economic terms.

Venezuela

At Punta del Este, among the strongest advocates of agrarian reform were the delegates of Venezuela, where eighteen months earlier President Rómulo Betancourt had promulgated a far-reaching agrarian reform law. Betancourt and his Democratic Action party had been elected on a program of democratic social reform in 1958, after the overthrow of President Marcos Pérez Jiménez. Pérez' military dictatorship had given high priority to promoting foreign oil investments, which swelled the state coffers; it also spent heavily on public works, including what is probably the world's most expensive highway in cost per mile (from La Guaira to Caracas) and what is without any doubt at all the most expensive and luxurious officers' club in the world (at a cost of over $8 million). But General Pérez Jiménez felt he had little to gain by investing in peasants.

By 1959 the restoration of political liberties and, soon after, the nearby triumphant Cuban revolution had unleashed radical currents in Venezuela. Betancourt took over during widespread rural agitation and invasions of estates by landless peasants, some led by the governing party's own rural union organizers. Venezuela's cities were filling up with poor rural migrants.

Betancourt, a tough, canny politician, had been elected with strong rural support. He and other Venezuelan moderates saw that only legal changes in land tenure could maintain the stable political situation necessary for the success of this oil-rich country's development program. The Venezuelan government has therefore invested close to $400 million in agrarian reform since 1959, settling 140,000 peasant families on their own land. Although this program has affected only about 5 percent of Venezuela's farmland, it has calmed the countryside and added organized peasant support to the democratic political consensus that has kept Venezuela stable for a decade of sustained economic development.

Apart from the recent mechanization of commercial farming, Venezuelan agriculture still closely resembles what it was forty years ago, when Venezuela was still a low-income agricultural country depending on exports of coffee, cacao, and cattle for its meager foreign trade. The oil boom broke this pattern dramatically, propelling Venezuela to the top ranks of world petroleum exporters in two decades and kicking off its domestic industrialization. Oil has given this country the highest per capita income in Latin America, close to $900 a year. Venezuela is thus in the income range of the developed countries, but this statistical datum does not reveal the profound imbalance of income distribution between the modern, high-productivity sector and the backward agricultural masses and their urban cousins, the migrants.

Venezuela's national accounts value its annual gross domestic product at close to $8 billion, of which agriculture generates about 7.5 percent. This share is produced by 700,000 rural workers, more than one-third of the active labor force, and only about 20 percent of these rural workers have benefited directly from the agrarian reform. Their overall productivity has certainly risen, and so has their income, but there are many small subsistence farmers and landless laborers among them. Comparing the contribution of agriculture and of industry to domestic product on a per capita basis, the agricultural workers are four times less productive than Venezuela's 340,000 industrial workers (including many small artisans) and eighty times less productive than the country's labor elite, the 40,000 oil workers. Naturally, there is a vast difference in the ratio of capital to labor between agriculture and the oil industry, which generates one-quarter of Venezuela's domestic output.

Agrarian reform experts continue to debate the return on Venezuela's large investment in peasant settlements. Critics point out that the Agrarian Reform Institute spent more than $100 million buying private land that it then gave to the peasants without charge. The government has also subsidized the extension of credit to the peasants for farm production. The figures of the Agriculture and Livestock Bank show that in an eight-year period it has ·recovered only half the production loans made to peasants in the agrarian reform program. More than $100 million is outstanding. The peasant settlements have been fairly successful with corn, but their productivity levels in rice, sugar, vegetable oils, poultry, dairy products, and beef cattle have been well below those of private commercial farmers under a successful (and subsidized) program to make Venezuela self-sufficient in food supplies. Critics also argue that the rate of rural migration to Venezuela's booming cities and industrial centers has not slowed measurably since the agrarian reform began.

But the program can be seen in proper perspective only as part of a larger national political decision. The investment in agrarian reform has served to integrate, at least partially, a society in transition, reducing the yawning gap between the very modern, highly capitalized oil sector and a traditional, productively backward agricultural sector. The Venezuelan authorities used a single program both to promote commercial farming and to alleviate rural poverty through a significant investment of domestic resources on behalf of the landless peasant, and thus obviated some of the opposition of the commercial farmers to agrarian reform.

However, with an annual income of well over one billion dollars from oil exports, Venezuela has a singular advantage over nearly all its neighbors. Even Mexico's $700 million net income each year from tourism is not comparable, since it is

The agrarian impasse

not paid directly to the state. Venezuela's oil income provides a steady source of public savings so that the development authorities can invest in agrarian reform without squeezing the necessary funds out of the private sector through taxation. Most Latin American countries do not enjoy this political luxury and must look to other sources of capital for what Venezuela buys with its oil income.

Chile

The governments of poorer and hence more typical Latin American countries than Venezuela encounter serious difficulties in mounting a peaceful agrarian reform effort. For a capital-starved country with narrow financial options, an agrarian reform effort obviously requires diversion of resources from other claimants, who will therefore oppose the project. Resistance is particularly strong if arable land is limited and changes in land-tenure policy may cause food production to falter. This opposition goes deeper than the stereotype of the landlord resisting expropriation of his ancestral domain with its accompanying seigneurial perquisites as W. Arthur Lewis views it: "Of all social classes the most reactionary is the class of great landowners. . . . Nowadays the power of the great landowners has been broken all over the world except in the Middle East and Latin America, and so Latin America is the most politically reactionary of all the continents.[5]

In Latin America today these *hacendados* retain political influence at local levels, but power in the sense of economic leverage has long since passed to urban banking, industry, and government.

The great landlord, as such, is unable to set prices for the produce from his estate, because many urbanized Latin American countries have adopted controlled, low-price food policies designed to please urban consumers. If the landlord's crop is for export, the central bank takes a large part of the foreign exchange he earns at fixed exchange rates to pay for industrial imports. And he usually has to buy farm machinery and fertilizer produced by domestic industrialists behind protective tariff walls at prices well above the world market.

5. W. Arthur Lewis, closing remarks, Conference on Inflation and Growth (mimeographed), Rio de Janeiro, 1963.

The bankers and industrialists of the new elite may be as reactionary as the landlord when it comes to government investment in the peasant, but for different reasons. These reasons usually include low regard for social investment (as opposed to economic development investment) and a general opposition to any new government spending that may lead to higher taxation of the private sector. If the party in power appears to be seeking populist strength through an agrarian reform that will mobilize the peasants politically, elite resistance stiffens. This is what happened in Chile.

President Eduardo Frei came to power in 1964. His party, the Christian Democrats, had offered Chile's nine million people a "revolution in freedom" as an alternative to the platform of the Communist-Socialist Popular Front. This "revolution in freedom" included an agrarian reform that would settle 100,000 peasants on their own land during Frei's six years in office.

In 1965 Chile was reported to have 10.2 million acres of land under cultivation, of which 3.2 million were irrigated lands in the central valley, watered by the melting snows of the Andes. Theodore W. Schultz, professor of agricultural economics at the University of Chicago, has described the Chilean central region as, next to California, "probably the best piece of farm real estate in the world."[6] The central region produces in wheat, corn, potatoes, orchard fruits, grapes, dairy products, cattle, and truck farming about 70 percent of Chile's agricultural output. It is also the center of Chile's agrarian reform dispute, because it consists for the most part of large estates operated by tenants, sharecroppers, or hired laborers who own tiny family plots that the *hacendados* have sold to them to retain a ready supply of cheap labor.

The proponents of land reform say that the system of estates is grossly inefficient, lends itself to exploitation of the rural laborer, and is responsible for a steady rise in Chile's net food imports, which cost $115 million, close to 20 percent of total imports, in 1967. According to Frei, "It is impossible to obtain an increase in production and productivity when the whole basic structure of landholding, credit, and marketing lends

6. Theodore W. Schultz, speaking at the Round Table on Agricultural Development, Inter-American Development Bank, Washington, D.C., 1967.

itself to stagnation and the concentration of income and opportunities in the hands of a few."[7]

The large farm operators respond by pointing to official statistics that show that between 1950 and 1962, production of foodstuffs, aside from beef and milk, increased at a rate of close to 5 percent a year, well above the 3 percent population growth rate. The big farmers say that if the government eliminated consumer-oriented price controls and financed production inputs and new irrigation works adequately, Chilean food production would increase to satisfy demand. They oppose the use of scarce credit to finance agrarian reform for peasants, who, according to the big farmers, are not productive.

When Frei took office an Agrarian Reform Corporation already existed under an earlier law. This law did not satisfy the Christian Democrats, however, because it required cash payment for expropriated land (rather than deferred payment in long-term bonds) and specifically exempted farms of any size that were productively operated. The old law also left the traditional irrigation water rights untouched, and its system of land valuation favored the landlord.

The Christian Democratic agrarian reform law fixed a basic family farm unit of 192 acres of irrigated land; any farm larger than this was subject to expropriation. It provided for payment primarily in twenty-five-year negotiable bonds, partially readjustable against inflation, and it based purchase value on the low valuation traditionally claimed by landlords for land-tax payments. It nationalized all irrigation water.

During the ensuing congressional debate, Minister of Finance Sergio Molina disclosed that under the agrarian reform plan the settlement of 98,000 peasants over a ten-year period would require an investment of more than $1 billion, of which about 10 percent would be for land. Some of the investment would be financed by repayments from the peasants for land credit and improvements over a twenty-five-year span. The rest would require annual budget allocations for the Agrarian Reform Corporation (CORA); thus every year the program would be up for review by a hostile Congress.

It took three years to fight the law through Chile's multiparty

7. Eduardo Frei Montalva, Annual Message to Congress, Santiago, Chile, September 1966.

Congress. Meanwhile, CORA began buying up estates from land-lords willing to sell. With these properties and some government land, CORA managed to form 279 agrarian reform cooperative settlements with 9,313 peasant families by July 1968. It was far behind Frei's scheduled goal of 100,000 families by 1970. Officials began to speak privately of perhaps 40,000 by the end of 1970, and even this estimate seemed too optimistic, as reports circulated that CORA was in deep financial difficulties. Confidential CORA documents appeared indicating peasant failure to make payments on credits advanced, nondelivery of produce by the settlements, and large losses of cattle by death and disappearance. In Venezuela such problems merely provoked criticism. In Chile they became a weapon with which opponents of agrarian reform struck at the heart of the program —future financing.

Another new government agency, the Institute for Agriculture and Livestock Development (INDAP), worked with small farmers and organized rural labor unions. It was in competition with the Marxist-oriented rural unions and an independent Christian rural worker union. Between the three, they organized more than 100,000 rural workers. Under a new law requiring rural collective bargaining, these unions negotiated labor contracts that generally doubled wages in the central region and brought rural wages into line with unskilled urban wages. To the 100,000 rural workers covered by contracts, this change was more significant than the agrarian reform program itself.

INDAP was headed by Jacques Chonchol, a Chilean agricultural economist who had been an adviser to the Cuban Agrarian Reform Institute in 1960–1961. Within the Christian Democratic party he was a leading advocate of mobilizing peasants and the urban poor into a decisive electoral force. The application of this radical line to agrarian reform provoked the organized opposition of farmowners, particularly the medium-sized farmers in the central region and the southern provinces. The National Agrarian Society, representing the big landowners who lived in Santiago and held positions on the boards of directors of banks and industries, had tried to collaborate with Frei in putting through a moderate agrarian reform law. The private farmers who dealt directly with INDAP rural union organizers in the provinces were more hostile.

In the congressional elections in 1969, leading up to the presidential election of 1970, agrarian reform was a major political issue. The Christian Democrats, who had hoped to capitalize on the increased registration and political mobilization of the peasants, suffered defeat at the hands of conservative National party candidates backed by the same propertied, taxpaying rural and urban voters who had backed Frei in 1964 against the Popular Front. Small urban proprietors, shopkeepers, and professionals had apparently become less concerned with rural social reforms than with high taxes and defense of property rights.

The Chilean agrarian reform ran into political complications it might have avoided or reduced if its primary objective had been to promote efficient farm production, regardless of the size of the farm. Such a policy objective would have brought the expropriation and taxation powers of the state to bear against inefficient estates. Price incentives for production would have increased the income of large, efficient farms, but the spread of rural unions and of rural collective bargaining would probably have increased labor's share of this income. Expanded credit and technical assistance to small farmers, coupled with a strong government price-support policy and co-operative marketing, would have raised the income of small holders. Investment in agriculture would thus have helped meet chronic domestic food shortages and promoted exports of seasonal fruits and vegetables, for which Chile has great opportunities.

Some officials of the Ministry of Agriculture and CORA favored this approach. However, the left wing of the Christian Democratic party was committed to breaking the political power base of the traditional commercial agrarian sector, which it blamed for much of Chile's inequitable social structure. This group was therefore hostile to any measures, no matter how economically rational, that might enhance the economic status and political power of the larger commercial estates. The left wing generally regarded ownership of extended acreage, particularly farms run by corporations, as an inherent social evil, and sought to replace it, through the "revolution in freedom," with collective or cooperative forms of farm ownership. The agricultural authorities never fully accepted this ideological position, but the left wing was strong enough to prevent them from publicly announcing which properties were to be expropriated and which exempted. This uncertainty accentuated the hostility of private farmers toward agrarian reform.

The agrarian reform fight gave the U.S. mission in Chile some awkward moments. The ambassador during the first half of the Frei administration was Ralph Dungan, a former White House aide to President Kennedy, who brought to Chile the spirit and ideology of the New Frontier. He did not hesitate to speak out in favor of the goals of social reform inherent in the Alliance for Progress. While the agrarian reform law was being hotly debated, *Ercilla*, Chile's major weekly magazine, published an interview with Dungan in which he said the United States believed in agrarian reform "as an act of humanity." Although he maintained that the program should provide just compensation for expropriated land, he also declared, "The rights of private property are not unlimited."[8] At a dinner party a few months later, a wealthy Chilean said to Dungan, "This country is going communist, and you are to blame."[9]

In fact, Dungan and his AID mission were trying to persuade the Chilean authorities to improve conditions for private commercial farmers. A U.S. advisory mission from California working with the planning staff of the Ministry of Agriculture was urging the government to free agricultural prices from depressing controls that always lagged behind inflation. One purpose of this measure was to help establish incentives for increased use of imported fertilizer, financed by a $3.6 million U.S. loan. The mission believed that through widespread use of fertilizer, Chilean farmers could produce enough food to cut down on food imports, including $40 million a year in U.S. food shipments under Public Law 480.

Price incentives would clearly benefit the peasants who had become producers on their own under the agrarian reform. But the Chilean left interpreted U.S. insistence on price incentives as an attempt to reinforce the position of the conservative landowners, who opposed the agrarian reform program. Moreover, since the Christian Democratic political base was essentially

8. Ralph Dungan, "Reforma agraria sin diplomacia," *Ercilla*, January 5, 1966, pp. 4–5. In the same issue Raúl Cardinal Silva Henríquez, archbishop of Santiago, gave equal backing to the agrarian reform law; his moral authority was enhanced by the fact that only a few weeks earlier the church had turned over its last four rural estates to peasants under a church-sponsored land reform.

9. Interview with Ralph Dungan, Santiago, Chile, September 1966.

urban and higher prices for farmers would raise urban food prices, at least in the short run, opposition to the AID conditions within the Ministry of Agriculture was considerable. The U.S. priorities, perfectly rational from a production standpoint, were impractical in the context of Chilean politics. Yet Chilean politics was not helping to grow more food.

In 1968 U.S. food gifts to Chile were providing school lunches for 800,000 children a day. An estimated 1.9 million persons —one-quarter of Chile's population—were receiving U.S. food aid through voluntary agencies, particularly Caritas. The food grants are a measure of the inadequacies of Chilean production.

Alliance assistance to Chilean agriculture has come, for the most part, from the annual $80 million U.S. program loan, which generates local currency for the Chilean regular budget, which includes investments for agricultural development. A $23 million agricultural-sector loan was signed in 1967.

The most direct Alliance contributions to Chilean agrarian reform have come from the Inter-American Development Bank, which has loaned $10 million to INDAP for a supervised credit program to small farmers and $8 million to CORA to help finance peasant settlements. At the end of 1968 the IDB also authorized a $10 million drought-relief loan to finance small rural public works and irrigation systems, some of which have benefited agrarian reform sites.

Colombia

From the late 1940s to the late 1950s, Colombia was shaken by one of the worst outbreaks of rural violence in its history. During this period, known as *la violencia*, an estimated 100,000 people were killed. *La violencia* was a twilight civil war dispersed through the villages and valleys of this mountainous country with its many tiny farms. The conflict fed on the murderous hatred between Liberal and Conservative party supporters, but underlying this political factionalism was usually a struggle for land. After an episode of violence, the members of the victorious faction would seize or buy cheaply the properties of those killed or driven from the land in terror.

In 1953, in an attempt to halt the bloodshed, General Gustavo Rojas Pinilla took power, but his military dictatorship was not compatible with Colombia's strong tradition of rule by political party. The Colombians ultimately adopted a national coalition system of government, dividing cabinet posts and governor-ships equally between the Liberals and Conservatives, allowing the two parties equal representation in Congress, and establishing a four-year presidency held alternately by a Liberal and a Conservative.

In 1958, when this system was established, Colombia was still in the grip of *la violencia.* Rural bandits terrorized the highways and haciendas. They were organized in guerrilla units of up to two hundred men, and in some areas the effective government was the local bandit chieftain, who sometimes advocated a political position. Some of these chieftains have gained national renown, like the Sicilian bandit-heroes. The most famous of the Colombians, Tirofijo (a *nom de guerre* that means Sureshot), is still being pursued by army counterinsurgency forces and is reported to have visited Cuba in recent years.

Alberto Lleras Camargo, a Liberal, became the first president of the coalition government in 1958. He and most of the Colombian political leadership recognized the urgent need for agrarian reform to pacify the rural areas, where more than half of Colombia's eighteen million people live. A broadly representative national commission drafted the agrarian reform bill, calling for the creation of an agency with strong powers to redistribute land. The bill went to Congress just before the Punta del Este meeting and was enacted in 1962: The man most responsible for the preparation of the law and the organization of the program was Carlos Lleras Restrepo, who became the second Liberal president of the national coalition in 1966.

The Agrarian Reform Institute (INCORA) grew steadily even during the Conservative presidency of Guillermo León Valencia (from 1962 to 1966), despite opposition from Conservative rural interests. Enrique Peñaloza, head of INCORA from its inception, had worked with Lleras Restrepo and was deeply committed to the success of the program. Peñaloza is a lawyer and economist from Bogotá. Although he has no background in agriculture, his remarkable talent for administration and his political acumen deserve much of the credit for INCORA's accomplishments.

An example of Peñaloza's work is the case of Sumapaz, a village of twelve hundred families on an isolated, grassy plateau at an altitude of twelve thousand feet in the central Andean range, about ninety miles from Bogotá. During *la violencia*, Sumapaz became an "independent republic" under the leadership of a Communist, Juan de la Cruz Varela. Peñaloza personally negotiated peace terms with Varela, including grants of land titles to the farmers of Sumapaz and construction of a twenty-mile road from the isolated village to the highway leading to Bogotá. Since then, INCORA has granted more than seven hundred titles, along with supervised credit, and the villagers are working on the road that will carry their potatoes and wool to market in Bogotá. Military patrols now make token visits to Sumapaz without violence. "The most important thing the agrarian reform has accomplished so far is that it has prevented bloodshed," says Peñaloza.[10]

In addition to providing land titles and supervised credit to seventy thousand peasants to date, INCORA is also carrying out seventeen major irrigation projects that will double the number of acres under irrigation. Private land benefited by these projects is automatically subject to expropriation for redistribution. The effect of irrigation on the production value of these lands is dramatic. In one of the project districts in Tolima, two hundred new holders paid off their land debts to INCORA with their first two rice crops. INCORA now has under its control more than a million acres of land suitable for farming, and expects to include close to 200,000 peasants in its production programs by the end of the Lleras Restrepo administration in 1970.

On January 1, 1968, the government issued a major new law under which farms owned by absentee landlords and operated by tenants may be expropriated and turned over to the tenants. The government plans to make sixty thousand tenants into owners of the land they work. The government has also authorized the issuance of $100 million in agrarian reform bonds to finance INCORA's expanded programs. Colombia's new agrarian reform effort is among the most significant yet made in Latin America to break the landlord's hold on peasants.

Since *la violencia*, Colombia's broad public consensus on the need for agrarian reform extends even to the military. The army has suffered thousands of casualties in the long struggle against the bandits and has learned about the acute rural social problem and about local tensions over landownership from di-

---

10. Interview with Enrique Peñaloza, Bogotá, August 1968.

rect experience. It now takes a dim view of proprietors who seek to use force against peasants on their lands. The army high command regularly reports to INCORA any complaint of land invasions or other rural conflicts it receives. If an INCORA investigation finds that the conflict arises out of land-title fights between a large landlord and neighboring peasants, or that tenancy conditions are exploitative, the government will enforce the expropriation or rural labor laws. The Colombian military has developed the relatively sophisticated doctrine that internal security in rural areas requires social justice rather than simple repression.

Peñaloza, who became Colombia's minister of agriculture late in 1968, believed that agrarian reform must be based on sound productive investment. He refused to put INCORA money into projects that seemed unlikely to produce a good rural family income within a few years for the peasants awarded land. Nor did he have the illusion that agrarian reform alone could solve the Colombian rural employment problem. He remarked: "If all the land under cultivation in Colombia now were divided up into lots big enough to give a peasant family an annual income of six hundred dollars, this would accommodate one million, two hundred thousand families. By the time we were finished, there would be another million families without land." Peñaloza believed Colombia could eliminate chronic unemployment only through diversified economic development, including expansion of industry and mining, combined with agrarian reform and effective birth control.

Colombia has been fairly successful in attracting external financing under the Alliance for its agrarian program. INCORA and other agricultural agencies have obtained about $40 million in USAID funds for supervised credit to small farmers, cattle development, and technical assistance from the University of Nebraska. The IDB has made six loans totaling more than $40 million for irrigation, farm machinery imports, crop diversification, and supervised credit.

Brazil

In the mid-1960s the U.S. government became seriously concerned about agriculture in the developing countries. Lester Brown's landmark study, *Man, Land, and Food*, appearing in 1963, had shown that U.S. surplus food production would soon be inadequate to make up the food deficits of other nations. Soaring population in southeast Asia and Africa was outstripping food production, and dramatic increases in agricultural productivity were urgently needed in all the developing countries.

In April 1966 Secretary of Agriculture Orville Freeman paid an official visit to Brazil to examine the state of its agriculture and to impress on its officials the need for international cooperation to meet the food demands of the swiftly expanding world population. Brazil has more than a million square miles of arable land. It has also been undergoing a very rapid increase in population, but a combination of good commercial farms in the south and gradual extension of the farming area in less fertile regions has kept food production ahead of demand. Freeman wanted to find out how much Brazil could increase its exports, particularly in corn, rice, and beef cattle.

The U.S. Department of Agriculture had assigned to Brazil twenty-one technicians on marketing, pricing, credit, and resource surveys, the largest agricultural-sector mission of any U.S. aid team in the world. Under U.S.-financed contracts, three Brazilian universities were overhauling their agricultural schools with assistance from American universities such as Purdue, which sent teams of faculty members to teach at Brazilian universities and accepted Brazilian graduate students who would eventually form the faculties of modernized agricultural schools in Brazil. The United States also financed soil and plant research centers in São Paulo, Brasília, and the Northeast. The agriculture mission did not, however, include a rural sociologist, a specialist in small-farm management, or any other personnel who might have contributed ideas on land tenure and the income situation of the peasants to U.S. government discussions of agriculture in Brazil.

Brazil is one of fifteen Latin American countries listed by the Alliance for Progress as having adopted agrarian reform laws and established agrarian reform agencies. Under the government of President Goulart (who owned five big cattle ranches) the Ministry of Agriculture made a serious effort to formulate an agrarian reform plan. But the more radical sectors of the government, primarily urban labor leaders and intellectuals, took over this project and tried to enforce a law authorizing expropriation of farmlands on either side of new highways. Their efforts served only to generate support among rural conservatives for the military opposition that ultimately toppled Goulart.

The military government of President Castelo Branco set up an agrarian reform agency (IBRA) that spent two years carrying out a cadastral survey. The survey showed that Brazil contained more than three million farm properties, of which two-thirds were subsistence plots so badly managed that erosion was spreading across the country. The purpose of the survey was to justify enactment of a tax law penalizing large, badly exploited farms, but the taxation system subsequently adopted has generated smaller revenues than the landowners had been paying to the municipalities before its enactment. Although the government has started a handful of colonization projects, it has made no serious attempt to expropriate land or carry out an agrarian reform in the areas where densely concentrated subsistence farms and landless peasants are major problems.

One such area is the sugarcane zone of the Northeast. On this stretch of heavily populated coastal land more than forty sugar mills and their surrounding plantations provide a livelihood for some 250,000 people. This region, around the port city of Recife, is where the Portuguese and Dutch installed the plantations that brought the first African slaves to Brazil. The inhabitants have been growing sugar there for nearly four hundred years. The big sugar factories installed in the early decades of this century served in their time to modernize the backward Northeast. During the worldwide depression, however, sugar prices collapsed. After World War II, many of the sugar-mill and plantation owners began investing heavily in more lucrative industrial and construction projects in the south of Brazil. With few exceptions, the sugar mills are now inefficient. Agricultural practice is very wasteful of land, steadily extending sugarcane acreage to make up for low productivity. The whole system is based on the availability of cheap labor.

All the sugar that the United States buys from Brazil, about 400,000 tons a year, comes from the Northeast. Under the U.S. Sugar Act, the United States buys its Brazilian quota at a preferential price of more than six cents a pound (the world free-market price is two and a half cents). Brazil uses part of this bonus to subsidize the Northeast sugar industry, which has much higher production costs than does São Paulo's more modern sugar industry. Thus, in effect, the Northeast sugar economy survives in its present form on a U.S. subsidy.

The Northeast is the scene of the peasant unrest that inspired President Kennedy's concern in 1961. Freeman visited it during his 1966 tour of Brazil. In the interim, the military regime had found its own solutions for the region's problems. The government had jailed and then exiled Governor Miguel Arraes of Pernambuco, who had enforced minimum-wage laws in the rural areas. It had fired Celso Furtado from his post as head of the Northeast Development Agency; he left Brazil to teach in the United States and France. The regime had dispersed the Peasant Leagues, and their leader, Francisco Julião, had fled to Mexico. By 1966 the conservative businessmen and landowners were resting more easily. And the peasants of the sugarcane zone and the tenants of the cotton and produce farms continued to subsist in poverty, disease, and ignorance.

In a cool, tiled mansion, as servants in white jackets served tropical fruit drinks, Freeman met with Guillermo Martins and other members of the old Pernambuco family that owns the Catende sugar mill and plantation. This property occupies 25,000 acres at the outskirts of Recife, a city of a million people, where undeveloped land sells for more than $100 an acre. Mr. Martins and his brother-in-law, an army colonel and former head of the Pernambuco state police, lamented to Mr. Freeman that sugar was not a good business and that they barely broke even on the operation. Freeman tried without success to find out from them how much it cost to produce a pound of sugar at Catende. They seemed puzzled at this question, and the most he could determine was that the Brazilian government adjusted its subsidy to cover whatever costs the mill owners said had gone into producing the sugar. "It sounds to me as though everyone in sugar should be getting rich," said Freeman.

At the dilapidated mill and on the dirt roads leading through the fields of green cane, Freeman stopped to talk with workers and tenant farmers. One worker, a mechanic at the mill for six years, said that he earned $7 a week, on which he supported a wife and four children. He said he didn't send the children to school because he couldn't afford to buy the required uniforms. Mr. Martins said the sugar company didn't make enough money to provide the uniforms.

Freeman also met a peasant who rented five acres of land for

$25 a year. Tilling his plot and cutting cane, he maintained a family of ten children. He said he grew cassava, oranges, and coconuts for the market, in addition to the food crops he kept for family needs. He added that he and his sons could work three times as much land if it could be had, but that no land was available where he lived "at prices a poor man can pay." He had never received any credit from a bank, nor had he ever seen an extension agent. Ants destroyed much of his crops, but he said he could not afford to buy insecticides. Freeman came away from his day on the sugar plantation feeling "quite disturbed."[11]

At the same time, the USAID regional office for the Northeast and Brazilian officials were discussing an agrarian reform plan for the sugar zone. A U.S.-financed study by a firm of consultants, Hawaiian Agronomics, showed that the Northeast could produce its annual·900,000 tons of sugar at lower costs on half the land by means of intensive cultivation and proper investment in farm mechanization, transportation, irrigation, and mill improvements. The study sought not only to increase agricultural productivity but also to mitigate the desperate poverty of the peasants. U.S. and Brazilian technicians in the Northeast drew up a plan for a sugar rehabilitation program under which land released from sugar could become small family farms for tenants and landless peasants, producing food, poultry, and dairy products for better paid sugar workers and for Recife's urban markets. The plantations were to contribute the land to the agrarian reform agency in return for financing for modernization of sugar production. Estimating that the sugar plan might displace 100,000 peasants and their families, the planners suggested a large parallel social investment program that would provide literacy courses and vocational training to prepare peasants for industrial jobs, and employ others in public works projects in the region. The study proposed an initial three-year effort at a cost of $160 million, to be financed half by USAID and half by Brazil.

The plan never got beyond the drawing board. The plantation owners refused to give up any of their land voluntarily. Brazilian federal officials were unable to agree on the organization of the strong executive agency needed to coordinate a complex

11. Interviews with Orville Freeman, Recife and São Paulo, April 1966.

program involving heavy expenditures in agriculture, education, public works, and community development. And U.S. officials did not really push the Brazilian authorities to accept the program. The United States could, for example, have applied leverage through the sugar quota, withholding the full preferential price for sugar imports unless Brazil undertook an effective agrarian reform in the sugar zone. Or it could have tied program-loan disbursements to implementation of an effective agrarian reform. It did neither.

As the U.S. Congress reduced Alliance for Progress funds, USAID officials gradually found themselves unable even to consider financing on the scale required for agrarian reform in the Northeast sugar region. And left to their own inclinations, the Brazilian authorities chose to handle the peasant problem in the Northeast through political repression rather than agrarian reform.

The purpose of agrarian reform

The Alliance for Progress was to bring about agrarian reform, but political vacillation by some countries, outright desertion by others, and shifting priorities in the United States have delayed the integration of the rural masses into Latin American society. Since its establishment the IDB has made agricultural development loans in nearly every Latin American country, totaling more than $600 million, of which the primary source is the bank's "soft loan" Fund for Special Operations, maintained by government contributions. (The United States has provided about 65 percent of the $1.5 billion allotted to this fund.) The bank is thus participating in a variety of programs to build local institutions for agrarian reform and rural development. The Mexican agricultural agencies and the Colombian Agrarian Reform Institute have established successful programs in supervised credit, research, extension, and irrigation for the benefit of small farmers. These successes have additional value as examples of what other developing countries can accomplish.

During the period of the Alliance, however, U.S. government and inter-American development agency officials have come to construe agriculture as the "farm problem" rather than the "peasant problem." The Kennedy administration's political emphasis on changes in land tenure to prevent violent agrarian upheavals has given way to an economic emphasis on expansion of agricultural production to feed a rapidly multiplying population. The development of modern agriculture is clearly a prime necessity, not only to increase production of food, but to raise Latin America's agricultural exports; but if food production takes precedence over integrating the peasant into the social fabric of these modern nations, the modernization of agriculture itself may give rise to new and destructive political conflicts. Clifton R. Wharton, Jr., former director of the Agricultural Development Council of the Rockefeller Foundation, has articulated this problem:

Among the farmers of any developing country, there are already existing differential levels of development. There are always a few farmers who are technologically advanced, highly profit oriented, and relatively well to do; and then there are the masses who are quite poor and living at the threshold of subsistence.

The governments of these nations have limited capital and human resources. Given the race between food and population, the governments face the following alternatives which pose a serious dilemma in the use of these limited resources. Either they can invest in the "growth points" in the economy, the more responsive farmers who will produce the food, and meet the race. But if they invest in the more responsive area, they are immediately faced with the fact that they are increasing the maldistribution of income because the "growth points" are the better farmers. Increased maldistribution of income leads immediately to the increased possibility of political instability among the poorer, more numerous farmers because only the richer farmers are growing and being aided.

On the other hand, if the governments invest in the slower growing points or not as much in the advanced growing points, they may lose the race between food and population because per capita incomes will go down. Then, again, the government will face a problem of political instability due to reduced incomes and food availability.[12]

Because of the particularly sharp inequalities of landownership in many Latin American countries, agricultural modernization may well add to the insecurity of the marginal peasant. The few farmers who own the sizable tracts of fertile, well-watered land and have an established position in the market will flourish as new resources and technology modify the traditional agriculture. Even the middle farmers may greatly increase production and force the peasant out of his marginal position in the market. This process, accompanied by advances in farm mechanization, forces tenants to become agri-

---

12. Clifton R. Wharton, paper submitted to conference on "The World Food Problem: Private Investment and Government Cooperation," New York, April 12–13, 1967.

cultural laborers competing for work with the landless peasants. Overall rural income increases, but the income gap widens between the larger farmers and the peasants.

There is no easy way out of this dilemma. Many Latin American countries simply do not have enough land to provide a productive family unit for every peasant. Even Venezuela, with its ambitious, socially oriented agrarian reform, has not stemmed the flow of rural migrants to the cities in search of better income opportunities and the amenities of modern life.

The solution obviously involves a clear distinction between the economic and social purposes of agrarian reform, and simultaneous funding for both. This distinction involves the willingness to make social investments in subsistence farmers which are just not "bankable." The organization of a small peasant cooperative may require outlays of capital and personnel that will never be recovered. But without technical and marketing assistance, the peasants would be unable to obtain or fulfill a production contract with, for example, a fruit packer or vegetable canning plant. This business would go instead to large farm operators working with tenants or hired laborers. Each nation must thus make a political decision to bring the peasants into the national community, the commonwealth; some Latin American countries find this decision difficult to reach. The countries that do reach it and develop public institutions to deal with the peasant problem need international financing on very flexible terms to support domestic efforts.

The development of these public institutions involves issues far beyond those of farm productivity and income distribution. For instance, birth rates in rural areas are extremely high. Moreover, the literate urban populations of Latin America have far greater access to birth control information and contraceptives than do the isolated, illiterate peasants. But a government cannot expect to bring effective family planning to rural areas without ending its overall abandonment of the peasants and supplying them with functional public institutions providing other useful services. An agrarian reform institute, coupled with a rural public health service, is the logical agency to channel to the peasants the birth control information and materials already available to Latin America's middle classes.

In Venezuela, Colombia, and Chile, the parties in power have undertaken agrarian reform because they considered it essential to achieve a more equitable society by moderate means. In Venezuela extraordinary oil revenues have carried this program forward without excessive political stress. In Colombia, *la violencia* has created a national consensus in favor of agrarian reform. The program has, however, encountered significant resistance in Chile, which has had neither the extraordinary resource base with which Venezuela is blessed nor the national trauma from which Colombia has suffered.

If the program planners in these three countries had seen agrarian reform in strictly technical terms, seeking only to achieve higher production values, none of the programs would have achieved their present momentum. This statement is not intended to suggest that agrarian reform is antithetical to increases in production. The entire debate within the development community as to whether agrarian reform is conducive to or destructive of short-term production gains misses the point. Agrarian reform must be seen as a means to the ends of social justice and political viability, within a larger context to which short-term economic efficiency is also relevant but not necessarily decisive.

Agrarian reform and social integration

The strategy of an effective agrarian reform must combine an improvement in rural income distribution, based on efficient production, with a manpower utilization policy that accepts as inevitable the displacement of many families now barely subsisting on the land, and is prepared to invest in their welfare and training for employment.

Through agricultural modernization Latin America can increase its production of food and raw materials and thus not only meet the rising demands of domestic consumption but also export more of the agricultural products in which the region enjoys some competitive advantage. And to the extent that agrarian reform increases the overall income of the rural sector, the program's political acceptability also increases.

Agrarian reform must also deal with the extraordinary level of disguised unemployment in rural areas. Perhaps ten million landless laborers and peasants on dwarf holdings in Latin America are marginal to the market economy and modern society. With their families, they represent some sixty million people, a quarter of the Latin American population. These

The agrarian impasse

agricultural workers need a level of income on which their families can live in communities that provide at least public education and health services.

The road to achievement of these two goals is not drastic land redistribution on the model of what in the United States has been called forty acres and a mule, and in Latin America is more likely to be ten acres and a hoe; unskilled peasants given minimum-sized family plots to work will only slightly improve their own income position and almost certainly will be unable to increase production of food and raw materials for the market.

Some countries simply have nowhere near enough arable land to supply every peasant who is a candidate for land with a family farm that could provide an acceptable income for a skilled owner-operator. In other countries that have abundant undeveloped land, the economic and social costs of colonization, weighed against prospects for marketable production, are prohibitively high. Unless its object is to create subsistence farms in the wilderness, colonization of these lands is, with a few exceptions, impractical.

Therefore, unless Latin America abandons private ownership oriented to a competitive market for centrally planned economies based on state ownership, its agrarian reform strategy requires, as a start, the establishment of realistic profit incentives for farmers. Without these incentives, farmers, large or small, will not make use of credit and the variety of purchased inputs, from fertilizer to marketing services, that are necessary to increase production and distribution by modern methods. But the relatively few large farmers will receive most of the income gains arising from agricultural modernization unless the public authorities provide for more equitable distribution of income among rural producers. A technically oriented program of land-tenure changes can serve this purpose by making tenant farmers the owners of the land they now work or by making land available to peasants who have a demonstrable capability for market production. Equally necessary for this purpose is effective enforcement of rural labor laws to maintain minimum wage standards for agricultural workers similar to those in industrialized urban areas.

The large farmer still has a natural advantage over the small farmer and peasant settled on land through expropriation or colonization. An effective program must place the small farmer in a competitive position from which he has access to a fair share of the increased rural income. Agrarian reform institutes must therefore have independent control of a large share of rural credit so that they can extend credit and technical assistance and set up cooperative arrangements to provide machinery, inputs, and marketing services to small producers.

Agricultural modernization will certainly give an added push to rural migration. This migration will continue, in any case, while the disequilibrium in income between the cities and the countryside remains pronounced. It may be modified by transfers of public funds to the rural areas, but not reversed. Moreover, as rational land use and investment make some farms more productive, the marginal producers will be squeezed out of their precarious positions and some peasants will be forced to seek nonfarm jobs.

But an effective program can turn the rural outflow to more productive purposes than it has so far served. It can, for example, promote the installation in rural areas, or in smaller towns, of industrial plants to process food and agricultural raw materials. This approach would require specialized development financing and social investment in literacy and vocational training to prepare the sons and daughters of peasant families for industrial and office jobs. A successful town development program would increase rural income opportunities for some of the rural people who would otherwise migrate to the cities. Public works programs could also employ part of the rural labor force to build farm-to-market roads and other construction projects in provincial towns. In this capacity peasants would be more productive than they can be now as surplus labor on inefficient farms.

A serious agrarian reform effort thus goes beyond the farm, land, and food problem, because only a national economic and social integration program can deal with these issues effectively. The great shift of Latin America's population from a rural to an urban base has transferred many of the countryside's poverty problems to the cities. Improved communications and transportation have broken the dikes that have contained the traditional rural society and have generated mobility toward the urban centers of income. But the flow exceeds the present capability of the cities to provide urban services and employment opportunities, and soaring population intensifies the pressing demands for education, health care, and new jobs.

Today many agencies of public administration, from agrarian reform institutes to economic development banks and municipal housing boards, are attempting to deal with this problem. The quality of these agencies varies greatly, but in general they work independently, without coordination or an institutionalized perspective on the fundamental problem of a mobile population. Each Latin American country might consider establishing a presidential-level national integration council to develop a dynamic overall policy on the problems of transition. Such a council could have both public and private representation and make political decisions to guide the national planning authorities and the agencies.

The success of this integrated approach in a Latin American country that is ready to implement it may depend on substantial and timely transfers of external resources. The IDB and World Bank are moving in this direction through loans for supervised credit, irrigation, colonization, and rural community development, but these efforts are largely diffuse and not sufficiently articulated within national integration programs. USAID's agricultural-sector loans are oriented basically toward production and not toward the population shift, which is the key social problem of agrarian reform. This shift involves millions of peasant families. It is complex and expensive. By conventional lending standards, the improvement of rural manpower utilization is not a sound investment; that sort of thing requires concessional long-term loans or grants. This money has not been available. The cost of continuing to skirt the problem, however, is the sacrifice of another, more numerous generation of marginal peasants to miserable lives outside the modern community. The Alliance cannot survive such a failure.

Peru

A national commitment to bring the peasant into the commonwealth seems to require both a certain amount of prior stress and a general acceptance of change in the society as a whole. It is no accident that the Peruvian military junta has given high priority to agrarian reform. The junta has sought to justify its seizure of power by pointing out the overriding need for structural reform in Peruvian society. To remain in power it had to identify itself with an issue that would support this justification, capture the Peruvian imagination, and thus provide itself with a politically viable popular base. That issue was agrarian reform. During the Belaúnde administration the United States was, of course, prevented by the IPC dispute from providing extensive assistance to Peru. But on the few occasions when it could consider such assistance, the U.S. government chose not to support Belaúnde's proposed agrarian reform program, which, although inadequate, did represent a serious effort, the first in Peruvian history.

The Peruvian decree of June 24, 1969, affected not only Peruvian land but U.S. landholders as well. The first expropriations were the lush sugar lands on the coast, among whose owners was W. R. Grace and Company. In taking this action the Peruvian junta dramatically raised the issue of agrarian reform in the hemisphere and once again emphasized its essentially social and political imperative. One cannot help wondering whether things might have been different for Belaúnde and Frei, and Peru and Chile, if the United States had recognized that imperative earlier.

The urban revolution

Latin America, traditionally associated
with rural influences, will definitively
and irreversibly be a predominantly
urban region. We must agree that
in great measure the solutions to be
provided for the development problems
of Latin America will have to
be urban solutions.
Felipe Herrera, 1966

13.

The most vivid and socially dynamic form of marginal living in Latin America is the urban squatter settlement. Nearly every major city has a profusion of shantytowns alongside its modern, high-rise buildings and gracious residential neighborhoods.

The shanties begin where the pavement ends. They cluster beyond the water mains, streets, power lines, telephone wires, public schools, and municipal hospitals that bind together the urban core. The invaders move in along the railroad tracks and beside city dumps, where they pick over the refuse for paper, metal, and other salable scrap. They build on steep hillsides or along river beds that have been condemned as unsafe or unhealthy for habitation. At the edges of the swiftly expanding cities they occupy vacant areas between the corn and cotton fields or around the old sugar plantations that have become more valuable for urban real estate speculation than for farming.

The shanties represent a desperate effort by the marginal poor to gain a foothold in the modern social order of Latin America.

Their struggle for living space and economic opportunity in the cities has moments of violence and heroism.

When the squatters move in, the first shacks go up with stunning speed, often overnight. They use the cheapest materials at hand: bamboo, straw mats, wattle, tarpaper, old boards, rusty tin. The construction may look haphazard, but the squatters are usually following a plan. They help each other stake out lots of equal size. If the terrain permits, they lay out future street space. Often, as soon as their miserable dwellings go up, they set small national flags flying bravely from the rooftops.

Once entrenched, men, women, and children together will fight and hold their ground against the police or the hired guards sent by the landowners to drive them off. Once their territory is secured, they build for greater permanence with stone, adobe, wooden frames, and cement. They have then moved in for good.

With their bizarre patchwork of building materials and harlequin house fronts, the shantytowns appear both picturesque and pathetic, like a hobo's garb pulled from a gentleman's trash can. But these settlements are at the center of an urban revolution that is changing the lives of millions of people, of both urban and rural origin. In some metropolitan areas, such as Rio de Janeiro and Lima, squatter settlements hold close to 25 percent of the population, and the figure is rising.

The urban population explosion

In no other region of the world has the rural-to-urban population shift been so great or the growth of city populations through high urban birth rates so rapid as in Latin America.

Using towns of 2,000 or more people as a benchmark for urbanization, ECLA has found that in 1950, when Latin America had a population of 156 million, 39 percent (61 million people) were city dwellers. In 1960, when the population was 200 million, the urban component had risen to 46 percent (95 million people). ECLA's projected figures indicate that in 1975, of 291 million Latin Americans, 54 percent will be city dwellers. In Argentina, Uruguay, Chile, and southern Brazil, where industrialization and urban concentration have been going forward together for several decades, the urban proportion already exceeds 70 percent.

The ECLA study shows that during the decade between 1950 and 1960, the urban growth rate was 55 percent, with many large cities growing 6 to 7 percent a year, while the rural population rose only 12 percent during the entire period. The average annual growth rate was 4.5 percent for the cities, 1.6 percent for the rural areas, and thus about 3 percent for the region as a whole. These figures mean that half the population increment in the rural areas has been migrating to the cities.[1]

The squatters are part of a historic process that involves population growth, rural migration, urban expansion, industrialization, and the spread of information that stimulates aspirations for new job opportunities, education, and political representation.

The population of Caracas, the capital of Venezuela, has nearly doubled during the past ten years and now approaches two million. This opulent city, filled with modern high-rise apartment buildings and traversed by expressways, occupies a long valley where real estate sells for $10 to $50 a square foot. But the hillsides are studded with shantytown *ranchos* that have served as reception camps for migrants coming in from the countryside in search of city work.

Many migrants have left the land given them under Venezuela's substantial agrarian reform program to become peddlers or taxi drivers in the city. The law forbids an agrarian reform beneficiary to sell his lot, but he can easily work out clandestine payment arrangements with neighboring farmers who want more land. Despite Venezuela's expensive investment in agrarian reform, the rural population is attracted to the disproportionate share of national income retained by the cities.

Some semiskilled rural migrants find urban employment at union-regulated wages in construction or industry, and a bit of the urban wealth filters down to those who become gardeners, laundresses, garbage collectors, pushcart vendors, junk collectors, and minstrels. The cities also offer career opportunities for what the Caracas newspapers call "antisocial" elements—professional beggars, prostitutes, and specialized petty thieves who make a living by stealing and selling automobile

---

1. United Nations Economic Commission for Latin America, *Social Change and Social Development Policy in Latin America*, E/CN 12/826 (February 1969), p. 34.

hubcaps and windshield wipers. This group in turn creates jobs for parking-lot attendants and car watchers. Such are the sources of urban income for which most migrants have fled from the farms. In the diversity of the city, the migrants find at least the illusion of greater financial opportunities, along with access to social advantages not available in the country, from first-aid clinics to movie theaters. But the newcomers to the city, or those who seek relief from slum rent sharks by creating shantytown communities, remain politically, economically, and socially marginal to the organized urban structures.

The urban crucible

The crisis of urban growth affects, above all, the metropolitan conglomerates—Mexico City, Bogotá, Caracas, Lima, Rio de Janeiro, São Paulo, Santiago, and Buenos Aires—that function as command posts for their nations or regions of influence. These cities are the seats of administrative, economic, and military institutions that wield power. They also contain the major universities and attract most of the creative intellectuals. Through their control of the communications media, which propagate news, commercial propaganda, and cultural innovation, they begin to urbanize awareness and taste in the outlying regions even before the migrants set out for the city. In the depths of the Amazon, Caiapo Indians, their bodies and faces painted crimson and black with vegetable dyes, have transistor radios and listen with rapt attention to a Beatles record being broadcast by a São Paulo radio station, 1,200 miles to the south.

Planned city growth is the result of major decisions made by the ruling sectors of a nation. Many of these decisions are financial and technical, but as in all aspects of Latin American development, the basic decision is political; it determines the place of the marginal poor in the community.

In these great cities of Latin America the confrontation of the incorporated and the marginal sectors of society engenders urban political attitudes with national implications. These attitudes, whether radical and innovative or conservative and repressive, will have a decisive influence on Latin American political development. For the urban problem consists of the alienation of a segment of the population whose frustrations have an increasing potential for political instability.

Bricks and mortar

The Charter of Punta del Este sought "to increase the construction of low-cost houses for low-income families in order to replace inadequate and deficient houses and to reduce housing shortages; and to provide necessary public services to both urban and rural centers of population."

When the Alliance began, most Latin American capitals already could display several generations of public housing projects going back to the 1930s, when social security first came to the region, inspired by either Mussolini or the New Deal. Most of the countries also had institutions that were nominally designed to finance low-cost housing. In fact, their loans went mainly to the white-collar government employees or upper tier of organized labor, such as bank clerks, who had considerably more political leverage with the housing institutions than the unorganized poor. The soaring inflation of the period immediately before the Alliance gutted many of these institutions financially. Housing assistance under the Alliance consisted initially of revitalizing the public housing institutions with massive transfusions of very long-term, low-interest capital.

In the first years of the Alliance, construction of low-cost units was the easiest type of social investment, with both visible impact and a quick stimulating effect on employment. The first big loan of the Alliance, announced three days after the Punta del Este meeting, was a $7.6 million housing loan to Panama, followed within a few weeks by housing loans of $22.8 million to Peru and $15.2 million to Colombia. Between 1961 and 1965 the IDB made housing loans in fourteen countries, devoting more than 40 percent of the Social Progress Trust Fund to investments in low-cost housing projects. USAID and the IDB made loans totaling close to $500 million to finance the building of about 500,000 small houses. USAID provided housing investment guarantees covering $450 million in U.S. private investment to turn out 90,000 units of middle-income housing. In many cities of Latin America the hand-clasp symbol of the Alliance stood before row on row of new little brick or cement houses occupied by families selected for need. Official U.S. visitors who went to see what the Alliance had accomplished in Latin America were often taken to see future homeowners working in cooperative self-help teams to dig foundations and raise walls for houses built with U.S. aid. U.S.-

financed central funds provided backing for savings and loan associations, and the volume of savings by aspirants to home-ownership rose dramatically. Through this financial system thousands of thrifty families of modest income could obtain the long-term credit to purchase a home of their own. In Peru alone the savings and loan associations, known as *mutuales*, rapidly attracted deposits of more than $10 million.[2]

USAID country missions, particularly those with large local-currency balances on hand from U.S. PL 480 commodity sales, took a crash-program approach to housing projects. Ciudad Kennedy, a satellite city of Bogotá, for which President Kennedy laid the cornerstone during his visit to Colombia in December 1961, was constructed in a few months. This community now holds more than 200,000 people. But until 1969, when Bogotá's mayor acquired a fleet of Soviet buses to serve Ciudad Kennedy, the residents suffered acute transportation problems for lack of planning of access roads and bus routes to the new community to go along with the houses.

Governor Carlos Lacerda of Guanabara, an ebullient politician with presidential ambitions in those days, ordered the eradication of some shantytowns in the heart of Rio de Janeiro. He planned to relocate the occupants in two housing projects, Villa Alianza and Villa Kennedy, far on the outskirts of Rio, financed by counterpart funds from U.S. wheat sales accumulated in Brazil, in a model program of slum clearance and community development. The eradication of the shanties actually brought more satisfaction to luxury apartment owners, who got rid of unwanted neighbors, and to real estate developers interested in the cleared properties, than to the uprooted shantytown dwellers. In the next election Lacerda's opponents capitalized on the discontent of the transplanted families over the lack of employment opportunities near the new housing sites. The bus fare for the round trip to the city, where many kept their old jobs as domestic help or peddlers, cost one quarter of the average family's monthly income.

In Lima, Peru, the same problems led to public protests by

---

2. Labor-union housing cooperatives also received Alliance financing. AFL-CIO teams in Latin America tried to work out housing projects organized in cooperation with local unions and financed by U.S. union pension funds. Except in Venezuela, however, this program has had only limited success, because of administrative weaknesses, union politics, and regulations that require relatively high interest rates.

the new occupants and legislative investigations of the satellite-city project launched by Premier Pedro Beltrán, a presidential aspirant in late 1961; his model community, called Ventanilla, was fifteen miles from the capital in the middle of a sandy desert.

By 1965 these adverse public reactions to new Alliance projects had inspired a critical reassessment of the crash-program approach, and the sobering realization that it was barely making a dent in the squatter problem.

In 1965 the IDB estimated that the shortage of decent housing in Latin America amounted to fourteen million dwellings. The bank's experts calculated that Latin America needed 300,000 new houses each year just to keep pace with the growth in the number of families seeking dwelling space.[3] External financing of housing construction under the Alliance has produced about 100,000 units a year during the past decade. Information on licensed domestic housing construction in Latin America is sketchy, but it does not suggest that the number of new houses reaches 300,000 a year. The IDB based its estimate on conventional U.S. concepts of housing, using standards and quality specifications for building materials, design, space, sanitary facilities, and public services that are simply unrealistic in view of the income levels of the poor majorities in Latin America. So defined, the housing problem is insoluble, and has undoubtedly worsened during the period of the Alliance.

The Alliance approach to housing primarily utilized government-administered low-cost housing development projects and the new decentralized government-guaranteed savings and loan associations, which finance housing construction initiated by individuals or cooperatives. This approach is based on the experience of the U.S. and western European countries, which of course enjoy much higher levels of income and savings than Latin America. In Latin America, these programs have helped to solve the problems of salaried people with stable jobs. The Alliance has done very little for squatters or slum dwellers.

The average unit of low-cost housing under the Alliance has cost between $1,500 and $2,000. A contract in this amount

---

3. *El BID y la vivienda* (Washington, D.C.: Inter-American Development Bank, 1965).

represents a financial commitment that many squatter families, unfamiliar with long-term credit operations, are unwilling to assume. Payments of $10 to $15 a month are technically within the means of even an unskilled wage earner if he is regularly employed, as many of the new homeowners are. But the public housing institutions have encountered very high levels of evasion from the occupants of low-cost housing, with arrears in some projects amounting to 50 percent. Delays in recovering investment have badly weakened the ability of these institutions to make new housing starts. The institutions were not prepared for the special problems and responsibilities involved in effective expansion of low-cost housing, both in administration and in social work necessary to adapt the squatter or migrant to public housing conditions. A number of the public housing institutions, particularly in Brazil and Colombia, have made administrative improvements and manage their resources more effectively now than they did during the early days of the Alliance. But these measures still do not meet Latin America's need for policies that come to grips with urban problems and the visible proliferation of squatter communities.

The Alliance has approached urban housing as production of units, rather than as development of the urban community. As one former USAID official put it, "We turned the job of social integration over to brick-and-mortar people."

The magnitude and nature of urban growth in Latin America make it impossible, according to any realistic estimate of available domestic and foreign resources, to provide a home for every poor family. However, some rather radical changes in attitudes toward squatters, urban land use, real estate taxation, city planning, and integrated economic and social investments in metropolitan areas can make Latin American cities function better as social institutions for bringing people into the modern industrial society.

Urban planning

In April 1966 a Washington consulting firm, Regional and Urban Planning Implementation, Inc. (RUPI), hired to review the Alliance housing program and make policy recommendations on urban problems, turned in its report to AID in Washington. According to RUPI, without effective steps toward more orderly urbanization, Latin America's major cities would give rise

to political tensions in an exorbitant degree. Urban masses crowded into intolerable environments . . . are politically more volatile than a discontented rural population. . . . The critical point for political explosions among the urban poor is much lower than among the rural poor, even though the latter are often in point of fact still poorer.[4]

The report recommended that USAID finance comprehensive metropolitan-area development plans in Mexico City and Lima, not only to coordinate the efforts of public and private housing bodies, but also to draw the citizens of the community, individually and through private organizations, into orderly participation in the growth of the cities.

On the basis of the RUPI report, USAID in Washington sent out instructions to field missions encouraging attention to urban community problems and consultations with local authorities on metropolitan development. These instructions caused particular excitement in the U.S. mission in Rio de Janeiro.[5] In January 1966 torrential rains had produced disaster in Rio's shantytowns. Rockslides had thundered through hillside settlements and floods had inundated the squatter districts beside low-lying canals and mud flats. More than four hundred people were killed and tens of thousands were homeless. This calamity had awakened the well-to-do sectors of the population to the death, disease, and poverty in their midst, and they had responded generously.

Food, clothing, and medicines poured in from voluntary contributors. Socially prominent women ferried mud-caked evacuees in their automobiles and operated food kitchens in their homes. Teenage daughters of wealthy families bathed and fed infants of shantytown mothers. In the emergency, people of all

4. Regional and Urban Planning Implementation, Inc., "Urban Development in Peru" (Washington, D.C., April 30, 1966), pp. 3–4. The report was drafted by Charles Haar, who was about to become assistant secretary of the new Department of Housing and Urban Development.

5. According to a Brazilian urban development study, in 1965 the population of Rio de Janeiro was 3.8 million and that of the metropolitan area 5.7 million; projected population in the year 2000 is 8.4 million in the city and 18 million in the metropolitan area. The study also estimates that public services and community development to accommodate this growth, including construction of 470,000 low-cost housing units, would require an investment of $7 billion. See *Guanabara: A Plan for Urban Development* (Rio de Janeiro: Constantine Doxiades Associates, November 1965), pp. v–vi.

classes acted as a community. When the emergency subsided, city life returned to its old social compartments, but a residue of political concern for the shantytowns remained.

A few months later, a USAID consultant team arrived in Brazil, led by Bernard Wagner (who later became a USAID housing adviser in Vietnam). The team found some interest among the young economic planners of the Guanabara state administration in a metropolitan development authority for Rio, embracing not only housing but transportation, industrial promotion, and land-use control. The planners were also receptive to the fresh approach of rehabilitating or upgrading existing squatter settlements, rather than trying to eradicate them and push the squatters out of the city. The team accepted the estimate of Anthony Leeds (an anthropologist at the University of Texas who has studied Rio's squatter settlements for years) that the investment in housing, stores, community facilities, and other improvements made by the squatters was worth at least $50 million, which would be lost through eradication. The mission recommended a $4.9 million USAID contribution to help organize a Guanabara metropolitan authority and to carry out several rehabilitation projects in squatter settlements, with strong emphasis on training of staff and technical personnel, rather than large material investments.[6]

USAID in Rio followed up with a $100,000 grant from local-currency funds and some strenuous efforts by David M. Trubek, the AID housing officer, to form the nucleus of a metropolitan development authority. But the measures necessary to vest powers and resources in a development authority became entangled in Guanabara state and national politics.

The program has survived on a small scale, however; squatter rehabilitation projects in four shantytowns were beginning in 1969. Some of the proposals of the Wagner report have been adopted by the Brazilian National Housing Bank, which has mobilized more than $1 billion in local resources for a major construction program aimed at building 400,000 houses a year. It is too early to say, however, if the bank, which has emphasized setting up a financial market for contract construc-

6. Agency for International Development, "Guanabara Housing and Urban Development," July 1, 1966.

tion, will also promote urban development geared to the mass of low-income families.

In 1966 the Chilean government established the first Ministry of Housing and Urbanization in Latin America. After two years in office, the Frei government had realized that it could not reach its housing target, 360,000 new publicly financed houses between 1964 and 1970. The new ministry made a substantial shift away from private contract construction toward self-help housing, assisting organized squatter settlement on land acquired for that purpose by the state. The Colombian government has also adopted this approach.

But as this new realism has taken hold, less and less U.S. long-term public money has been available for urban problems. Issues other than housing have acquired higher priority in Washington. President Johnson found housing problems less worrisome than mass illiteracy and the increasing demand for subsidized U.S. food imports in some Latin American countries. The word that came out of the White House was for USAID to concentrate its efforts on education and agriculture, with quiet support for population control. Housing, except for the investment-guarantee program supported by U.S. builders, was largely shelved, and urban problems were turned over to the IDB and the World Bank. The Alliance's lack of support for urban development is one of its most serious shortcomings today.

Urban problems and radical politics

The RUPI report's warning of political turmoil in Latin America's major cities is not mere speculation. Urban problems have been known to produce major political upheavals in the region. One of the first cities to receive a massive influx of both rural and foreign immigrants was Buenos Aires. Between the two world wars industrialization around Argentina's capital and main port concentrated a full third of its population in the metropolitan area of an otherwise heavily agricultural country. The conservative, military-backed Argentine governments of the 1930s repressed democratic political and labor activities, preventing Argentina's moderate reform parties, the middle-class Radicals and the white-collar Socialists, from bringing about the political integration of the poorer new urban masses.

As the dissatisfactions of this rootless and resentful new working class sought expression and found no outlet, they became the basis for a political and social convulsion that has done lasting damage to Argentina's national life.

Close to seven million people live in the Buenos Aires metropolitan area. Its gracious architecture and spacious urban plan compare favorably with those of Madrid or Washington. On the other hand, its *villas de miseria* (literally, towns of misery) are typical of Latin America's urban slums and shantytowns. Those near the Río de la Plata football stadium are hidden behind high walls put up by the city. Many others are in the outlying industrial areas of Buenos Aires. From these working-class settlements by the stockyards and oily canals, and in the crowded sections where the poor pay high rent for one-room flats in subdivided old houses, Colonel Juan Domingo Perón and his first wife, Evita, a one-time actress, recruited the *descamisados,* "the shirtless ones," who voted his populist dictatorship to power in 1945 through a free election. He ruled for ten years before the army revolted and ended his regime.

Peronism proved to be an economic and moral failure. Perón and his clique of favorites ran a corrupt regime that squandered Argentina's accumulated wealth. But he did not forget his constituency. Through strong labor unions, officially sponsored social clubs, and vacation colonies, Perón's regime gave the Argentine working class a sense of social participation and security. These sentiments are so strong that Peronists remain today the largest single political force in Argentina, representing at least one-third of the voters. Peronism has been kept out of power only by repeated military intervention, the most recent instance of which, in mid-June 1970, ousted the increasingly authoritarian Juan Carlos Onganía, who had come to consider himself superior to the military chiefs who had installed him, and replaced him with a junta headed by Brigadier General Marcelo Levingston. It was the eighth military coup in Argentina over the past three decades.

Cuba offers another example of the urban potential for political radicalism. The Cuban revolution was not, as some mythmakers would have it, an agrarian uprising rooted in the revolutionary resentments of the peasants of the Sierra Maestra. The most active elements in the movement, including Fidel Castro, acquired their revolutionary convictions as they grew up in the major cities of Cuba.

The corruption and political violence in Havana and the chronic unemployment and administrative neglect in Santiago de Cuba produced more recruits for the guerrilla forces in the hills than any peasant discontent. And in these cities and Santa Clara, Cuba's three centers of university education, the violence of the police against rebellious students turned not only the students but the whole educated middle class into a force for rebellion against the Batista dictatorship.

To be sure, peasants joined the movement, but they didn't lead it. Moreover, no operation of this type could have succeeded without a continuing urban resistance and an underground support apparatus that kept the movement militarily supplied in the rural areas and politically militant in the cities. These urban centers were always the ultimate target of the revolution, and after it triumphed, urban radical thinking made the new regime's policy decisions. In Cuba's agrarian reform program, for example, the urban objective of national economic modernization under central planning imposed the decision to hold expropriated land in technically managed state farms; the peasants would have preferred to receive title to the land individually, as in fact they had been led to expect.

One cannot view the political violence and student radicalism in Brazil's major cities without being reminded of the political protest, repression, and radicalization that ultimately reached revolutionary proportions in Batista's Cuba.

Greater Lima

In Lima the squatter problem has acquired an increasingly political character. Conditions in this city vividly illustrate the effects of urban growth in Latin America.

In recent years Peru has enjoyed substantial economic growth. With major expansion in exports of cotton, sugar, fish meal, iron ore, copper, silver, lead, and zinc, export earnings have climbed to $650 million, a relatively large income for Peru's twelve million people. This growth has benefited some lesser cities such as Piura, Chiclayo, and Chimbote in the coastal region, but the bulk of the new wealth has flowed to the capital.

Lima is the megalopolis of Peru. In a country with an area of

482,000 square miles, equal in size to the six countries of the European Common Market, half the national wealth is contained in the four hundred square miles of the Lima-Callao metropolitan area. The commercial agriculture, mining, and fishing activities of the provinces are directed largely from central offices in the capital. The industry of the metropolitan area turns out 60 percent of national manufactures and pays 73 percent of industrial wages. Lima provides 55 percent of government employment. Banking is so concentrated that 90 percent of public and private credit operations take place in Lima. Callao is the port of entry for 80 percent of imports, and Lima's commercial establishments and shopkeepers handle 65 percent of the nation's retail trade.

All major highways and airline routes seem to lead to Lima. Peru is split from north to south by the soaring Andean range, and it is often easier to get from one highland city to another by way of Lima, on the Pacific coast, than over the treacherous mountain roads. These roads, opened during the precolonial Inca empire for the messenger-runners of the Sun King (whose administrative center was in the mountain city of Cuzco), have now become trucking routes by which foodstuffs and migrants travel from the sierra to the highways leading to the coast.

In a study published in 1963, the Peruvian National Planning Institute estimated that on the coast the per capita share of national income was $600 a year, while in the sierra, the home of the highland Indians, it was $90. This income imbalance has produced a dynamic population shift. The number of new arrivals in the Lima metropolitan area each year is an estimated 75,000, equivalent to the entire population of Huancayo, the largest city of the central sierra.

In 1940 the population of the Lima-Callao metropolitan area was 645,000; in 1961 it was 1,846,000; in 1968 it reached 2.2 million. The estimated population figure for 1980 is 5.8 million, close to one-third of the estimated population of all Peru by that time.[7]

President Fernando Belaúnde Terry came to power in 1963, greatly concerned over Peru's lopsided income distribution and

7. *Plan de desarrollo metropolitano, Lima-Callao, esquema director 1967– 80* (Lima, 1967), pp. 52, 161.

the avalanche of migration toward Lima. Belaúnde filled the marble halls of the Pizarro presidential palace with papier-maché models of big irrigation projects, relief maps of jungle highways, and photographs of his frequent trips to remote villages, where he inaugurated new schools and community health centers. The purpose of these projects was to stem the flow of migrants to Lima, but just outside the palace gates, mocking Belaúnde's efforts, were spreading squatter settlements, core city slums, and an urban crisis for which no solution was in sight.

7 de Octubre

On the night of October 7, 1963, shortly after Belaúnde took office, a small group of squatters invaded a steep, rocky hillside within a mile of the presidential palace. The invaders were the poorest and worst situated residents of an older settlement called El Agustino, led by a religious mystic known as Poncho Negro. The new district, which the squatters named 7 de Octubre, is now a community of 40,000 people. The huts and shanties clinging to the hillside have spread steadily, despite the efforts of the landowner at the foot of the hill, with his gangs of hired toughs, to dislodge the squatters from what he claims is his property.

From their hillside, the squatters of 7 de Octubre look down on a large, flat tract of land that the owner has hastily irrigated and planted in corn because land under cultivation cannot be expropriated. At the foot of the hill, a large electric pump draws irrigation water from a recently drilled well that is kept under guard. The settlement has neither running water nor electricity.

The squatters have not threatened the flat land, which is legally protected, but they are well entrenched on the undeveloped hillside, where the owner's claim is questionable at best. Through community efforts they have built a neat, four-room schoolhouse, which the government has staffed with teachers despite the protests of the owner. The squatters, who have brought to their new home the highlander's artisan skills, have also built strong supporting walls of fitted stone for roadways up the hillside on which trucks bring barrels of water and deliver food supplies, cement, charcoal, beer, and other articles in demand. In some areas the squatters are digging trenches and laying pipe for a sewer. But the municipality has offered to 7 de Octubre neither public services nor recognition of permanence nor another more suitable housing site.

Santa Rosa

On New Year's Eve 1964 a group of Lima construction workers had a stag party to greet the incoming year. Over bottles of beer they discussed their major housing problem: high rent for badly overcrowded flats in the deteriorating, subdivided old houses that are Lima's slum tenements. That night they talked about invading a sandy, uncultivated gully near the Pan-American Highway north of the capital, where several automobile assembly plants and other new factories were going up. In July 1965 the group—about four hundred men, women, and children—made their move. At first they met no resistance as they put up their provisional shelters of reed mats, carefully marking out lots and broad roadways under the direction of a community committee. They received friendly visits from Father Louis Berger, one of three French Roman Catholic priests running the neighboring parish at Piedra Lisa.

Then the owner of the large corn and cotton fields at the foot of the gully moved against the invaders. He fenced off the access road to the gully with barbed wire and sent his peons to drive back any squatters seeking to leave or enter. The squatters massed for attack, with the priest in the front ranks. After a two-hour battle with rocks and clubs the squatters carried the day, drove off the peons, and tore down the fence.

The community, called Santa Rosa in honor of the patroness of Lima, now holds 1,200 families. They have built a church, a community center, and a well-laid-out football field. Many of the original mat houses have been converted into solid structures of adobe, brick, and cement building blocks. In 1966 the squatters received into the community two Peace Corps volunteers, a married couple who worked with the women on handicrafts, a small but useful source of extra income. The volunteers lived with the squatters in a flimsy shack, which has been empty since they left at the end of their assignment. "That's the way it will stay until someone else comes who wants to help us. We call that shack the American embassy," says Teófilo Pereda, president of the community association and one of the original group of construction workers who led the invasion.[8]

Trends in squatter settlements

The origins of Santa Rosa and 7 de Octubre are typical of the beginnings of all 267 squatter settlements counted in Lima in 1968.[9] Four of these settlements are now so big that they are recognized as municipal districts and have their own mayors. Yet even with this status, Pampa de Comas, a settlement containing 100,000 people, many two- and three-story buildings, and a number of stores and small factories, has not yet been able to obtain a waterworks system or home electricity from the city public services.

In San Martín de Porres (named for a Peruvian Negro saint), the most influential of the settlements-turned-municipalities, the government has issued provisional property titles that will become permanent if the settlers pay for water and sewer installations. The squatters don't pay property taxes, but block committees have pooled their resources and volunteer work to build four hundred blocks of sidewalks, with an estimated value of $200,000. In the waterless settlements, the annual purchases of water from tank trucks that deliver to these districts are estimated at over $2 million. If these resources could be captured for a long-term financial operation, they would easily pay for the needed expansion of public water services. "But there are too many opposing interests. Many people in the city still don't want to see that we have dug our foundations deep and are here to stay," says Alberto Díaz Jiménez, who started the sidewalk-building block committees.[10]

In 1968, a new settlement called Año Nuevo attracted more than usual attention. The 1,500 families involved, coming out of the Comas settlement, took over land legally held by the influential Álvarez Calderón family, who had been holding the inherited tract for the steady increase in real estate values around Lima. (Undeveloped land in Peru has been virtually untaxed and the profit expectation of real estate speculators in

8. Interview with Teófilo Pereda, Lima, August 1968.
9. In 1956, one of the first squatter surveys counted fifty-six settlements (José Matos Mar, "Estudios de Barriadas Limeñas," Departamento de Antropología, Universidad de San Marcos, Lima, 1956).
10. Interview with Alberto Díaz Jiménez, Lima, August 1968.

rural land around Lima is 300 percent of investment.) Until Año Nuevo, the squatters had restricted their invasions to government-owned land or uncultivated tracts on which the state had residual claims in the absence of a clear private title. Carlos Delgado, a leading Peruvian urbanist, commented:

A subtle but important change is perceptible in the attitude of the invaders toward traditional respect for private property. It appears that there is a growing tendency to challenge the inviolability of property, particularly in barren lots, in the face of the vast numbers of the dispossessed who are struggling to obtain a piece of land for a home.[11]

Ramón Carcamo: A slum

About ten thousand people live jammed together in the huts, hovels, and alleyways of a two-block compound called Ramón Carcamo in the center of Lima. The residents of Ramón Carcamo used to pay rents of $5 or $6 a month for one-room units in which families of six or eight people cook and eat and sleep. If the family owns a bed, it is usually reserved for the parents and the smallest children; the rest sleep on the floor. In 1963 they formed an association to put water taps in each alley. The proprietor refused to install the taps. In 1965 the tenants decided to pay no further rent.

Ramón Carcamo represented a potential rental income of $85,000 a year and had great real estate value because it is located on the Avenida Argentina, the main thoroughfare from Lima to Callao. Its owner was Lisardo Alzamora Silva, a former dean of the San Marcos University Law School (the most prestigious law school in Peru) and an alternate justice of the Peruvian Supreme Court. He tried to have the tenants evicted by police action, which the tenants resisted en masse and successfully. Soon afterward, Congress pushed through a special law by which the state bought the compound for $950,000 in cash. "That's the kind of deals the politicians make behind the backs of the people. The owner taught half the lawyers in Peru, so he got his money, but Ramón Carcamo remains just the same as it was," says Fidel Rojas Sánchez, a

11. Carlos Delgado, "Tres planteamientos en torno a problemas de urbanización acelerada en áreas metropolitanas: el caso de Lima," mimeographed (Centro Interdisciplinario de Desarrollo Urbano y Regional, Universidad Católica de Chile, Santiago, March 1968), p. 28.

business-machine salesman who is the president of the community association.[12]

By current estimate, some 500,000 people are living in slum conditions in Lima. A visit to these human corrals explains the appeal of the squatter settlement: it is both a step up in the world and an escape from slumlord rental payments. If no more slum residents have become squatters, it is only because land opportunities for new settlements are farther and farther away from the places of employment that keep the slum dwellers in the city. In the new chemical, textile, and fish-meal factories near Ramón Carcamo, the largely unskilled laborers who live there earn about $60 a month, a living wage by Peruvian standards. For a squatter, a steady income at this level will finance the gradual building, piece by piece, of a solid dwelling, without complicated administration or interest payments.

Lima's urban policy

Between 1949 and 1967, 31,000 homes were built in the Lima metropolitan area and 11,000 in the interior through public financing. Two-thirds of these homes were built after 1961, during the Alliance. But in the same period, Lima squatters built close to 100,000 homes. Carlos Delgado observes, "By comparison, the contribution of the squatters to the solution of the housing problem has been much greater than the contribution organized by society through the state."[13]

In 1966 the Washington consulting firm Regional and Urban Planning Implementation, Inc., delivered a performance report to USAID on Alliance housing in Peru. It noted that, under laws passed in 1961, the Peruvian National Housing Board had the authority to acquire land and provide financial and technical assistance to settlers for self-help housing construction and community services, but that the board's "plans for extensive expropriation of private land around Lima have been put off because of a shortage of government funds and opposition from the landowners." Moreover, according to RUPI, in administering an IDB housing loan, the board had fallen short

---

12. Interview with Fidel Rojas Sánchez, Lima, August 1968.
13. Delgado, "Tres planteamientos," p. 11.

by 9,000 units of an originally planned 30,000 low-cost houses. "The complexities of administering the loan and present difficulties of recapturing from the beneficiaries the money lent may have caused the JNV [the housing board] to lose much of its interest in self-help housing. . . . Its emphasis at the present time is on promotion of private contractor-built construction."[14] The RUPI report conveyed the failure of nerve among officials applying the urban development approach to the assimilation of squatters and the triumphant reinstatement of speculative landowners and building contractors.

The consequences of an ineffectual urban policy were brought home to Lima in 1968, when the squatters' settlements began to organize a citywide protest movement. A central figure in this movement was León Velarde, the colorful mayor of San Martín de Porres, who had begun to think of himself as a possible presidential candidate someday. Supported by other settlement leaders and assisted by Communist organizers, he began planning a march on the presidential palace to demand homeowner titles for squatters and the expropriation of land for new settlements. The government was seriously alarmed at the prospect of the march, and the military regarded it as a security problem.

Months before, Juan Cardinal Landazurri Ricketts, archbishop of Lima, concerned with the social and political problems in the settlements, had named a progressive young Jesuit, the Most Reverend Luis Bambaren, as auxiliary bishop to work full time on squatter areas. Bishop Bambaren now assembled a group of urbanists, lawyers, and settlement leaders, who drafted texts of decrees authorizing the issuance of property titles to squatters and simplifying expropriation procedures with long-term payment to the affected owners. The government accepted the drafts and issued them as executive decrees under a state of emergency. The squatters called off the march.

A new look at squatters

In the past decade squatters have been building more homes and urbanizing more people throughout Latin America than

---

14. Regional and Urban Planning Implementation, Inc., "Urban Development in Peru."

---

the official housing institutions. The housing goals of the Charter of Punta del Este require Alliance action on behalf of *all* the people, and not just a segment of the "upper poor." Alliance officials can channel the most energetic building and urbanizing activity in Latin America to meet these goals by utilizing a part of the funds and technical assistance designated for housing to support and orient the squatter settlement process. This approach would imply a shift in emphasis on the part of housing authorities, from building "minimum decency" units to integrating new migrants into urban society in stages that would begin with planned squatter settlements.

This shift requires a new political recognition of the inexorability of the rural migration to the cities, the integrative potential of the squatter settlement, and the responsibility of urban society to the new migrants. The conventional Latin American middle-class attitude toward the squatters is a combination of repugnance and fear. The policy preference that results from this attitude is that the squatter settlements should be eradicated and that migrants should be excluded from the city. Middle-class horror at shantytown conditions is partially relieved by the token solution of building a few low-cost housing developments. The urban propertied sectors oppose the more radical measures necessary for true urban reform. These measures would place in the hands of urban planning authorities the means of regulating land use in cities where real estate speculation has distorted patterns of occupancy. Legislation for the expropriation of urban land (with long-term payment to owners) and realistic taxes on undeveloped urban property are long overdue in most countries. The staff of an effective urban development agency would consist of professional urban planners, engineers, economists, and social workers with a practical commitment to urban development, rather than the career bureaucrats, contractors, and politicians who have until now run Latin America's urban housing institutions. An effective urban development agency would have to include in its overall plan a set of policies responsive to the needs and self-help capabilities of families at very low income levels.

A growing number of urban specialists see the squatter settlements as a desirable and creative form of urbanization, given the low income level of the waves of migrants entering the cities. William Mangin, a professor of anthropology at Syracuse

University, and John C. Turner, a professor of city planning at the MIT-Harvard Joint Center for Urban Studies, have concluded, on the basis of more than a decade of studies in Peru, Venezuela, and other countries, that

squatter communities . . . are highly successful solutions to the problem of mass urbanization in South America and elsewhere. . . .

Instead of chaos and disorganization [the settlements] represent thousands of people living together in an orderly fashion with no police protection or public service. . . .

Many of the [squatter] residents rapidly identify themselves as respectable property owners once they have consolidated their seizure of the land. In effect, they have succeeded en masse in forcing their way into patterns of control [of land] that have been dominant in South America for decades.[15]

According to Turner, only by working with the squatters can governments hope to fill the housing needs of Latin America's cities:

No housing agency in any newly urbanizing country can even begin to make an impression on the "housing problem" without the active participation of the people [squatters] themselves. As their resources cannot be metamorphosed into money, they cannot be collected by the State and then used at the State's discretion. These "popular" resources consist mainly of initiative, effort, skills and very small savings, difficult to collect or mobilize unless one works with those who have them.[16]

A RUPI report points out the financial benefits of this approach:

The great advantage which self-help housing offers is not the saving of labor costs through participation of the occupant—it is the lack of necessity to hire a private contractor. It has been estimated that the cost of a house can be reduced by forty to fifty percent through the use of self-help, and of that saving one-fifth is reduced labor costs and four-fifths the absence of profit to a contractor. Given the shortage, and thus the high price, of professional builders, self-contracting and self-construction clearly must be the answer to the national low-cost housing shortage.[17]

Government can use the savings of this self-help approach to benefit squatters through a credit program for the purchase of building materials. Several squatter communities in Lima and elsewhere have formed successful credit cooperatives for this

15. William Mangin and John C. Turner, "The Barriada Movement," *Progressive Architecture*, May 1968, pp. 153–62.

16. John C. Turner, "Uncontrolled Urban Settlement Problems and Policies," *UN International Social Development Review*, no. 1: *Urbanization: Development Policies and Planning*, 1968, p. 128.

17. Regional and Urban Planning Implementation, Inc., "Urban Development in Peru," p. 14.

purpose; the programs are run by members of the settlements with the supervision of a trained credit manager.

The physical infrastructure

To utilize the creative potential of the squatter communities, the cities of Latin America must extend their public services to the consolidated squatter districts and thus place an added burden on their already inadequate finances. In 1968 Galo Plaza, secretary general of the Organization of American States and former president of Ecuador, commented, "It is apparent that urbanization is taking place in Latin America without necessary investments in urban infrastructure and adequate planning. Aside from housing itself, gaps in water supplies, gas, electricity, drainage, transportation, schools, and hospitals are growing every year."

An illustration of these problems is São Paulo, Brazil. Greater São Paulo is today the center of the largest industrial complex in Latin America. In 1920 this city contained 540,000 people spread over an area larger than Paris'. By 1964 São Paulo and its adjoining municipalities comprised a packed conglomerate of five million people.

Meanwhile, without government regulation of urbanization, São Paulo land speculators had turned squatter settling into a profitable venture:

The period of massive immigration began a form of urban land occupation that has brought the worst consequences for the city. Real estate proprietors would sell part of their land cheaply for the establishment of a housing nucleus, whose members would then demand from the municipal authorities the provision of public services (at least streets, light, and water). If these demands were met, the proprietor would then sell the rest of his land, now increased in value by the proximity of public services, at great profit. This cycle, characterized by real estate speculation, stimulated the metropolitanization of São Paulo services.[18]

After this process of explosive migration and land speculation had taken its toll, inflation moved in to deplete the city's remaining financial resources. In 1950, when São Paulo had little more than two million people, it raised municipal revenues of $60 million. By 1964, when Brazil's annual cost-of-living increase had hit a record 75 percent, municipal revenues, based on fixed-rate taxes, had dropped in real terms to $38 million

18. Jorge Wilhelm, *São Paulo Metropole 1965* (São Paulo, 1965).

while the population had risen to five million. The city administration was near paralysis.

José Vicente Faria Lima was the mayor of São Paulo from 1965 to 1969. Through a remarkable tax reform, including increases of up to 600 percent in land valuations, he managed to increase annual city revenues to more than $200 million. With these funds he launched a long overdue attack on acute problems, particularly transportation and primary education. But even with these increased revenues, São Paulo is no better off than it was in 1950, with municipal revenue per capita of about $30 a year. And planners expect the population of greater São Paulo to reach ten million by 1980.

Mayor Faria Lima made a practice of receiving neighborhood committees once a week to hear their complaints and receive petitions. Invariably the requests were for some form of public service: the paving of an access road to a settlement where rainstorms made a quagmire of the red dirt streets, a school to accommodate more children than school district planners had dreamed the district could hold, at least one telephone line for a neighborhood so people could call a doctor at night in case of emergency.

In the mayor's office a map, completed in 1963, showed in detail all the streets and byways then known to the city authorities. The mayor frequently found that a settlement of several thousand people, represented by a delegation standing in the mayor's office asking for essential services, didn't even appear on the map. Such is the speed of urban growth.

São Paulo's urban planning office has received aid under the Alliance through a U.S.-funded technical assistance grant. The IDB has authorized one of its largest loans for São Paulo, an $83 million long-term credit for expansion of waterworks. The World Bank, which has made a major contribution in recent years to urban development in Bogotá, is now giving special attention to São Paulo. The coordination of a comprehensive urban development plan for greater São Paulo will be difficult, however, if not impossible, without an authority that can go beyond technical planning to regulate land use, establish an autonomous basis for financing public works, and provide guidance and incentives to public and private investors in the city's development.

Education:
the tinderbox

The population of 1980, on the average,
will have spent a good deal more time
in school than the population of today.
At best, this can mean a population
much better equipped to take part in a
striving for development and for a more
equitable and democratic social order.
At worst, it can mean a population
explosively frustrated, and divided
by the failure of maldistributed,
inappropriate, and low-quality
schooling to produce the status
and occupational rewards for
which it was sought.
United Nations Economic
Commission for
Latin America, 1969

Of all the Alliance targets, educational reform was the most strongly influenced by the example of Castro's Cuba. Although many of his claims at Punta del Este were sheer propaganda, Che Guevara was not boasting idly when he said that Cuba had vastly expanded its education program and would eliminate adult illiteracy within the year. The literacy program was already under way. More than 100,000 high school and university students had gone into rural areas and small towns in supervised "literacy brigades," teaching their elders to read and write.

In 1961 Cuba's educational reforms had been widely publicized and had had considerable impact on public opinion in Latin America. They broke with the traditional Latin American educational structure, which had served only the core society. Young students particularly were enthusiastic about Cuba's system of full scholarships for secondary and university education. The literacy brigades made education a new element of popular integration, teaching urban students about rural realities through firsthand experience, while teaching peasants to read and do sums. Lacking the fiscal and technical means simply to expand the existing system, the Cubans adopted experimental teaching methods in order to democratize education. They made this effort because they recognized the political effect of educating the people and regarded it as essential to the success of the revolution. Few Latin American countries have placed a comparable value on social integration.

The Latin American educational systems have traditionally followed the French model, designed for a rather narrow elite group. The constitutions of virtually all the Latin American countries promise a free primary education to every school-age child, but few countries even come close to keeping this promise. The elitist character of the system becomes even more apparent at the secondary level.

In most Latin American countries most of the secondary schools are privately run (in many cases by religious orders) and charge relatively high fees. Only the children of parents who can afford to pay these fees over an extended period of time are able to complete the secondary course and arrive at the university level. The secondary schools accordingly serve to filter the children of the lower classes out of the educational system. Beyond the secondary level, most of the universities either are free or charge relatively low tuition. Society thus subsidizes university education for students whose parents are affluent enough to see them through the secondary course.

Outside the formal educational system is a large mass of adult illiterates (over fifteen years of age), most of whom are also outside the money economy.

Obviously some children of working-class families do rise through the system. Latin America also has some private universities charging relatively high fees. Relatively few children of the truly peripheral masses, however, obtain even the most rudimentary education, and only a tiny fraction of these make it through the secondary system to the university.

In most Latin American countries the percentage of students in rural schools who finish the sixth grade is only half that of students in urban schools; the dropouts are heavily concentrated in the countryside, where either school attendance is not compulsory or truancy laws are laxly enforced. Moreover, 65 percent of Latin American teachers work in urban areas, and the remaining 35 percent include a substantial number of lay teachers, who frequently staff rural schools.[1] Thus in Latin America, even more than in the United States or western Europe, education is a social and political matter.

At the close of the Alliance decade, although some countries were doing much more for education than others, the educational goals of the charter were still far from being realized. By the late 1960s, with an adult literacy rate of 66.1 percent in the region as a whole, the elimination of adult illiteracy was no longer even a serious topic of conversation among development officials. The elementary school dropout rate was so high that the Alliance goal of at least six years of primary school education for every child had also become visionary.

This is not to say that no progress has been made. In virtually all Latin American countries the number of children and young persons attending school has substantially increased. Between 1960 and 1967 the percentage of children of primary school age (five to fourteen) enrolled in schools rose from 49.8 percent to 56.8 percent, from 24 million to 36 million. In 1967, however, over 27 million children, 740,000 more than in 1960, were not even enrolled in primary school. Moreover, of those who enter the system, less than 30 percent of primary school students and 35 percent of middle-level students reach the last year of their studies.

Venezuela, Peru, Chile, and Costa Rica have earmarked as much as 5 percent of the gross national product for education, an impressive commitment by any standards. The investment by the Latin American countries in primary education has been much greater than the assistance received from external sources. U.S. direct support to education in the period 1961–1968 totaled only $157 million (although this figure does not include some important local-currency counterpart funds applied to education programs). In fiscal 1968, AID loaned $70 million in Latin America for educational improvements, including a $32 million loan to Brazil for a project in secondary

---

1. U.S. House of Representatives, Subcommittee on Inter-American Affairs of the Committee on Foreign Affairs, *New Directions for the 1970's: Toward a Strategy of Inter-American Development, Hearings,* 91st Cong., 1st sess. (Washington, D.C.: U.S. Government Printing Office, 1969), pp. 701–705; cited hereafter as *New Directions.*

education that has not yet got off the ground because the Brazilian government delayed signing the loan contract until December 1969.

Nowhere, in fact, has the inadequacy of Latin America's educational systems been more apparent than in Brazil. The United States has tried to work with Brazil at all levels of its educational system, with disappointing results. This failure has done much to postpone achievement of the Alliance goals; Brazil, with its large low-income population, accounted for 43 percent of the Latin American children of primary school age (five to fourteen) who were not enrolled in school in 1967. Between 1960 and 1967, the number of five-to-fourteen-year-olds not in school decreased by 218,000 in Chile; in Brazil, it increased by 600,000. The events behind these statistics tell a great deal about commitment to the Alliance.

Education in Brazil

The Brazilian educational system has not stood still during the Alliance years. But it has also not adapted rapidly enough to Brazil's explosive population growth (3 percent a year) and urbanization rates (5 percent a year in Rio and São Paulo), and to the ambitions of a rising urban middle class that is exceedingly education-minded. When the Alliance began, the system was in trouble at all three levels; since then demand for education and frustration at the pace of change have become central to Brazil's social and political turmoil.

The dominant fact about education in Brazil in recent years is the explosive growth in school enrollment. Between 1950 and 1968, elementary enrollment doubled, secondary enrollment almost quadrupled, and higher education more than tripled.

This dramatic increase has placed enormous strain on a system originally designed to serve an elite. As a result the system does not remotely meet the quantitative demand for education, nor does it function with a minimally acceptable degree of efficiency.

According to the Brazilian constitutions of both 1946 and 1966, every child is entitled to four years of free primary education. But only two-thirds of Brazilian children in the elementary school-age group (seven to eleven) are ever enrolled. Of those who enroll in the first grade, only 50 percent make it to the second grade. No more than 19 percent of the children enrolled in the first grade between 1952 and 1955 reached the fourth grade.

The secondary system is divided into two levels: the *gymnasio*, which covers four years, and the *collegio*, which covers three additional years. In 1956, 70 percent of the secondary schools were privately operated, accessible only to those who could afford the fees for seven years. By the end of 1965, however, only 52 percent of secondary school students were enrolled in the private system. The public secondary schools have absorbed most of the huge growth in enrollment, but the system is not yet able to enroll more than half of those who wish to attend, and it continues to discriminate economically. In 1965 the public schools accepted only 39 percent of the candidates for admission; the private schools accepted 60 percent of their applicants. Near-tragic street scenes mark registration time in Rio de Janeiro as hysterical parents find their children denied places in the school system.

Table 14.1

Students enrolled in the Brazilian education system, 1950–1968

year	educational level		
	elementary	*secondary*	*higher*
1950	5,000,000	540,000	44,000
1965	10,000,000	2,480,000	180,000
1968	11,600,000	3,300,000	258,000

SOURCE: Statistics from the three-year plan of the Brazilian government during the administration of President Artur da Costa e Silva (1967–1969) and an unclassified AID loan paper, AID/DCL/P-726.

Only one-third of the students who enter the *gymnasio* make it through to the *collegio* level, and the average number of *collegio* graduates is less than 80,000 per year. The system thus wastes two-thirds of the potential middle-level and professional manpower potentially available from the *collegio* level. The number of those who remain within the system is inadequate to the development needs of a nation of ninety million people. Higher education enrolls no more than 2.5 percent of Brazilians between the ages of nineteen and twenty-five.

In recent years, though, university enrollment too has been

growing rapidly. From 1947 to 1965 the average annual growth rate was 9.5 percent; since 1965 it has climbed to 20 percent. But distribution of enrollment among the various curricula has not changed markedly. In 1964 the faculties of philosophy (liberal arts) enrolled the largest number of university students (23 percent). Law enrolled the second largest number (22 percent), followed by engineering (15 percent), economics (10 percent), and medicine (10 percent). These five fields enrolled 80 percent of all students.

Each year for the past four, the system has graduated approximately twenty thousand students, of whom approximately two thousand are engineers. In 1964 the Brazilian universities had a total of 735 agriculture and veterinary graduates, nowhere near the number needed to improve the functioning of Brazil's agricultural economy.[2]

But perhaps the most serious problem at the university level is that of the qualified rejects, or *excedentes* (overflow); that is, students who have passed the entrance examinations but for whom the system has no room. Each year the *excedentes* can usually be found camped on the patio of the Ministry of Education and Culture, demanding that room be made for them within the university system. The government's responses to these demands have ranged from a proposal that the *excedentes* be shipped to a little-used university in the once flourishing but now virtually deserted city of Manaus to the suggestion, made by a former minister of education in the Castelo Branco regime, of burning their records.

Brazil: Politics and literacy

In all of Latin America only Bolivia and Guatemala have higher adult illiteracy rates (68 percent and 62 percent respectively) than Brazil. Of the Brazilian population aged fifteen and older, 39 percent are illiterate, i.e., cannot read or write a simple note. Most of this group live in the Northeast.

Brazil's Northeast is a nine-state region that bulges out into the South Atlantic toward Africa. It was the first region in Brazil colonized by the Portuguese, some four hundred years ago. Its plantation agriculture and backland ranches keep the good lands in the hands of wealthy families. Landless laborers

---

2. Unclassified AID loan paper AID/DLC/P-726.

and sharecroppers populate the rural districts. Traditionally the large landholder is referred to honorifically (as in our southern states) as the *coronel*. The local police chief, judge, and notary are usually indebted to the *coronel* for their jobs. The small merchants, cattle dealers, and parish priests of the interior look to him for leadership. In disputes with small landholders over water rights or with tenants over contracts, the *coronel* may hire the gunmen who abound in the region to protect his position. The *coronel* jealously guards his social and economic advantages. He has no interest in the improvement of any part of his district or municipality, unless, like a public road, for example, it brings benefit to his property. He sends his children to private schools and thus sees no need for rural public schools. He can send to the nearest large town for a doctor and thus doesn't need a rural public health service. As a result, of the Northeast's 29 million people, 60 percent are illiterate, and their infant mortality rate is one of the highest in the world.

The most important state in the Northeast is Pernambuco, whose capital city is Recife. Until 1959 the politics of Pernambuco, like those of the other states of the Northeast, had been dominated by the Social Democratic party (PSD), the party of the *coroneles*. In the Pernambuco gubernatorial election of 1959, a schism within the PSD opened the way to victory for Cid Sampaio, the candidate of the National Democratic Union (UDN) party. Sampaio, supported by industrial and banking interests in Recife, set out to break the interior power base of the PSD by appointing his own men to the key positions of police chief, judge, and notary.

Simultaneously the federal government organized a regional development agency (SUDENE) to promote economic development and make the region less vulnerable to catastrophic droughts. The head of SUDENE was Celso Furtado, a native of the Northeast state of Paraíba. He quickly gathered around him a core of enthusiastic though inexperienced young people determined to change the region's centuries-old economic structure. The creation of SUDENE, combined with the end of the PSD's traditional dominance in Pernambuco, created a political ferment that spread to other states in the Northeast. The language of politics began to focus on development, industrialization, workers' rights, and agricultural modernization, superseding the traditional political rivalries based upon family. New political personalities appeared, speaking the language of the new politics.

One of the new faces was that of Miguel Arraes.[3] Arraes was the son of a small shopkeeper in an interior town in the state of Ceará. After studying law at the University of Recife, he had become an economist on the staff of the government sugar agency. (His wife was Cid Sampaio's sister-in-law.) Arraes was a key figure in Sampaio's campaign; then he entered politics on his own. As his political star rose, Arraes became increasingly concerned about the great dichotomy in living and social conditions between the small group of dominant landholders and the large numbers of the impoverished in the rural areas. With powerful support from the Brazilian Labor party, Arraes was elected mayor of Recife.[4]

Arraes became mayor at a time when Recife's intellectuals were increasingly preoccupied with popular culture and social integration. Germain Coelho, a scholarship student who had recently returned from France, had organized a group of young professors at the University of Recife to "develop the creativity of the people."[5] This group embarked upon a series of projects including popular theater, folk art, and adult education. They had also campaigned enthusiastically for Arraes. Once elected, Arraes invited them to form a nongovernmental movement to promote popular culture, providing assistance in the form of a famous house that had been the rallying point for resistance to the Dutch in the seventeenth century.

The organization, called Movimento Cultural Popular (MCP), was a link between the intellectual, politically radicalized elite of Recife and the illiterate, politically unsophisticated migrants from the rural interior. Arraes' political base was among this populist mass. The increasing political and social consciousness deliberately fostered by the MCP and its em-

---

3. The best books on the rise of Arraes and the period of his influence in the Northeast are Antonio Callado, *No tempo de Arraes* (Rio de Janeiro: José Álvaro, 1964), and Adison de Barros, *Ascensão e queda de Miguel Arraes* (Rio de Janeiro: Editora Ecuador, 1965).

4. Although Sampaio represented primarily the industrial and banking interests, and Arraes the labor interests, both men sought Communist party assistance in their campaigns, a relatively common practice among mainstream political figures in Latin America, where the Communists are noted for their skill as political campaign organizers.

5. Interview with Paulo Freire, Cambridge, Mass., October 23, 1969.

Education: the tinderbox

phasis upon literacy as a key to the vote all worked to his political advantage.

The MCP emphasized two basic ideas: first, that the people could change their fate through the vote; and second, that they were part of the struggle between the rich and the poor. The literacy manuals related these highly political ideas to life experiences that people could understand:

"The *sertanejo* [one who lives in the backlands] lives in the *sertão*. His life is hard. His vote can serve to change his fate."
"The arm of the citizen is his vote."
"Are you from the city of Recife?"
"Yes, I am a *citizen* of Recife."

The movement also promoted popular culture:

"The *batucada* [the rhythm of the drums] is the music of the people."
"The samba is the dance of the people."

and the significance of economic issues:

"With the high cost of living, a good salary protects the worker's family."
"A people without bread is a people without health."

Impressed by the effect of the MCP program in Recife, Sampaio sought a program of his own, and eventually organized the Promoção Popular to compete with the MCP. He also took advantage of a literacy program initiated in the early 1960s by the Protestant evangelical churches in northeastern Brazil. These churches, determined to avoid the mistakes that they felt the Protestant missionaries had made in mainland China, combined the practical and the evangelical in an approach that asserted that through literacy people could improve their economic standard of living—and incidentally achieve a direct communion with God.

The social and political ferment also spread to the Catholic church. In 1958 a group of Brazilian bishops had decided that the church should sponsor an adult literacy program, which they called the Movimento Educação Brasileiro (MEB). Dom Eugénio Salles, bishop of Natal, initiated a literacy-by-radio program that emphasized agrarian reform, organization of the rural workers, and participation of the masses in political life, themes that at that time were almost revolutionary in northeastern Brazil.

The popular cultural movements, the literacy programs of

the Catholic and Protestant churches, and the competition among the politicians of the core society began to pull the marginal elements of northeastern Brazil into the political and cultural mainstream of Brazilian society.

In 1962, aided by an aroused citizenry and a catchy campaign song called "Zé Ninguém" ("Joe Nobody"), Arraes was elected governor of Pernambuco. One of his first acts was to prohibit the police, for the first time, to act as agents of the landowners in their developing struggle with the workers and tenants. The state government also gave tacit support to the rural labor unions being organized in the sugar zone. In 1963 the Brazilian Congress passed legislation establishing a minimum wage in the rural areas. The rural unions demanded that this wage be paid in cash and, since the police had been neutralized, were able to strike for this demand without fear of retaliation. Arraes organized a state-owned company to sell staple items such as overalls to the sugar workers at low prices. With the government's encouragement, the workers were challenging the traditional domination of the *coroneles* in the sugar zone and the deep interior.

Arraes terminated state financial support of Sampaio's Promoção Popular program and tried to extend the MCP to the interior. But he found that the key workers on the program in Recife were not willing to move to the isolated towns and villages of the interior.

One of those who had been involved in the MCP was Paulo Freire, a forty-two-year-old philosophy and education professor in charge of the cultural extension service at the University of Recife. Freire had developed new techniques to promote literacy. He criticized the literacy programs then in use because, regardless of their political content, they depended heavily on rote learning. He believed that literacy instruction should foster an active dialogue between student and teacher, rather than continue the traditional relationship, which encouraged student passivity. The task was not simply to eliminate illiteracy but to help the ordinary man develop a sense of responsibility for his own fate. The great challenge, said Freire, was to overcome centuries of "democratic inexperience." Democracy and democratic education, he felt, sprang from the belief "that man is master of his fate," that he "not only can but must discuss his problems—the problems of his country, of his continent, of the world, of his work—the problems of democracy itself."[6]

In 1962 and 1963 the USAID mission in the Northeast and SUDENE agreed to finance a program of basic adult education and elementary school expansion. Over $37 million was eventually committed to this program. The secretary of education of the state of Rio Grande do Norte asked Freire to develop an adult education program as part of the USAID-SUDENE education program. Freire insisted upon two conditions: that the state set up the project agreement with the University of Recife rather than with himself, and that students from the University of Rio Grande do Norte participate in the project. In 1963 and early 1964, the Freire technique was utilized in two states, Alagôas and Rio Grande do Norte. Approximately four thousand people were enrolled.

A dynamic figure within the university, Freire attracted students and imbued them with a sense of personal involvement in the program. He believed that the students should not start a program unless the people clearly wanted it and considered it relevant to their needs. Before starting a literacy course in a community, a cadre of students would conduct a house-to-house inquiry and hold informal meetings to determine whether the community was receptive to the program. If it was, the students would catalog the words commonly used in the community, selecting the ones with the greatest emotional content. Returning to the university, they would draw up a basic vocabulary of about seventeen words designed for the particular locale. They also developed simple visual aids, charts, and slides to go along with the vocabulary. The process was time-consuming, painstaking, and clumsy. But the content had the great virtue of relevance to the living language and life situations of the community.

Once the basic vocabulary and visual aids were developed, a student monitor would bring them back to the community and initiate a literacy class. But the meetings between the monitor and the participants were not "classes" in the conventional sense, with an active teacher instructing passive students. The role of the student monitor was to provoke a dialogue with the

---

6. Paulo Freire, *Educação como práctica de liberdade* (Rio de Janiero: Editora Civilização Brasileira, 1962), p. 96.

participants, to challenge them. For example, in one class a participant complained about the local *coronel* and said that the government should do something about him.

The student monitor replied, "But what are you doing to help yourself? Why don't you organize your neighbors?"

According to reports, some monitors even brought in the words of President Kennedy: "Ask not what your country can do for you but what you can do for your country."

Each course ran a total of forty hours. In the second class the participants were encouraged to write words. Once they could write fifteen or twenty words, they were told to try compositions. According to one observer, "It was thrilling. The people became intellectually drunk with words."[7] The program was significant not only because it brought literacy to illiterates but also because it engaged the imaginations of students from relatively well-off families in what amounted to a Brazilian domestic peace corps. It brought them into contact with the previously anonymous people of the interior, spanning what had seemed until then an unbridgeable gap between the core society's intellectual leadership and the primitive masses. In 1960 a university student from a good Recife family would scarcely have considered going into the *sertão* to teach illiterates how to read and write. In 1963 a substantial number of students were participating in the Freire program, and their work had to some extent become socially acceptable.

The literacy movement had a more solid foundation than social idealism. Literacy was the key to the vote. Through the literacy movement the politicians of the core society saw a means of consolidating and extending their political base. Arraes initiated the MCP program in the *favelas* of Recife in part because he thought the program would serve his political interests. Sampaio supported the Protestant literacy program not out of a love of either Protestants or illiterates, but because he was in political competition with Arraes. The Catholic church was drawn into an arena it had neglected for centuries by fear that continued neglect would cause it to lose adherents to the Protestants and the "atheist" political left.

This competition for the allegiance of Zé Ninguém was par-

---

7. Interview with Philip Schwab (educational director, USAID mission in northeastern Brazil, 1961–1965), Washington, D.C., July 23, 1968.

Education: the tinderbox

ticularly propitious for the Freire program. It invested the have-nots with an individual importance they had never had before. It gave Freire's message, that they could change their fate and that each of them had an individual responsibility to do so, a certain plausibility. As the focus of the major core institutions (the political leadership, the church, and the university), Zé Ninguém was something completely new in Brazilian life.

The USAID mission in Recife, however, found two faults with the program. First, Freire had failed to develop written materials to complement the verbal part of the program. The AID mission felt that whatever was gained through the forty-hour course had a tendency to be lost later. (Freire argued that in the initial stages it was more important to maintain the enthusiasm and momentum, that rationalization would come later.) Second, the program was increasingly political. The conflicts between the landowners and workers were becoming more intense. The discussions that were so vital to the Freire method inevitably dealt with these conflicts. Many of the students had radical political views. Freire (a devout Roman Catholic) and his program were charged with fomenting unrest, with being communist-inspired.

The Paulo Freire program was indeed subversive in its basic technique of deliberate provocation and in its purpose of developing a critical faculty, creating a sense of the capacity and moral responsibility of the individual to change his life and the world around him. In a hierarchical, paternalistic society where the *coronel*'s word was law, this emphasis upon critical thinking and individual and community action was destructive of traditional values. The Freire program was revolutionary in the most profound sense of the term.

In January 1964, dissatisfaction with Freire's pedagogical technique and uneasiness about the program's political content led the AID mission to terminate its financial support of the program (just three months before the coup against Goulart). This act was merely one manifestation of an insistence on rationality and order in a situation of revolutionary change. In 1963 Ambassador Lincoln Gordon, the embodiment of cultivated rationality, met with Arraes in the governor's palace. Gordon tried to explain how the uncontrolled wage increases in the sugar zone were contributing to the Brazilian inflation.

Arraes failed completely to grasp these macro-economic relationships, but he did understand that, in the *sertão* and the sugar zone, to elevate Joe Nobody into a somebody was to make a revolution in Brazil. Gordon (and the U.S. development economists in charge of the AID program) had no more affinity with that revolution than Arraes had with Gordon's sophisticated economics.

Once the United States realized that the social change taking place in northeastern Brazil was inherently disorderly and even potentially revolutionary, it backed off and shifted its concentration to the core society, hoping that by gradual expansion the core would eventually take in the marginals.

The ABC Crusade

Shortly after taking office, the Castelo Branco government permitted the evangelical church group to reopen its literacy program under the name of the ABC Crusade. The program, which is devoid of political content, trains Recife's *favela* residents to teach their neighbors. At first attendance was poor, but the USAID mission made PL 480 agricultural commodities available as part of the program, and those who attended regularly got free food. By the end of 1968 the Crusade had reached 250,000 adults and adolescents.

The program consists of three phases. The first phase takes five months and teaches a basic vocabulary of seven hundred words. (Some students have emerged with two-thousand-word vocabularies.) The second and third phases include mathematics, social studies, natural sciences, hygiene, and education. The program is equivalent to the first and second years of elementary education. In the more advanced phases the program does not rely on *favela* residents, but hires trained teachers to conduct the classes.

The ABC Crusade has expanded beyond the Recife area into other large cities of the Northeast. In 1967 the government contemplated extending the program to the southern states of Guanabara and Rio de Janeiro. In 1968 the government decided to include the ABC Crusade as the literacy segment of its new educational reform program. The fate of this program depends on the commitment of the Brazilian government to the goal of widespread adult literacy. In 1970 that commitment was still very much in doubt, and so was the future of the ABC Crusade.

University reform

Brazil's universities are not like those of the United States; they are patterned after those of France. Brazilian universities consist of independent faculties of law, medicine, philosophy, science, and the like, each of which has its own libraries, laboratories, and courses. A number of faculties may be physically located in the same section of a city, but each remains a separate entity. If a student decides after two or three years that he prefers another career, he has to start over in the new faculty, with no credit given for his previous work.

The traditional university in Brazil is highly autocratic. Within every department of each faculty one man is the *catedrático*, the lifetime holder of the *catedra*, or departmental chair. He may never show up for classes. His work is usually handled by badly paid assistants. For all practical purposes he is an absolute monarch.

Darcy Ribeiro, chief of Goulart's civil staff, was a young anthropologist and educator of avowedly Marxist views, passionately committed to fundamental changes in the educational structure. Ribeiro initiated Brazil's first serious university reform effort, the establishment of the University of Brasília in 1962.[8]

This institution abandoned Brazil's traditional university structure to adopt that of U.S. universities. The key features that distinguished it from other Brazilian universities were:

1. A totally integrated administrative structure with the faculties subject to central control.
2. Elimination of the *catedráticos*.
3. A basic system of two years of general studies to be followed by specialization.
4. Full-time faculty and students.
5. Campus dormitories and an attempt to attract students from throughout the nation.

---

8. The proposal for the establishment of a modern university in Brasília went back to the late 1950s. In 1959 the Kubitschek government had approached the International Cooperation Administration (ICA), AID's predecessor agency in Brazil, for a $20 million grant to help in establishing the university; ICA had dismissed the proposal without further consideration.

Ribeiro used his influence to obtain funds for the new university, and from all over Brazil it attracted top teachers and students, many of whom had leftist political orientation. Brasília acquired a reputation not only for its innovative university structure but also for the political radicalism of its academic community.

The Goulart regime used student organizations as political instruments, but student leaders also became political figures in their own right, with direct access to Goulart's office. University reform thus became embroiled in Brazil's political turmoil in the early sixties.

The Goulart regime's support of educational reform had been part of its attempt to extend political power to the marginals. The military government under Castelo Branco associated the educational innovations of the Goulart regime with Goulart's attempt to shift the political balance of power. The government terminated Paulo Freire's literacy program, arrested Freire, and exiled him to Chile, where he became an adviser to the education program of the Frei government. The government also arrested Darcy Ribeiro and eventually exiled him to Uruguay. Paulo de Tarso, a former minister of education under Goulart, who had provided federal support for the Freire program, was also exiled to Chile. Since the coup that ousted Goulart, Brazil's most important export to Chile has been its leading educators!

The government purged the faculty and students at the University of Brasília of "subversive" elements. In a September 1968 issue of the *Jornal do Brasil*, Carlos Castelo Branco,[9] one of Brazil's most respected political columnists, wrote:

The military that occupied the Federal Capital at the end of March 1964 never pardoned the University the fact of having been founded by Darcy Ribeiro. Nor were they ever reconciled to the innovative spirit that dominated it. Although frustrated, it was the pilot experience of a profound university reform that still has not occurred but is taking its first steps.[10]

The budgets of the postcoup government have assigned a low priority to education. Between 1963 and 1967, education as a percentage of total federal budgeted expenditures declined

9. No relative of President Humberto Castelo Branco.
10. Carlos Castelo Branco, "A Meta è fechar a universidade" (The Purpose Is to Close the University), *Jornal do Brasil*, September 27, 1968.

from 9.2 percent to 7.4 percent. The Ministry of Education and Culture (MEC) is the primary agency through which federal resources flow into the educational sector. MEC expenditures account for about 93 percent of federal spending for education, 35 to 40 percent of total public-sector expenditures for education, and roughly 30 percent of total resources for formal education. The ministry devotes between 13 and 17 percent of federal expenditures for education to primary education (transferring most of these resources to other levels of government, primarily to muncipal government). Secondary education receives 20 to 25 percent. Higher education receives the largest share (40 to 50 percent) of these resources, most of which go to the federal universities located throughout the country, although state and private institutions also receive shares. Between 1964 and 1968 the government's disbursements were irregular, however—some states and universities received their annual allowances two years late—because the budget treated education as a residual item that could be cut when retrenchment was necessary. It was almost constantly necessary in the period following Goulart's ouster by the military. Only after the student riots of June and August 1968 did the government begin to change its educational policy. Since then it has made a significant allocation of resources for education.

The failure of the military governments of Castelo Branco and Costa e Silva to deal effectively with public secondary education is more difficult to explain. Although the radical left had made the private secondary school system an object of attack in the period before the coup, secondary education was never as directly linked with subversion as the University of Brasília and the literacy programs. Moreover, secondary education is of great concern to the Brazilian urban middle class, which substantially supported the coup against Goulart. A program of investment in public secondary education facilities might have engendered support for the regime among a segment of the population painfully affected by economic stabilization measures. In a speech at Santa Maria University in Rio Grande do Sul in 1965, Castelo Branco accurately spelled out the social consequences of Brazil's secondary education system in great detail. Yet aside from a fairly ineffectual scholarship program for children of union workers, the government made virtually no attempt to cope with the problem.

One explanation for this neglect is that the Castelo Branco government, believing it could achieve economic stabilization within a relatively short time, subordinated everything else to that objective, with encouragement from the U.S. government, the IMF, and the IBRD. But the government could have made a reassuring start on educational reform without massive investments, merely by indicating commitment and direction through a modest but well-publicized concrete program.

The indifference of the Castelo Branco government toward this issue reflects the basic ambivalence of the Brazilian elite on the social question. For the issue of secondary education involves more than the technical problems of training teachers, building schools, buying equipment. It involves access to economic and social opportunity. The present system of secondary school education supported by relatively steep fees significantly limits the social and economic mobility of the lower classes, as does the entire educational structure. This structure has begun to change, but the leadership of Brazilian society has not yet fully committed itself to an expansion of the educational system that would substantially broaden the base of opportunity. Its failure to do so has provided a focus for the opposition of Brazilian students to the postcoup military governments.

Education and dictatorship

The Calabouco (Dungeon) restaurant is a rather shabby, government-subsidized student restaurant in downtown Rio de Janeiro. Early in 1968 the Calabouco was a gathering place for radical student leaders who opposed the Costa e Silva regime. As part of a general austerity program, the government determined to end its subsidy of student restaurants. On April 1, 1968, the students held a demonstration in front of the Calabouco to protest this decision. The police broke up the demonstration and a police officer shot to death an eighteen-year-old student, Edson Souto. Other students picked up his body, carried it on their shoulders through the streets of Rio to the State Assembly Building, and placed it on the speaker's podium, bloody shirt and all.

Eight days later, thousands of students attended a mass for Edson Souto at the Candelaria Church in downtown Rio. As they emerged at the conclusion of the mass, police on horseback charged up the church steps. But a row of priests, arms linked together, placed themselves between the oncoming mounted police and the students, successfully preventing further bloodshed. This event placed the church firmly on the side of the students and against the government.

Early in June 1968, office workers in Rio's downtown buildings rained chairs, desks, ashtrays, and anything else that was handy on police trying to break up another student demonstration against cuts in the education budget and the finance minister's failure to release funds designated for the universities.

On July 7, from ten thousand to fifty thousand people (depending on who was counting), including middle-class women, priests, students, professors, and artists, marched down the Avenida Rio Branco, Rio's main thoroughfare, in a disciplined protest against the government's education policy. They were chanting, "Down with the dictatorship!"

In August the First Army was mobilized in the streets of Rio with tanks, armored cars, steel helmets, and bayonets to prevent a student demonstration. On August 29, in search of four students, police invaded the University of Brasília and without provocation clubbed faculty members, students, and a federal deputy who had raced to the university to protect his children. No one could say who had given the order to invade the university or why the four students were wanted.

In October, two students were shot to death in Rio in a demonstration protesting the arrest of seven hundred student leaders at a clandestine convention of the outlawed National Student Union (UNE).

Education has become the most explosive political issue facing the Brazilian government, and the students have spearheaded opposition to the regime. If, as they believe, the inadequacy and inequities of Brazilian education are characteristic of Brazilian society as a whole, those who demand university reform must also cry out, "Down with the dictatorship!"

The events of 1968 and pressure from the students, joined more recently by a significant part of the younger clergy and the middle class in the urban centers, finally persuaded the government to take its first steps toward changing its education policy. In the summer of 1968 the finance minister committed himself to release the budgeted education funds. In July 1968 the government appointed a commission to implement a program of university reform. The commission presented its proposal to the Congress in September 1968. The government has drawn up a three-year program including expansion of facilities at the secondary level, a mass literacy campaign, and modernization of the university structure, to be financed by funds designated exclusively for the educational sector. It is too soon to tell whether these plans will amount to more than a paper exercise, like so many previous ones in Brazil.

The United States involvement

Although the United States has never made education or agrarian reform a condition of program-loan disbursement, it has provided some assistance for Brazilian education. Part of the $131 million special loan for the Northeast in 1962, based on the recommendations of the Merwin Bohan mission, was to finance a crash program in primary education. As a first step in expanding and improving elementary education, USAID in Rio advanced cruzeiros received from the sale of PL 480 agricultural commodities for school construction. AID expected these funds, the cruzeiro equivalent of $37 million, to pay for building 17,000 elementary school classrooms. The program also provided for extensive teacher training, the organization of state planning units, and adult education (under which heading AID supplied funds for the Paulo Freire program).

Of the planned 17,000 classrooms, only 3,000 were ultimately built. Before the cruzeiros earmarked for school construction could be spent, the Brazilian inflation peaked. Between May 1963 and August 1965 the exchange rate fell from 600 cruzeiros to the dollar to 1,825, and building costs in the Northeast more than tripled.

USAID's inaccurate estimates and poor planning contributed to the failure of the program. The Northeast is Brazil's most backward region; its public administration is poor and graft is endemic. The size of the nine-state area presented an obstacle to on-site inspection of elementary school construction, and some of the finished products failed to meet AID contract specifications. A U.S. General Accounting Office auditing team found cracked walls and decaying buildings only two years after construction. Moreover, Brazilian state governments, lacking both the administrative capacity to train teachers for the newly opened schools and stable sources of revenue with which to pay them, often found themselves with schools but no teachers.

Still, the program did produce some positive results. For the first time the northeastern states established education planning offices staffed by trained personnel, where previously the state secretary of education had often not known just how many schools were operating or how many teachers on the payroll really existed. The states also established departments of supervision and curriculum and teacher-training centers. These agencies function, of course, with varying degrees of effectiveness, but they have value merely as an institutional basis for educational planning that simply did not exist before.

The wastage of funds was due more to inflation than to anything else. But both the U.S. Congress and the General Accounting Office severely criticized USAID's management of the program. Their concern about possible misuse of the U.S. taxpayers' money is justifiable. Undoubtedly the AID administrators of the program made mistakes, but just as undeniably they have learned from them. Moreover, the cost of working in administratively underdeveloped areas such as northeastern Brazil is inevitably high; expensive errors are the price of modernization.

Since 1966 these financial and technical issues have declined in importance as obstacles to U.S. support of Brazilian education. By that time, AID in Brazil had become concerned with the lack of progress in education. Despite its decision not to make education reform a condition of program-loan disbursement, AID pressed for a lending program to assist secondary education, and in 1968 authorized a $32 million loan for expansion and modernization of secondary education facilities in four southern states.

A team of U.S. and Brazilian technicians had prepared the loan application and plan, working jointly under the auspices of the Ministry of Education and Culture. Their project was highly ambitious. It was to accelerate the flow of students through the *gymnasios*, to reform the secondary school curriculum, to train teachers, and to establish a new type of *gymnasio*, which was to offer vocational and technical training, as opposed to the classical academic curriculum of the traditional *gymnasio*.

The quantitative targets of the loan were the construction of 272 new *gymnasios*, the conversion of thirty more, and the establishment of eight model *gymnasios*. The project was to train more than 9,600 teachers, to upgrade the skills of 4,400 school personnel, and to increase pupil enrollment by 250,000 over a three-year period. The Brazilian government was to guarantee a financial contribution equivalent to AID's $32 million loan during the period of the loan disbursement. The government was also to commit itself to maintain the budgetary appropriation for education at an agreed level. AID had set up similar conditions in Chile and Colombia for educational loans.

USAID in Washington authorized the loan in June 1968, but not until December 1969 was the loan contract signed. As the Brazilian negotiators raised one technical objection after another, the suspicion gained ground in AID that the Brazilians did not really want the loan. Perhaps they felt that the reforms contemplated were too radical and the financial conditions onerous (although the highest levels of the Brazilian government had already approved the loan conditions). But they may also have feared the political consequences of U.S. involvement in the educational sector. This issue had already prevented execution of one agreement between USAID and the MEC, for U.S. technical assistance at the university level.

In May 1966 a group of U.S. universities known as the Midwest Consortium (the University of Wisconsin, Michigan State University, the University of Illinois, and Indiana University) entered into an AID-financed agreement to help the MEC formulate a university reform program. The agreement itself seemed perfectly innocuous, but Brazilian students attacked it as "cultural imperialism," and a weak minister of education and an indifferent Brazilian government failed to defend it. Because of this failure, in 1968 John Tuthill, the U.S. ambassador, insisted that the agreement be canceled.

The agreement itself contained weaknesses, among them the inaccurate assumption that the Brazilian project staff would include personnel with training and technical skills equivalent to those of the American team. Disagreement within the U.S. team also worked against effective implementation of the agreement. But the students who attacked the project were not primarily concerned about these mistakes. Many who demonstrated against the agreement admitted that they had not even read it. As leaders of the opposition to Brazil's present regime, they opposed all manifestations of U.S. support for that regime, including the MEC-USAID agreement. In this context the merits of a particular agreement were—and are—irrelevant. When AID attempted to collaborate with a government ostensibly friendly to the United States on a project intended to benefit its students, it was foiled by those students because they were opposed to the government. In short, education is not, as the United States would like it to be, a purely technical problem; it cannot be isolated from its political context.

The Inter-American Development Bank has loaned $25 million in Brazil for university expansion. The funds have been primarily allocated to building construction and the provision of laboratory equipment for six universities. Some critics complain that the loan has provided brick and mortar rather than educational reform. However, the multilateral IDB loan has not aroused violent student opposition, as did the bilateral USAID technical assistance.

Chile

The Chilean and Venezuelan governments have carried out the most far-reaching education reforms in Latin America (outside of Cuba).

The Frei government, which came to power in Chile in 1964, made educational reform one of its first priorities. President Eduardo Frei assembled a team of young administrators and appointed Patricio Rojas, a thirty-one-year-old medical school graduate, as undersecretary of education. Rojas had been president of Chile's National Federation of Students and had initiated a project to establish a student fellowship and assistance program. During the 1964 presidential campaign, he had headed Frei's task force for education.

The Ministry of Education, one of the political power centers of the new regime, initially emphasized the goal of a quantitative increase in enrollment. In December 1964 the national census showed that slightly over 185,000 children of school age were receiving no formal education. The government undertook a crash program and in 1965 enrolled some 175,000 new primary school students.[11] In 1965 and 1966, 6,600 pri-

---

11. Chile's average annual increase had been 40,000; the 1965 increase was over four times that average (*New Directions*, p. 784).

---

mary school teachers were trained, one third more than had been trained in any previous two-year period. In 1965 over six thousand classrooms were constructed, with a potential capacity of half a million students. The government had adopted a policy of favoring less developed areas and marginal groups in the society, and therefore located over a thousand of these classrooms in rural areas, where the rate of school enrollment was lowest and illiteracy highest.

The government equipped the schools with kitchens and utensils, and in 1965 alone the schools served 800,000 breakfasts and 400,000 lunches. The schools also provided uniforms for those students who could not afford them. At the secondary level the government provided 17,500 scholarships in 1965 and 20,000 in 1966. At the university level the government made 2,000 student loans in 1965 and 2,500 in 1966. Enrollment in the educational system increased within two years from 20 percent of the school-age population to 25 percent. In 1966 an estimated 100,000 illiterates achieved an acceptable degree of proficiency in reading and writing.[12]

In real terms, total public-sector expenditures on education increased by nearly 25 percent in 1965, 17 percent in 1966, and 15 percent in 1967. Current-account expenditures on education have remained fairly constant at 19.5 percent of total public-sector current expenditures, but capital expenditures on education have increased from 4 percent to 6 percent of total public-sector capital expenditures.

In addition to expanding physical facilities and expenditures, the Chilean educational planners intend to overhaul the entire system of education, and have formulated a five-year plan for this purpose. On the primary level it involves a major campaign to reduce the dropout rate by means of a modernized curriculum, the introduction of guidance and testing systems, and an automatic promotion system designed to move students expeditiously through their primary schooling.[13] The plan will also expand Chile's primary school program gradually from six to eight years of basic general education. In 1966 the schools added the new seventh year and thus retained an estimated

12. Report of the Executive Committee of the Christian Democratic party to the Christian Democratic party congress, April 1966.
13. Before 1965, 62 percent of those enrolled in the first year dropped out before completing the sixth year.

Education: the tinderbox

25,000 students who would otherwise have dropped out. The government hoped to have all children of primary school age enrolled for a minimum of eight years of education by 1970.

At the secondary level the objective is a reduction of the dropout rate from 75 percent to 35 percent. The secondary level has traditionally consisted of five tracks—general academic, industrial, agricultural, commercial, and technical education—with no lateral movement between them. The five-year plan calls for the establishment of a dual track system: a college preparatory track and a vocational track teaching middle-level technical skills for immediate employment. The system will integrate the curricula of the two tracks and maintain lateral mobility between them.

The plan also calls for a completely modernized curriculum providing three years of basic education followed by four years of middle-level academic or vocational education. Courses at the secondary level will make intensive use of teaching materials. The plan will also expand in-service teacher training, improve teacher preparation, and introduce testing, guidance, and evaluation throughout the system.[14]

The Ministry of Education in Santiago has traditionally dominated Chile's highly centralized educational system. It has not effectively coordinated its primary, secondary, and vocational education programs and its administrative, supervisory, planning, and operational functions. The plan calls for a decentralized administrative structure and the creation of eight to ten regional educational districts by 1970. Each district director will administer all public education institutions within his district and be responsible for developing educational programs adapted to specific district needs. The Ministry of Education will continue to provide supervision and financial support for these districts but will relinquish most administrative responsibilities.

Chile's human resources and political commitment have justified AID support of its educational reform program. AID has made two loans totaling more than $20 million of a projected $50–70 million commitment over five years. This assistance will enable Chile to accomplish in four to six years an educational reform that would otherwise take ten years.

14. See *New Directions*, p. 784.

Venezuela: money isn't everything

Between 1957 and 1966, the Venezuelan population enrolled in the educational system increased from 12.7 percent to 20.9 percent. (See Table 14.2.) This expansion is all the more re-

Table 14.2

Students enrolled in the Venezuelan educational system, 1957–1958 and 1965–1966

(thousands of students)

educational level	academic year		interannual increment of the period	increment in the period
	1957–1958	*1965–1966*		
Primary	751.1	1,481.0	8.9	97.17
Middle	82.8	295.4	17.2	256.76
Higher	10.6	45.8	20.0	332.07
Venezuelan population	6,635,942	8,722,212		

SOURCE: "Educación: la gran urgencia" (a report made for the Ministry of Education by the Institute for Economic and Social Development, Caracas, 1968).

markable because 54.5 percent of Venezuela's population is less than fifteen years of age.[15]

Like Frei, Betancourt gave educational priority to bringing the children of primary school age into the system. Between 1957 and 1960, primary school enrollment increased from 750,000 to 1,250,000. By the end of 1961 the primary school enrollment deficit had virtually disappeared, and thereafter the annual increase in enrollment remained relatively stable at 3.5 percent per year, keeping pace with population growth. But a recent report by the Venezuelan educational authorities on the efficiency of the educational system reveals the emergence of a new problem: As enrollment has risen, so has the dropout rate. Table 14.3 shows the retention rate of the system. The children whom the system expanded to include from 1957 to 1960 came for the most part from the marginal sectors of society which the system had never really reached. A special effort would have been required to keep them from dropping out again. The report also shows the strain that rapidly expanded

15. All statistics on the Venezuelan educational system cited in this section are taken from "Educación: la gran urgencia" (a report made for the Ministry of Education by the Institute for Economic and Social Development, Caracas, 1968).

Table 14.3

Percentage of students retained in Venezuelan
elementary schools, 1956–1960 and 1960–1965

grades	1956–1960 (N=242,203)	1960–1965 (N=463,711)
2	59.4%	58.4%
3	54.7	52.1
4	49.2	42.4
5	41.0	34.7
6	33.4	28.0

SOURCE: "Educación: la gran urgencia" (a report made for the Ministry of Education by the Institute for Economic and Social Development, Caracas, 1968).

enrollment placed on the supply of qualified teachers and facilities. "Almost half of the children that do have the toughness or experience, upon finding themselves in class with fifty or more students, with teachers in many cases without experience and with a difficult student body, disappear between the first and second grade." The report concludes that quantitative improvement (enrollment of more students at the primary level) was not accompanied by a qualitative improvement through which the system could retain a higher percentage of the students—this despite the fact that Venezuela's educational expenditures more than tripled between 1957 and 1966, rising from 5.6 percent to 17.5 percent of total budgetary expenditures.

The report calculates the cost of primary school education through the sixth grade at $414 per capita. A 75 percent dropout rate from an entering class of 400,000 students results in a loss to Venezuela of approximately $124 million. Even in a country with the huge financial resources of Venezuela, this expense is intolerable. In poorer countries it is unthinkable.

Education and the Alliance

In August 1966 President Johnson announced that education, agriculture, and health were high-priority objectives of the Alliance for Progress. This announcement enabled AID to overcome the Treasury Department's opposition to education projects that required local-currency financing and justified AID's pursuit of goals other than monetary stabilization. In 1968 AID authorized over $70 million in education-sector lending. (AID had never before loaned more than $25 million for education in any one fiscal year.) The Inter-American Development Bank has concentrated its lending in higher education. The $100 million it has provided in this sector has facilitated the expansion of universities in every Latin American country.

The lending agencies usually require countries receiving loans for education to match those loans with domestic resources additional to those normally programmed for educational investment. Thus the financial resources committed to education have been growing. But they are nowhere near enough to reach the goals of the Alliance for Progress: elimination of adult illiteracy, a minimum six-year primary education for every school-age child, and modernization of the secondary and higher education systems in Latin America.

The achievement of these goals probably will require not only a technological breakthrough such as educational television (AID made its first pilot educational TV loan in El Salvador in 1968), but also a political mystique that mobilizes the energy of both the students (as Castro did in Cuba and as began to happen in northeastern Brazil in 1963) and the marginals themselves.

After the Alliance

A decade of the Alliance for Progress has yielded more shattered hopes than solid accomplishment, more discord than harmony, more disillusionment than satisfaction. The progress has been halting, painful, and uneven, and the nations allied are discontented, restless, and tense. Without the Alliance the Latin American experience in the 1960s might have been even more turbulent. But the Alliance was unable to impose reconciliation on the fundamental conflicts it sought to overcome. It was a dramatic and noble crusade, deriving from excessive idealism and overoptimism a momentum that was slowly but indisputably dissipated in encounters with harsh realities—economic, political, social.

To be sure, most proponents of the Alliance in the United States considered themselves hardheaded and realistic. They viewed stepped-up support by Washington for national development in Latin America not only as a constructive and generous gesture toward the developing republics to the south, but as an essential and reasonable means of protecting the vital security interest of the United States. As they conceived it, the Alliance could counteract the appeal of Castroism to Latin America's once docile masses of workers and peasants by offering them economic benefits and social reform within a democratic political framework. In retrospect, the program designed to kill two birds with one stone has hit neither squarely. It has not removed the danger of revolution and it has not brought significant economic, social, and political advancement to the poor of Latin America.

Some of the internal contradictions of the Alliance were apparent even at its birth. The Pentagon had little confidence in the ability of reformers to maintain political stability in Latin America. The United States business community pointed out that the emphasis on reform was likely to produce economic instability and a poor climate for U.S. investment. And a great deal of the original enthusiasm for the Alliance was lost once the Cuban missile crisis reduced the appeal of Castroism in Latin America and its ability to arouse fear in Washington. Within the first few years of the decade, the reformist elements in Latin America proved less effective than their supporters in the United States had hoped, and administration officials learned that development in Latin America was a far more complex, expensive, and far-reaching process than reconstruction had been in western Europe.

Conventional development assistance usually serves to accelerate the economic growth of the recipient country. The economic benefits will tend to follow the recipient country's existing pattern of income distribution; unless they are accompanied by social or political restructuring, they will go primarily to those who already hold wealth and power. The Alliance principle of distributing the benefits of economic growth throughout a society by means of social and political reforms was new to both development economists and loan officials in the United States. But experience soon showed them that social and political reforms were indeed destabilizing. Thus they gradually narrowed their focus to monetary stabilization and economic growth, in which they achieved significant advances, particularly toward the end of the decade. In education and agriculture they turned their efforts away from adult literacy and agrarian reform, to technical education and agricultural production. These changes reflect not only an increasing technocratic orientation but a shift of political concern from bettering the lives of the marginal masses to protecting the key elements of the core society.

At the end of the 1960s U.S. policy in Latin America had virtually abandoned the Alliance principle, even though recent events and current conditions made it clear that without a deliberate effort to integrate the marginals into the economic, social, and political core, there was no hope for continuing stability in Latin America.

The destabilizing element is not the capacity of the poor for autonomous action. People debilitated by disease and illiteracy are rarely active politically. They lack both the energy and the perspective to initiate and organize a campaign. But their presence in growing numbers and conditions of desperation and misery outside the framework of society constitutes a *potential* force that, if activated, could destroy the delicate structure of the core.

The catalyst that could activate this potential is also present. It consists of dissident members of the core society who, motivated by compassion, opportunism, or nationalist frustration, rage against the social order and preach its overthrow. The revolutionary purpose of these dissidents, reinforced by the numerical strength of the disenfranchised masses, is the specter that continues to haunt the core societies of Latin America.

The Alliance planners viewed the solution of this problem as a simple struggle between the forces of good (democratic left) and evil (Castro and communism). In fact, the moral and political options were and are a great deal more complex.

One option is represented by Cuba, which has had nearly ten years since Punta del Este to demonstrate the effectiveness of its approach to development. Far from achieving the 10 percent annual growth rate promised by Che Guevara and Fidel Castro, it has produced in the decade what is generally depicted as economic disaster. But there is another side to the Cuban picture. Cuba has come closer to some of the Alliance objectives than most Alliance members. In education and public health, no country in Latin America has carried out such ambitious and nationally comprehensive programs. Cuba's centrally planned economy has done more to integrate the rural and urban sectors (through a national income distribution policy) than the market economies of the other Latin American countries.

Brazil represents a second option: economic growth concentrated within the core society, managed by a coalition of the military and apolitical technocrats. This coalition is in turn supported by the industrial and financial leadership, the rural landowning elite, and an important part of the middle class. It controls the marginals and the core dissidents—students, populist politicians, the younger clergy, a restive labor leadership —largely through political repression. But this repression has a cost. It forces an increasingly activist opposition to use extra-institutional channels for the expression of its discontent; and the bank robberies and urban terrorism of the dissidents provoke the government to even more brutal repression. In September 1969, as we have seen, youthful terrorists kidnapped the U.S. ambassador to Brazil, C. Burke Elbrick, who, they said, "represents in our country the interests of imperialism, which, allied to the great bosses, the big ranchers, and the big national bankers, maintain the regime of repression. . . . They have created the wage squeeze, the unjust agrarian situation, the institutionalist repression."[1] Elbrick was freed only after the kidnappers had humiliated the regime by obtaining the release of fifteen political prisoners. The Brazilian authorities later caught several of his captors and tortured two of them to death.

A part of the Peruvian military has chosen a third route. Peru's military government is carrying out a social reform program and has negotiated new and more advantageous contracts with U.S. business interests, while taking restrictive measures against the press and the judiciary. The Peruvian option thus involves the establishment of a populist type of military government, but one which has not yet abandoned private investment as a stimulus to growth. As one Peruvian military officer described it:

When one is pursued by a herd of maddened bulls one has three options. One is to kneel, close the eyes, and pray. The second is to fight the bulls, which is as good as the first option. The third is to lead the stampeding herd into terrain that is more advantageous to the pursued.
The masses in Latin America are starting to stampede. We the military are the only ones who are capable of leading them—and us—into safe ground.[2]

Chile, Colombia, and Venezuela have undertaken a fourth option. The governments of all three countries have deliberately adopted a national policy of keeping the political process open while advancing social integration and economic growth. Expensive, messy, unevenly successful at best, this option is the one to which all the signatories of the Charter of Punta del Este originally committed themselves in 1961.

The question for the United States now is: Where do we go from here in Latin America?

---

1. "Text of Manifesto from Kidnappers of U.S. Ambassador to Brazil," *New York Times*, September 6, 1969, p. 2.
2. H. J. Maidenberg, "Chaos Hovers Over Latin Lands," *New York Times*, January 26, 1970, p. 49.

The Rockefeller report

President Nixon made no mention of the American republics to the south in his inaugural address. On his first day in the White House, however, he asked Galo Plaza, secretary general of the Organization of American States and former president of Ecuador, what the United States should do in Latin America. At Plaza's suggestion, he asked Governor Nelson Rockefeller to go on a mission to the Latin American countries and sound out their leaders.

Rockefeller agreed on condition that he be given a free hand in organizing the mission and making recommendations. He made the journey, accompanied by an advisory staff of twenty-three experts, in May and June 1969.

The Rockefeller mission was in no sense a pleasure jaunt. Student demonstrations in growing intensity met the emissaries on their way. In Tegucigalpa, Honduras, one student was killed. In Quito, Ecuador, students seized the streets behind the presidential palace; tear gas filled the air; the Rockefeller party had to come in from the airport by back roads, accompanied by armed troops, to a hotel where paratroopers in full combat dress were standing guard in the corridors. The president of Bolivia, the next stop on the itinerary, confined his meeting with the governor to the airport. The governments of Venezuela and Chile canceled the visits altogether, fearing the disorders they assumed would otherwise take place. Peru declined to receive the governor when the State Department announced its cancellation of arms sales in retaliation for Peru's seizure of U.S. fishing vessels.

In preparation for Rockefeller's visit, the Brazilian government forbade the press to publish information that might reflect adversely on the mission—including news of disturbances in other countries. Before Rockefeller arrived the Brazilian authorities picked up several thousand students, civilian politicians, known troublemakers, and people who were listed as subversive for obscure reasons, and detained them until he left. In Argentina the Onganía government, already tense as a result of disturbances in Córdoba and the most successful general strike in Argentine history (neither of which had anything to do with the Rockefeller mission), welcomed the governor reluctantly. During his stay, thirteen supermarkets belonging to the Rockefeller-controlled International Basic Economy Corporation (IBEC) were destroyed in a coordinated midnight bombing attack. On the day of Rockefeller's meeting with General Onganía, Augusto Vandor, a moderate labor leader who had opposed the call for a general strike to protest Rockefeller's visit, was assassinated. (The strike itself did not take place.)

In Uruguay, fire-bombing caused an estimated $1 million in damage to the General Motors building. The Uruguayan government moved its meeting with Rockefeller from downtown Montevideo to Punta del Este. In Santo Domingo, in the Dominican Republic, four people were killed by trigger-happy soldiers. As the mission prepared to leave Santo Domingo it received a warning message from Dominican terrorists: "They shall not pass." Frogmen patrolled the waters spanned by the Duarte Bridge, a famous landmark of the 1965 revolution. The heat was stifling but the mission members kept their bus windows tightly shut and held briefcases against the windows as protection against possible shattering glass. Surrounded by truckloads of armed troops with rifles and submachine guns pointing in all directions, the buses sped over the bridge. Soldiers, sailors, marines, and air force personnel were stationed fifteen feet apart all along the route out of the city.

Only in Paraguay and Haiti were enthusiastic crowds turned out (by presidential order) to greet the governor.

On September 2, 1969, Rockefeller delivered his official report to President Nixon. It was a comprehensive critique of U.S. policy in the hemisphere:

The United States has allowed a special relationship it has historically maintained with the other nations of the Western Hemisphere to deteriorate badly.[3]

Failure to maintain that special relationship would imply failure of our capacity and responsibility as a great power. If we cannot maintain a constructive relationship in the Western Hemisphere, we will hardly be able to achieve a successful order elsewhere in the world. Moreover, failure to maintain this special relationship would create a vacuum in

---

3. *The Rockefeller Report on the Americas* (Chicago: Quadrangle Books, 1969), p. 21. (The report was written by Governor Nelson Rockefeller and his chief aides: James M. Cannon, Hugh Morrow, and William Butler, vice-president of the Chase Manhattan Bank. They also sent copies for comment to George Woods, former president of the World Bank and the First Boston Corporation, who was traveling in Portugal. No other members of the mission saw the report in draft or final form before it was released to the public.)

this hemisphere and facilitate the import in the region of hostile foreign powers.[4]

Rockefeller declared, "Forces of anarchy, terror, and subversion are loose in the Americas."[5] Praising the idealism of Latin American youth, he also noted that the "very fact of their idealism makes some of the young vulnerable to subversive penetration and to exploitation as a revolutionary means for the destruction of the existing order."[6] Finding labor and the church equally idealistic and vulnerable, he concluded, "Clearly, the opinion in the United States that communism is no longer a serious factor in the Western Hemisphere is thoroughly wrong."[7]

Rockefeller proposed the establishment of a civilian-directed Western Hemisphere Security Council to combat subversion. He also urged, in general terms, a more pragmatic approach to governments that had come to power through military coups, for even the military, he found, were

often becoming a major force for constructive social change in the hemisphere. . . . In this connection, special mention should be made of the appeal to the new military, on a theoretical level, of Marxism: (1) it justifies, through its elitist-vanguard theories, government by a relatively small group or single institution (such as the Army) and, at the same time, (2) produces a rationale for state-enforced sacrifices to further economic development.

One important influence counteracting this simplistic Marxist approach is the exposure to the fundamental achievements of the U.S. way of life that many of the military from the other American countries have received through the military training programs which the U.S. conducts in Panama and the United States.[8]

He recommended that the United States increase, rather than decrease, both its grants for the training of security forces and its sales of military equipment to Latin American countries, but he also observed that the large U.S. military assistance missions in the field were too conspicuous and should therefore be reduced in size. These measures would hold "the new military" for the United States in the decade ahead.

---

4. *Ibid.*, p. 39.
5. *Ibid.*, p. 60.
6. *Ibid.*, p. 30.
7. *Ibid.*, p. 35.
8. *Ibid.*, pp. 32–33.

Rockefeller also surveyed the economic relations between the Americas:

Just as the other American republics depend upon the United States for their capital equipment requirements, so the United States depends on them to provide a vast market for our manufactured goods, and as these countries look to the United States for a market for their primary products whose sale enables them to buy equipment for their development at home, so the United States looks to them for raw materials for our industries on which depend the jobs of many of our citizens.

But these forces of economic interdependence are changing and must change. An increasing flow of two-way trade in industrial products must supplement the present interchange of manufactured goods and primary products.[9]

In other words, to win the allegiance of the younger, more modern-minded Latin American entrepreneurs, the United States must offer them access to its markets on reasonable terms and should make vigorous efforts to persuade the other industrialized nations to extend generalized preferences to all developing nations for manufactured and semimanufactured goods. Here the report made one of its boldest recommendations: that until such agreement could be reached, the United States should extend preferences to the developing nations (primarily Latin American) that were not receiving special treatment from other industrialized nations.

With respect to debt financing, the report proposed that those countries whose indebtedness prevented them from maintaining the level of imports necessary for development should postpone servicing such debts in dollars and reserve an equivalent amount of local currency to finance internal development during the grace period. (This earmarking of local currencies would require a reshuffling of internal monetary accounts if it were not to be inflationary.)

The report did not comment on quantitative needs or funding for development assistance, but dealt with the conditions under which such assistance should be provided. It recommended:

1. A review of the freight rates fixed by the North American Maritime Conferences for merchandise carried from the United States to Latin America and abandonment of the

---

9. *Ibid.*, p. 38.

requirement that 50 percent of the cargoes financed by U.S. aid be carried on U.S. bottoms.

2. Self-help, country performance criteria, and a three-to-five-year commitment basis for program loans.
3. Financing of most public works projects through the multinational and regional lending institutions.
4. Removal from United States assistance programs of restrictions interfering with development.
5. The unrestricted use of assistance funds by borrowers to purchase goods anywhere in the Western Hemisphere.
6. Repeal of the Pelley, Conte, Hickenlooper, Symington, and Roess Amendments, which affect extension of assistance to countries that purchase sophisticated weapons, or seize U.S. fishing boats operating without a license, or expropriate without due compensation.

Governor Rockefeller also proposed a major reorganization of U.S. government agencies dealing with Latin America. He recommended the creation of a new position within the State Department, a secretary of Western Hemisphere affairs, who would report directly to the president and the secretary of state. He proposed the creation of an Institute of Western Hemisphere Affairs to take over the economic and social aspects of development now handled by the State Department, and he sought to obtain more involvement of the White House by establishing an economic and social development agency in the executive office of the president and a special office of Western Hemisphere affairs on the staff of the National Security Council.

The *Rockefeller Report* was a highly perceptive, intelligent, and imaginative response on the part of U.S. business leadership having interests in Latin America to the problem of potential revolutionary social change in Latin America. Though showing no lack of compassion for the plight of Latin America's marginals, Rockefeller sought primarily to preserve U.S. political, military, and above all economic dominance in the hemisphere. His recommendations amounted to a strategy of timely adaptation of economic policies and flexible accommodation to the emergence of a new military and a growing entrepreneurial class. Underlying his report was the assumption on which U.S. policy in the hemisphere has traditionally been based: that the United States must continue to dominate Latin America and that any basic change in the established structure of Latin American society would be detrimental to the security interests of the United States. Although Rockefeller condemned the paternalism that he felt had permeated the development assistance program, his report expressed a much more fundamental paternalism—a belief that the government of the United States has the ultimate responsibility of maintaining order in the hemisphere.

The report never articulated the extent of this responsibility in the context of the revolutionary change that it described. But if the security interest is indeed as vital as Rockefeller maintained, and the subversive threat as dire, then over the next decade U.S. policy in Latin America must inevitably include increasing support of repressive authoritarian military regimes and more interventions along the lines of the 1965 intervention in the Dominican Republic.

The President's speech

Governor Rockefeller's report did not, however, constitute the policy of the Nixon administration. On the contrary, the new president had his own views on what should be done, as he made clear in an address to the Inter-American Press Association at the end of October 1969. In this speech, entitled "Action for Progress for the Americas," he committed the United States to a liberal system of generalized tariff preferences for all developing countries, including Latin America: "We will seek adoption from all the industrialized countries of a scheme with broad product coverage and with no ceilings on preferential imports."[10] The United States had never done more than promise to consider a liberal system of tariff preferences; it had never publicly committed itself to "broad product coverage" and "no ceilings on preferential imports." Nixon had adopted this position after a bitter struggle in the executive branch and despite the opposition of the Commerce and Agriculture Departments. He did not institute the interim measure of unilateral preferences for Latin America which Rockefeller had recommended. He did, however, express his

10. White House press release, October 31, 1969.

determination to take this step if after a reasonable time no movement was forthcoming on generalized preferences. (He did not define a reasonable time.)

On tied loans, the president had in June abolished the "additionality" requirements. He now freed United States aid dollars further to allow purchases anywhere in the hemisphere. President Nixon accurately described this measure as "one of those things people kept saying ought to be done." Moreover, the amount of purchases was estimated to be relatively small, about $30 million a year, and the dollars still had to return to the United States under specific procedures.

He also proposed that a multilateral inter-American agency be given an increasing share of responsibility for development assistance decisions, suggesting that either "CIAP could be given this function, or an entirely new agency could be created." He recommended that CIAP "conduct a periodic review of U.S. economic policies as they affect the other nations of the hemisphere." Endowing CIAP or some other organization with decision-making rather than merely consultative functions would be a new departure for the United States, for the history of the Committee of Nine and of CIAP itself shows that the United States has traditionally been unwilling to relinquish any decision-making powers.

Not surprisingly, the president endorsed the leading role of the private sector in economic development, but he added, "Each government must make its own decision on the place of private investment, domestic and foreign, in its development process. . . . We will not encourage U.S. private investment where it is not wanted or where local political conditions face it with unwarranted risks."[11]

Nixon did not adopt the Rockefeller recommendations for government reorganization, but he did propose to raise the rank of the State Department official in charge of inter-American affairs from assistant secretary to undersecretary, "thus giving the hemisphere special representation."

Nor did Nixon adopt the hard-line anticommunist rhetoric of the *Rockefeller Report*. Although he said that the United States was proud of its own domestic system and expressed hope that

11. *Ibid.*

"eventually most, perhaps even all, of the world's people would share what we consider to be the blessings of a genuine democracy," he also added:

"Nevertheless, we recognize that enormous, sometimes explosive forces for change are operating in Latin America. These create instabilities and bring changes in governments. On the diplomatic level we must deal realistically with governments in the inter-American system as they are. We have of course a preference for democratic procedures and we hope that each government will help its people to move forward to a better, fuller, and freer life."[12]

The limits of the political tolerance implicit in this statement are still to be tested. If Chile elects a government that includes Communists in its cabinet, will the CIA incite the Chilean army to undertake a coup? If the Dominican Republic erupts into another blood bath from which a government of the left emerges, will the United States intervene as it did in 1965? The assumptions implicit in the *Rockefeller Report* would justify intervention in both cases, but by mid-1970 the actual posture of the Nixon administration was not yet clear.

On the whole, the differences between the Rockefeller approach and the Nixon approach to Latin American affairs are probably more metabolic than political. Both favor trade liberalization, elimination of restrictions on aid funds, U.S. private investment in Latin America, a special position for inter-American affairs within the U.S. government, and pragmatism in dealing with internal political developments in the Latin American countries. But on each issue Nixon has proposed a less activist approach than Rockefeller. The president's speech added up to a somewhat less energetic or ostentatious version of traditional U.S. policy toward Latin America. Only time will test the consistency of Nixon's actions as president with his 1958 policy recommendation for the United States in Latin America: "A distant handshake for dictators, an enthusiastic *abrazo* for democratic leaders."

The disenchanted liberals

Some voices in the United States have begun to urge termination of the U.S. political role in Latin America altogether. Appalled by the intervention in the Dominican Republic in 1965 and by the uncritical support given to military governments in

---

12. *Ibid.*

Brazil, such U.S. liberals as Senators Frank Church (chairman of the Latin American Subcommittee of the Senate Foreign Relations Committee) and J. William Fulbright have come to believe that the most constructive thing the United States can do is to get out of Latin America and let social revolution run its course. Speaking in Mexico City in August 1969, Senator Church condemned the country performance standards of the economists who dominate AID and recommended termination of the U.S. bilateral aid program in the hemisphere. Both Church and Fulbright feel that the United States should continue to supply financial assistance to Latin America, but only through such multinational channels as the World Bank and the Inter-American Development Bank.

In 1968 Teodoro Moscoso also roundly condemned United States policy in the hemisphere, recommending the abolition not only of the bilateral aid program, but also of the CIA establishment. He also called for a drastic reduction of U.S. embassy representation—in effect, a diminution of Washington's presence.

Many Latin American liberals, despairing of the Alliance, now look to a reformist-minded military to carry out the task of social integration in Latin America. Speaking informally before the Center for Inter-American Studies in New York City in October 1969, Senator Church observed that more fundamental change may be occurring in Peru than has taken place in Chile and Colombia under Frei and Lleras Restrepo.

Despair is not a totally unreasonable response to the sorry record of inter-American relations in the past decade. A policy based on despair, however, is probably no more conducive to democracy and social justice in Latin America than the Alliance itself has been. Foreign assistance supplied exclusively by the Inter-American Development Bank and the World Bank, for example, seems unlikely to serve those objectives. The IDB has done much in the field of social reform, but it must be politically neutral in the allocation of funds among its member countries. The World Bank offers even less promise of encouraging social reform unless Mr. McNamara undertakes—and wins approval for—a fundamental reorientation of the bank's policies.

Nor would the termination of U.S. assistance programs have a liberalizing effect on Latin America. These programs are not the sole manifestation of the U.S. presence, or even the most important one. If they were removed, the massive U.S. business and military communities would still remain. The business community, by the nature of its associations in Latin American society, tends to favor social stability and financial orthodoxy —which in Latin America today are invariably accompanied by conservative, authoritarian government. The political impact of the business presence thus reflects not a mindless reflex but a reasoned pursuit of business interests. The military presence of the United States serves the same purpose.

Finally, Latin America's reformist military establishments have not yet proved themselves reliable agents of continuing social integration. The noble rhetoric of the Peruvian military government may represent something less than an irrevocable commitment to social change. Instead it may be used to justify acts motivated by more parochial considerations. For example, the Peruvian government, although carrying out a genuine and badly needed agrarian reform program, has begun its implementation not in the areas of greatest need, but in the sugar zone where the APRA labor unions are strongest and the foreign companies most vulnerable. More important, the military government's increasingly restrictive measures against the press early in 1970 and its purge of the judiciary do not indicate that its policies will become more liberal, particularly if the regime runs into economic difficulties. On the contrary, its early reformist surge could well degenerate into a more traditional tyranny. Yet a great many people in Latin America have, like U.S. liberals, come to view the Peruvian option as their only hope for change. A number of progressive Brazilians, repelled by the repressiveness of the government, the misery of the marginals, and the terrorist acts of the dissidents, have begun to insist that social reform depends on the younger Brazilian military and have abandoned their hopes for representative political institutions. The loss of this hope is one of the great tragedies of the Alliance period and one for which the United States is at least in part responsible. But it is not necessarily irreversible.

The policy reconsidered

The United States may still make a significant contribution to Latin American development. But it must learn from the mistakes it has made during the Alliance decade and build on its successes. In effect, the United States has to recognize its limitations. Instead of setting targets that cannot be reached or making promises that cannot be kept, it should undertake more modest commitments that will be sustainable over time and relatively invulnerable to other demands and constraints on what, after all, are finite resources.

But the key to an appropriate United States policy toward Latin America is the distinction between development objectives and security considerations. The failures of the Alliance result in large part from a failure to make this distinction. Traditionally, of course, the issue of security has played a leading role in the formulation of policy. In the form of the Castro threat it was present at the birth of the Alliance, and it has played a dominant role, certainly in Brazil, since 1964. Security considerations obviously motivated the United States military intervention in the Dominican Republic and were behind other less overt maneuvers elsewhere during the decade. And they are implicit in both the *Rockefeller Report* and the Nixon speech.

The U.S. security interest in Latin America, as traditionally conceived, consists of three propositions:

1 (dating from the Monroe Doctrine in the early nineteenth century): The United States must keep potentially hostile extracontinental powers out of the hemisphere in order to deny them a geographically convenient base from which to attack.

2 (dating from the days of Elihu Root in the early twentieth century): The United States, having become a capital surplus nation, must seek outlets for this surplus, generally abroad and particularly in Latin America (because of its geographic proximity and Christian heritage).[13]

3 (dating from the onset of the cold war in the late 1940s): The political apostasy of a Latin American country would cause the United States to lose face, weaken its influence in other parts of the world, and undermine the confidence of important European countries in the ability of the United States

---

13. This concern to maintain a worldwide "open door" for United States capital has received its most sophisticated—and critical—treatment at the hands of the revisionist U.S. historians, notably William Appleton Williams, who presents it, in *The Tragedy of American Diplomacy* (New York: Dell, 1962), as the unifying principle of U.S. foreign policy.

to lead the "free world" struggle against the monolithic communist bloc.

All of these propositions are open to question. The first provides justification for U.S. intervention in Latin America, on the grounds that a Latin American country, particularly one in the Caribbean area, could provide a site for Soviet missiles, as Cuba did in 1962. But the United States now has three major delivery systems that can destroy the Soviet Union: the intercontinental ballistic missile (ICBM) system, the submarine-launched Polaris-Poseidon nuclear missile system, and the intercontinental bomber force of the Strategic Air Command. Any one of these can deliver much more than the 400 megatons that former Secretary of Defense Robert McNamara estimated would eliminate three-fourths of the Soviet Union's industrial capacity and nearly one-third of its population.

In view of this nuclear strike capability, the Pentagon itself will concede that Latin America has little or no strategic value in a nuclear confrontation. And even if the establishment of Soviet missile sites in the hemisphere offered some marginal advantage, neither the Soviet Union nor potential host countries in Latin America would consider it worth the risk of another Cuban missile crisis. Moreover, the United States, with its modern satellite detection devices, could discover and interdict such an installation.

The second proposition has served to justify the Hickenlooper Amendment and the role of the U.S. government in the IPC dispute. It has also generated an inordinate fear of Latin American nationalists and leftists. But although nationalism may alter the terms of investment and trade, it cannot affect the need of developing countries for capital and technology. In any case, the political coloration of a regime does not necessarily determine its receptiveness to U.S. capital. Rumania and Yugoslavia need and want U.S. capital and technology. Mexico expropriated U.S. oil companies during its period of "left nationalism" in the late 1930s, but within a decade the two countries reached an accommodation that restored a heavy flow of U.S. private investment to Mexico under conditions of political stability. The basic logic of trade and geography dictates a continuing commercial relationship between Latin America and the United States.

The third proposition assumes the continuing existence of a

monolithic, hostile communist bloc that could extend its power through alliances with revolutionary regimes in Latin America. But the Chinese-Soviet rivalry and territorial conflict and the rising tide of nationalism, especially in the developing countries, have completely discredited this assumption. The Soviet intervention in Czechoslovakia revealed still another schism within the communist world. It was also a manifestation of the Soviet Union's almost obsessive fear of Germany, conditioned by a long history of incredibly bloody invasions. No comparable historical threat compels the United States to intervene in the Latin American countries.

Of course, the United States must be free to act against any credible threat to its security (for example, a new attempt on the part of a hostile power to install offensive missiles capable of changing the balance of terror). The Rio Treaty of 1947 states that foreign intervention affecting the security, territorial integrity, or political independence of any American republic is an act of aggression, to be repelled by the collective security measures of the American states. The military capability of the United States gives this treaty its protective force but does not justify unilateral intervention by the United States in the domestic political disorders of Latin American countries. On the other hand, when asked by a legitimately constituted Latin American government for assistance in dealing with a domestic disorder, the United States may judge the request on its merits (largely by evaluating the legitimacy of the government involved) and act accordingly.

The lessons of the Alliance

What considerations, then, should shape future United States policy in the hemisphere? By and large, the major lesson of the Alliance is that the reach of the United States should not exceed its grasp. Between the overambitious idealism of its development goals and the pointless obsessiveness of its concern for security, the United States really undermined the Alliance before it could get started. When the security issue lost its urgency and when other problems arose to demand higher priority—the war in Vietnam, the need to defend the dollar, the pressure of protectionist lobbies, the domestic urban crisis—the Alliance was deflated and distorted. The resulting situation is the worst of both worlds. The people of the United States feel that their generosity has not been appreciated and, in view of both domestic inflation and pressing domestic needs, appear unwilling to do more, while Latin Americans generally resent the restrictions placed on use of the funds made available, as well as the patronizing attitude with which they were often provided.

It may not be possible to reconstitute the Alliance as a set of ideals with quantitative targets and a precise timetable. It certainly does not appear either wise or realistic to do so. But if the United States is to participate constructively in Latin America's economic and social development, the executive leadership of the United States must establish clear priorities among conflicting policies and then see that these priorities are explained to Congress and the public, so that its programs can serve their purpose and function effectively. This emphasis on clear choices and explanations may help to produce reasonable, long-term commitments in specific areas where a little help can go a long way.

Another lesson of the Alliance is that a profound and perhaps very painful readjustment is taking place in Latin America, one that the United States may influence in minor ways but cannot begin to dominate or direct. Basic relationships—economic, political, and social—are being strained, broken down, rebuilt, and strained again, a process that must continue until it produces a new balance. In all likelihood, the upheaval that began before the Alliance but accelerated under it will become even more pronounced in the years ahead, so that further upheaval and experimentation and change will be the rule rather than the exception. Already various forms of authoritarian government have emerged; others are almost sure to follow. The United States, as a democracy dedicated to constitutional processes and civil liberties, cannot provide financial assistance to authoritarian regimes without calling its own political system into question. This limitation on policy may make an Alliance impossible, but it is a real and practical constraint that springs from the nature of democracy.

Unquestionably, the readjustment process will affect the United States in both its political relationships and its property holdings in Latin America. These effects are inevitable, in part simply because the United States has such ties to a region undergoing basic change, and in part because Latin American societies, deeply divided in so many ways, often find a degree of unity—real or spurious—in an aggressive nationalism. This spirit is likely to manifest itself in·attacks on United States holdings, as it already has in Peru and Bolivia. The lesson that the Alliance has taught in this critical area is that the United States must learn to live with and expect change, and that its response should be flexible and measured rather than excessively rigid or tough. In fact, long before the Alliance, the United States learned that it could accommodate such revolutionary change; in both Mexico and Bolivia it accepted new property relationships without permanent damage to its own interests.

It is safe to predict that in the coming decade inter-American relationships will face fresh uncertainties and harsh tests that demand policies much more effective than those of the Alliance decade. Policy-makers must use greater realism and sophistication in both the making and the implementation of commitments. They must also deepen their awareness of and sensitivity to the internal conflicts afflicting the varied social classes of Latin America. And they must achieve a profound and sure understanding of just what constitutes the national interest of the United States in its relations with its sister republics.

Back to democratic development

A fresh start should not mean a renunciation of the Alliance and all that it implies. On the contrary, it should build on the basic cornerstone of the Alliance, which was designed to improve living standards for the teeming masses of Latin America within the framework of democratic institutions. This objective is idealistic but not fanciful. In fact, the attainment of the Alliance ideal requires that the United States acknowledge its own limitations and its own national interest, which lies in assisting those countries determined to undertake economic and social reforms while strengthening the democratic process.

The political leaders of a few Latin American countries, motivated by enlightened self-interest, a sense of justice, or both, have made the decision to begin incorporating the previously neglected masses into society. The Chilean and Colombian governments, implementing this decision within a framework of representative political institutions, have asked the United States to support their difficult and expensive enterprise.

The United States is under no military compulsion to assist any of the Latin American countries. But since the resources available for foreign development assistance are not infinite, the United States cannot allocate them indiscriminately, wastefully, or for uses that are inconsistent with its own principles. The proper function of these resources is to help less wealthy countries solve the difficult problems of development with a minimum of human suffering and without violating the basic American ideological commitment to an open and just society. The United States can freely devote its assistance funds to this purpose rather than to purchasing collaboration by sending in the Marines, as in the Dominican Republic, or by arranging for military disruptions of the political process, as in Guatemala.

The United States need not lecture, threaten, or dictate policy to governments seeking assistance. The present leadership of Brazil, for instance, is entitled to choose its course, however mistaken it may seem, without hectoring from the United States. The United States, on the other hand, is entitled to withhold financing from programs that depend upon political oppression and negative social policies. And if the Brazilian government makes such financing a condition for the granting of privileges to the United States, then the United States must weigh those privileges against the consequences of supporting a repressive military dictatorship.

Having made the decision to support democratic development in Latin America, the United States must recognize that its aid alone cannot produce reform. Title IX of the Foreign Assistance Act suggests that aid funds may promote grass-roots small-scale private development: "In carrying out programs authorized in this chapter, emphasis shall be placed on assuring maximum participation in the task of economic development on the part of the people of the developing countries, through the encouragement of democratic private and local governmental institutions."

This objective is unexceptionable. Governments that want to encourage community development through small, locally directed private institutions may find the Title IX approach congenial. Other governments may not. No foreign aid program can bring about democratic, modernizing change in a significant degree without the political support of the national government.

The assumption that the United States knows how to promote grass-roots organizations in another society also smacks of arrogance. One thing our experience in the Alliance clearly demonstrates is how little we know about the interaction of economic, social, and political conditions in developing countries and about the consequences of specific decisions for one sector or another. External assistance, whether capital or technical, is important, but it cannot substitute for Latin American leadership in dealing with such issues as population policy, agrarian reform, and urban development.

On what basis, then, should the United States organize its assistance program? A country that is to receive assistance must already have an effective political leadership, a reasonable economic management capability, and a sufficient social consensus on objectives. The United States can provide none of these essentials. But it can provide a part of the necessary incremental capital resources and, when requested, a modest amount of technical assistance. That is what its program should be designed to do.

Multilateral channels

The existing international lending institutions, the World Bank group and the Inter-American Development Bank, are essential sources of financing for Latin American development. These institutions are technical, apolitical, and experienced in public development financing. Both depend heavily on the U.S. government and U.S. capital markets for their funds. The World Bank and its affiliated "soft loan" International Development Association have shown increasing interest in Latin America and have extended financing from conventional "infrastructure" and agriculture loans to education, urban problems, and community development.

The IDB, although not yet on a par with the World Bank in its professional studies and operations, is now the most important source of financing for Latin America. Among other valuable assets, it has a growing cadre of economists and operational personnel who have acquired special knowledge of Latin American problems. The IDB is more flexible and experimental than the World Bank. Its flexibility has won it the respect and gratitude of the Latin American authorities. And since the state of the art of developmental economics is still quite primitive, the IDB's experimentation, particularly in the area of social investment, serves to extend knowledge of the development process.

Because Latin America's economic growth in itself serves U.S. foreign aid purposes, the United States should channel most of its public development assistance through multilateral institutions. But these institutions can fulfill their functions effectively only if the United States respects their decisions. The United States has on occasion had the U.S. director of the IDB or the World Bank hold up technically approved loans to Peru, for example, because of the IPC dispute or Peruvian purchases of sophisticated military aircraft. This interference blurs the distinction between bilateral and multilateral aid and impairs the effectiveness of both. Countries in situations that are politically unpalatable for a United States bilateral aid program (such as the IPC case in Peru) may nonetheless meet the technical lending criteria of the international financing institutions. In view of Latin America's highly fluid political situation, both the World Bank and the IDB can function effectively only by retaining their essentially apolitical integrity and utilizing only technical criteria for the allocation of their resources.

U.S. bilateral aid

A bilateral foreign assistance program, on the other hand, cannot be depoliticized. The United States is by definition a political entity. Its decision to provide massive balance-of-payments support to a government as part of a development program is a political decision. Implicit in U.S. financial support for the Frei government's development program in Chile, for example, is political support of the Frei government. Officials of the United States government have asserted that financial support of Brazil's military regime merely serves long-term development objectives in Brazil and does not constitute endorsement of the Brazilian government's politically repressive acts. But all informed segments of the Brazilian public simply assume that behind this financial support is political approval of the Brazilian government. And they have no concrete reason to think otherwise.

Those who administer the bilateral program must therefore recognize the political consequences of their decisions. They must decide whether a country has the political leadership, the economic management capability, and the will to carry out a program of social reform and economic development within the framework of representative political institutions. Having reached a favorable decision, they should then work with the recipient government to determine the amount of assistance that is needed, its duration, the country's own resource contribution, and the procedures by which the country can draw on funds.

AID (phased down to a relatively small staff capable of administering a public capital assistance program) should make its funds available in the form of program loans. And since the consequences of a nation's program of monetary, fiscal, exchange-rate, and social reform primarily devolve not upon AID but upon that nation's government, the recipient government and not AID should determine the details of that program. If the country's economic or political situation deteriorates to the point where its government seems unable or unlikely to carry on its development program effectively, the United States should so inform the country and terminate its assistance.

Both Rockefeller and Nixon have criticized the present restrictions on foreign aid funds. Removing these restrictions would considerably increase the effectiveness of a politically and socially oriented assistance program. Ideally, the Congress should permit AID to authorize funds for more than a year at a time, so that recipient governments can rely on a fairly specific amount of assistance for the duration of a long-term program. Balance-of-payments constraints should also be minimized. If the Vietnam war ends, the United States procurement rule will probably become unnecessary. In any case, the Treasury Department should not be permitted to interfere with AID lending. The "positive lists," the fifty-fifty shipping, small business notification, and other such promotional uses of aid should be abolished.

Technical assistance

AID's massive technical assistance programs are a carry-over from the fifties. Most of them have outlived their usefulness in Latin America and go on primarily out of inertia. The one field in which U.S. technical assistance is vitally needed, however, is education (particularly higher education). One of the most effective channels for this assistance may be the Latin American Scholarship Program of American Universities (LASPAU), formed in 1965. LASPAU offers up to four years of scholarship support to carefully selected transfer applicants from Latin American universities. AID finances the program but United States universities administer it, working directly with their Latin American counterparts. LASPAU students usually obtain bachelor's and master's degrees in the United States. The program envisions assured teaching positions for the students upon their return to the sponsoring Latin American universities. In 1968 approximately four hundred LASPAU students were enrolled in United States universities. In 1969 six hundred were enrolled. An expanded LASPAU-type program and concentration of technical assistance in the one field where the United States contribution is unquestionably useful—provided the political circumstances permit—should replace AID's present diffuse technical assistance effort.

Military assistance

Recent history suggests a correlation between the probability of United States intervention in a Latin American country and the influence of the CIA-Defense establishment in that country. The work of the intelligence and military communities focuses their attention on the dangers of communist activity in the hemisphere, to which they respond by preparing contingency plans in tempting detail. Like the business community, the CIA and the military have a direct and abiding interest in Latin American affairs. But the United States government must base its policy decisions on a broader view of conditions in Latin America. The United States would be well advised to terminate its military assistance missions in Latin America, to maintain contact with the Latin American military through well-selected military attachés working under the close policy guidance of the United States ambassador, and to limit procurement of arms. The United States military assistance program in Latin

America, costing $60 million a year, has accomplished very little of its stated purpose: to guide Latin American military thinking toward democratic norms.

The United States cannot control the turbulence through which Latin America must pass in the coming years. It can help or hinder the course of social change, but it cannot start, stop, or alter it.

Change was, in fact, the basis of the Alliance for Progress—change not only in Latin American society, but also in U.S. foreign policy. The Alliance represented innovation in both its approach to national development and its identification of the United States with concern for democracy and social justice. This innovative effort was subverted not by communism but by two preoccupations, technocracy and the U.S. security interest, with which many Latin Americans today identify the United States.

The Alliance experience has discredited these preoccupations as a basis for government policy. The narrow, technocratic approach to development as economic growth has not enhanced the quality of life in Latin America, and the hot pursuit of the U.S. security interest has not enhanced the security of the United States (or at least of U.S. citizens abroad, if the kidnapping of Ambassador Elbrick in Brazil and the murders of three U.S. diplomats in Guatemala have any significance).

In short, only through a commitment to support development in its economic, social, and political aspects can the United States help bring stability to all the Americas. Fulfilling this commitment would demand intelligence, imagination, and the courage to make and acknowledge mistakes when necessary—qualities that do not seem to be highly developed in U.S. policymakers today. But it would also resolve at last the conflict between morality and pragmatism that has distorted United States policy, both foreign and domestic, throughout its history.

Address by John F. Kennedy at a White House reception for members of Congress and for the diplomatic corps of the Latin American republics, March 13, 1961[1]

It is a great pleasure for Mrs. Kennedy and for me, for the Vice President and Mrs. Johnson, and for the members of Congress to welcome the ambassadorial corps of our hemisphere, our long-time friends, to the White House today. One hundred and thirty-nine years ago this week the United States, stirred by the heroic struggle of its fellow Americans, urged the independence and recognition of the new Latin American republics. It was then, at the dawn of freedom throughout this hemisphere, that Bolívar spoke of his desire to see the Americas fashioned into the greatest region in the world, "greatest," he said, "not so much by virtue of her area and her wealth, as by her freedom and her glory."

Never in the long history of our hemisphere has this dream been nearer to fulfillment, and never has it been in greater danger.

The genius of our scientists has given us the tools to bring abundance to our land, strength to our industry, and knowledge to our people. For the first time we have the capacity to strike off the remaining bonds of poverty and ignorance—to free our people for the spiritual and intellectual fulfillment which has always been the goal of our civilization.

Yet at this very moment of maximum opportunity, we con-

Reprinted from *Public Papers of the Presidents of the United States, 1961* (Washington, D.C.: U.S. Government Printing Office, 1962), pp. 170–81.

1. The President spoke in the East Room at the White House. Immediately following his speech, the President's words were translated and broadcast in Spanish, Portuguese, and French, as well as in English, to the nations of the south by the Voice of America.

The text of the Act of Bogotá, adopted September 13, 1960, by a Special Committee to Study the Formulation of New Measures for Economic Cooperation, is published in the *Department of State Bulletin*, vol. 43, p. 537.

front the same forces which have imperiled America throughout its history—the alien forces which once again seek to impose the despotisms of the Old World on the people of the New.

I have asked you to come here today so that I might discuss these challenges and these dangers.

We meet together as firm and ancient friends, united by history and experience and by our determination to advance the values of American civilization. For this New World of ours is not a mere accident of geography. Our continents are bound together by a common history, the endless exploration of new frontiers. Our nations are the product of a common struggle, the revolt from colonial rule. And our people share a common heritage, the quest for the dignity and the freedom of man.

The revolutions which gave us birth ignited, in the words of Thomas Paine, "a spark never to be extinguished." And across vast, turbulent continents these American ideals still stir man's struggle for national independence and individual freedom. But as we welcome the spread of the American revolution to other lands, we must also remember that our own struggle—the revolution which began in Philadelphia in 1776, and in Caracas in 1811—is not yet finished. Our hemisphere's mission is not yet completed. For our unfulfilled task is to demonstrate to the entire world that man's unsatisfied aspiration for economic progress and social justice can best be achieved by free men working within a framework of democratic institutions. If we can do this in our own hemisphere, and for our own people, we may yet realize the prophecy of the great Mexican patriot Benito Juárez, that "democracy is the destiny of future humanity."

As a citizen of the United States let me be the first to admit that we North Americans have not always grasped the significance of this common mission, just as it is also true that many in your own countries have not fully understood the urgency of the need to lift people from poverty and ignorance and despair. But we must turn from these mistakes—from the failures and the misunderstandings of the past—to a future full of peril, but bright with hope.

Throughout Latin America, a continent rich in resources and in the spiritual and cultural achievements of its people, millions of men and women suffer the daily degradations of poverty and hunger. They lack decent shelter or protection from disease. Their children are deprived of the education or the jobs which are the gateway to a better life. And each day the problems grow more urgent. Population growth is outpacing economic growth; low living standards are further endangered; and discontent—the discontent of a people who know that abundance and the tools of progress are at last within their reach—that discontent is growing. In the words of José Figueres, "once dormant peoples are struggling upward toward the sun, toward a better life."

If we are to meet a problem so staggering in its dimensions, our approach must itself be equally bold—an approach consistent with the majestic concept of Operation Pan America. Therefore I have called on all people of the hemisphere to join in a new Alliance for Progress—*Alianza para Progreso*—a vast cooperative effort, unparalleled in magnitude and nobility of purpose, to satisfy the basic needs of the American people for homes, work and land, health and schools—*techo, trabajo y tierra, salud y escuela.*

First, I propose that the American republics begin on a vast new ten-year plan for the Americas, a plan to transform the 1960s into a historic decade of democratic progress.

These ten years will be the years of maximum progress, maximum effort, the years when the greatest obstacles must be overcome, the years when the need for assistance will be the greatest.

And if we are successful, if our effort is bold enough and determined enough, then the close of this decade will mark the beginning of a new era in the American experience. The living standards of every American family will be on the rise, basic education will be available to all, hunger will be a forgotten experience, the need for massive outside help will have passed, most nations will have entered a period of self-sustaining growth, and though there will be still much to do, every American republic will be the master of its own revolution and its own hope and progress.

Let me stress that only the most determined efforts of the American nations themselves can bring success to this effort. They and they alone can mobilize their resources, enlist the energies of their people, and modify their social patterns so that all, and not just a privileged few, share in the fruits of growth. If this effort is made, then outside assistance will give vital impetus to progress; without it, no amount of help will advance the welfare of the people.

Thus if the countries of Latin America are ready to do their part, and I am sure they are, then I believe the United States, for its part, should help provide resources of a scope and magnitude sufficient to make this bold development plan a success —just as we helped to provide, against equal odds nearly, the resources adequate to help rebuild the economies of western Europe. For only an effort of towering dimensions can ensure fulfillment of our plan for a decade of progress.

Secondly, I will shortly request a ministerial meeting of the Inter-American Economic and Social Council, a meeting at which we can begin the massive planning effort which will be at the heart of the Alliance for Progress.

For if our Alliance is to succeed, each Latin nation must formulate long-range plans for its own development, plans which establish targets and priorities, ensure monetary stability, establish the machinery for vital social change, stimulate private activity and initiative, and provide for a maximum national effort. These plans will be the foundation of our development effort, and the basis for the allocation of outside resources.

A greatly strengthened IAECOSOC, working with the Economic Commission for Latin America and the Inter-American Development Bank, can assemble the leading economists and experts of the hemisphere to help each country develop its own development plan—and provide a continuing review of economic progress in this hemisphere.

Third, I have this evening signed a request to the Congress for $500 million as a first step in fulfilling the Act of Bogotá. This is the first large-scale inter-American effort, instituted by my predecessor, President Eisenhower, to attack the social barriers which block economic progress. The money will be used to combat illiteracy, improve the productivity and use of the land, wipe out disease, attack archaic tax and land-tenure structures, provide educational opportunities, and offer a broad range of projects designed to make the benefits of increasing abundance available to all. We will begin to commit these funds as soon as they are appropriated.

Fourth, we must support all economic integration which is a genuine step toward larger markets and greater competitive opportunity. The fragmentation of Latin American economies is a serious barrier to industrial growth. Projects such as the Central American Common Market and free-trade areas in South America can help to remove these obstacles.

Fifth, the United States is ready to cooperate in serious, case-by-case examinations of commodity market problems. Frequent violent change in commodity prices seriously injures the economies of many Latin American countries, draining their resources and stultifying their growth. Together we must find practical methods of bringing an end to this pattern.

Sixth, we will immediately step up our Food for Peace emergency program, help establish food reserves in areas of recurrent drought, help provide school lunches for children, and offer feed grains for use in rural development. For hungry men and women cannot wait for economic discussions or diplomatic meetings—their need is urgent, and their hunger rests heavily on the conscience of their fellow men.

Seventh, all the people of the hemisphere must be allowed to share in the expanding wonders of science—wonders which have captured man's imagination, challenged the powers of his mind, and given him the tools for rapid progress. I invite Latin American scientists to work with us in new projects in fields such as medicine and agriculture, physics and astronomy, and desalinization, to help plan for regional research laboratories in these and other fields, and to strengthen cooperation between American universities and laboratories.

We also intend to expand our science teacher training programs to include Latin American instructors, to assist in establishing such programs in other American countries, and translate and make available revolutionary new teaching materials in physics, chemistry, biology, and mathematics, so that the young of all nations may contribute their skills to the advance of science.

Eighth, we must rapidly expand the training of those needed to man the economies of rapidly developing countries. This means expanded technical training programs, for which the Peace Corps, for example, will be available when needed. It also means assistance to Latin American universities, graduate schools, and research institutes.

We welcome proposals in Central America for intimate cooperation in higher education—cooperation which can achieve a regional effort of increased effectiveness and excellence. We are ready to help fill the gap in trained manpower, realizing that our ultimate goal must be a basic education for all who wish to learn.

Ninth, we reaffirm our pledge to come to the defense of any American nation whose independence is endangered. As its confidence in the collective security system of the OAS spreads, it will be possible to devote to constructive use a major share of those resources now spent on the instruments of war. Even now, as the government of Chile has said, the time has come to take the first steps toward sensible limitations of arms. And the new generation of military leaders has shown an increasing awareness that armies cannot only defend their countries; they can, as we have learned through our own Corps of Engineers, help to build them.

Tenth, we invite our friends in Latin America to contribute to the enrichment of life and culture in the United States. We need teachers of your literature and history and tradition, op-
•portunities for our young people to study in your universities, access to your music, your art, and the thought of your great philosophers. For we know we have much to learn.

In this way you can help bring a fuller spiritual and intellectual life to the people of the United States, and contribute to understanding and mutual respect among the nations of the hemisphere.

With steps such as these, we propose to complete the revolution of the Americas, to build a hemisphere where all men can hope for a suitable standard of living, and all can live out their lives in dignity and in freedom.

To achieve this goal political freedom must accompany material progress. Our Alliance for Progress is an alliance of free governments, and it must work to eliminate tyranny from a hemisphere in which it has no rightful place. Therefore let us express our special friendship to the people of Cuba and the Dominican Republic, and the hope they will soon rejoin the society of free men, uniting with us in common effort.

This political freedom must be accompanied by social change. For unless necessary social reforms, including land and tax reform, are freely made—unless we broaden the opportunity for all of our people—unless the great mass of Americans share in increasing prosperity—then our alliance, our revolution, our dream, and our freedom will fail. But we call for social change by free men—change in the spirit of Washington and Jefferson, of Bolívar and San Martín and Martí—not change which seeks to impose on men tyrannies which we cast out a century and a half ago. Our motto is what it has always been: Progress, yes; tyranny, no—*progreso, sí; tiranía, no!*

But our greatest challenge comes from within—the task of creating an American civilization where spiritual and cultural values are strengthened by an ever broadening base of material advance; where, within the rich diversity of its own traditions, each nation is free to follow its own path toward progress.

The completion of our task will, of course, require the efforts of all governments of our hemisphere. But the efforts of governments alone will never be enough. In the end, the people must choose and the people must help themselves.

And so I say to the men and women of the Americas—to the *campesino* in the fields, to the *obrero* in the cities, to the *estudiante* in the schools—prepare your mind and heart for the task ahead; call forth your strength and let each devote his energies to the betterment of all, so that your children and our children in this hemisphere can find an ever richer and freer life.

Let us once again transform the American continent into a vast crucible of revolutionary ideas and efforts—a tribute to the power of the creative energies of free men and women, an example to all the world that liberty and progress walk hand in hand. Let us once again awaken our American revolution until it guides the struggle of people everywhere—not with an imperialism of force or fear, but the rule of courage and freedom and hope for the future of man.

Special message to the Congress
requesting appropriations for
the Inter-American Fund
for Social Progress and
for reconstruction in Chile,
March 14, 1961

To the Congress of the United States:
On September 8, 1960, at the request of the Administration,

the Congress authorized the sum of $500 million for the Inter-American Fund for Social Progress. On the basis of this authorization the United States, on September 12, 1960, subscribed to the Act of Bogotá, along with eighteen other American republics.

In the same bill the Congress authorized $100 million for the long-term reconstruction and rehabilitation of those areas of southern Chile recently devastated by fire and earthquake.

I now request that Congress appropriate the full amount of $600 million.

The Act of Bogotá marks a historic turning point in the evolution of the Western Hemisphere. For the first time the American nations have agreed to join in a massive cooperative effort to strengthen democratic institutions through a program of economic development and social progress.

Such a program is long overdue. Throughout Latin America millions of people are struggling to free themselves from the bonds of poverty and ignorance. To the North and East they see the abundance which modern science can bring. They know the tools of progress are within their reach. And they are determined to have a better life for themselves and their children.

The people of Latin America are the inheritors of a deep belief in political democracy and the freedom of man—a sincere faith that the best road to progress is freedom's road. But if the Act of Bogotá becomes just another empty declaration —if we are unwilling to commit our resources and energy to the task of social progress and economic development— then we face a grave and imminent danger that desperate peoples will turn to communism or other forms of tyranny as their only hope for change. Well-organized, skillful, and strongly financed forces are constantly urging them to take this course.

A few statistics will illustrate the depth of the problems of Latin America. This is the fastest growing area in the world. Its current population of 195,000,000 represents an increase of about 30 percent over the past ten years, and by the 1980s the continent will have to support more than 400,000,000 people. At the same time the average per capita annual product is only $280, less than one-ninth that of the United States— and in large areas, inhabited by millions of people, it is less than $70. Thus it is a difficult task merely to keep living standards from falling further as population grows.

Such poverty inevitably takes its toll in human life. The average American can expect to live seventy years, but life expectancy in Latin America is only forty-six, dropping to about thirty-five in some Central American countries. And while our rate of infant mortality is less than 30 per thousand, it is more than 110 per thousand in Latin America.

Perhaps the greatest stimulus to our own development was the establishment of universal basic education. But for most of the children of Latin America education is a remote and unattainable dream. Illiteracy extends to almost half the adults, reaching 90 percent in one country. And approximately 50 percent of school-age children have no schools to attend.

In one major Latin American capital a third of the total population is living in filthy and unbearable slums. In another country 80 percent of the entire population is housed in makeshift shacks and barracks, lacking the privacy of separate rooms for families.

It was to meet these shocking and urgent conditions that the Act of Bogotá was signed. This act, building on the concept of Operation Pan America, initiated by Brazil in 1958, introduced two important new elements to the effort to improve living standards in South America.

First, the nations of Latin America have recognized the need for an intensive program of self-help—mobilizing their domestic resources and undertaking basic reforms in tax structure, in land ownership and use, and in education, health, and housing.

Second, it launches a major inter-American program for the social progress which is an indispensable condition to growth —a program for improved land use, education, health, and housing. This program, supported by the special fund which I am asking Congress to appropriate, will be administered primarily through the Inter-American Bank, and guided by greatly strengthened regional institutions.

The $500 million Inter-American Fund for Social Progress is only the first move toward carrying out the declarations of the Act of Bogotá; and the act itself is only a single step in our program for the development of the hemisphere, a program I have termed the Alliance for Progress—*Alianza para Progreso.* In addition to the social fund, hemispheric development will require substantial outside resources for economic development, a major self-help effort by the Latin American nations themselves, inter-American cooperation to deal with the problems of economic integration and commodity markets and other measures designed to speed economic growth and improve understanding among the American nations.

Social progress and economic development

The fund which I am requesting today will be devoted to social progress. Social progress is not a substitute for economic development. It is an effort to create a social framework within which all the people of a nation can share in the benefits of prosperity and participate in the process of growth. Economic growth without social progress lets the great majority of the people remain in poverty, while a privileged few reap the benefits of rising abundance. In addition the process of growth largely depends on the existence of beneficial social conditions. Our own experience is witness to this. For much of our own great productivity and industrial development is based on our system of universal public education.

Thus the purpose of our special effort for social progress is to overcome the barriers of geographical and social isolation, illiteracy and lack of educational opportunities, archaic tax and land-tenure structures, and other institutional obstacles to broad participation in economic growth.

Self-help and internal reform

It is clear that the Bogotá program cannot have any significant impact if its funds are used merely for the temporary relief of conditions of distress. Its effectiveness depends on the willingness of each recipient nation to improve its own institutions, make necessary modifications in its own social patterns, and mobilize its own domestic resources for a program of development.

Even at the start such measures will be a condition of assistance from the social fund. Priorities will depend not merely on need, but on the demonstrated readiness of each government to make the institutional improvements which promise lasting social progress. The criteria for administration of the funds by the Inter-American Development Bank and the ICA will explicitly reflect these principles.

For example: the uneven distribution of land is one of the gravest social problems in many Latin American countries. In some nations 2 percent of the farms account for three-quarters of the total farm area. And in one Central American country, 40 percent of the privately owned acreage is held in one-fifth of 1 percent of the number of farms. It is clear that when land ownership is so heavily concentrated, efforts to increase agricultural productivity will benefit only a very small percentage of the population. Thus if funds for improving land usage are to be used effectively, they should go only to those nations in which the benefits will accrue to the great mass of rural workers.

Examples of potential areas of progress

When each nation demonstrates its willingness to abide by these general principles, then outside resources will be focused on projects which have the greatest multiplying effect in mobilizing domestic resources, contributing to institutional reform, and reducing the major obstacles to a development in which all can share.

In housing, for example, much can be done for middle-income groups through improved credit mechanisms. But, since the great majority of family incomes are only $10 to $50 a month, until income levels as a whole are increased, the most promising means of improving mass housing is through aided self-help projects—projects in which the low-income worker is provided with low-cost materials, land, and some technical guidance, and then builds the house with his own labor, repaying the cost of materials with a long-term mortgage.

Education is another field where self-help efforts can effectively broaden educational opportunities—and a variety of techniques, from self-help school construction, where the entire village contributes labor, to the use of local people as part-time teachers, can be used.

In the field of land use there is no sharp demarcation between economic and social development. Improved land use and rural living conditions were rightly given top place in the Act of Bogotá. Most of the Latin American peoples live and work on the land. Yet agricultural output and productivity have lagged far behind both industrial development and urgent needs for consumption and export.

As a result, poverty, illiteracy, hopelessness, and a sense of injustice—the conditions which breed political and social unrest—are almost universal in the Latin American countryside.

Thus there is an immediate need for higher and more diversified agricultural production, better distribution of wealth and income, and wider sharing in the process of development. This can be partly accomplished through establishing supervised rural credit facilities, helping to finance resettlement in new lands, constructing access roads to new settlement sites, conducting agricultural surveys and research, and introducing agricultural extension services.

Administration of the Inter-American Fund for Social Progress

It is fundamental to the success of this cooperative effort that the Latin American nations themselves play an important role in the administration of the social fund.

Therefore, the major share of the funds will be administered by the Inter-American Development Bank (IDB)—an organization to which nearly all the American republics belong.

Of the total $500 million, $394 million will be assigned to the IDB, to be administered under a special trust agreement with the United States. The IDB will apply most of these funds on a loan basis with flexible terms, including low interest rates or repayment in local currency. The IDB's major fields of activity will be land settlement and improved land use, housing, water supply, and sanitation, and technical assistance related to the mobilizing of domestic financial resources.

In order to promote progress in activities which generally are not self-liquidating and therefore not appropriate for loan financing, the sum of $100 million will be administered by the International Cooperation Administration (ICA). These funds will be applied mainly on a grant basis for education and training, public health projects, and the strengthening of general governmental services in fields related to economic and social development. Funds administered by the ICA will also be available to assist projects for social progress in dependent territories which are becoming independent, but are not yet members of the IDB.

Up to $6 million more is to be used to help strengthen the Organization of American States (OAS). To reinforce the movement toward adequate self-help and institutional improvement, the Inter-American Economic and Social Council (IAECOSOC) of the OAS is strengthening its secretariat and its staff. It is also working out cooperative arrangements with the United Nations Economic Commission for Latin America (ECLA) and the IDB. These three regional agencies will work together in making region-wide studies, and in sponsoring conferences directed toward bringing about tax reform, improved land use, educational modernization, and sound national development programming.

Many of the nations of the Americas have already responded to the action taken at Bogotá by directing attention to their most pressing social problems. In the brief period since the meeting at Bogotá, United States embassies and operations missions, after consultation with Latin American governments, have already reported proposals for social development projects calling for external assistance totaling about $1.225 billion. A preliminary selection from this list shows some $800 million worth of projects which are worthy of early detailed examination by the bank and the ICA.

In the bank's area of activity these selected projects total $611 million, including $309 million for land use and improved rural living conditions, $136 million in the field of housing, and $146 million for water supply and sanitation.

Selected proposals in fields to be administered by the ICA total $187 million, of which $136 million are for education and training, $36 million for public health, and $15 million for public administration and other assigned responsibilities.

So that each recipient nation will live up to the principles of self-help and domestic reform outlined above, funds will not be allocated until the operating agency receives assurances that the country being aided will take those measures necessary to ensure that the particular project brings the maximum social progress. For the same reason we can make no firm forecast of the rate at which the funds will be committed. Thus, if they are to be used most efficiently and economically, they must be made available for obligation without limitation as to time.

Urgency of the need

Under ideal conditions, projects for social progress would be undertaken only after the preparation of integrated country plans for economic and social development. Many nations, however, do not possess even the most basic information on their own resources or land ownership. Revolutionary new social institutions and patterns cannot be designed overnight. Yet, at the same time, Latin America is seething with discontent and unrest. We must act to relieve large-scale distress immediately if free institutions are to be given a chance to work out long-term solutions. Both the bank and the ICA are ready to begin operation immediately. But they must have the funds in hand if they are to develop detailed projects, and stimulate vital measures of self-help and institutional improvement.

The Bogotá conference created a new sense of resolve—a new determination to deal with the causes of the social unrest which afflicts much of the hemisphere. If this momentum is lost, through failure of the United States to act promptly and fully, we may not have another chance.

The role of private organizations

Inter-American cooperation for economic and social progress is not limited to the actions of government. Private foundations and universities have played a pioneering role in identifying critical deficiencies and pointing the way toward constructive remedies. We hope they will redouble their efforts in the years to come.

United States business concerns have also played a significant part in Latin American economic development. They can play an even greater role in the future. Their work is especially important in manufacturing goods and providing services for Latin American markets. Technical expertness and management skills in these fields can be effectively transferred to local enterprises by private investment in a great variety of forms, ranging from licensing through joint ventures to ownership.

Private enterprise's most important future role will be to assist in the development of healthy and responsible private enterprise within the Latin American nations. The initiation, in recent years, of strikingly successful new private investment houses, mutual investment funds, savings and loan associations, and other financial institutions is an example of what can be done. Stimulating the growth of local suppliers of components for complex consumer durable goods is another example of the way in which domestic business can be strengthened.

A major forward thrust in Latin American development will create heavy new demands for technical personnel and specialized knowledge—demands which private organizations can help to fill. And, of course, the continued inflow of private capital will continue to serve as an important stimulus to development.

Chilean reconstruction and rehabilitation

Last May more than five thousand Chileans were killed when fire and earthquake devastated the southern part of that republic. Several of the American republics, including the United States, provided emergency supplies of food, medicine, and clothing to the victims of this disaster. Our country provided almost $35 million in emergency grants and loans.

However, these emergency efforts did not meet the desperate need to rebuild the economy of an area which had suffered almost $400 million worth of damage. In recognition of this need, Congress authorized $100 million for long-term reconstruction and rehabilitation. Since then the people of Chile have been patiently rebuilding their shattered homes and communications facilities. But reconstruction is severely hampered by lack of funds. Therefore, I am asking the Congress to appropriate the $100 million so that the task of rebuilding the economy of southern Chile can proceed without delay.

JOHN F. KENNEDY

Declaration to the peoples of America

Assembled in Punta del Este, inspired by the principles consecrated in the Charter of the Organization of American States, in Operation Pan America, and in the Act of Bogotá, the representatives of the American republics hereby agree to establish an Alliance for Progress: a vast effort to bring a better life to all the peoples of the continent.

This Alliance is established on the basic principle that free men working through the institution of representative democracy can best satisfy man's aspirations, including those for work, home and land, health and schools. No system can guarantee true progress unless it affirms the dignity of the individual which is the foundation of our civilization.

Therefore the countries signing this declaration in the exercise of their sovereignty have agreed to work toward the following goals during the coming years:

To improve and strengthen democratic institutions through application of the principle of self-determination by the people.

To accelerate economic and social development, thus rapidly bringing about a substantial and steady increase in the average income in order to narrow the gap between the standard of living in Latin American countries and that enjoyed in the industrialized countries.

To carry out urban and rural housing programs to provide decent homes for all our people.

To encourage, in accordance with the characteristics of each country, programs of comprehensive agrarian reform, leading to the effective transformation, where required, of unjust structures and systems of land tenure and use; with a view to replacing latifundia and dwarf holdings by an equitable system of

Reprinted from *Alliance for Progress: Special Documents Emanating from the Special Meeting of the Inter-American Economic and Social Council at the Ministerial Level, Held at Punta del Este, Uruguay, from August 5 to 17, 1961*, OEA/Ser. H./XII.1, rev. (Washington, D.C.: Pan American Union, 1961), pp. 3–16.

property so that, supplemented by timely and adequate credit, technical assistance and improved marketing arrangements, the land will become for the man who works it the basis of his economic stability, the foundation of his increasing welfare, and the guarantee of his freedom and dignity.

To assure fair wages and satisfactory working conditions to all our workers; to establish effective systems of labor-management relations and procedures for consultation and cooperation among government authorities, employers' associations, and trade unions in the interests of social and economic development.

To wipe out illiteracy; to extend, as quickly as possible, the benefits of primary education to all Latin Americans; and to provide broader facilities, on a vast scale, for secondary and technical training and for higher education.

To press forward with programs of health and sanitation in order to prevent sickness, combat contagious disease, and strengthen our human potential.

To reform tax laws, demanding more from those who have most, to punish tax evasion severely, and to redistribute the national income in order to benefit those who are most in need, while, at the same time, promoting savings and investment and reinvestment of capital.

To maintain monetary and fiscal policies which, while avoiding the disastrous effects of inflation or deflation, will protect the purchasing power of the many, guarantee the greatest possible price stability, and form an adequate basis for economic development.

To stimulate private enterprise in order to encourage the development of Latin American countries at a rate which will help them to provide jobs for their growing populations, to eliminate unemployment, and to take their place among the modern industrialized nations of the world.

To find a quick and lasting solution to the grave problem created by excessive price fluctuations in the basic exports of Latin American countries on which their prosperity so heavily depends.

To accelerate the integration of Latin America so as to stimulate the economic and social development of the continent. This process has already begun through the General Treaty of Economic Integration of Central America and, in other countries, through the Latin American Free Trade Association.

This declaration expresses the conviction of the nations of Latin America that these profound economic, social, and cultural changes can come about only through the self-help efforts of each country. Nonetheless, in order to achieve the goals which have been established with the necessary speed, domestic efforts must be reinforced by essential contributions of external assistance.

The United States, for its part, pledges its efforts to supply financial and technical cooperation in order to achieve the aims of the Alliance for Progress. To this end, the United States will provide a major part of the minimum of $20 billion, principally in public funds, which Latin America will require over the next ten years from all external sources in order to supplement its own efforts.

The United States will provide from public funds, as an immediate contribution to the economic and social progress of Latin America, more than $1 billion during the twelve months which began on March 13, 1961, when the Alliance for Progress was announced.

The United States intends to furnish development loans on a long-term basis, where appropriate running up to fifty years and in general at very low or zero rates of interest.

For their part, the countries of Latin America agree to devote a steadily increasing share of their own resources to economic and social development, and to make the reforms necessary to assure that all share fully in the fruits of the Alliance for Progress.

Further, as a contribution to the Alliance for Progress, each of the countries of Latin America will formulate a comprehensive and well-conceived national program for the development of its own economy.

Independent and highly qualified experts will be made available to Latin American countries in order to assist in formulating and examining national development plans.

Conscious of the overriding importance of this declaration, the signatory countries declare that the inter-American community is now beginning a new era when it will supplement its institutional, legal, cultural, and social accomplishments with immediate and concrete actions to secure a better life, under freedom and democracy, for the present and future generations.

The Charter of Punta del Este

Establishing an Alliance for Progress
within the framework
of Operation Pan America

Preamble

We, the American republics, hereby proclaim our decision to unite in a common effort to bring our people accelerated economic progress and broader social justice within the framework of personal dignity and political liberty.

Almost two hundred years ago we began in this hemisphere the long struggle for freedom which now inspires people in all parts of the world. Today, in ancient lands, men moved to hope by the revolutions of our young nations search for liberty. Now we must give a new meaning to that revolutionary heritage. For America stands at a turning point in history. The men and women of our hemisphere are reaching for the better life which today's skills have placed within their grasp. They are determined for themselves and their children to have decent and ever more abundant lives, to gain access to knowledge and equal opportunity for all, to end those conditions which benefit the few at the expense of the needs and dignity of the many. It is our inescapable task to fulfill these just desires— to demonstrate to the poor and forsaken of our countries, and of all lands, that the creative powers of free men hold the key to their progress and to the progress of future generations. And our certainty of ultimate success rests not alone on our faith in ourselves and in our nations but on the indomitable spirit of free man which has been the heritage of American civilization.

Inspired by these principles, and by the principles of Operation Pan America and the Act of Bogotá, the American republics hereby resolve to adopt the following program of action to establish and carry forward an Alliance for Progress.

Title I

Objectives of the Alliance for Progress

It is the purpose of the Alliance for Progress to enlist the full energies of the peoples and governments of the American republics in a great cooperative effort to accelerate the economic and social development of the participating countries of Latin America, so that they may achieve maximum levels of well-being, with equal opportunities for all, in democratic societies adapted to their own needs and desires.

The American republics hereby agree to work toward the achievement of the following fundamental goals in the present decade:

1. To achieve in the participating Latin American countries a substantial and sustained growth of per capita income at a rate designed to attain, at the earliest possible date, levels of income capable of assuring self-sustaining development, and sufficient to make Latin American income levels constantly larger in relation to the levels of the more industrialized nations. In this way the gap between the living standards of Latin America and those of the more developed countries can be narrowed. Similarly, presently existing differences in income levels among the Latin American countries will be reduced by accelerating the development of the relatively less developed countries and granting them maximum priority in the distribution of resources and international cooperation in general. In evaluating the degree of relative development, account will be taken not only of average levels of real income and gross product per capita, but also of indices of infant mortality, illiteracy, and per capita daily caloric intake.

It is recognized that, in order to reach these objectives within a reasonable time, the rate of economic growth in any country of Latin America should be not less than 2.5 percent per capita per year, and that each participating country should determine its own growth target in the light of its stage of social and economic evolution, resource endowment, and ability to mobilize national efforts for development.

2. To make the benefits of economic progress available to all citizens of all economic and social groups through a more equitable distribution of national income, raising more rapidly the income and standard of living of the needier sectors of the population, at the same time that a higher proportion of the national product is devoted to investment.

3. To achieve balanced diversification in national economic structures, both regional and functional, making them increasingly free from dependence on the export of a limited number

of primary products and the importation of capital goods while attaining stability in the prices of exports or in income derived from exports.

4. To accelerate the process of rational industrialization so as to increase the productivity of the economy as a whole, taking full advantage of the talents and energies of both the private and public sectors, utilizing the natural resources of the country, and providing productive and remunerative employment for unemployed or part-time workers. Within this process of industrialization, special attention should be given to the establishment and development of capital-goods industries.

5. To raise greatly the level of agricultural productivity and output and to improve related storage, transportation, and marketing services.

6. To encourage, in accordance with the characteristics of each country, programs of comprehensive agrarian reform leading to the effective transformation, where required, of unjust structures and systems of land tenure and use, with a view to replacing latifundia and dwarf holdings by an equitable system of land tenure so that, with the help of timely and adequate credit, technical assistance, and facilities for the marketing and distribution of products, the land will become for the man who works it the basis of his economic stability, the foundation of his increasing welfare, and the guarantee of his freedom and dignity.

7. To eliminate adult illiteracy and by 1970 to assure, as a minimum, access to six years of primary education for each school-age child in Latin America; to modernize and expand vocational, technical, secondary, and higher educational and training facilities; to strengthen the capacity for basic and applied research; and to provide the competent personnel required in rapidly growing societies.

8. To increase life expectancy at birth by a minimum of five years, and to increase the ability to learn and produce, by improving individual and public health. To attain this goal it will be necessary, among other measures, to provide adequate potable water supply and sewage disposal to not less than 70 percent of the urban and 50 percent of the rural population; to reduce the present mortality rate of children less than five years of age by at least one-half; to control the more serious communicable diseases, according to their importance as a cause

of sickness, disability, and death; to eradicate those illnesses, especially malaria, for which effective techniques are known; to improve nutrition; to train medical and health personnel to meet at least minimum requirements; to improve basic health services at national and local levels; and to intensify scientific research and apply its results more fully and effectively to the prevention and cure of illness.

9. To increase the construction of low-cost houses for low-income families in order to replace inadequate and deficient housing and to reduce housing shortages; and to provide necessary public services to both urban and rural centers of population.

10. To maintain stable price levels, avoiding inflation or deflation and the consequent social hardships and maldistribution of resources, always bearing in mind the necessity of maintaining an adequate rate of economic growth.

11. To strengthen existing agreements on economic integration, with a view to the ultimate fulfillment of aspirations for a Latin American common market that will expand and diversify trade among the Latin American countries and thus contribute to the economic growth of the region.

12. To develop cooperative programs designed to prevent the harmful effects of excessive fluctuations in the foreign exchange earnings derived from exports of primary products, which are of vital importance to economic and social development; and to adopt the measures necessary to facilitate the access of Latin American exports to international markets.

Title II
Economic and Social Development

CHAPTER I. BASIC REQUIREMENTS FOR ECONOMIC AND
SOCIAL DEVELOPMENT

The American republics recognize that to achieve the foregoing goals it will be necessary:

1. That comprehensive and well-conceived national programs of economic and social development, aimed at the achievement of self-sustaining growth, be carried out in accordance with democratic principles.

2. That national programs of economic and social development be based on the principle of self-help—as established

in the Act of Bogotá—and on the maximum use of domestic resources, taking into account the special conditions of each country.

3. That in the preparation and execution of plans for economic and social development, women should be placed on an equal footing with men.

4. That the Latin American countries obtain sufficient external financial assistance, a substantial portion of which should be extended on flexible conditions with respect to periods and terms of repayment and forms of utilization, in order to supplement domestic capital formation and reinforce their import capacity; and that, in support of well-conceived programs, which include the necessary structural reforms and measures for the mobilization of internal resources, a supply of capital from all external sources during the coming ten years of at least $20 billion be made available to the Latin American countries, with priority to the relatively less developed countries. The greater part of this sum should be in public funds.

5. That institutions in both the public and private sectors, including labor organizations, cooperatives, and commercial, industrial, and financial institutions, be strengthened and improved for the increasing and effective use of domestic resources, and that the social reforms necessary to permit a fair distribution of the fruits of economic and social progress be carried out.

CHAPTER II. NATIONAL DEVELOPMENT PROGRAMS

1. Participating Latin American countries agree to introduce or strengthen systems for the preparation, execution, and periodic revision of national programs for economic and social development consistent with the principles, objectives, and requirements contained in this document. Participating Latin American countries should formulate, if possible within the next eighteen months, long-term development programs. Such prógrams should embrace, according to the characteristics of each country, the elements outlined in the Appendix.

2. National development programs should incorporate self-help efforts directed toward:

   a. Improvement of human resources and widening of opportunities by raising general standards of education and health; improving and extending technical education and professional training with emphasis on science and technology; providing adequate remuneration for work performed, encouraging the talents of managers, entrepreneurs, and wage earners; providing more productive employment for underemployed manpower; establishing effective systems of labor relations, and procedures for consultation and collaboration among public authorities, employer associations, and labor organizations; promoting the establishment and expansion of local institutions for basic and applied research; and improving the standards of public administration.

b. Wider development and more efficient use of natural resources, especially those which are now idle or underutilized, including measures for the processing of raw materials.

c. The strengthening of the agricultural base, progressively extending the benefits of the land to those who work it, and ensuring in countries with Indian populations the integration of these populations into the economic, social, and cultural process of modern life. To carry out these aims, measures should be adopted, among others, to establish or improve, as the case may be, the following services: extension, credit, technical assistance, agricultural research and mechanization; health and education; storage and distribution; cooperatives and farmers' associations; and community development.

d. More effective, rational, and equitable mobilization and use of financial resources through the reform of tax structures, including fair and adequate taxation of large incomes and real estate, and the strict application of measures to improve fiscal administration. Development programs should include the adaptation of budget expenditures to development needs, measures for the maintenance of price stability, the creation of essential credit facilities at reasonable rates of interest, and the encouragement of private savings.

e. Promotion through appropriate measures, including the signing of agreements for the purpose of reducing or eliminating double taxation, of conditions that will encourage the flow of foreign investments and help to increase the capital resources of participating countries in need of capital.

f. Improvement of systems of distribution and sales in order to make markets more competitive and prevent monopolistic practices.

CHAPTER III. IMMEDIATE AND SHORT-TERM ACTION MEASURES

1. Recognizing that a number of Latin American countries, despite their best efforts, may require emergency financial assistance, the United States will provide assistance from the funds which are or may be established for such purposes. The United States stands ready to take prompt action on applications for such assistance. Applications relating to existing situations should be submitted within the next sixty days.

2. Participating Latin American countries should, in addition to creating or strengthening machinery for long-term development programming, immediately increase their efforts to accelerate their development by giving special emphasis to the following objectives:

a. The completion of projects already under way and the initiation of projects for which the basic studies have been made, in order to accelerate their financing and execution.

b. The implementation of new projects which are designed:
   (1) To meet the most pressing economic and social needs and benefit directly the greatest number of people;
   (2) To concentrate efforts within each country in the less developed or more depressed areas in which particularly serious social problems exist;
   (3) To utilize idle capacity or resources, particularly underemployed manpower; and
   (4) To survey and assess natural resources.

c. The facilitation of the preparation and execution of long-term programs through measures designed:
   (1) To train teachers, technicians, and specialists;
   (2) To provide accelerated training to workers and farmers;
   (3) To improve basic statistics;
   (4) To establish needed credit and marketing facilities; and
   (5) To improve services and administration.

3. The United States will assist in carrying out these short-term measures with a view to achieving concrete results from the Alliance for Progress at the earliest possible moment. In connection with the measures set forth above, and in accordance with the statement of President Kennedy, the United States will provide assistance under the Alliance, including assistance for the financing of short-term measures, totaling more than $1 billion in the year ending March 1962.

CHAPTER IV. EXTERNAL ASSISTANCE IN SUPPORT OF NATIONAL DEVELOPMENT PROGRAMS

1. The economic and social development of Latin America will require a large amount of additional public and private financial assistance on the part of capital-exporting countries, including the members of the Development Assistance Group and international lending agencies. The measures provided for in the Act of Bogotá and the new measures provided for in this charter are designed to create a framework within which such additional assistance can be provided and effectively utilized.

2. The United States will assist those participating countries whose development programs establish self-help measures and economic policies and programs consistent with the goals and principles of this charter. To supplement the domestic efforts of such countries, the United States is prepared to allocate resources which, along with those anticipated from other external sources, will be of a scope and magnitude adequate to realize the goals envisaged in this charter. Such assistance will be allocated to both social and economic development and, where appropriate, will take the form of grants or loans on flexible terms and conditions. The participating countries will request the support of other capital-exporting countries and appropriate institutions so that they may provide assistance for the attainment of these objectives.

3. The United States will help in the financing of technical assistance projects proposed by a participating country or by the General Secretariat of the Organization of American States for the purpose of:

    a. Providing experts contracted in agreement with the government to work under their direction and to assist them in the preparation of specific investment projects and the strengthening of national mechanisms for preparing projects, using specialized engineering firms where appropriate;

b. Carrying out, pursuant to existing agreements for cooperation among the General Secretariat of the Organization of American States, the Economic Commission for Latin America, and the Inter-American Development Bank, field investigations and studies, including those relating to development problems, agrarian reform and rural development, health, cooperatives, housing, education and professional training, and taxation and tax administration; and

c. Convening meetings of experts and officials on development and related problems.

The governments or above-mentioned organizations should, when appropriate, seek the cooperation of the United Nations and its specialized agencies in the execution of these activities.

4. The participating Latin American countries recognize that each has in varying degree a capacity to assist fellow republics by providing technical and financial assistance. They recognize that this capacity will increase as their economies grow. They therefore affirm their intention to assist fellow republics increasingly as their individual circumstances permit.

CHAPTER V. ORGANIZATION AND PROCEDURES

1. In order to provide technical assistance for the formulation of development programs, as may be requested by participating nations, the Organization of American States, the Economic Commission for Latin America, and the Inter-American Development Bank will continue and strengthen their agreements for coordination in this field, in order to have available a group of programming experts whose service can be used to facilitate the implementation of this charter. The participating countries will also seek an intensification of technical assistance from the specialized agencies of the United Nations for the same purpose.

2. The Inter-American Economic and Social Council, on the joint nomination of the secretary general of the Organization of American States, the chairman of the Inter-American Committee on the Alliance for Progress, the president of the Inter-American Development Bank, and the executive secretary of

the United Nations Economic Commission for Latin America, will appoint a panel of nine high-level experts, exclusively on the basis of their experience, technical ability, and competence in the various aspects of economic and social development. The experts may be of any nationality, though if of Latin American origin an appropriate geographical distribution will be sought. They will be attached to the Inter-American Economic and Social Council, but will nevertheless enjoy complete autonomy in the performance of their assigned duties. For administrative purposes and the purposes of better organization of its work, the panel shall elect from among themselves a coordinator. The secretary general of the Organization of American States and the coordinator shall conclude the agreements of a technical or administrative nature necessary for operations.

Four, at most, of the nine members may hold other remunerative positions that in the judgment of the officials who propose them do not conflict with their responsibilities as independent experts. The coordinator may not hold any other remunerative position. When not serving as members of ad hoc committees, the experts may be requested by the coordinator to perform high-level tasks in connection with planning, the evaluation of plans, and execution of such plans. The panel may also be requested to perform other high-level, specific tasks in its advisory capacity to the Inter-American Committee on the Alliance for Progress by the chairman of that committee, through the coordinator of the panel, provided such tasks are not incompatible with the functions set forth in paragraph 4. In the performance of such tasks the experts shall enjoy unquestioned autonomy in judgments, evaluations, and recommendations that they may make.

The experts who perform their duties during only part of the year shall do so for a minimum of 110 days per year and shall receive a standard lump-sum payment in proportion to the annual remuneration, emoluments, and benefits of the other members of the panel.

That proportion shall be set by the secretary general within the authorizations provided in the budget of the OAS.

Each time the coordinator requires the services of the members of the panel, they shall begin to provide them within a reasonable period.

The appointment of the members of the panel will be for a

period of at least one and not more than three years, and may be renewed.

3. Each government, if it so wishes, may present its program for economic and social development for consideration by an ad hoc committee, composed of no more than three members drawn from the panel of experts referred to in the preceding paragraph together with one or more experts not on the panel, if the interested government so desires, provided that the number of such experts shall not exceed the number of those drawn from the panel. The experts who compose the ad hoc committee will be appointed by the secretary general of the Organization of American States at the request of the interested government and with its consent. The chairman of such ad hoc committee shall be one of the members of the panel of experts.

4. The committee will study the development program, exchange opinions with the interested government as to possible modifications, and, with the consent of the government, report its conclusions to the Inter-American Committee on the Alliance for Progress, to the Inter-American Development Bank, and to other governments and institutions that may be prepared to extend external financial and technical assistance in connection with the execution of the program. At the request of the interested government, the panel will also reevaluate the development program.

5. In considering a development program presented to it, the ad hoc committee will examine the consistency of the program with the principles of the Act of Bogotá and of this charter, taking into account the elements in the Appendix.

6. The general secretariat of the Organization of American States will provide the technical and administrative services needed by the experts referred to in paragraphs 2 and 3 of this chapter in order to fulfill their tasks, in accordance with the agreements provided for in Point 2. The personnel for these services may be employed specifically for this purpose or may be made available from the permanent staffs of the Organization of American States, the Economic Commission for Latin America, and the Inter-American Development Bank, in accordance with the present liaison arrangements between the three organizations. The general secretariat of the Organization of American States may seek arrangements with the United Nations secretariat, its specialized agencies, and the inter-

American specialized organizations for the temporary assignment of necessary personnel.

7. A government whose development program has been the object of recommendations made by the ad hoc committee with respect to external financing requirements may submit the program to the Inter-American Development Bank so that the bank may undertake the negotiations required to obtain such financing, including the organization of a consortium of credit institutions and governments disposed to contribute to the continuing and systematic financing, on appropriate terms, of the development program. However, the government will have full freedom to resort through any other channels to all sources of financing, for the purpose of obtaining, in full or in part, the required resources.

The ad hoc committee shall not interfere with the right of each government to formulate its own goals, priorities, and reforms in its national development programs.

The recommendations of the ad hoc committee will be of great importance in determining the distribution of public funds under the Alliance for Progress which contribute to the external financing of such programs. These recommendations shall give special consideration to Title I.1.

The participating governments and the Inter-American Committee on the Alliance for Progress will also use their good offices to the end that these recommendations may be accepted as a factor of great importance in the decisions taken, for the same purpose, by inter-American credit institutions, other international credit agencies, and other friendly governments which may be potential sources of capital.

8. The Inter-American Economic and Social Council will review annually the progress achieved in the formulation, national implementation, and international financing of development programs; and will submit to the Council of the Organization of American States such recommendations as it deems pertinent.

Appendix
Elements of national development programs

1. The establishment of mutually consistent targets to be aimed at over the program period in expanding productive ca-

pacity in industry, agriculture, mining, transport, power, and communications, and in improving conditions of urban and rural life, including better housing, education, and health.

2. The assignment of priorities and the description of methods to achieve the targets, including specific measures and major projects. Specific development projects should be justified in terms of their relative costs and benefits, including their contribution to social productivity.

3. The measures which will be adopted to direct the operations of the public sector and to encourage private action in support of the development program.

4. The estimated cost, in national and foreign currency, of major projects and of the development program as a whole, year by year over the program period.

5. The internal resources, public and private, estimated to become available for the execution of the program.

6. The direct and indirect effects of the program on the balance of payments, and the external financing, public and private, estimated to be required for the execution of the program.

7. The basic fiscal and monetary policies to be followed in order to permit implementation of the program within a framework of price stability.

8. The machinery of public administration—including relationships with local governments, decentralized agencies, and nongovernmental organizations, such as labor organizations, cooperatives, business and industrial organizations—to be used in carrying out the program, adapting it to changing circumstances and evaluating the progress made.

Title III
Economic integration of Latin America

The American republics consider that the broadening of present national markets in Latin America is essential to accelerate the process of economic development in the hemisphere. It is also an appropriate means for obtaining greater productivity through specialized and complementary industrial production, which will, in turn, facilitate the attainment of greater social benefits for the inhabitants of the various regions of Latin America. The broadening of markets will also make possible the better use of resources under the Alliance for Progress. Consequently, the American republics recognize that:

1. The Montevideo Treaty (because of its flexibility and because it is open to the adherence of all of the Latin American nations) and the Central American Treaty on Economic Integration are appropriate instruments for the attainment of these objectives, as was recognized in Resolution No. 11 (III) of the Ninth Session of the Economic Commission for Latin America.

2. The integration process can be intensified and accelerated not only by the specialization resulting from the broadening of markets through the liberalization of trade but also through the use of such instruments as the agreements for complementary production within economic sectors provided for in the Montevideo Treaty.

3. In order to insure the balanced and complementary economic expansion of all of the countries involved, the integration process should take into account, on a flexible basis, the condition of countries at a relatively less advanced stage of economic development, permitting them to be granted special, fair, and equitable treatment.

4. In order to facilitate economic integration in Latin America, it is advisable to establish effective relationships between the Latin American Free Trade Association and the group of countries adhering to the Central American Economic Integration Treaty, as well as between either of these groups and other Latin American countries. These arrangements should be established within the limits determined by these instruments.

5. The Latin American countries should coordinate their actions to meet the unfavorable treatment accorded to their foreign trade in world markets, particularly that resulting from certain restrictive and discriminatory policies of extracontinental countries and economic groups.

6. In the application of resources under the Alliance for Progress, special attention should be given not only to investments for multinational projects that will contribute to strengthening the integration process in all its aspects, but also to the necessary financing of industrial production, and to the growing expansion of trade in industrial products within Latin America.

7. In order to facilitate the participation of countries at a relatively low stage of economic development in multinational

Latin American economic cooperation programs, and in order to promote the balanced and harmonious development of the Latin American integration process, special attention should be given to the needs of these countries in the administration of financial resources provided under the Alliance for Progress, particularly in connection with infrastructure programs and the promotion of new lines of production.

8. The economic integration process implies a need for additional investment in various fields of economic activity, and funds provided under the Alliance for Progress should cover these needs as well as those required for the financing of national development programs.

9. When groups of Latin American countries have their own institutions for financing economic integration, the financing referred to in the preceding paragraph should preferably be channeled through these institutions. With respect to regional financing designed to further the purposes of existing regional integration instruments, the cooperation of the Inter-American Development Bank should be sought in channeling extraregional contributions which may be granted for these purposes.

10. One of the possible means for making effective a policy for the financing of Latin American integration would be to approach the International Monetary Fund and other financial sources with a view to providing a means for solving temporary balance-of-payments problems that may occur in countries participating in economic integration arrangements.

11. The promotion and coordination of transportation and communications systems is an effective way to accelerate the integration process. In order to counteract abusive practices in relation to freight rates and tariffs, it is advisable to encourage the establishment of multinational transport and communication enterprises in the Latin American countries, or to find other appropriate solutions.

12. In working toward economic integration and complementary economies, efforts should be made to achieve an appropriate coordination of national plans, or to engage in joint planning for various economies through the existing regional integration organizations. Efforts should also be made to promote an investment policy directed to the progressive elimination of unequal growth rates in the different geographic areas,

particularly in the case of countries which are relatively less developed.

13. It is necessary to promote the development of national Latin American enterprises, in order that they may compete on an equal footing with foreign enterprises.

14. The active participation of the private sector is essential to economic integration and development, and except in those countries in which free enterprise does not exist, development planning by the pertinent national public agencies, far from hindering such participation, can facilitate and guide it, thus opening new perspectives for the benefit of the community.

15. As the countries of the hemisphere still under colonial domination achieve their independence, they should be invited to participate in Latin American economic integration programs.

Title IV
Basic export commodities

The American republics recognize that the economic development of Latin America requires expansion of its trade, a simultaneous and corresponding increase in foreign exchange incomes received from exports, a lessening of cyclical or seasonal fluctuations in the incomes of those countries that still depend heavily on the export of raw materials, and the correction of the secular deterioration in their terms of trade.

They therefore agree that the following measures should be taken:

CHAPTER I. NATIONAL MEASURES

National measures affecting commerce in primary products should be directed and applied in order to:

1. Avoid undue obstacles to the expansion of trade in these products;
2. Avoid market instability;
3. Improve the efficiency of international plans and mechanisms for stabilization; and
4. Increase their present markets and expand their area of trade at a rate compatible with rapid development.

Therefore:

A. Importing member countries should reduce and if possible eliminate, as soon as feasible, all restrictions and discriminatory practices affecting the consumption and importation of primary products, including those with the highest possible degree of processing in the country of origin, except when these restrictions are imposed temporarily for purposes of economic diversification, to hasten the economic development of less developed nations, or to establish basic national reserves. Importing countries should also be ready to support, by adequate regulations, stabilization programs for primary products that may be agreed upon with producing countries.

B. Industrialized countries should give special attention to the need for hastening economic development of less developed countries. Therefore, they should make maximum efforts to create conditions, compatible with their international obligations, through which they may extend advantages to less developed countries so as to permit the rapid expansion of their markets. In view of the great need for this rapid development, industrialized countries should also study ways in which to modify, wherever possible, international commitments which prevent the achievement of this objective.

C. Producing member countries should formulate their plans for production and export, taking account of their effect on world markets and of the necessity of supporting and improving the effectiveness of international stabilization programs and mechanisms. Similarly they should try to avoid increasing the uneconomic production of goods which can be obtained under better conditions in the less developed countries of the continent, in which the production of these goods is an important source of employment.

D. Member countries should adopt all necessary measures to direct technological studies toward finding new uses and by-products of those primary commodities that are most important to their economies.

E. Member countries should try to reduce, and, if possible, eliminate within a reasonable time export subsidies and other measures which cause instability in the markets for basic commodities and excessive fluctuations in prices and income.

CHAPTER II. INTERNATIONAL COOPERATION MEASURES

1. Member countries should make coordinated and if possible joint efforts designed:

   a. To eliminate as soon as possible undue protection of the production of basic products;
   b. To eliminate taxes and reduce domestic prices which discourage the consumption of imported basic products;
   c. To seek to end preferential agreements and other measures which limit world consumption of Latin American basic products and their access to international markets, especially the markets of western European countries in process of economic integration, and of countries with centrally planned economies; and
   d. To adopt the necessary consultation mechanisms so that their marketing policies will not have damaging effects on the stability of the markets for basic commodities.

2. Industrialized countries should give maximum cooperation to less developed countries so that their raw material exports will have undergone the greatest degree of processing that is economic.

3. Through their representation in international financial organizations, member countries should suggest that these organizations, when considering loans for the promotion of production for export, take into account the effect of such loans on products which are in surplus in world markets.

4. Member countries should support the efforts being made by international commodity study groups and by the Commission on International Commodity Trade of the United Nations. In this connection, it should be considered that producing and consuming nations bear a joint responsibility for taking national and international steps to reduce market instability.

5. The secretary general of the Organization of American States shall convene a group of experts appointed by their respective governments to meet before November 30, 1961, and to report not later than March 31, 1962, on measures to provide an adequate and effective means of offsetting the effects of fluctuations in the volume and prices of exports of basic products. The experts shall:

   a. Consider the questions regarding compensatory financing raised during the present meeting;
   b. Analyze the proposal for establishing an international fund for the stabilization of export receipts contained in the Report of the Group of Experts to the Special Meeting of the Inter-American Economic and Social Council, as well as any other alternative proposals;
   c. Prepare a draft plan for the creation of mechanisms for compensatory financing. This draft plan should be circulated among the member governments and their opinions obtained well in advance of the next meeting of the Commission on International Commodity Trade.

6. Member countries should support the efforts under way to improve and strengthen international commodity agreements and should be prepared to cooperate in the solution of specific commodity problems. Furthermore, they should endeavor to adopt adequate solutions for the short- and long-term problems affecting markets for such commodities so that the economic interests of producers and consumers are equally safeguarded.

7. Member countries should request other producer and consumer countries to cooperate in stabilization programs, bearing in mind that the raw materials of the Western Hemisphere are also produced and consumed in other parts of the world.

8. Member countries recognize that the disposal of accumulated reserves and surpluses can be a means of achieving the goals outlined in the first chapter of this title, provided that, along with the generation of local

resources, the consumption of essential products in the receiving countries is immediately increased. The disposal of surpluses and reserves should be carried out in an orderly manner, in order to:

a. Avoid disturbing existing commercial markets in member countries; and
b. Encourage expansion of the sale of their products to other markets.

However, it is recognized that:

a. The disposal of surpluses should not displace commercial sales of identical products traditionally carried out by other countries; and
b. Such disposal cannot substitute for large-scale financial and technical assistance programs.

IN WITNESS WHEREOF this charter is signed in Punta del Este, Uruguay, on the seventeenth day of August, nineteen hundred sixty-one.

The original texts shall be deposited in the archives of the Pan American Union, through the secretary general of the special meeting, in order that certified copies may be sent to the governments of the member states of the Organization of American States.

INDEX

Adair, Charles, 101
AFL-CIO, 85
Agency for International Development, 109–110, 111, 113, 115, 117–127, 151, 152, 158, 197–198, 200, 201, 205, 281, 298–300, 305–306, 329; and U.S. Congress, 114–115, 124, 127
Agrarian reform, 9–10, 69, 201, 203, 216, 227–230, 247–250; in Bolivia, 9; in Chile, 233–239; in Colombia, 239–242; in Cuba, 226–227, 267; failure in Brazil, 9, 243–247; in Guatemala, 38, 83; in Mexico, 9, 224; in Peru, 9, 99, 253–254; and social integration, 250–253; in Venezuela, 9, 230–233, 249
Agriculture: U.S. loans for, 117–120, 125–128
Agudelo Villa, Hernando, 109
Ahumada, Jorge, 29
AID. See Agency for International Development.
Aid, regional: economic considerations for, 15–16
Aldrich, Richard, 71
Alessandri, Jorge, 91
Alexander, Robert, 54
Allende, Salvador, 91, 93
Alliance for Progress, 307–309, 331; aims of, 8–13, 33, 60, 133, 162, 203–204, 216–217, 219; Committee of Experts, 69, 70; directed against Castro regime, 60, 95, 219; disillusionment with, 13, 321; and divided interests in U.S. government, 112–113; financing of, 65–66; financing under, 111, 133–134, 138–140; lessons of, 323–325; loses popularity in Latin America, 97; results, 13–16; support of

monetary stabilization, 137; and U.S. Congress, 15, 60–61, 66, 110, 120. See also Punta del Este.
Almeida Magalhaes, Rafael de, 146
Alzamora Silva, Lisardo,, 272
American and Foreign Power Company, 145–146
American Popular Revolutionary Alliance, 54
AMFORP. See American and Foreign Power Company.
Amoedo, Julio, 60
Anaconda Copper, 157, 158
Andean Group, 181–182
Anderson, Robert D., 42–43
APRA. See American Popular Revolutionary Alliance.
Arbenz Guzman, Jacobo, 32, 38, 83
Arévalo, Juan José, 38, 83, 84, 85
Argentina, 14; at conference of Punta del Este, 68, 69; debt service, 135; election of 1963, 96–97; foreign investments in, 19, 141; Frente Justicialista, 80; governments of 1930's, 265–266; inflation in, 135; military coups in, 77, 79–80, 96–97, 105–106; military involvement in industry, 178; obstacles to common market in, 177–178; Onganía government in, 97, 105; per capita income, 17; Peronists in, 79–80, 266; population, 222; Union Civica Radical (UCR) party, 79, 80
Arias, Arnulfo, 100–107
Arosemena, Carlos Julio, 86
Arraes, Miguel, 286, 288, 291–292
Automobile assembly plants, 21–22

Balance of payments, 116
Balance of trade, 134–135
Bambaren, Bishop Luis, 274
Bay of Pigs, 59–60
Belaúnde Terry, Fernando, 81, 82, 98, 99, 146–147, 148, 150, 152, 155, 156, 268–269
Bell-Dantas agreement, 193
Bell, David, 50, 88, 113, 115, 193
Beltrán, Pedro, 68, 261
Berle, Adolf, Jr., 52–53, 54, 55–56, 60, 109
Betancourt, Ernesto, 52, 63 (n. 4)
Betancourt, Rómulo, 7, 48, 53, 54, 55, 57, 60, 62, 84, 85, 197, 230, 231
Black, Eugene, 41–42
Bogotá, 260
Bolivia, 32; agrarian reform in, 9; foreign investments in, 19; military coups in, 93–94, 226; Nationalist Revolutionary Movement (MNR), 94; peasants, 225; per capita income, 17, 225; revolution in, 225; U.S. aid in, 93–94, 226
Bosch, Juan, 85–86
Boti, Regino, 48, 49
Braden Copper, 157
Braden, Spruille, 32
Brazil, x, 14, 18; Castelo Branco government in, 96, 195–200, 244, 296; CIA in, 89; at conference of Punta del Este, 70, 73; Costa e Silva dictatorship, 102–103, 196, 200, 209, 296; debt service, 135; development, 176; economic planning in, 13; education in, 282–301; evaluation of development, 206, 207; fall of Goulart government, 88–91, 95, 97, 194; female employment in, 222; Fifth Institutional Act, 102, 103, 200; foreign investments in, 19, 141, 143–146; GNP, 10, 190, 192; Goulart government, 192–194, 243, 294; growth, 309; housing in, 260, 264–265; illiteracy in, 284; inflation, 10, 135, 189, 194, 196, 277; Kubitschek government, 190–191; literacy programs,

286–293; military coups in, 78, 89–91, 104–105, 194; military involvement in industry, 178; Ministry of Planning, 211; "new left," 192–193; no agrarian reform in, 9, 243–247; Northeast, 245–247, 284, 298; Northeast Development Agency, 227; per capita income, 18; population, 223; Quadros government, 191–192; repression in, 309–310; resignation of Quadros, 77, 78; sugar industry, 244–247; U.S. aid in, 15, 36, 37, 88, 101, 105, 117–120, 123–124, 137, 197–198, 200, 207, 298–300, 301; U.S. military intervention in, 13; universities, 293–298
Briggs, Ellis, 61
Brizola, Leonel, 143–144, 145, 192, 193, 194
Bronheim, David, 115, 128
Buenos Aires, 24, 265, 266
Business Group for Latin America, 159
Businessmen: united with leftists against U.S., 107

Campos, Roberto de Oliveira, 39, 96, 195–197
Caracas, 257; Declaration of, 84; Nixon attacked in, 44
Carcano, Miguel, 50
Cárdenas, Lázaro, 224
Castelo Branco, Carlos, 294
Castelo Branco, Humberto, 145; administration of, 96, 195–200
Castillo Armas, Carlos, 38, 84
Castro, Fidel, 6, 46–47; proposes U.S. aid to Latin America; and Soviet missiles in Cuba, 83
Castro Gutiérrez, Edgar, 210, 211
Catholic church: population, 222–223; social protest by, 106–107
Central Programming Office, 126
Chenery, Hollis, 140, 201–202
Chile, 8; agrarian reform in, 9, 92, 233–239, 249, 250; Christian Democratic party, 14, 28

Chile—*continued*
(n. 14), 91, 92, 93, 157, 158, 234, 237, 238–239; economic planning in, 13; education in, 301–303; election of 1964, 91–93; evaluation of performance, 206, 207; food imports, 22; foreign aid in, 91; foreign investments in, 19; *Frente de Acción Popular* (FRAP) party, 91, 92, 93; housing in, 265, 267–274; inflation in, 10–11, 135, 189; nationalization of copper companies, 157–158; obstacles to common market in, 178; per capita income, 18; planning in, 211; population policy, 221; U.S. aid in, 36, 91, 123, 125–128, 137, 155, 204, 239, 303; U.S.-owned copper companies in, 92

Chonchol, Jacques, 236

Church, Frank, 319

CIA, 32, 38, 59, 60; in Brazil, 89; in Dominican Republic, 85; in Guatemala, 32, 38, 84, 85

CIAP. *See* Comité Interamericana de la Alianza para el Progreso.

Coffee prices, 133, 183

Cold war, 32; in Chilean elections, 91; inter-American relations in, 37

Cole, Charles, 92, 93

Colombia; agrarian reform in, 9, 239–242, 249, 250; evaluation of performance, 207; food imports, 22; foreign investments in, 19; GNP, 10; housing in, 260; Liberal party, 28 (n. 14); obstacles to common market in, 177; planning in, 13, 208, 210–211; population policy, 221; social reform in, 14, 310; U.S. aid in, 123, 137, 155, 208–209, 242; U.S. aid to, 204

Comité Interamericana de la Alianza para el Progreso, 129–131

Committee of Nine, 108, 109, 111, 128, 130

Committee of 21; meeting of May 1959, 46–47

Common Market, Central American, 181

Common Market, European, 167

Common market, Latin American, 11, 18, 169–173; obstacles to, 175–180; role of IDB in, 180–181. *See also* Latin American Free Trade Association.

Consensus of Viña del Mar, 183–184

Consumption, 20, 24–25

Costa e Silva, Artur da, 102–103, 223

Costa Rica, population of, 222

Council for Latin America, 159–160

Coups, military, 77; in Argentina, 77, 79–80, 96–97, 105–106; in Bolivia, 93–94; in Brazil, 78, 89–91, 104, 105; in Dominican Republic, 85–86; in Ecuador, 86; in Guatemala, 84–85; in Honduras, 86; in Panama, 100–101; in Peru, 77, 80–82, 98–100, 154–156, 310; U.S. policy on, 86–87

Creole Petroleum Company, 150

Cuba, 7, 29; agrarian reform in, 226–227, 267; diplomatic relations with Soviet Union, 51; education in, 279–280; foreign investments in, 19, 133; proposes U.S. development fund in Latin America, 47, 48–49; at Punta del Este Conference, 64–65, 66–67; revolution in, 46, 47–48, 266–267, 309; seeks allegiance of other Latin American nations, 48, 56; seizure of U.S.-owned businesses by, 135; signs barter agreement with People's Republic of China, 51; Soviet missiles in, 82–83; U.S. breaks off commercial and diplomatic relations with, 48, 51; in World War II, 32

Dantas, Santiago, 89, 193, 194

Delfin Neto, Antonio, 103, 209

Goulart, João, 78, 88–90, 144, 145; administration of, 192–194

Governments: constitutional vs. authoritarian, 27–28; military, 15

Grace, Peter, 82

Greece, 202

Grieve, Jorge, 109

Gross National Product (GNP), and "marginals," 26–27; prescribed by Alliance, 26. *See also under individual countries.*

Growth, export, 20–21

Growth points, 24, 25, 26

Growth rate, 21; economic, 8; population, 8, 21

Guatemala, 83; agrarian reform in, 38, 83; Arbenz government of, 38, 83; assents to invasion of Cuba, 60; CIA in, 32, 38, 84, 85; military coup in, 84–85; U.S. military intervention in, 13

Guevara, Ernesto "Che," 38, 64–65, 66–67, 69, 78

Guido, José María, 80

Gulf Oil Company, 226

Haedo, Eduardo Víctor, 70

Haiti: per capita income, 17–18

Haya de la Torre, Víctor Raúl, 54, 80, 82

Health, public, 10, 217

Helder Camara, Dom, 106

Herrera, Felipe, 39, 57, 71, 171, 172, 180, 255

Hickenlooper Amendment. *See* Foreign Assistance Act.

Highway maintenance: U.S. loans for, 124

Hirshtritt, Ralph, 123

Honduras: per capita income, 17; population policy, 221

Hornbostel, Peter, 118–119

Housing, 10, 217, 259–262, 275; in Brazil, 260, 264–265; in Chile, 265; in Colombia, 260; in Peru, 260–261; U.S. loans for, 123, 259, 261

Huachipato steel mills, 36, 177

Hull, Cordell, 36

Humphrey, George, 39, 41

IAECOSOC. *See* Inter-American Economic and Social Council.

IDB. *See* Inter-American Development Bank.

Illía, Arturo, 96

Immigration, European: into Latin America, 20

Imports, 20, 21, 22, 164; demand for, 164; food, 22; substitution for, 21

Income: distribution, 26; export, 12–13, 20, 21, 133, 163; inequalities, 23, 218–219; per capita, 17, 18, 23, 218, 225; redistribution, 28; trade, 165

Income, national, 8

Indebtedness, public, 132, 135

Industrialists, 21

Industrialization, 9, 21–22

Inflation, 187–189; in Argentina, 135; in Brazil, 10, 135, 189, 194, 196, 277; in Chile, 10–11, 135, 189; in Colombia, 10, 135, 189; in Peru, 153

Intelligentsia, 29

Inter-American Development Bank, 6, 40, 41, 43, 45, 70, 71, 110, 136, 170, 180–181, 212, 229, 242, 247, 261, 319, 327–328

Inter-American Economic and Social Council, 62, 69, 70, 110, 129

Inter-American relations: from World War II to 1961, 36–58

International Coffee Agreement, 133, 183

International Harvester, 127

International Monetary Fund, 47, 195, 205, 208

International Petroleum Company, 147, 149, 150, 153, 154, 156, 160

International Telephone and Telegraph, 143–145, 173

Investment, private, in Latin America: called for in Charter of Punta del Este, 71–72; European, 19; predominance of, 179–180; U.S., 12, 19, 21–22, 30, 132–133, 135–137, 141–161

Irwin, John D., 156

Javits, Jacob, 173
John Deere Company, 125, 126, 127
Johnson, Lyndon B.: approach to Alliance for Progress, 87–88; calls second conference at Punta del Este, 97–98; designates priorities in Alliance for Progress, 122; and fall of Goulart government, 90; initiates "new commitments procedure" for AID loans, 120; quoted, 167, 173, 224; statement at Punta del Este, 173–174

Katzenbach, Nicholas, 155
Kennecott Copper, 157
Kennedy, Jacqueline, 34
Kennedy, John F.: administration of and inter-American relations, 32–33, 72; on agrarian reform, 227; Alliance for Progress speech, 49; approves Brazilian purchase of public utilities, 145; assassination of, 87, 151; authorizes invasion of Cuba, 59; on coup in Dominican Republic, 95; interest in Latin America, 49–50, 109–110; message to Punta del Este conference, 65; opposes Hickenlooper Amendment, 144; policy speech of March 13, 56–58, 221; popularity in Latin America, 87; proposes Alliance for Progress, 6, 7, 34–36, 52, 186; quoted, 34, 82, 95, 186; supports Goulart, 193; Tampa speech, 51–52
Kenya: per capita income, 8
Korry, Edward, 158
Krieger Vasena, Adelberto, 96, 106
Kubitschek, Juscelino, 44–45, 46, 90, 102, 109 (n. 1), 128, 190; development of promotion program, 190–191

Labor unions, 20
Lacerda, Carlos, 144, 145, 260
Landazurri Ricketts, Juan Cardinal, 274

Land redistribution. See Agrarian reform.
Latin American Free Trade Association (LAFTA), 181–182
Latin American task force, 52–56
Leeds, Anthony, 264
Levingston, Marcelo, 266
Levinson, Jerome I., vii
Lewis, W. Arthur, 188
Lima, 24, 260, 267–274
Linder, Harold, 122
Lippmann, Walter, 170–171
Lleras Camargo, Alberto, 7, 61–62, 128, 130, 220, 240
Lleras Restrepo, Carlos, 39, 42, 123, 208, 210, 240, 241
Loans: balance-of-payments, 133; development, 212, 247–248, 253; net disbursement, 138–140; reduced restrictions on, 184, 329
Loeb, James, 81–82

Magalhães Pinto, José, 89
Maleccorto, Ernesto, 109
Mangin, William, 275, 276
Man, Land, and Food, 242
Mann, Thomas C., 12, 45, 58, 72–73, 87–88, 94, 151
Maquera, Eusebio, 215
Marginals, 26–27, 29, 216
Mariani, Clemente, 73
Marighella, Carlos, 104
Marshall, George C., 37
Marshall Plan, 5, 116, 200–201
Martin, Edwin, 66, 86–87, 97, 110, 150
Marxists, 29
Mayobre, José Antonio, 56, 172
McNamara, Robert, 168, 223
Médici, Emilio Garrastazú, 105
Merchant Marine Act, 116–117
Mexico, 14; agrarian reform in, 9, 224; Cárdenas period, 224–225; at conference of Punta del Este, 68; debt service, 135; foreign investments in, 19–20, 133; growth in, 225; obstacles to common market in, 177; peasantry, 225; per capita income, 18; political system, 208; population of, 222; price stability in, 189

Mexico City, 24
Meyer, Karl, 52
Military expenditures: by under-developed countries, 154–155
Molina, Sergio, 235
Montenegro, Julio César, 85
Mora, José A., 57
Morales Carrión, Arturo, 54
Moscoso, Teodoro, 54, 81–82, 87, 110, 111, 150, 151, 160, 319
Mourão Filho, Olympio, 89
MR. *See* Office of Material Resources.
Muñoz Marín, Luis, 53, 54, 85

National development programs, 108–109, 110–111, 186–187; standard for, 202–203, 204–212
National Security Council, 59
Nationalism, 107, 178–179
Nicaragua: assents to invasion of Cuba, 60
Ninth Inter-American Conference (Bogotá, 1948), 37
Nixon, Richard M.: "Action for Progress for the Americas" speech, 316–318; election of, 106; goodwill tour of Latin America (1958), 44–46
Noriega Morales, Manuel, 109

OAS. *See* Organization of American States.
Odría, Manuel, 81
Office of Material Resources, 117, 118, 119, 126
Oliver, Covey C., 98, 101
Onganía, Juan Carlos, 96–97, 106, 266
Onís, Juan de, vii
Operation Bootstrap, 54
Operation Pan-America, 45
Organization of American States, 30
Ovando Candia, Alfredo, 226
Overby, Andrew, 41

Pakistan: per capita income, 18; political systems of, 206
Palmer, Donald, 200, 201, 202

Panama: foreign investments in, 19; military coup in, 100–101; U.S. aid in, 123; U.S. military assistance in, 100
Panama Canal Company, U.S., 19
Paraguay: at conference of Punta del Este, 70; development, 176; per capita income, 17
Passman, Otto E., 115
Pastrana Borrero, Misael, 14
Paz Estenssoro, Victor, 93, 94
Pazos, Felipe, 57, 63, 66 (n. 6), 109, 186–187
Peñaloza, Henrique, 240, 241, 242
People's Republic of China: barter agreement with Cuba, 51; trade with, 168
Peralta, Azurdia Enríque, 85
Pereira Neto, Father Henrique, 106
Pérez, Jiménez, Marcos, 230
Perloff, Harvey, 109
Pernambuco, 285
Perón, Evita, 266
Perón, Juan Domingo, 32, 266
Peru, 14, 18; *Acción Popular* party, 148; agrarian reform in, 9, 99, 253–254; *Alianza Popular Revolucionaria Americana* (APRA) party, 80–82, 148, 149, 152–153, 154; at conference of Punta del Este, 68, 69; expropriation of U.S. businesses, 99; foreign investments in, 19–20, 133, 141; growth, 267; housing in, 260–261; income imbalance, 268; inflation in, 153; military coups in, 77, 80–82, 98–100, 154–155, 310; nationalization of oilfields, 147, 153, 154, 155–156; U.S. aid to, 155, 160; war college of, 99
Planning, 13, 28–29; urban, 262–265. *See also* National development programs.
Plaza, Galo, 277, 311
Poor, the. *See* Marginals.
Population, 220–223, 249; urban, 256–258. *See also under individual cities.*

Prado, Manuel, 77, 81
Prebisch, Raúl, 24, 39, 57, 72, 129–130, 170, 172
Program planning, 201
Puerto Rico, 53, 54
Punta del Este: charter of, 8, 9, 10, 11, 12, 67–69, 108–109, 163, 170, 186, 206, 228, 259, 275; first conference of, 64–73; preparations for, 62–63; second conference of, 97–98; Stevenson mission prior to, 61–62. *See also* Alliance for Progress.

Quadros, Jânio, 60, 70, 77, 78, 90; administration of, 191–192
Quitandinha, 38; meeting of, 38–42, 185

Radical politics, 29–30
Ranis, Gustav, 201
Regional integration programs, 18. *See also* Common market, Latin American.
Regional and Urban Planning Implementation, Inc., 262–263, 273–274, 276
Reid Cabral, Donald, 86
Report of the Experts, 40–41
Revolution. *See* Radical politics.
Revolutionaries, 32; middle-class, 33
Revolutionary Movement of October 8, 104
Ribeiro, Darcy, 293, 294
Rio de Janeiro, 260, 263–264
Rio de Janeiro Treaty of Reciprocal Assistance (1947), 37, 38, 323
Roa, Raúl, 48
Robinson, John, 93
Rockefeller, David, 61, 159, 172, 204
Rockefeller, Nelson, 108, 311–312
Rockefeller Report, 9, 312–316, 318
Rogers, William, 128, 156
Rojas Pinilla, Gustavo, 239
Roosevelt, Franklin D., 31, 32
Root, Elihu, 30
Rosenstein-Rodan, Paul, 109
Rosenthal, Benjamin, 124

Rubottom, Roy, 44–45, 47
Ruggles, Richard, 66 (n. 6)
RUPI. *See* Regional and Urban Planning Implementation, Inc.
Rusk, Dean, 58, 90

Sáez, Raúl, 109, 128, 157
Samudio, David, 101
San Marcos University (Lima): riot at, 44
Santiago, 24
Sanz de Santamaría, Carlos, 130, 172
São Paulo, 24, 277–278
Savings, domestic, 11
Schlesinger, Arthur, Jr., 51, 56, 63
Schmidt, Augusto Federico, 46
Self-help, 185–186
Servan-Schreiber, Jean Jacques, 142
Shantytowns, 25–26, 255–256, 263–264, 266
Silvert, Kalman, 24
Social Progress Trust Fund, 48
Social sectors, 23, 26–27. *See also* Marginals.
Society, Latin America: stability of, 27
Sol Castellanos, Jorge, 57, 109
Soviet Union: diplomatic relations with Cuba, 51; female employment, 222; Latin American trade with, 168, 169
Squatters, 274–278. *See also* Shantytowns; *individual cities.*
Standard Oil of New Jersey, 147, 149
Stevenson, Adlai: Latin American mission, 61

Tariff: preferences, 167–168; protective, 177
Tax collections, 11
Tenth Inter-American Conference (Caracas, 1954), 38
Tomic, Radomiro, 158
Trade: diversification, 8–9
Trujillo, Rafael, 31, 32, 48, 85
Turbay Ayala, Julio César, 62
Turner, John C., 276
Tuthill, John C., 198–199, 300

Unemployment, 9

United Fruit Company, 19, 38, 83

United States: agrees to blockade of Dominican Republic, 48; bilateral program, 328–329; breaks off commercial and diplomatic relations with Cuba, 48, 51; breaks off, then resumes relations with Peru, 81, 82; business interests, 159–160; competes with Cuba for allegiance in Latin America, 56, 62; Commerce Department, 112, 127; Congress, 15, 60–61, 66, 110, 120; Democratic party, 50; Department of Agriculture, 112, 243; draft of Act of Punta del Este, 69; economic pressures against Latin American governments, 14; financial commitment to Latin America, 11–12, 62, 65; influence on consumption, 24–25; intervention in Latin America, 31, 33, 318–319, 325–327; liberal movement for disengagement from Latin America, 318–320; military assistance, 330–331; objectives in Latin America, 31, 32; opposition to, 14; policy in Latin America during Alliance for Progress, 77–78, 97; policy on military coups, 86–87, 106; political and economic influence in Latin America, 30–31, 320; preparation for Punta del Este Conference, 63; public economic cooperation with Latin America, 5–6; security interest in Latin America, 321–323; sends Marines to Dominican Republic, 85; State Department, 109–110, 160, 200, 202; supports Frei government in Chile, 93; supports Lleros Restrepo re-

forms, 204; technical assistance, 330; Treasury Department, 112, 120–125, 127

Uruguay: at conference of Punta del Este, 70; population, 222

USAID, 136, 137, 263, 264, 265, 291

Valdez, Gabriel, 183

Van Dyke, Stuart, 124

Vargas, Getulio, 53, 90

Vaughan, Jack, 198

Velarde, León, 274

Velasco Alvarado, Juan, 99

Velasco Ibarra, José María, 86

Venezuela, 14; *Acción Democrática*, 28 (n. 14), 55; agrarian reform in, 9, 230–233, 249; Christian Democratic party, 28 (n. 14); demands blockade of Dominican Republic, 48; education in, 304–305; foreign investments in, 19, 133; obstacles to common market in, 177; oil income, 232–233, 250; per capita income, 17; price stability in, 189; social reform in, 310; urban population, 257–258

Vietnam War, 15

Villeda Morales, Ramón, 86

Volkswagen (Brazil), 177

Volta Redonda steel mills, 36

Welles, Sumner, 50

Wessin y Wessin, General, 95

Wharton, Clifton R., Jr., 248

Whitaker, Arthur, 54

Williams, G. Mennen, 55

Worker-priests. *See* Catholic church.

World Bank, 41–42, 47, 49, 319, 327, 328

World War II, 21, 32

Ydígoras Fuentes, Miguel, 84, 85

JEROME LEVINSON was born in New York City in 1931 and studied at Harvard University and the Harvard Law School. He was a Fulbright Scholar at the University of Bombay in 1956–1957. After four years as an attorney in New York, Mr. Levinson joined the Department of Justice in 1960 and went to the Agency for International Development in 1962, where he served as head of the Chile-Bolivia capital projects program. In 1964 he was appointed assistant director of AID in Brazil, and in 1966 he became deputy director of the Office of Capital Development for the Alliance for Progress, a post in which he was responsible for administering and managing all capital lending in Latin America.

JUAN DE ONÍS was born in 1927 and studied at Williams College and Columbia University. A working journalist throughout his career, he was with the United Press for six years, first in the United States and later in Rio de Janeiro and Buenos Aires, before joining the *New York Times* in 1957. From 1958 to 1961 he was head of the Buenos Aires bureau with responsibility for Uruguay, Chile, Bolivia, and Argentina; from 1961 to 1967 he was head of the Rio bureau, with responsibility for Peru, Colombia, Venezuela, and Brazil. His reporting in Brazil won him the Ed Stout Memorial Award of the Overseas Press Club in 1963 and the Maria Moore Cabot Award from Columbia University the same year. Mr. de Onís is now chief of the *Times's* bureau in Mexico City.